PMP®: Project Management Professional Study Guide, 2nd Edition

Project Management Professional Exam Objectives

SYBEX®

PMP®:
Project Management
Professional
Study Guide
2nd Edition

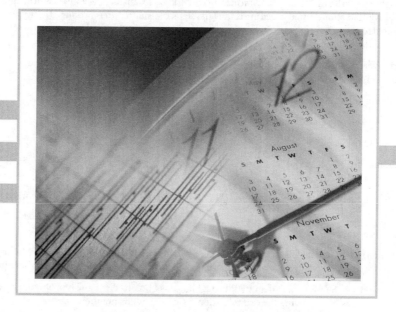

Kim Heldman, PMP

San Francisco • London

SYBEX

Associate Publisher: Neil Edde
Acquisitions Editor: Elizabeth Peterson
Developmental Editor: Heather O'Connor
Production Editor: Lori Newman
Technical Editor: Patti Jansen
Copyeditor: Sarah Lemaire
Compositor: Scott Benoit
Graphic Illustrator: Scott Benoit
CD Coordinator: Dan Mummert
CD Technician: Kevin Ly
Proofreaders: Laurie O'Connell, Amy Rasmussen, Nancy Riddiough
Indexer: Ted Laux
Book Designer: Bill Gibson, Judy Fung
Cover Design and Illustration: Richard Miller, Calyx Design
Cover Photographs: Getty Images, Duncan Smith, and Comstock Images

An earlier version of this book was published under the title PMP: Project Management Study Guide, 2nd Edition © 2002 SYBEX Inc.

First edition copyright © 2002 SYBEX Inc.

Library of Congress Card Number: 2003115677

ISBN: 0-7821-4323-7

Screen reproductions produced with FullShot 99. FullShot 99 © 1991-1999 Inbit Incorporated. All rights reserved.

FullShot is a trademark of Inbit Incorporated.

The CD interface was created using Macromedia Director, COPYRIGHT 1994, 1997-1999 Macromedia Inc. For more information on Macromedia and Macromedia Director, visit http://www.macromedia.com.

TRADEMARKS: SYBEX has attempted throughout this book to distinguish proprietary trademarks from descriptive terms by following the capitalization style used by the manufacturer.

Manufactured in the United States of America

10 9 8 7 6 5 4 3 2 1

SYBEX

To Our Valued Readers:

Thank you for looking to Sybex for your PMP exam prep needs. Since publishing the first edition of our *PMP: Project Management Professional Study Guide* in April 2002, Sybex has earned the respect of thousands of PMP candidates for providing accurate and accessible instruction on the skills and knowledge demanded by companies large and small.

Just as the Project Management Institute is committed to establishing measurable standards for certifying project management professionals, Sybex is committed to providing those individuals with the skills needed to meet those standards. For the second year in a row, readers such as yourself voted Sybex as winner of the "Best Study Guides" category in the 2003 CertCities Readers Choice Awards.

The author and editors have worked hard to ensure that the new edition you hold in your hands is comprehensive, in-depth, and pedagogically sound. We're confident that this book will exceed the demanding standards of the certification marketplace and help you, the PMP certification candidate, succeed in your endeavors.

As always, your feedback is important to us. If you believe you've identified an error in the book, please send a detailed e-mail to support@sybex.com. And if you have general comments or suggestions, feel free to drop me a line directly at nedde@ysbex.com. At Sybex we're continually striving to meet the needs of individuals preparing for certification exams.

Good luck in pursuit of your PMP certification!

Neil Edde
Associate Publisher—Certification
Sybex, Inc.

Software License Agreement: Terms and Conditions

To BB, my forever love, for your ever-continuing encouragement and support.

—Kimmie

Acknowledgments

A very special thank you to Elizabeth Peterson for taking a chance on the first edition of this book and for giving me the opportunity to write it. Thank you again for the opportunity to revise and update it. Elizabeth, you're the best!

This book clearly fits the definition of a project, and the team at Sybex is the best project team on earth to work with. I appreciate all the hard work and dedication everyone on the team put into producing this book. I especially want to thank Heather O'Connor. Her suggestions for improvements and enhancements were excellent. She was instrumental in helping me clarify difficult passages and in making the information flow logically. She did a great job fulfilling the role of project manager as well by keeping everyone on schedule and keeping us all working according to the project plan.

Thank you to Sarah Lemaire, Susan Berge, and Lori Newman for their eye for detail. And thanks to all the behind-the-scenes team members, including Scott Benoit, the compositor and graphic illustrator, and the proofreaders, Laurie O'Connell, Amy Rasmussen, and Nancy Riddiough.

This book was made much stronger due to the expertise Patti Jansen, the technical editor, lent during her reviews. Patti graciously answered my questions concerning issues where *A Guide to the PMBOK* seemed fuzzy, and she contributed many good comments that I incorporated into the text. Thank you, Patti, for another terrific job and for your excellent contributions.

Thanks also to Claudia Baca who served as the technical editor on the first edition of this book. Her contributions to the first version of the book were incorporated into this edition as well.

None of this would have been possible without the continued support and encouragement from my best friend in the whole world, BB. I love you, and there's no one else I'd rather spend the rest of my life with. Thank you to Bob and Terri, our best friends in all the earth, for your support and prayers—they're always coveted. Thank you, B&T, for being closer to us than a brother—we love you! Thanks to my sister Jill and her hubby John, and to Sam, Promise, and Destiny for their cheerleading behind the scenes. Thank you Mom and Dad for giving me the love of reading; some of my best memories are storytime. And thanks also to the greatest adult children on the planet: Jason, Leah (our adopted daughter), Noelle, and Amanda. And I can't forget the two best grandchildren anywhere in the universe—Kate and Juliette. Thank you for your understanding of my limited availability and for your encouragement and enthusiasm.

Contents at a Glance

Contents

Chapter   3   Creating a Project Charter   73

Introduction

This book was designed for anyone thinking of taking the Project Management Professional (PMP) exam sponsored by the Project Management Institute (PMI). This certification is growing in popularity and demand in all areas of business. PMI has experienced explosive growth in membership over the last few years, and more and more organizations are recognizing the importance of PMP certification.

This book assumes you have knowledge of general project management practices, but not necessarily specific *A Guide to the Project Management Body of Knowledge (PMBOK)* practices. It's written so that you can skim through areas you are already familiar with, picking up the specific *A Guide to the PMBOK* terminology where needed to pass the exam. Those of you with no formal training in project management but lots of experience will find the project management processes and techniques defined in such a way that you'll recognize things you've always done and be able to identify them with *A Guide to the PMBOK* process names or methodologies.

PMI offers the most recognized certification in the field of project management, and this book deals exclusively with their procedures and methods. There are many methods of project management, each with its own terminology, tools, and procedures. If you're familiar with another organized project management methodology, don't assume you already know the *A Guide to the PMBOK* processes. I strongly recommend you learn all of the processes—their key inputs, tools and techniques, and outputs. Take the time to memorize the key terms found at the end of every chapter as well. Sometimes just understanding the definition of a term will help you answer a question. It might be that you've always done that particular thing or used the methodology described but called it by another name. Know the name of each process and its primary purpose.

An Exam Essentials section appears at the end of every chapter to highlight the topics you'll most likely find on the exam and help you focus on the most important material covered in the chapter so that you'll have a solid understanding of those concepts. However, it isn't possible to predict what questions will be covered on your particular exam, so be sure to study everything in the chapter.

Like the exam itself, this study guide is organized in terms of process groups and the natural sequence of events a project goes through in its life cycle. By contrast, other study guides organize their material by knowledge area—Human Resource Management, Communications Management, and so on—and it can be confusing when studying for the exam to map the processes in each knowledge area to process groups.

Review questions are provided at the end of every chapter. You can use these to gauge your understanding of the subject matter before reading the chapter and to point out the areas where you need to concentrate your study time. If you can answer at least 80 percent of the review questions, you can probably feel comfortable moving on to the next chapter. If you can't answer that many correctly, reread the chapter, or the section that seems to be giving you trouble, and try the questions again.

Don't rely on studying the review questions exclusively as your study method. The questions you'll see on the exam will be different than the questions presented in the book. There are 200 randomly generated questions on the PMP exam, so it isn't possible to cover every potential exam question in the Review Questions section of each chapter. Make sure you understand the concepts behind the material presented in each chapter and memorize all the formulas as well.

What Is the PMP Certification?

PMI was founded in 1969 and first started offering the Project Management Professional (PMP) certification exam in 1984. PMI is accredited as an American National Standards Institute (ANSI) standards developer and also has the distinction of being the first organization to have their certification program attain International Organization for Standardization (ISO) 9001 recognition.

PMI boasts a worldwide membership of over 100,000, with members from 125 different countries. Local PMI chapters meet regularly and allow project managers to exchange information and learn about new tools and techniques of project management or new ways to use established techniques. I encourage you to join a local chapter and get to know other professionals in your field.

PMI is the leader in project management practices and is the most widely recognized organization and certification in the field. PMI strives to maintain and promote standards and ethics in this field and offers publications, training, seminars, chapters, special interest groups, and colleges to further the project management discipline.

Why Become PMP Certified?

The following benefits are associated with becoming PMP certified:

- It demonstrates proof of professional achievement.
- It increases your marketability.
- It provides greater opportunity for advancement in your field.
- It raises customer confidence in you and your company's services.

Demonstrates Proof of Professional Achievement

PMP certification is a rigorous process that documents your achievements in the field of project management. The exam tests your knowledge of the disciplined approaches, methodologies, and project management practices as described in *A Guide to the PMBOK*, published by the Project Management Institute.

You are required to have several years of experience in project management before sitting for the exam, as well as 35 hours of formal project management education. Your certification assures employers and customers that you are well grounded in project management practices and disciplines. It shows that you've got the hands-on experience and a mastery of the processes and disciplines to manage projects effectively and motivate teams to produce successful results.

Increases Your Marketability

Many industries are realizing the importance of project management and its role in the organization. They are also seeing that simply proclaiming a head technician to be a "project manager" does not make it so. Project management, just like engineering, information technology, and a host of other trades, has its own specific qualifications and skills. Certification tells potential employers you've got the skills, experience, and knowledge to drive successful projects and ultimately improve the company's bottom line.

Certification will always make you stand out above the competition. If you're certified and you're competing against a project manager without certification, chances are you'll come out as the top pick. As a hiring manager, all other things being equal, I will always opt for the candidate who has certification over the candidate who doesn't have it. Certification tells potential employers you have gone the extra mile. You've spent time studying techniques and methods as well as employing them in practice. It shows dedication to your own professional growth and enhancement and to adhering to and advancing professional standards.

Provides Opportunity for Advancement

PMP certification displays your willingness to pursue growth in your professional career and shows that you're not afraid of a little hard work to get what you want. Potential employers will interpret your pursuit of this certification as a high-energy, success-driven, can-do attitude on your part. They'll see that you're likely to display these same characteristics on the job, which will help make the company successful. Your certification displays a success-oriented, motivated attitude that will open up opportunities for future career advancements in your current field as well as in new areas you might want to explore.

Raises Customer Confidence

Just as the PMP certification assures employers that you've got the background and experience to handle project management, customers are also assured they have a competent, experienced project manager at the helm. Certification will help your organization sell customers on your ability to manage their projects. Customers, like potential employers, want the reassurance that those working for them have the knowledge and skills necessary to carry out the duties of the position and that professionalism and personal integrity are of utmost importance. Individuals who hold these ideals will translate their ethics and professionalism to their work. This enhances the trust customers will have in you, which in turn will give you the ability to influence them on important project issues.

How to Become PMP Certified

There are several requirements you need to fulfill in order to sit for the PMP exam. PMI has detailed the certification process quite extensively at their website. Go to www.pmi.org and click the Professional Development and Careers tab to reveal the Certifications selection to get the latest information on certification procedures and requirements.

As of the date of this publication, you are required to fill out an application to sit for the PMP exam. You can submit this application online at `http://certificationapp.pmi.org`. You also need to document 35 hours of formal project management education. This might include college classes, seminars, workshops, or training sessions. Be prepared to list the class titles, location, date, and content.

In addition to filling out the application and documenting your formal project management training, there is one additional set of criteria you'll need to meet to sit for the exam. These criteria fall into two categories. You need to meet the requirements for only one of these categories:

- Category 1 is for those who hold a baccalaureate degree. You'll need to provide proof, via transcripts, of your degree with your application. In addition, you'll need to complete verification forms—found at the PMI website—that show 4500 hours of project management experience that spans a minimum of three years and no more than six years.

- Category 2 is for those who do not hold a baccalaureate degree but do hold a high school diploma or equivalent. You'll need to complete verification forms documenting 7500 hours of project management experience that spans a minimum of five years and no more than eight years.

The exam fee at the time of this publication is $405 for PMI members in good standing and $555 for non-PMI members. Testing is conducted at Prometric centers. You can find a center near you at the PMI website. You have six months from the time PMI receives and approves your completed application to take the exam. You'll need to bring a form of identification such as a driver's license with you to the Prometric center on the test day. You will not be allowed to take anything with you into the testing center. You will be given a calculator, pencils, and scrap paper by the center. You will turn in all scrap paper, including the notes and squiggles you've jotted during the test, to the center upon completion of the exam.

The exam is scored immediately, so you will know if you've passed at the conclusion of the test. You're given four hours to complete the exam, which consists of 200 randomly generated questions that cover the following process groups and areas: Initiation, Planning, Executing, Controlling, Closing, and Professional Responsibility. All unanswered questions are scored as wrong answers, so it benefits you to guess at an answer if you're stumped on a question.

After you've received your certification, you'll be required to earn 60 professional development units (PDUs) every three years to maintain certification. Approximately one hour of structured learning translates to one PDU. The PMI website details what activities constitute a PDU, how many PDUs each activity earns, and how to register your PDUs with PMI to maintain your certification. As an example, attendance at a local chapter meeting earns one PDU.

Who Should Buy This Book?

If you are serious about passing the PMP exam, you should buy this book and use it to study for the exam. This book is unique in that it walks you through the project processes from beginning to end, just as projects are performed in practice. You will benefit from reading this book by learning specific *A Guide to the PMBOK* processes and techniques coupled with real-life scenarios that describe how project managers in different situations handle problems and the various issues all project managers are bound to encounter during their career. This study guide describes in detail the exam objective topics in each chapter and has attempted to cover all of the important project management concepts.

How to Use This Book and CD

We've included several testing features, both in the book and on the companion CD-ROM. Following this Introduction is an assessment test that you can use to check your readiness for the actual exam. Take this test before you start reading the book. It will help you identify the areas you may need to brush up on. The answers to the assessment test appear after the last question of the test. Each answer includes an explanation and a note telling you in which chapter this material appears.

As mentioned, to test your knowledge as you progress through the book, there are review questions at the end of each chapter. As you finish each chapter, answer the review questions and then check to see if your answers are right—the correct answers appear on the pages following the last question. You can go back to reread the section that deals with each question you got wrong to ensure that you answer the question correctly the next time you are tested on the material. You'll also find 240+ flashcard questions on the CD for on-the-go review. Download them right onto your Palm device for quick and convenient reviewing.

In addition to the assessment test and the review questions, you'll find two bonus exams on the CD. Take these practice exams just as if you were actually taking the exam (i.e., without any reference material). When you have finished the first exam, move on to the next exam to solidify your test-taking skills. If you get more than 85 percent of the answers correct, you're ready to go ahead and take the real exam.

Additionally, if you are going to travel but still need to study for the PMP exam, and you have a laptop with a CD-ROM drive, you can take this entire book with you just by taking the CD. This book is in PDF (Adobe Acrobat) format so it can be easily read on any computer.

The Exam Objectives

Behind every certification exam, you can be sure to find exam objectives—the broad topics in which the exam developers want to ensure your competency. The official PMP exam objectives are listed in this section.

 Exam objectives are subject to change at any time without prior notice and at PMI's sole discretion. Please visit the Certification page of PMI's website, www.pmi.org, for the most current listing of exam objectives.

Domain 1.0: Initiation

The objectives for the Initiation domain are as follows:

1. Determining project goals.
2. Determining deliverables.

3. Determining process outputs.

4. Documenting project constraints.

5. Documenting project assumptions.

6. Defining strategy.

7. Identifying performance criteria.

8. Determining resource requirements.

9. Defining budget.

10. Producing formal documentation.

Domain 2.0: Planning

The objectives for the Planning domain are as follows:

1. Refining a project.

2. Creating a WBS.

3. Developing a resource management plan.

4. Refining time and cost estimates.

5. Establishing project controls.

6. Developing a project plan.

7. Obtaining plan approval.

Domain 3.0: Execution

The objectives for the Execution domain are as follows:

1. Committing resources.

2. Implementing resources.

3. Managing progress.

4. Communicating progress.

5. Implementing quality assurance procedures.

Domain 4.0: Control

The objectives for the Control domain are as follows:

1. Measuring performance.

2. Refining control limits.

3. Taking corrective action.

4. Evaluating effectiveness of corrective action.

5. Ensuring plan compliance.

6. Reassessing control plans.

7. Responding to risk event triggers.
8. Monitoring project activity.

Domain 5.0: Closing

The objectives for the Closing domain are as follows:

1. Obtaining acceptance of deliverables.
2. Documenting lessons learned.
3. Facilitating closure.
4. Preserving product records and tools.
5. Releasing resources.

Domain 6.0: Professional Responsibility

The objectives for the Professional Responsibility domain are as follows:

1. Ensuring integrity.
2. Contributing to knowledge base.
3. Applying professional knowledge.
4. Balancing stakeholder interests.
5. Respecting differences.

Tips for Taking the PMP Exam

Here are some general tips for taking your exam successfully:

- Get to the exam center early so that you can relax and review your study materials.

- Read the exam questions very carefully. Make sure you know exactly what the question is asking and don't be tempted to answer too quickly.

- Unanswered questions score as wrong answers. It's better to guess than to leave a question unanswered.

- If you're not sure of an answer, use a process of elimination to identify the obvious incorrect answers first. Narrow the remaining choices down by referring back to the question, looking for key words that might tip you off to the correct answer.

- You'll be given scratch paper to take with you to the exam station. As soon as you get to your place, write down all the formulas and any other memory aids you used while studying before starting the exam. That way you can relax a little, because you won't have to remember the formulas when you get to those questions on the exam—you can simply look at your scratch paper.

- Visit the PMI website at www.pmi.org for the latest information regarding certification and to find a testing site nearest you.

Assessment Test

1. Which performance measurement tells you how much more of the budget is required to finish the project?

    A. ETC

    B. EV

    C. AC

    D. EAC

2. Which of the following compression techniques increases risk?

    A. Crashing

    B. Resource leveling

    C. Fast tracking

    D. Lead and lag

3. You are a project manager for Waterways Houseboats, Inc. You've been asked to perform a benefit/cost analysis for two proposed projects. Project A costs $2.4 million, with potential benefits of $12 million and future operating costs of $3 million. Project B costs $2.8 million, with potential benefits of $14 million and future operating costs of $2 million. Which project should you recommend?

    A. Project A, because the cost to implement is cheaper than Project B.

    B. Project A, because the potential benefits plus the future operating costs are less in value than the same calculation for Project B.

    C. Project B, because the potential benefits minus the implementation and future operating costs are greater in value than the same calculation for Project A.

    D. Project B, because the potential benefits minus the costs to implement are greater in value than the same calculation for Project A.

4. These diagrams rank-order factors for corrective action by frequency of occurrence. They are also a type of histogram.

    A. Control charts

    B. Process flowcharts

    C. Scatter diagrams

    D. Pareto diagrams

5. You've been assigned as a project manager on a research and development project for a new dental procedure. You've published the scope statement and are working on the scope management plan. What is the purpose of the scope management plan?

   A. The scope management plan describes and documents a scope baseline to help make future project decisions.

   B. The scope management plan decomposes project deliverables.

   C. The scope management plan describes how project scope changes will be incorporated into the project and how project scope will be managed.

   D. The scope management plan describes how cost and time estimates can be composed for project scope changes.

6. What is one of the most important skills a project manager can have?

   A. Negotiation skills

   B. Influencing skills

   C. Communication skills

   D. Problem-solving skills

7. The project manager has the greatest influence over quality during which process?

   A. Quality Planning

   B. Quality Assurance

   C. Quality Control

   D. Quality Change Control

8. Project managers have the highest level of authority and the most power in which type of organizational structure?

   A. Projectized

   B. Strong matrix

   C. Functional

   D. Balanced matrix

9. You are the project manager for Heartthrobs by the Numbers Dating Services. You're working on an updated Internet site that will display pictures as well as short bios of prospective heartbreakers. You have your activity list and resource requirements in hand and are planning to use qualitatively based durations and reserve time to determine activity durations. Which of the following statements is true?

   A. You are using inputs of the Activity Duration Estimating process.

   B. You are using tools and techniques of the Cost Estimating process.

   C. You are using tools and techniques of the Activity Duration Estimating process.

   D. You are using inputs of the Cost Estimating process.

10. You are a project manager who has recently held a project team kickoff meeting where all the team members were formally introduced to each other. Some of the team members know each other from other projects and have been working with you for the past three weeks during the Planning processes. Which of the following statements is true?

   A. Team building begins once all the members of the team are identified and introduced to each other. This team is in the storming stage of Team Development.

   B. Team building begins at the Planning process. This team is in the storming stage of Team Development.

   C. Team building begins once all the members of the team are identified and introduced to each other. This team is in the forming stage of Team Development.

   D. Team building begins at the Planning process. This team is in the forming stage of Team Development.

11. Project managers spend what percentage of their time communicating?

   A. 90

   B. 85

   C. 75

   D. 50

12. All of the following statements are true regarding configuration management except:

   A. Configuration management requires all acceptance decisions to be made through the CCB.

   B. Configuration management serves as a change control system.

   C. Configuration management describes the physical characteristics of the product of the project.

   D. Configuration management controls changes to the characteristics of an item.

13. Which of the following project-scheduling techniques allows for conditional and probabilistic treatment?

   A. GERT

   B. CPM

   C. PERT

   D. CPM and PERT

14. Which of the following contracts should you use for projects that have a degree of uncertainty and require a large investment early in the project life cycle?

   A. Fixed price

   B. Cost reimbursable

   C. Lump sum

   D. Unit price

15. You are the project manager for Lucky Stars Candies. You've identified the deliverables and requirements and documented them where?

  A. In the scope statement, which will be used as an input to the Scope Definition process.

  B. In the scope definition document, which is used as an input to the Scope Planning process.

  C. In the WBS, which is an output of the Scope Planning process.

  D. In the WBS, which is a tool and technique of the Scope Definition process.

16. All of the following statements are true regarding Ishikawa diagrams in the Quality Planning process except:

  A. Ishikawa diagrams are also called cause-and-effect diagrams.

  B. Ishikawa diagrams are also called fishbone diagrams.

  C. Ishikawa diagrams are a tool and technique of this process.

  D. Ishikawa diagrams are an output of this process.

17. The primary function of the Closing process is to:

  A. Formalize lessons learned and distribute this information to project participants.

  B. Perform audits to verify the project results against the project requirements.

  C. Formalize project completion and disseminate this information to project participants.

  D. Perform post-implementation audits to document project successes and failures.

18. What is the purpose of the project charter?

  A. To recognize and acknowledge the project sponsor

  B. To recognize and acknowledge the existence of the project and commit organizational resources to the project

  C. To acknowledge the existence of the project team, project manager, and project sponsor

  D. To describe the selection methods used to choose this project over its competitors

19. Which performance measurement tells you what the projected total cost of the project will be at completion?

  A. ETC

  B. CPI

  C. SPI

  D. EAC

20. People are motivated by the need for achievement, power, or affiliation according to which theory?

  A. Expectancy Theory

  B. Achievement Theory

  C. Contingency Theory

  D. Theory X

21. You are a project manager working in a foreign country. You observe that some of your project team members are having a difficult time adjusting to the new culture. You provided them training on cultural differences and the customs of this country before arriving, but they still seem uncomfortable and disoriented. Which of the following statements is true?

   A. This is the result of working with teams of people from two different countries.

   B. This condition is known as culture shock.

   C. This is the result of jet lag and travel fatigue.

   D. This condition is known as global culturalism.

22. The project management knowledge areas:

   A. Include Initiation, Planning, Executing, Controlling, and Closing.

   B. Consist of nine different areas that bring together processes that have things in common.

   C. Consist of five different processes that bring together phases of projects that have things in common.

   D. Include Planning, Executing, and Controlling processes as these three processes are commonly interlinked.

23. You are the project manager for a construction company that is building a new city and county office building in your city. You recently looked over the construction site to determine if the work to date was conforming to the requirements and quality standards. Which tool and technique of Quality Control are you using?

   A. Performance measurements

   B. Inspection

   C. Sampling

   D. Prevention

24. Which of the following statements is true regarding Administrative Closure?

   A. Administrative Closure occurs at the end of a project phase and at the end of the project.

   B. Administrative Closure occurs at the end of the project phase only.

   C. Administrative Closure occurs at the end of the project only.

   D. Administrative Closure is performed prior to Contract Closeout.

25. You are the project manager for the Heart of Texas casual clothing company. Your project involves installing a new human resources system. You've identified the risks associated with this project and are ready for the next step. What is the next step?

   A. You will evaluate the risks and assign probabilities and impacts using Qualitative and/or Quantitative Risk Analysis.

   B. You will use the Delphi technique to confirm the risks you've detailed and identify others you may have missed.

   C. You must evaluate the risks and assign probabilities and impacts using both Qualitative Risk Analysis, which comes first, and then Quantitative Risk Analysis.

   D. You will define the steps to take to respond to the risks and detail them in the risk response plan.

26. The project sponsor has approached you with a dilemma. The CEO announced at the annual stockholders meeting that the project you're managing will be completed by the end of this year. The problem is that this is six months prior to the scheduled completion date. It's too late to go back and correct her mistake, and stockholders are expecting implementation by the announced date. You must speed up the delivery date of this project. Your primary constraint before this occurred was the budget. What actions can you take to help speed up the project?

   A. Hire more resources to get the work completed faster.

   B. Ask for more money so that you can contract out one of the phases you had planned to do with in-house resources.

   C. Utilize negotiation and influencing skills to convince the project sponsor to speak with the CEO and make a correction to her announcement.

   D. Examine the project plan to see if there are any phases that can be fast tracked, and then revise the project plan to reflect the compression of the schedule.

27. During your project meeting, a problem was discussed and a resolution to the problem was reached. During the meeting, the participants started wondering why they thought the problem was such a big issue. Some time after the meeting, you received an e-mail from one of the meeting members saying they've changed their mind about the solution reached in the meeting and need to resurface the problem. The solution reached during the initial project meeting is an example of which of the following conflict resolution techniques?

   A. Confrontation

   B. Forcing

   C. Smoothing

   D. Storming

28. You are the project manager for Heartthrobs by the Numbers Dating Services. You're working on an updated Internet site that will display pictures as well as short bios of prospective heart-breakers. You've just completed your project staff assignments and published the project team directory. Which process are you in?

  A. Resource Planning

  B. Organizational Planning

  C. Project Development Planning

  D. Staff Acquisition

29. Which of the following describes the Executing process?

  A. Project plans are put into action.

  B. Project performance measurements are taken and analyzed.

  C. Project plans are developed.

  D. Project plans are published.

30. Each of the following statements describes an element of the Scope Definition process except:

  A. Breaking down the major deliverables of the project into smaller, manageable components

  B. Supporting detail

  C. Decomposition

  D. Improving the accuracy of time and cost estimates

31. Which of the following are tools and techniques of the Initiation process?

  A. Project selection methods and expert judgment

  B. Project selection criteria and expert judgment

  C. Constraints and assumptions, and expert judgment

  D. Expert judgment and project charter

32. Your project involves the research and development of a new food additive. You're ready to release the product to your customer when you discover that a minor reaction might occur in people with certain conditions. The reactions to date have been very minor, and no known long-lasting side effects have been noted. As project manager you should:

  A. Do nothing because the reactions are so minor that very few people will be affected.

  B. Inform the customer that you've discovered this condition and tell them you'll research it further to determine its impacts.

  C. Inform your customer that there is no problem with the additive except for an extremely small percentage of the population and release the product to them.

  D. Tell the customer you'll correct the reaction problems in the next batch, but you'll release the first batch of product to them now to begin using.

xxxAssessment Test

33. According to *A Guide to the PMBOK*, the project manager is identified and assigned during which process?

   A. As an input to the Initiation process

   B. As an input to the Planning process

   C. As an output of the Initiation process

   D. As an output of the Scope Planning process

34. All of the following statements are true regarding the ADM method except:

   A. The ADM method is a tool and technique of Activity Sequencing.

   B. The ADM method uses one time estimate to determine durations.

   C. The ADA method is also called AOA.

   D. The ADA method is rarely used today.

35. You have been assigned to a project that will allow job seekers to fill out applications and submit them via the company website. You report to the VP of human resources. You are also responsible for screening applications for the information technology division and setting up interviews. The project coordinator has asked for the latest version of your changes to the online application page for his review. Which organizational structure do you work in?

   A. Functional organization

   B. Weak matrix organization

   C. Projectized organization

   D. Balanced matrix organization

36. What type of organization experiences the least amount of stress during project closeout?

   A. Projectized

   B. Functional

   C. Weak matrix

   D. Strong matrix

37. You work for a company that writes billing software programs for the communication industry. You've just been assigned a new project. The customer is located in a distant country that limits the number of foreigners allowed into the country. You identify this risk in your risk management plan. The critical point during the project is installation and setup. You might do which of the following given these circumstances?

   A. Use a design of experiments technique to develop a contingency plan.

   B. Develop a cause-and-effect diagram that identifies the contract type you should use for a project like this.

   C. Use sensitivity analysis to assist you in developing the appropriate risk response for this situation.

   D. Develop a contingency plan for installation.

38. You are working on a project that will upgrade the phone system in your customer service center. You have used bottom-up estimating techniques to assign costs to the project activities and have determined the cost baseline. Which of the following statements is true?

   A. You have completed the Cost Estimating process and now need to complete the Cost Budgeting process to determine the project's baseline.

   B. You have completed the Project Plan Development process and established a project baseline to measure future project performance against.

   C. You have completed the Cost Estimating process and now need to complete the Project Plan Development process to establish a project baseline to measure future project performance against.

   D. You have completed the Cost Budgeting process, and the cost baseline will be used to measure future project performance.

39. You know that PV = 470, AC = 430, EV = 480, EAC = 500, and BAC = 525. What is VAC?

   A. 70

   B. 20

   C. 25

   D. 30

40. All of the following statements are true of the project Closing processes except:

   A. Probability for success is greatest in the project Closing processes.

   B. The project manager's influence is greatest in the project Closing processes.

   C. The stakeholders' influence is least in the project Closing processes.

   D. Risk is greatest in the project Closing processes.

41. You are refining the product description for your company's new line of ski boots. Which of the following statements is true?

   A. You are in the Initiation process of your project and know that the product description will contain more detail in this stage and that a decreasing amount of detail will be added to it as the project progresses.

   B. You are in the Planning process of your project and know that the product description will contain less detail in this stage and greater detail as the project progresses.

   C. You are in the Initiation process of your project and know that the product description should contain the most detail possible at this stage, because this is critical information for the Planning process.

   D. You are in the Initiation process of your project and know that the product description will contain less detail in this stage and greater detail as the project progresses.

42. This process applies evaluation criteria to the bids and proposals received from potential vendors.

   A. Solicitation

   B. Contract Administration

   C. Source Selection

   D. Quality Assurance

43. All of the following are tools and techniques of the Integrated Change Control process except:

   A. Configuration management

   B. Performance measurements

   C. Change requests

   D. Additional planning

44. You need to convey some very complex, detailed information to the project stakeholders. The best method of communicating this kind of information is:

   A. Verbal

   B. Vertical

   C. Horizontal

   D. Written

45. You have just prepared an RFP for release. Your project involves a substantial amount of contract work detailed in the RFP. Your favorite vendor drops by and offers to give you and your spouse the use of their company condo for your upcoming vacation. It's located in a beautiful resort community that happens to be one of your favorite places to go for a getaway. What is the most appropriate response?

   A. Thank the vendor but decline the offer because you know this could be considered a conflict of interest.

   B. Thank the vendor and accept. This vendor is always offering you incentives like this, so this offer does not likely have anything to do with the recent RFP release.

   C. Thank the vendor, accept the offer, and immediately tell your project sponsor so they're aware of what you're doing.

   D. Thank the vendor but decline the offer because you've already made another arrangement for this vacation. Ask them if you can take a rain check and arrange another time to use the condo.

46. PERT is:

   A. The longest path

   B. A weighted average technique

   C. A simulation technique

   D. Widely used in practice to determine schedule durations

47. What are the Scope Planning process tools and techniques?

   A. Benefit/cost analysis, work breakdown structure templates, expert judgment, and supporting detail

   B. Product analysis, benefit/cost analysis, alternatives identification, and expert judgment

   C. Product analysis, work breakdown structure templates, supporting detail, and expert judgment

   D. Benefit/cost analysis, alternatives identification, supporting detail, and expert judgment

48. You are a project manager for Swirling Seas Cruises food division. You're considering two different projects regarding food services on the cruise lines. The initial cost of Project Fish'n for Chips will be $800,000, with expected cash inflows of $300,000 per quarter. Project Picnic's payback period is six months. Which project should you recommend?

   A. Project Fish'n for Chips, because its payback period is two months shorter than Project Picnic's.

   B. Project Fish'n for Chips, because the costs on Project Picnic are unknown.

   C. Project Picnic, because Project Fish'n for Chips' payback period is four months longer than Project Picnic's.

   D. Project Picnic, because Project Fish'n for Chips' payback period is two months longer than Project Picnic's.

49. You are the project manager for Xylophone Phonics. They produce children's software programs that teach basic reading and math skills. You're performing cost estimates for your project and don't have a lot of details yet. Which of the following techniques should you use?

   A. Analogous estimating techniques, because this is a form of expert judgment that uses historical information from similar projects.

   B. Bottom-up estimating techniques, because this is a form of expert judgment that uses historical information from similar projects.

   C. Monte Carlo Analysis, because this is a modeling technique that uses simulation to determine estimates.

   D. Parametric modeling, because this is a form of simulation used to determine estimates.

50. As a PMP, one of your responsibilities is to ensure integrity on the project. When your personal interests are put above the interests of the project or when you use your influence to cause others to make decisions in your favor without regard for the project outcome, this is considered:

   A. Conflict of interest

   B. Using professional knowledge inappropriately

   C. Culturally unacceptable

   D. Personal conflict issue

51. Your project is in the Scope Definition process. You've just completed the WBS. Which of the following statements is true?

    A. The WBS breaks the project deliverables down to a level where alternatives identification can be used to determine how level two assignments should be made.

    B. The WBS breaks the project deliverables down to a level where project constraints and assumptions can be easily identified.

    C. The WBS breaks the project deliverables down to the work package level where product analysis can be documented.

    D. The WBS breaks the project deliverables down to the work package level where cost and time estimates can be easily determined and quality control measurements can be determined.

52. The product description, strategic plan, project selection criteria, and historical information are considered:

    A. Inputs to the project Planning process

    B. Inputs to the project Overview process

    C. Inputs to the project Initiation process

    D. Inputs to the project Execution process

53. What are decision models?

    A. Project selection criteria

    B. Project selection methods

    C. Project selection committees

    D. Project resource and budget selection criteria

54. Performance reporting tools and techniques include all of the following except:

    A. Earned value analysis

    B. Statistical sampling

    C. Variance analysis

    D. Performance reviews

55. Which of the following statements is true regarding constraints and assumptions?

    A. Constraints restrict the actions of the project team, and assumptions are considered true for planning purposes.

    B. Constraints are considered true for planning purposes, and assumptions limit the options of the project team.

    C. Constraints consider vendor availability and resource availability to be true for planning purposes. Assumptions limit the project team to work within predefined budgets or timelines.

    D. Constraints and assumptions are inputs to the Initiation process. They should be documented, because they will be used throughout the project Planning process.

56. You are the project manager for a construction company that is building a new city and county office building in your city. Your CCB recently approved a scope change. You know that scope change might come about as a result of all of the following except:

    A. Schedule revisions

    B. Product scope change

    C. Changes to the agreed-upon WBS

    D. Changes to the project requirements

57. What are the tools and techniques of the Quantitative Risk Analysis process?

    A. Checklists, flowcharting, and interviewing

    B. Interviewing, sensitivity analysis, decision tree analysis, and simulation

    C. Checklists, sensitivity analysis, decision tree analysis, and information-gathering techniques

    D. Interviewing, checklists, assumptions analysis, and risk probability impact

58. Name the ethical code you'll be required to adhere to as a PMP.

    A. *Project Management Policy and Ethics Guide*

    B. *Project Management Professional Standards and Ethics*

    C. *Project Management Code of Professional Ethics*

    D. *Project Management Professional Code of Professional Conduct*

59. You are the project manager for Xylophone Phonics. They produce children's software programs that teach basic reading and math skills. You are ready to assign project roles, responsibilities, and reporting relationships. Which project Planning process are you working on?

    A. Resource Planning

    B. Organizational Planning

    C. Staff Acquisition

    D. Human Resource Acquisition

60. Critical path tasks are those tasks that:

    A. Have equal pessimistic, optimistic, and most likely estimated times

    B. Have a float time of zero

    C. Have the same start date

    D. Have multiple early start dates and early finish dates

Answers to Assessment Test

1. **A.**   Estimate to completion (ETC) calculates how much more of the budget is needed to complete the project if everything continues at the current level of performance. For more information, please see Chapter 9.

2. **C.**   Fast tracking is a compression technique that increases risk and potentially causes rework. Fast tracking is starting two tasks previously scheduled to start one after the other at the same time. For more information, please see Chapter 7.

3. **C.**   Project B's benefit/cost analysis is a $9.2 million benefit to the company, compared to $6.6 million for Project A. Benefit/cost analysis takes into consideration the initial costs to implement and future operating costs. For more information, please see Chapter 3.

4. **D.**   Pareto diagrams rank-order important factors for corrective action by frequency of occurrence. For more information, please see Chapter 10.

5. **C.**   The scope management plan outlines how project scope will be managed and how changes will be incorporated into the project. For more information, please see Chapter 4.

6. **C.**   Negotiation, influencing, and problem-solving skills are all important for a project manager to possess. However, good communication skills are the most important skills a project manager can have. For more information, please see Chapter 1.

7. **B.**   Quality Assurance is the process where project managers have the greatest amount of influence over quality. For more information, please see Chapter 9.

8. **A.**   Project managers have the highest level of power and authority in a projectized organization. They also have high levels of power and authority in a strong matrix. However, a matrix organization is a blend of functional and projectized organizations. Therefore, the project manager does not have quite the same level of authority as they would in a projectized organization. For more information, please see Chapter 1.

9. **C.**   Qualitatively based durations and reserve time are two of the tools and techniques of the Activity Duration Estimating process. The other tools are expert judgment and analogous estimating. For more information, please see Chapter 5.

10. **D.**   Team building begins at the Planning process of your project. In this question, the team members have just been formally introduced to each other, so they are still in the forming stage of Team Development. For more information, please see Chapter 8.

11. **A.**   Project managers spend about 90 percent of their time communicating through status meetings, team meetings, e-mail, verbal communications, and so on. For more information, please see Chapter 8.

12. **A.**   Configuration management serves as a change control system; it describes the physical characteristics of the product, and it controls changes to the characteristics of the product or item. It tracks the changes requested and made and their status. For more information, please see Chapter 10.

13. **A.** GERT is the only technique that allows for conditional branching and looping, and probabilistic treatment. For more information, please see Chapter 7.

14. **B.** Cost reimbursable contracts are used when the degree of uncertainty is high and when the project requires a large investment prior to completion of the project. For more information, please see Chapter 6.

15. **A.** The scope statement contains an exhaustive list of the project deliverables, their requirements, and the measurable criteria used to determine project completion. The scope statement is an input to the Scope Definition process and is used to create the WBS. For more information, please see Chapter 4.

16. **D.** Cause-and-effect diagrams—also called Ishikawa or fishbone diagrams—show the relationship between the effects of quality problems and their causes. Cause-and-effect diagrams were developed by Kaoru Ishikawa. For more information, please see Chapter 6.

17. **C.** The primary function of the Closing process is to formalize project completion and disseminate this information to the project participants. For more information, please see Chapter 11.

18. **B.** The purpose of a project charter is to recognize and acknowledge the existence of a project and commit resources to the project. The charter names the project manager and project sponsor, but that's not its primary purpose. For more information, please see Chapter 3.

19. **D.** Estimate at completion (EAC) estimates the total cost of the project at completion based on the performance of the project to date. For more information, please see Chapter 9.

20. **B.** Achievement theory conjectures that people are motivated by the need for achievement, power, or affiliation. For more information, please see Chapter 8.

21. **B.** When people work in unfamiliar environments, culture shock can occur. Training and researching information about the country you'll be working in can help counteract this. For more information, please see Chapter 12.

22. **B.** The project management knowledge areas bring processes together that have commonalities. For example, Project Integration Management consists of the Project Plan Development, Project Plan Execution, and Integrated Change Control processes. For more information, please see Chapter 2.

23. **B.** Inspection involves physically looking at, measuring, or testing results to determine if they conform to your quality standards. Performance measurements are not part of the Quality Control process, and prevention is not an identified tool and technique of Quality Control. For more information, please see Chapter 10.

24. **A.** Administrative Closure occurs at the end of the project phase and at the end of the project itself. Administrative Closure is performed after Contract Closeout. It is the last process performed on your project. For more information, please see Chapter 11.

25. A. Since you've identified the risks, you've completed the Risk Identification process. The Delphi technique is a tool and technique of the Risk Identification process, so answer B is not correct. You will proceed to assign probabilities and impacts using Qualitative or Quantitative Risk Analysis, or both. You can use either process or both processes. They are not both required, therefore answer C is incorrect. For more information, please see Chapter 6.

26. D. Fast tracking is the best answer in this scenario. Budget was the original constraint on this project, so it's highly unlikely the project manager would get more resources to assist with the project. The next best thing is to compress phases to shorten the project duration. For more information, please see Chapter 1.

27. C. The smoothing technique does not usually result in a permanent solution. The problem is downplayed to make it seem less important than it is, which makes the problem tend to resurface later. For more information, please see Chapter 8.

28. D. The Staff Acquisition outputs are the assignment of project staff and project team directory. For more information, please see Chapter 5.

29. A. The Executing process takes published project plans and turns them into actions to accomplish the goals of the project. For more information, please see Chapter 1.

30. B. Supporting detail is an output of the Scope Planning process. For more information, please see Chapter 4.

31. A. Project Initiation has two tools and techniques: project selection methods and expert judgment. For more information, please see Chapter 3.

32. B. Honesty and truthful reporting are required of PMPs. In this situation, you would inform the customer of everything you know regarding the problem and work to find alternative solutions. For more information, please see Chapter 12.

33. C. According to *A Guide to the PMBOK*, the project manager is identified and assigned as an output of the Initiation process. In practice, project managers are often assigned at the beginning of this process. For more information, please see Chapter 2.

34. B. The arrow diagramming method (ADM)—also called activity on arrow (AOA)—uses more than one time estimate to determine project duration. For more information, please see Chapter 5.

35. B. Functional managers who have lots of authority and power working with project coordinators who have minimal authority and power characterizes a weak matrix organization. Project managers in weak matrix organizations are sometimes called project coordinators, project leaders, or project expeditors. For more information, please see Chapter 1.

36. C. Weak matrix organizational structures tend to experience the least amount of stress during the project closeout processes. For more information, please see Chapter 11.

37. D. You will develop a contingency plan that might include contracting with a vendor in the customer's country to perform the installation and setup should your team be unable to enter the country. Cause-and-effect diagrams are used during the Quality Planning process to map out problems and their causes. For more information, please see Chapter 6.

38. D.   The Cost Estimating and Cost Budgeting processes include bottom-up estimating techniques as well as analogous estimating, parametric modeling, and computerized tools. However, answer D is correct because the cost baseline is an output of the Cost Budgeting process and is used to measure and track the project throughout the remaining process groups. For more information, please see Chapter 7.

39. C.   VAC is calculated this way: VAC = BAC − EAC. Therefore, 525 − 500 = 25. For more information, please see Chapter 9.

40. D.   Risk is lowest during the Closing processes because you've completed the work of the project at this point. For more information, please see Chapter 11.

41. D.   Product descriptions are an input to the Initiation process and contain less detail now and more detail as the project progresses. For more information, please see Chapter 2.

42. C.   Source Selection receives bids and proposals from potential vendors and applies evaluation criteria to them to make a selection. For more information, please see Chapter 9.

43. C.   Change requests are an input to the Integrated Change Control process. The other tools and techniques of this process are change control system and project management information system. For more information, please see Chapter 10.

44. D.   Information that is complex and detailed is best conveyed in writing. A verbal follow-up would be good to answer questions and clarify information. Vertical and horizontal are ways of communicating within the organization. For more information, please see Chapter 8.

45. A.   The best response is to decline the offer. This is a conflict of interest, and accepting the offer puts your own integrity and the contract award process in jeopardy. For more information, please see Chapter 12.

46. B.   PERT is the Program Evaluation and Review Technique that uses weighted average and standard deviation to determine project durations. It is used for large, highly complex projects. For more information, please see Chapter 7.

47. B.   The tools and techniques of the Scope Planning process include product analysis, benefit/cost analysis, alternatives identification, and expert judgment. For more information, please see Chapter 4.

48. D.   The payback period for Project Fish'n for Chips is eight months. This project will receive $300,000 every three months, or $100,000 per month. The $800,000 will be paid back in eight months. For more information, please see Chapter 3.

49. A.   Analogous estimating—also called top-down estimating—is a form of expert judgment. Analogous estimating can be used to estimate cost or time and considers historical information from previous, similar projects. For more information, please see Chapter 5.

50. A.   A conflict of interest is any situation that compromises the outcome of the project or ignores the impact to the project to benefit yourself or others. For more information, please see Chapter 12.

51. D. The work package level is the lowest level in the WBS. Time and cost estimation is easily determined at this level, as are resource assignments. Quality control measurements can be determined at this level as well. For more information, please see Chapter 4.

52. C. Initiation process inputs include the product description, which describes the characteristics of the product; the strategic plan, which outlines the vision of the company; project selection criteria, which help determine how projects will be selected; and historical information regarding past projects of a similar nature. For more information, please see Chapter 2.

53. B. Decision models are project selection methods used as tools and techniques in Initiation. Decision models include benefit measurement methods and constrained optimization methods. For more information, please see Chapter 3.

54. B. Statistical sampling is a tool and technique of the Quality Control process. For more information, please see Chapter 9.

55. A. Constraints limit the options of the project team by restricting action or dictating action. Budget, time, and quality are the three most common constraints. Assumptions are presumed to be true for planning purposes. Always validate your assumptions. For more information, please see Chapter 2.

56. A. Scope changes will cause schedule revisions, but schedule revisions do not change the project scope. Project requirements are part of the scope statement, and therefore D is one of the correct responses. For more information, please see Chapter 10.

57. B. The Quantitative Risk Analysis process has four tools and techniques: interviewing, sensitivity analysis, decision tree analysis, and simulation. For more information, please see Chapter 6.

58. D. The *Project Management Professional Code of Professional Conduct* is published by PMI, and all PMPs are expected to adhere to its standards. For more information, please see Chapter 12.

59. B. The Organizational Planning process identifies project resources, documents roles and responsibilities of project team members and stakeholders, and documents reporting relationships. For more information, please see Chapter 5.

60. B. Critical path tasks are those tasks with zero float time. Float time, or slack time, is the amount of time between an activity's early start date and late start date. For more information, please see Chapter 7.

Chapter 1

What Is a Project?

THE PMP GENERAL EXAM CONTENT COVERED IN THIS CHAPTER INCLUDES:

- ✓ 1. Defining a project
- ✓ 2. Defining project management
- ✓ 3. Determining general management skills
- ✓ 4. Identifying organizational structures
- ✓ 5. Defining constraints
- ✓ 6. Defining assumptions
- ✓ 7. Defining project life cycles
- ✓ 8. Defining project management processes

Congratulations on your decision to study for and take the Project Management Institute (PMI)'s Project Management Professional (PMP) certification exam. This book was written with you in mind. The focus and content of this book revolve heavily around the information contained in *A Guide to the Project Management Body of Knowledge (PMBOK)*, published by PMI. I will refer to this guide throughout this book and elaborate on those areas that appear on the test. Keep in mind that the test covers all the project management processes, so don't skip anything in your study time.

When possible, I'll pass on hints and study tips that I collected while studying for the exam myself. Your first tip is to familiarize yourself with the terminology used in *A Guide to the PMBOK*. PMI has worked hard to develop and define standard project management terms, and these terms are used interchangeably among industries. For example, *resource planning* means the same thing to someone working in construction, information technology, or telecommunications. You'll find *A Guide to the PMBOK* terms explained throughout this book. Even if you are an experienced project manager, you might find that PMI uses specific terms for things that you call by another name. So, step one is to get familiar with the terminology.

This chapter lays the foundation for building and managing your project. We'll address project and project management definitions as well as organizational structures. Good luck!

Is It a Project?

The VP of marketing approaches you with a fabulous idea—"fabulous" because he's the big boss and because he thought it up. He wants to set up kiosks in local grocery stores as mini offices. These offices will offer customers the ability to sign up for new wireless phone services, make their wireless phone bill payments, and purchase equipment and accessories. He believes that the exposure in grocery stores will increase awareness of the company's offerings. After all, everyone has to eat, right? He told you that the board of directors has already cleared the project and he'll dedicate as many resources to this as he can. He wants the new kiosks in place in 12 stores by the end of next year. The best news is he's assigned you to head up this project.

Your first question should be, "Is it a project?" This may seem elementary, but confusing projects with ongoing operations happens often. According to *A Guide to the PMBOK*, page 4, "...a project is a temporary endeavor undertaken to create a unique product, service or result."

Quotations from *A Guide to the PMBOK* are cited in the text with the following abbreviation: *A Guide to the PMBOK:* Project Management Institute, *A Guide to the Project Management Body of Knowledge (PMBOK Guide)* 2000 Edition, Project Management Institute, Inc., 2000.

Projects versus Operations

Projects are temporary in nature, while operations are ongoing. Projects have definitive start dates and definitive end dates. The project is completed when the goals and objectives of the project are accomplished. Sometimes projects end when it's determined that the goals and objectives cannot be accomplished and the project is canceled. Operations involve work that is continuous without an ending date and often repeat the same process.

Projects exist to bring about a product or service that hasn't existed before. In this sense, a project is unique. However, don't get confused by the term *unique*. For example, Ford Motor Company is in the business of designing and assembling cars. Each model that Ford designs and produces can be considered a project. The models differ from each other in their features and are marketed to people with various needs. An SUV serves a different purpose and clientele than a luxury model. The design and marketing of these two models are unique projects. The actual assembly of the cars can be considered an operation—a repetitive process that is followed for most makes and models.

Determining the characteristics and features of the different car models is carried out through what *A Guide to the PMBOK* terms *progressive elaboration*. This means the characteristics of the product or service of the project (the SUV, for example) are determined incrementally and are continually refined and worked out in detail as the project progresses. These product characteristics typically start out very broad-based at the beginning of the project and are progressively elaborated into more and more detail over time. Keep in mind that product characteristics are progressively elaborated, but the work of the project itself stays constant.

Exam Spotlight

Progressive elaboration is a concept you may encounter on the exam.

A project is successful when it achieves its objectives and meets or exceeds the expectations of the stakeholders. *Stakeholders* are those folks with a vested interest in your project. They are the people who have something to either gain or lose as a result of the project.

Key stakeholders can make or break the success of a project. Even if all the deliverables are met and the objectives are satisfied, if your key stakeholders aren't happy—nobody's happy.

Stakeholders

The *project sponsor*, generally an executive in the organization with the authority to assign resources and enforce decisions regarding the project, is a stakeholder. The customer is a stakeholder, as are contractors and suppliers. The project manager, project team members, and the managers from other departments in the organization are stakeholders as well. It's important to identify all the stakeholders in your project up front. If you leave out an important stakeholder or their department's function and don't discover the error until well into the project, it could be a project killer.

Figure 1.1 shows a sample listing of the kinds of stakeholders involved on a typical project.

FIGURE 1.1   Project stakeholders

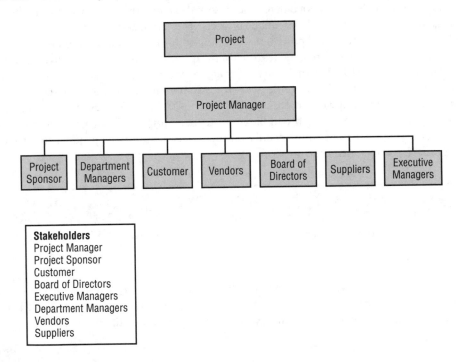

Many times, stakeholders have conflicting interests. It's the project manager's responsibility to understand these conflicts and try to resolve them. Be certain to identify and meet with all key stakeholders early in the project to understand all their needs and constraints. When in doubt, stakeholder conflicts should always be resolved in favor of the customer.

Project Characteristics

We've just learned that a project has several characteristics:

- Projects are unique.
- Projects are temporary in nature and have a definite beginning and ending date.
- Projects are completed when the project goals are achieved.
- A successful project is one that meets or exceeds the expectations of your stakeholders.

Using these criteria, let's examine the assignment from the VP of marketing to determine if it is a project:

Is it unique?   Yes, because the kiosks don't exist in the local grocery stores. This is a new way of offering the company's services to its customer base. While the service the company is offering isn't new, the way they are presenting their services is.

Does the project have a limited time frame?   Yes, the start date of this project is today, and the end date is the end of next year. It is a temporary endeavor.

Is there a way to determine when the project is completed?   Yes, the kiosks will be installed, and services will be offered from them. Once all of the kiosks are intact and operating, the project will come to a close.

Is there a way to determine stakeholder satisfaction?   Yes, the expectations of the stakeholders will be documented in the form of requirements during the planning processes. These requirements will be compared to the finished product to determine if it meets the expectations of the stakeholder.

Houston, we have a project.

What Is Project Management?

You've determined that you indeed have a project. What now? The notes you scratched out on the back of a napkin at coffee break might get you started, but that's not exactly good project management practice.

We have all witnessed this scenario—an assignment is made and the project team members jump directly into the project, busying themselves with building the product or service requested. Often, careful thought is not given to the project-planning process. I'm sure you've heard co-workers toss around statements like, "That would be a waste of valuable time" or "Why plan when you can just start building?" Project progress is rarely measured against the customer requirements. In the end, the delivered product or service doesn't meet the expectations of the customer! This is a frustrating experience for all those involved. Unfortunately, many projects follow this poorly constructed path.

Project management brings together a set of tools and techniques—performed by people—to describe, organize, and monitor the work of project activities. *Project managers* are the people responsible for managing the project processes and applying the tools and techniques used to carry out the project activities. All projects are composed of processes, even if they employ a haphazard approach. There are many advantages to organizing projects and teams around the project management processes endorsed by PMI. We'll be examining those processes and their advantages in depth throughout the remainder of this book.

Project management involves many skills and techniques. According to *A Guide to the PMBOK,* page 6, "Project management is the application of knowledge, skills, tools, and techniques to project activities to meet project requirements." It is the responsibility of the project manager to ensure project management techniques are applied and followed.

Exam Spotlight

Know the term *project management* as it's described in *A Guide to the PMBOK.*

Project management is a process that includes planning, putting the project plan into action, and measuring progress and performance. Planning is one of the most important functions you'll perform during the course of a project. It sets the standard for the rest of the project's life and is used to track future project performance. Before we begin the planning process, we'll need to look at some of the constraints found on all projects and define the term *programs.*

Project Constraints

In my organization, and I'm sure the same is true in yours, there are far more project requests than we have resources to work on them. In this case, resources are a constraint. You'll find a similar phenomenon occurs on individual projects as well. Almost every project you'll encounter must work within the triple constraint combination of time, money (resources), and quality. Usually one or two of the triple constraints, sometimes all three, are limited, which restricts the actions of the project team. You might work on projects where you have an almost unlimited budget (don't we wish!), but time is the limitation. The computer-programming changes required for the year 2000 are an example of a time-constrained project, because moving the date wasn't an option.

Other projects might present the opposite scenario. You have all the time you need to complete the project, but the budget is fixed. Still other projects may incorporate two or three of the constraints. Government agencies are notorious for starting projects that have at least two and sometimes all three constraints. For example, new tax law legislation is passed that impacts the computer programs, requiring new programs to calculate and track the tax changes. Typically, a due date is given when the tax law takes effect, and the organization responsible is required to implement the changes with no additions to budget or staff. In other words, they are told to use existing resources to accomplish the goals of the project. The specific requirements of the project are such that quality cannot be fudged to try to meet the time deadline.

As a project manager, one of your biggest jobs is to balance the project constraints while meeting or exceeding the expectations of your stakeholders. In most projects, you will usually be faced with balancing only one or two of the triple constraints. For example, if the project goal is a high-quality product, the saying goes, "I can give it to you fast or I can give to you cheap, but I can't give it to you fast and cheap."

Projects are not limited to the triple constraints, but these are typically the most burdensome restrictions you'll find on a project. We'll talk more about constraints in Chapter 2, "Initiating the Project."

Project Assumptions

Assumptions, for the purposes of project management, are things you believe to be true. For example, if you're working on a large construction project, you might make assumptions about the availability of materials. You may assume that concrete, lumber, drywall, and so on are widely available and reasonably priced. You may also assume that finding contract labor is either easy or difficult, depending on the economic times and the availability of labor in your locale. Each project will have its own set of assumptions, and they should be identified, documented, and updated throughout the project. We'll talk more about identifying and documenting project assumptions in Chapter 2.

Programs

Programs are groups of related projects that are managed using the same techniques in a coordinated fashion. When projects are managed collectively as programs, they capitalize on benefits that wouldn't be achievable if the projects were managed separately. Sometimes programs involve aspects of ongoing operations as well. This would be the case where a very large program exists with many subprojects under it—for example, building a new shopping mall. Many subprojects exist underneath this program such as excavation, construction, interior design, store placement, marketing, facilities management, etc. Each of the subprojects is really a project unto itself. Each subproject has its own project manager, who reports to a project manager with responsibility over several of the areas, who in turn reports to the head project manager over the entire program. After the structure itself is built, the management of the facility is considered the ongoing operations part of this program.

Defining Skills Every Good Project Manager Needs

Many times, organizations will knight their technical experts as project managers. The skill and expertise that made them stars in their technical fields are mistakenly thought to translate into project management skills. This is not necessarily so.

Project managers are generalists with many skills in their repertoire. They are problem solvers who wear many hats. Project managers might indeed possess technical skills, but technical skills are not a prerequisite for sound project management skills. Your project team should include a few technical experts, and these are the people whom the project manager will rely on for technical details. I have seen project managers with many years of experience in the construction industry successfully manage multi-million-dollar information technology projects. This is because project management techniques apply across industries and across projects. Understanding and applying good project management techniques, along with a solid understanding of general management skills, are career builders for all aspiring project managers.

Project managers have been likened to small-business owners. They need to know a little bit about every aspect of management. General management skills include every area of management from accounting to strategic planning to supervision, personnel administration, and more. General management skills are called into play on every project. But some projects require specific skills in certain application areas. Application areas are made up of categories of projects that have common elements due to the disciplines, regulations, or specific needs of the product the project has set out to produce, the customer, or the industry. For example, most governments have specific procurement rules that apply to their projects that wouldn't be applicable in the construction industry. The pharmaceutical industry is acutely interested in regulations set forth by the Food and Drug Administration, whereas the automotive industry has little or no concern for these regulations.

The general management skills listed in this section are the foundation of good project management practices. Your mastery of them (or lack thereof) will likely affect project outcomes. The various skills of a project manager can be broken out in a more or less declining scale of importance. We'll look at an overview of these skills now and discuss each in more detail in subsequent chapters.

Communication Skills

One of the single most important characteristics of a first-rate project manager is excellent communication skills. Written and oral communications are the backbone of all successful projects. Many forms of communication will exist during the life of your project. As the creator or manager of most of the project communication (project documents, meeting updates, status reports, etc.), it's your job to ensure that the information is explicit, clear, and complete so that your audience will have no trouble understanding what has been communicated. Once the information has been distributed, it is the responsibility of the person receiving the information to make sure they understand it.

There are many forms of communication and communication styles, which Chapter 8, "Developing the Project Team," covers in more depth.

Organizational Skills

Organizational and planning skills are probably the second most important skills a project manager can possess. Organization takes on many forms. As project manager, you'll have project documentation, requirements information, memos, project reports, personnel records, vendor quotes, contracts, and much more to track and be able to locate in a moment's notice. You will also have to organize meetings, put together teams, and perhaps manage and organize media release schedules, depending on your project.

Closely associated with organizational skills are time management skills. Take some time to attend a time management class if you've never attended one. They have some great tips and techniques to help you prioritize problems and interruptions, prioritize your day, and manage your time.

Planning is discussed extensively throughout the course of this book. There isn't any aspect of project management that doesn't first involve planning. Planning skills go hand in hand with organizational skills. Combining these two with excellent communication skills is almost a sure guarantee of your success in the project management field.

Budgeting Skills

Project managers establish and manage budgets and therefore need some knowledge of finance and accounting principles. Especially important in this skill area is the ability to perform cost estimates for project budgeting. There are different methods available to determine the project costs. They range from estimating individual activities and rolling the estimates up to estimating the project's cost in one big chunk. These methods will be discussed more fully in later chapters.

After a budget is determined, you can start spending. This sounds more exciting than it actually is. Reading and understanding vendor quotes, preparing or overseeing purchase orders, and reconciling invoices are budgeting skills that will be used by the project manager on most projects. These costs will be linked back to project activities and expense items in the project's budget.

Problem-Solving Skills

Show me a project, and I'll show you problems. All projects, in fact much of everyday life, have some problems. Isn't that what they say builds character? But I digress.

Problem solving is really a twofold process. First, you must define the problem by separating the causes from the symptoms. Often when defining problems, you end up just describing the symptoms instead of really getting to the heart of what's causing the problem. To avoid that, ask yourself questions like, "Is it an internal or external problem?" or "Is it a technical problem?" or "Are there interpersonal problems between team members?" or "Is it managerial?" or "What are the potential impacts or consequences?" These kinds of questions will help you to get to the cause of the problem.

Next, after the problem has been defined, you have some decisions to make. It will take a little time to examine and analyze the problem, the situation causing it, and the alternatives available.

After this analysis, the project manager will determine the best course of action to take and implement the decision. The timing of the decision is often as important as the decision itself. If you make a good decision but implement it too late, it may turn into a bad decision.

Negotiation and Influencing Skills

Effective problem solving requires negotiation and influencing skills. We all utilize negotiation skills in one form or another every day. For example, on a nightly basis I am asked, "Honey, what do you want for dinner?" Then the negotiations begin, and the fried chicken versus swordfish discussion commences. Simply put, negotiating is working with others to come to an agreement.

Negotiation on projects is necessary in almost every area of the project, from scope definition to budgets, contracts, resource assignments, and more. This may involve one-on-one negotiation or might involve teams of people, and it can occur many times throughout the project.

Influencing is convincing the other party that swordfish is a better choice than fried chicken, even if fried chicken is what they want. It's also the ability to get things done. Influencing requires an understanding of the formal and informal structure of all the organizations involved in the project.

Power and politics are techniques used to influence people to perform. *Power* is the ability to get people to do things they wouldn't do otherwise. It's also the ability to change minds and the course of events and to influence outcomes. We'll discuss power further in Chapter 8, "Developing the Project Team." *Politics* involve getting groups of people with different interests to cooperate creatively even in the midst of conflict and disorder.

These skills will be utilized in all areas of project management. Start practicing now because, guaranteed, you'll need these skills on your next project.

Leadership Skills

Leaders and *managers* are not synonymous terms. Leaders impart vision, gain consensus for strategic goals, establish direction, and inspire and motivate others. Managers focus on results and are concerned with getting the job done according to the requirements. Even though leaders and managers are not the same, project managers must exhibit the characteristics of both during different times on the project. Understanding when to switch from leadership to management and then back again is a finely tuned and necessary talent.

Team-Building and Human Resources Skills

Project managers will rely heavily on team-building and human resource management skills. Teams are often formed with people from different parts of the organization. These people may or may not have worked together before, so there may be some component of team-building groundwork that will involve the project manager. The project manager will set the tone for the project team and will help them work through the various team-forming stages to become fully functional.

An interesting caveat to the team-building role is that project managers many times are responsible for motivating team members who are not their direct reports. This has its own set of challenges and dilemmas. One way to help this situation is to ask the functional manager to allow you to participate in your project team members' performance reviews. Use the negotiation and influencing skills I talked about earlier to make sure you're part of this process.

A Mile Wide and an Inch Deep

Project managers are an interesting bunch. They know a little bit about a lot of things and are excellent communicators. Or, as one person said, they're "a mile wide and an inch deep." They have the ability to motivate people, even those who have no reason to be loyal to the project, and they can make the hard-line calls when necessary. Project managers can get caught in sticky situations that occasionally require making decisions that are good for the company (or the customer) but aren't good for certain stakeholders. These offended stakeholders will then drag their feet, and the project manager has to play the heavy in order to motivate and gain their cooperation again. Some organizations hire contract project managers to run their large, company-altering projects, just because they don't want to burn out a key employee in this role. Fortunately, that doesn't happen often.

Now that you've been properly introduced to some of the skills you need in your tool kit, you'll know to be prepared to communicate, solve problems, lead, and negotiate your way through your next project.

Understanding Organizational Structures

Just as projects are unique, so are the organizations in which they're carried out. The key to determining the type of organization you work in is by measuring how much authority senior management is willing to delegate to project managers. While uniqueness abounds in business cultures, all organizations are structured in one of three ways: functional, projectized, or matrix. Variations and combinations exist among these three structures, such as a projectized structure within a functional organization, and weak matrix, balanced matrix, and strong matrix organizations.

It pays to know and understand the organizational structure and the culture of the entity you're working with. Companies with aggressive cultures that are comfortable in a leading-edge position within their industry are highly likely to take on risky projects. Project managers who are willing to suggest new ideas and projects that have never been undertaken before are likely to receive a warm reception in this kind of environment. Conversely, organizational cultures that are risk averse and prefer the follow-the-leader position within their industry are highly unlikely to take on risky endeavors. Project managers with risk-seeking, aggressive styles are likely to receive a cool reception in a culture like this.

The level of authority the project manager enjoys is denoted by the organizational structure. For example, a project manager within a functional organization has little to no formal authority. And their title may not be project manager; instead they might be called a project leader, a project coordinator, or perhaps a project expeditor.

Let's take a look at each of these organizations individually to better understand how the project management role works in each one.

Functional Organizations

One common type of organization is the *functional organization*. Chances are you have worked in this type of organization. This is probably the oldest style of organization and is therefore known as the traditional approach to organizing businesses.

Functional organizations are centered on specialties and grouped by function; hence the term *functional organization*. As an example, the organization might have a human resources department, finance department, marketing department, etc. The work in these departments is specialized and requires people who have the skill sets and experiences in these specialized functions to perform specific duties for the department. Figure 1.2 shows a typical org chart for a functional organization.

FIGURE 1.2   Functional org chart

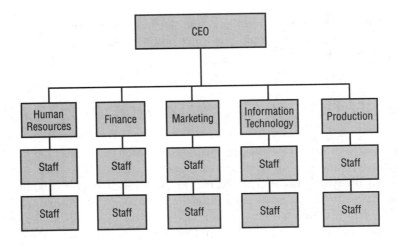

You can see that this type of organization is set up to be a hierarchy. Staff personnel report to managers who report to department heads who report to vice presidents who report to the CEO. In other words, each employee reports to only one manager; ultimately, one person at the top is in charge. Many companies today, as well as governmental agencies, are structured in a hierarchical fashion. In organizations like this, be aware of the chain of command. A strict chain of command may exist, and the corporate culture might dictate that you follow it. Roughly translated: *Don't talk to the big boss without first talking to your boss who talks to their boss who talks to the big boss.* Wise project managers should determine if there is a chain of command, how strictly it's enforced, and how the chain is linked before venturing outside of it.

Each department or group in a functional organization is managed independently and has a limited span of control. Marketing doesn't run the finance department or their projects, for example. The marketing department is concerned with their own functions and projects. If it were necessary for the marketing department to get input from the finance department on a project, the marketing team members would follow the chain of command. A marketing manager would speak to a manager in finance to get the needed information and then pass it back down to the project team.

Human Resources in a Functional Organization

Commonalities exist among the personnel assigned to the various departments in a functional organization. In theory, people with similar skills and experiences are easier to manage as a group. Instead of scattering them throughout the organization, it is more efficient to keep them functioning together. Work assignments are easily distributed to those who are best suited for the task when everyone with the same skill works together. Usually, the supervisors and managers of these workers are experienced in the area they supervise and are able to recommend training and career enrichment activities for their employees.

> Workers in functional organizations specialize in an area of expertise—finance or personnel administration, for instance—and then become very good at their specialty.

There is a clear upward career path for people in a functional organization. An assistant budget analyst may be promoted to a budget analyst and then eventually to a department manager over many budget analysts.

The Downside of Functional Organizations

Functional organizations have their disadvantages. If this is the kind of organization you work in, you probably have experienced some of them.

One of the greatest disadvantages for the project manager is that they have little to no formal authority. This does not mean that project managers in functional organizations are doomed to failure. Many projects are undertaken and successfully completed within this type of organization. Good communication, interpersonal, and influencing skills on the part of the project manager are required to bring about a successful project under this structure.

In a functional organization, the vice president or senior department manager is usually the one responsible for projects. The title of project manager denotes authority, and in a functional structure, that authority rests with the VP.

Managing Projects in a Functional Organization

Projects are typically undertaken in a divided approach in a functional organization. For example, the marketing department will work on their portion of the project and then hand it off to the manufacturing department to complete their part of the project, and so on. The work the marketing department does is considered a marketing project, while the work the manufacturing department does is considered a manufacturing project.

Some projects require project team members from different departments to work together at the same time on various aspects of the project. Project team members in this structure will more than likely remain loyal to their functional manager. The functional manager is responsible for their performance reviews, and their career opportunities lie within the functional department—not within the project team. Exhibiting leadership skills by forming a common vision regarding the project and the ability to motivate people to work toward that vision are great skills to exercise in this situation. As previously mentioned, it also doesn't hurt to have the project manager work with the functional manager in contributing to the employee's performance review.

Resource Pressures in a Functional Organization

Competition for resources and project priorities can become fierce when multiple projects are undertaken within a functional organization. For example, in my organization, it's common to have competing project requests from three or more departments all vying for the same resources. Thrown into the heap is the requirement to make, for example, mandated tax law changes, which automatically usurps all other priorities. This sometimes causes frustration and political infighting. One department thinks their project is more important than another and will do anything to get that project pushed ahead of the others. Again, it takes great skill and diplomatic abilities to keep projects on track and functioning smoothly. In a later chapter, we'll discuss the importance of gaining stakeholder buy-in, prioritization, and communication distribution to avert some of these problems.

Project managers have little authority in functional organizations, but with the right skills, they can successfully accomplish many projects. Table 1.1 highlights the advantages and disadvantages of this type of organization.

TABLE 1.1 Functional Organizations

Advantages	Disadvantages
Enduring organizational structure.	Project manager has little to no formal authority.
Clear career path with separation of functions, allowing specialty skills to flourish.	Multiple projects compete for limited resources and priority.
Employees have one supervisor with a clear chain of command.	Project team members are loyal to the functional manager.

Projectized Organizations

Projectized organizations are nearly the opposite of functional organizations. The focus of this type of organization is the project itself. The idea behind a projectized organization is to develop loyalty to the project, not to a functional manager.

Figure 1.3 shows a typical org chart for a projectized organization.

FIGURE 1.3 Projectized org chart

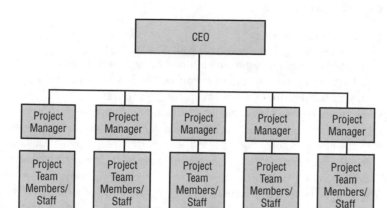

Organizational resources are dedicated to projects and project work in purely projectized organizations. Project managers almost always have ultimate authority over the project in this structure and report directly to the CEO. In a purely projectized organization, supporting functions like human resources and accounting might report directly to the project manager as well. Project managers are responsible for making decisions regarding the project and acquiring and assigning resources. They have the authority to choose and assign resources from other areas in the organization or to hire them from outside if needed. However, project managers in all organizational structures are limited by the triple constraints. For example, if the budget doesn't exist to hire additional resources, the project manager will have to come up with alternatives to solve this problem.

Teams are formed and often *collocated*, which means that team members physically work at the same location. Project team members report to the project manager, not to a functional or departmental manager. One obvious drawback to a projectized organization is that project team members may find themselves out of work at the end of the project. An example of this might be a consultant who works on a project until completion and then is put on the bench or let go at the end of the project. Some inefficiency exists in this kind of organization when it comes to resource utilization. If you have a situation where you need a highly specialized skill at certain times throughout the project, the resource you're using to perform this function might be idle during other times in the project.

In summary, projectized organizations are identified in several ways:

- Project managers have ultimate authority over the project.
- The focus of the organization is the project.
- The organization's resources are focused on projects and project work.
- Team members are collocated.
- Loyalties are formed to the project, not to a functional manager.
- Project teams are dissolved at the conclusion of the project.

You've been appointed project manager for your company's website design and implementation. You're working in a projectized organization, so you have the authority to acquire and assign resources. You put together your team, including programmers, technical writers, testers, and business analysts. Debbie, a highly qualified graphic arts designer, is also part of your team. Debbie's specialized graphic arts skills are needed only at certain times throughout the project. When she has completed the graphic design portion of the screen she's working on, there isn't anything else for her to do until the next page is ready. Depending on how involved the project is and how the work is structured, days or weeks might pass before Debbie's skills are needed. This is where the inefficiency occurs in a purely projectized organization. The project manager will have to find other duties that Debbie can perform during these down times. It's not practical to let her go and then hire her back when she's needed again.

In this situation, you might assign Debbie to other project duties when she's not working on graphic design. Perhaps she can edit the text for the web pages or assist with the design of the upcoming marketing campaign. You might also share Debbie's time with another project manager in the organization.

During the planning process, you will discover the skills and abilities of all your team members so that you can plan their schedules accordingly and eliminate idle time.

Matrix Organizations

Matrix organizations came about to minimize the differences between, and take advantage of, the strengths and weaknesses of functional and projectized organizations. The idea at play here is that the best of both organizational structures can be realized by combining them into one. The project objectives are fulfilled and good project management techniques are utilized, while still maintaining a hierarchical structure in the organization.

Employees in a matrix organization report to one functional manager and to at least one project manager. It's possible that employees could report to multiple project managers if they are working on multiple projects at one time. Functional managers pick up the administrative portion of the duties and assign employees to projects. They also monitor the work of their employees on the various projects. Project managers are responsible for executing the project and giving out work assignments based on project activities. Project managers and functional managers share the responsibility of performance reviews for the employee.

In a nutshell, functional managers assign employees to projects, while project managers assign tasks associated with the project in a matrix organization.

Project Focus in a Matrix Organization

Matrix organizations allow project managers to focus on the project and project work just like in a projectized organization. The project team is free to focus on the project objectives without distractions from the functional department.

Project managers should take care when working up activity and project estimates for the project in a matrix organization. The estimates should be given to the functional managers for input before publishing. The functional manager is the one in charge of assigning or freeing up resources to work on projects. If the project manager is counting on a certain employee to work on the project at a certain time, the project manager should determine their availability up front with the functional manager. Project estimates might have to be modified if it's discovered that the employee they were counting on is not available when needed.

Balance of Power in a Matrix Organization

As we've discussed, a lot of communication and negotiation takes place between the project manager and the functional manager. This calls for a balance of power between the two, or one will dominate the other.

In a strong matrix organization, the balance of power rests with the project manager. They have the ability to strong-arm the functional managers into giving up their best resources for projects. Sometimes, more resources than necessary are assembled for the project, and then project managers negotiate these resources among themselves, cutting out the functional manager altogether, as you can see in Figure 1.4.

FIGURE 1.4   Strong matrix org chart

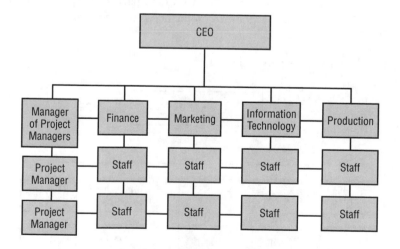

On the other end of the spectrum is the weak matrix (see Figure 1.5). As you would suspect, the functional managers have all the power in this structure. Project managers are really project coordinators or expeditors with part-time responsibilities on projects in a weak matrix organization.

Project managers have little to no authority, just like in the functional organization. On the other hand, the functional managers have a lot of authority and make all the work assignments. The project manager simply expedites the project.

FIGURE 1.5   Weak matrix org chart

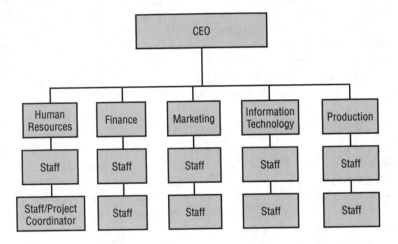

In between the weak matrix and the strong matrix is an organizational structure called the *balanced matrix* (see Figure 1.6). The features of the balanced matrix are what we've been discussing throughout this section. The power is balanced between project managers and functional managers. Each manager has responsibility for their parts of the project or organization, and employees get assigned to projects based on the needs of the project, not the strength or weakness of the manager's position.

FIGURE 1.6   Balanced matrix org chart

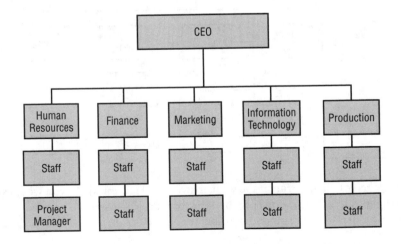

Matrix organizations have subtle differences, and it's important to understand their differences for the PMP exam. The easiest way to remember them is that the weak matrix has many of the same characteristics as the functional organization, while the strong matrix has many of the same characteristics as the projectized organization. The balanced matrix is exactly that—a balance between weak and strong, where the project manager shares authority and responsibility with the functional manager. Table 1.2 compares all three structures.

TABLE 1.2   Comparing Matrix Structures

	Weak Matrix	**Balanced Matrix**	**Strong Matrix**
Project Manager's Title:	Project coordinator, project leader, or project expeditor	Project manager	Project manager
Project Manager's Focus:	Split focus between project and functional responsibilities	Projects and project work	Projects and project work
Project Manager's Power:	Minimal authority and power	Balance of authority and power	Full authority and power
Project Manager's Time:	Part-time on projects	Full-time on projects	Full-time on projects
Organization Style:	Most like functional organization	Blend of both weak and strong matrix	Most like a projectized organization
Project Manager Reports to:	Functional manager	A functional manager, but shares authority and power	Manager of project managers

Most organizations today use some combination of the organizational structures described here. They're a composite of functional, projectized, and matrix structures. It's rare that an organization would be purely functional or purely projectized. For example, projectized structures can coexist within functional organizations.

In the case of a high-profile, critical project, the functional organization might appoint a special project team to work only on that project. The team is structured outside the bounds of the functional organization and the project manager has ultimate authority for the project. This is a workable project management approach and ensures open communication between the project manager and team members. At the end of the project, the project team is dissolved and the project members return to their functional areas to resume their usual duties.

Exam Spotlight

Organizational structure is a topic you may encounter on the exam.

Organizations are unique, as are the projects they undertake. Understanding the organizational structure will help you, as a project manager, with the cultural influences and communication avenues that exist in the organization to gain cooperation and successfully bring your projects to a close.

Understanding Project Life Cycles and Project Management Processes

Project life cycles are similar to the life cycle that parents experience raising their children to adulthood. Children start out as infants and generate lots of excitement wherever they go. However, not much is known about them at first. So you study them as they grow and assess their needs. Over time, they mature and grow (and cost a lot of money in the process), until one day the parents' job is done.

Projects start out just like this and progress along a similar path. Someone comes up with a great idea for a project and actively solicits support for the project. The project, after being approved, progresses through the intermediate phases to the ending phase, where the project is completed and closed out.

Project Life Cycles and Phases

All projects are divided into phases, and all projects, large or small, have a similar life cycle structure. At a minimum, a project will have a beginning or initiation phase, an intermediate phase or phases, and an ending phase. The number of phases depends on the project complexity and its industry. All the collective phases the project progresses through in concert are called the *project life cycle*.

The end of each phase allows the project manager, stakeholders, and project sponsor the opportunity to determine if the project should continue to the next phase. Project phases evolve through the life cycle in a series of *handoffs*. The end of one phase sequence typically marks the beginning of the next. For example, in the construction industry, feasibility studies often take place in the beginning phase of a project. The purpose of the feasibility study might be to determine if the project is worth undertaking and whether the project will be profitable for the construction company. The completion and approval of the feasibility study trigger the beginning of the planning phase, where requirements are documented and then handed off to the design phase, where blueprints are produced.

You will recognize phase completion, because each phase has a specific *deliverable*, or multiple deliverables, that marks the end of the phase. A deliverable is an output that must be produced to bring the phase or project to completion. Deliverables are tangible and can be measured and easily proved. For instance, a hypothetical deliverable produced in the beginning phase of our construction industry example would be the feasibility study. Deliverables might also include things like design documents, project budgets, blueprints, project schedules, prototypes, etc. This analysis allows those involved with the opportunity to determine if the project should continue to the next phase. The feasibility study might show that environmental impacts of an enormous nature would result if the construction project were undertaken at the proposed location. Based on this information, a go or no-go decision can be made at the end of this phase. The end of a phase also gives the project manager the ability to discover, address, and take corrective action against errors discovered during the phase.

End-of-phase reviews are called by many different names. My organization uses the term *gate review*. On page 11 of *A Guide to the PMBOK* they call these phase end reviews *phase exits*, *stage gates*, or *kill points*.

There are times when phases are overlapped to shorten or compress the project schedule. *A Guide to the PMBOK* terms this *fast tracking*. Fast tracking means that a later phase is started prior to completing and approving the phase, or phases, that come before it.

Most projects follow phase sequences that are completed within the project life cycle and as a result, have the following characteristics in common: In the beginning phase, which is where the Initiation process occurs, costs are low and there are few team members assigned to the project. As the project progresses, costs and staffing increase and then taper off at the closing phase. The potential that the project will come to a successful ending is lowest at the beginning of the project; its chance for success increases as the project progresses through its phases and life cycle stages. Risk is highest at the beginning of the project and gradually decreases the closer the project comes to completion. Stakeholders have the greatest chance of influencing the project and the characteristics of the product or service of the project in the beginning phases and have less and less influence as the project progresses.

To give you a better idea of when certain characteristics influence a project, refer to Table 1.3. A recap of the impacts in the beginning life cycle phase is shown here.

TABLE 1.3   Characteristics of the Initiation Process

Low Impact/Probability	High Impact/Probability
Costs	Risk
Staffing levels	Stakeholder influence
Chance for successful completion	

Project Management Processes

Project management processes, according to *A Guide to the PMBOK*, organize and describe the work of the project. These processes are performed by people and, much like the project phases, are interrelated and dependent on one another. For example, it would be difficult to identify specific project activities without first having an understanding of the project requirements.

PMI Process Groups

A Guide to the PMBOK documents five process groups in the project management process: Initiation, Planning, Executing, Controlling, and Closing. All of these process groups—with the exception of Initiation—have individual processes that collectively make up the group. For example, the Closing process group has two processes: Contract Closeout and Administrative Closure. Collectively, these process groups—including all their individual processes—make up the life cycle of a project. The life cycle starts with the Initiation process and progresses through all the processes in the Planning process group, the Executing process group, and so on until the project is successfully completed or it's canceled. All projects must complete the Closing processes, even if the project is killed. Phase sequences (the design phase handoff to manufacturing, for example) also occur within these life cycles. The project life cycles describe the work to be done within each cycle and the type of resources needed to perform the work. We'll look at an overview of each process here and go into more detail in later chapters.

Exam Spotlight

The five process groups are the heart of *A Guide to the PMBOK*. As you progress through this book, be certain you understand each of these processes as they're described in *A Guide to the PMBOK* also.

Initiation

The Initiation process, as its name implies, occurs at the beginning of the project or phase. Initiation acknowledges that a project, or the next project phase, should begin. Initiation grants the approval to commit the organization's resources to working on the project or phase.

Planning

Planning is the process of formulating and revising project goals and objectives and creating the project plans that will be used to achieve the goals the project was undertaken to address. Planning also involves determining alternative courses of action and selecting from among the best of those to produce the project's goals. This process group is where the project requirements are fleshed out and stakeholders are identified. Planning has more processes than any of the other project management process groups. The Executing, Controlling, and Closing process groups all rely on the Planning processes and the documentation produced during the Planning processes in order to carry out their functions. Project managers will perform frequent iterations of the Planning processes prior to project completion. Projects are unique, and as such, have never been done before. Therefore, Planning must encompass all areas of project management and consider budgets, activity definition, scope planning, schedule development, risk identification, staff acquisition, procurement planning, and more. The greatest conflicts a project manager will encounter in this process group are project prioritization issues.

Executing

The Executing process group involves putting the project plans into action. It's here that the project manager will coordinate and direct project resources to meet the objectives of the project plan. The Executing process keeps the project plan on track and ensures that future execution of project plans stays in line with project objectives. The Executing process group will utilize the most project time and resources, and as a result, costs are usually highest during the Executing process. Project managers will experience the greatest conflicts over schedules in this cycle.

Controlling

The Controlling process group is where project performance measurements are taken and analyzed to determine if the project is staying true to the project plan. If it's discovered that variances exist, corrective action is taken to get the project activities aligned with the project plan. This might require additional passes through the Planning process to realign to the project objectives.

Closing

The Closing process group is probably the most often skipped process in project management. Closing brings a formal, orderly end to a phase or to the project itself. Once the project objectives have been met, most of us are ready to move on to the next project. However, Closing is important, because all the project information is gathered now and stored for future reference. The documentation collected during Closing processes can be reviewed and utilized to avert potential problems on future projects. Contract closeout occurs here, and formal acceptance and approval are obtained from project stakeholders.

The Process Flow

The five process groups are *iterative* and should not be thought of as one-time processes. These processes will be revisited throughout the project life cycle several times as the project is refined. PMI calls this process of going back through the process groups an *iterative process*. The completion of each process allows the project manager and stakeholders to re-examine the business needs of the project and determine if the project is satisfying those needs. And it is another opportunity to make a go or no-go decision.

Figure 1.7 shows the five process groups in a typical project life cycle. Keep in mind that during phases of a project, the Closing phase can provide input to the Initiation phase. For example, once the feasibility study discussed earlier is accepted or closed, it becomes input to the Initiation phase of design and planning.

FIGURE 1.7 Project management process groups

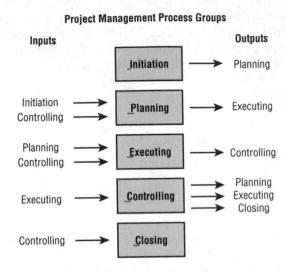

It's important to understand the flow of these processes for the exam. If you remember the processes and their inputs and outputs, it will help you when you're trying to decipher an exam question. Sometimes just understanding which process the question is asking about will help you determine the answer. One trick you can use to memorize these processes is to remember syrup of ipecac. (You probably have some of this poison antidote in your medicine cabinet at home.) When you sound out the first initial of each of the processes, it sounds like "ipecac"—IPECC (Initiation, Planning, Executing, Controlling, and Closing).

Processes exist within most of the process groups. For example, the Closing life cycle process group consists of two processes: Contract Closeout and Administrative Closure. Each process takes inputs and uses them in conjunction with various tools and techniques to produce outputs. It's outside the scope of this book to list all the inputs, tools and techniques, and outputs for each process in each process group. You'll find these detailed in *A Guide to the PMBOK*, and I highly recommend you get familiar with them.

Exam Spotlight

Understand each life cycle process group and each of the core and facilitating processes that make up these groups.

There are test questions regarding inputs, tools and techniques, and outputs of many of the processes within each process group. One way to keep them all straight is to remember that tools and techniques usually require action of some sort, be it measuring, applying some skill or technique, planning, or using expert judgment. Outputs are usually in the form of a deliverable.

Remember that a deliverable is characterized with results or outcomes that can be measured, are tangible, and are provable. Last but not least, outputs from one process sometimes serve as inputs to another process.

Establishing the Project Management Office

The concept of a *project management office*, sometimes referred to as the PMO, has been around for several years. You won't need to know anything about PMOs for the exam. However, in practice, you'll find many organizations are establishing PMOs in many different forms. The purposes of establishing a PMO, and its benefits, are many. The most common reason a company starts a project management office is to establish and maintain procedures and standards for project management methodologies to be used throughout the organization. In some organizations, project managers might work directly for the PMO and are assigned from this office to projects as they are initiated. The PMO, depending on its size and function, sometimes has experts available that assist project managers in project planning, estimating, and business assumption verification tasks. They serve as mentors to junior-level project managers and act as consultants to the senior project managers.

The PMO takes responsibility for maintaining and archiving project documentation. All project documentation and information is collected and tracked by the PMO for future reference. This office compares project goals with project progress and gives feedback to the project teams. This office also measures the project performance of active projects and suggests corrective actions. The PMO evaluates completed projects for their adherence to the triple constraints and asks the following: Did the project meet the time frames established, did it stay within budget, and was the quality acceptable?

Project management offices are becoming more common in organizations today, if for no other reason, simply to serve as a collection point for project documentation. Some PMOs are fairly sophisticated and prescribe the standards and methodologies to be used in all project phases across the enterprise. Still others provide all these functions and also offer project management consulting services. However, the establishment of a PMO is not required in order for you to apply good project management practices to your next project.

Summary

Phew! We covered a lot of ground in this chapter. We learned that projects exist to bring about a unique product or service. Projects are temporary in nature and have definite beginning and ending dates.

Stakeholders are those people or organizations that have a vested interest in the outcome of the project. Stakeholders include people like the project sponsor, the customer, key management personnel, the project manager, contractors, suppliers, and more. Projects are considered complete when the project meets or exceeds the expectations of the stakeholders.

Project management is a discipline that brings together a set of tools and techniques to describe, organize, and monitor the work of project activities. Project managers are the ones responsible for carrying out these activities.

Every project must work within constraints. The primary constraints that will affect all projects are the triple constraints of budget, time, and quality.

Project managers have a wide variety of skills. Not only should they be versed in the field they're working in, but in general management skills as well. Communication is the most important skill a project manager will use in the course of a project.

Organizational structures come in variations of three forms: functional, projectized, and matrix organizations. Functional organizations are traditional with hierarchical reporting structures. Project managers have little to no authority in this organization. Projectized organizations are structured around project work, and staff personnel report to project managers. Project managers have full authority in this organizational structure. Matrix organizations are a combination of the functional and projectized. A project manager's authority varies depending on the structure of the matrix, be it a weak matrix, a balanced matrix, or a strong matrix.

Projects progress along a life cycle path. The life cycle consists of phases, and the process groups in *A Guide to the PMBOK* are performed throughout the project's life cycle. The process groups described in *A Guide to the PMBOK* are Initiation, Planning, Executing, Controlling, and Closing.

Project management offices (PMOs) are a way to organize and establish standards for project management techniques within an organization. They can also serve as a project library, housing project documentation for future reference.

Exam Essentials

Be able to describe the difference between projects and operations.   A project is temporary in nature with a definite beginning and ending date. Operations are ongoing.

Be able to denote some of the skills every good project manager should possess.   Communication, budgeting, organizational, problem solving, negotiation and influencing, leading, and team building are skills a project manager should possess.

Be able to differentiate the different organizational structures and the project manager's authority in each.   Organizations are usually structured in some combination of the following: functional, projectized, and matrix (including weak matrix, balanced matrix, and strong matrix). Project managers have the most authority in a projectized organization and the least amount of authority in a functional organization.

Be able to name the five project management processes.   The five project management processes are Initiation, Planning, Executing, Controlling, and Closing.

Key Terms

You've learned a lot of new key words in this chapter. PMI has worked hard to develop and define standard project management terms that apply across industries. Here is a list of some of the terms you came across in this chapter:

balanced matrix

collocated

deliverable

fast tracking

functional organization

handoffs

iterative

leaders

managers

matrix organizations

politics

power

programs

progressive elaboration

project life cycle

project management

project management office

project managers

project sponsor

projectized organizations

projects

stakeholders

Review Questions

1. Which organization has set the de facto standards for project management techniques?

   A. PMBOK

   B. PMO

   C. PMI

   D. PMA

2. The VP of marketing approaches you and requests that you change the visitor logon screen on the company's website to include a username with at least six characters. This is considered:

   A. Project initiation

   B. Ongoing operations

   C. A project

   D. Project execution

3. Your company manufactures small kitchen appliances. They are introducing a new product line of appliances in designer colors with distinctive features for kitchens in small spaces. These new products will be offered indefinitely starting with the spring catalog release. Which of the following is true?

   A. This is a project because this new product line has never been manufactured and sold by this company before.

   B. This is an ongoing operation because the company is in the business of manufacturing kitchen appliances. Introducing designer colors and features is simply a new twist on an existing process.

   C. This is an ongoing operation because the new product line will be sold indefinitely. It's not temporary.

   D. This is not a project or an ongoing operation. This is a new product introduction not affecting ongoing operations.

4. Your company manufactures small kitchen appliances. They are introducing a new product line of appliances in designer colors with distinctive features for kitchens in small spaces. These new products will be offered indefinitely starting with the spring catalog release. In order to determine the characteristics and features of the new product line, you will have to perform which of the following?

   A. Fast tracking

   B. Consulting with the stakeholders

   C. Planning the project life cycle

   D. Progressive elaboration

5. A project is considered successful when:

   A. The product of the project has been manufactured.

   B. The project sponsor announces the completion of the project.

   C. The product of the project is turned over to the operations area to handle the ongoing aspects of the project.

   D. The project meets or exceeds the expectations of the stakeholders.

6. The VP of customer service has expressed concern over a project you're involved in. His specific concern is that if the project is implemented as planned, he'll have to purchase additional equipment to staff his customer service center. The cost is substantial and was not taken into consideration in the project budget. The project sponsor insists that the project must go forward as originally planned or the customer will suffer. Which of the following is true?

   A. The VP of customer service is correct. Since the cost was not taken into account at the beginning of the project, the project should not go forward as planned. Project initiation should be revisited to examine the project plan and determine how changes can be made to accommodate customer service.

   B. The conflict should be resolved in favor of the customer.

   C. The conflict should be resolved in favor of the project sponsor.

   D. The conflict should be resolved in favor of the VP of customer service.

7. Which of the following brings together a set of tools and techniques used to describe, organize, and monitor the work of project activities?

   A. Project managers

   B. *A Guide to the PMBOK*

   C. Project management

   D. Stakeholders

8. What are the triple constraints?

   A. Time, schedules, and quality

   B. Time, availability, and quality

   C. Time, money, and schedules

   D. Time, money, and quality

9. You are the project manager for a large construction project. The project objective is to construct a set of outbuildings to house the Olympic support team that will be arriving in your city 18 months from the project start date. You've been given a budget of $12 million to complete this project. Resources are easily attained. Which of the triple constraints is the primary constraint for this project?

    A. Time, because the date cannot be moved.

    B. Money, because the budget is set at $12 million.

    C. Resources, because they're not fixed.

    D. Quality, because the buildings have to be functional and safe.

10. You are the project manager for a large construction project. The project objective is to construct a set of outbuildings to house the Olympic support team that will be arriving in your city 18 months from the project start date. Resources are not readily available as they are currently assigned to other projects. Jack, an expert crane operator, is needed for this project two months from today. Which of the following skills will you use to get Jack assigned to your project?

    A. Negotiation and influencing skills

    B. Communication and organizational skills

    C. Communication skills

    D. Problem-solving skills

11. You are a project manager with technical expertise in the pharmaceutical industry. You've decided to try your hand at project management in the entertainment industry. Which of the following is true?

    A. You will likely be successful because communication skills are your strong suit. You anticipate having technical experts on your project team to address industry specifics that you're not familiar with.

    B. You will likely be successful because your organizational skills are excellent. You anticipate having technical experts on your project team to address industry specifics that you're not familiar with.

    C. You will probably be successful because you have a friend in the entertainment industry who has briefed you on all the important aspects of this project that you'll need to know. You anticipate having technical experts on your project team to address industry specifics that you're not familiar with.

    D. You will probably not be successful because you have little knowledge of the entertainment industry, even though you anticipate having technical experts on your project team to address industry specifics that you're not familiar with.

12. You are managing a project to install a new postage software system that will automatically print labels and administer postage for certified mailings, overnight packages, and other special mailing needs. You've attempted to gain the cooperation of the business analyst working on this project and need some answers. She is elusive and tells you that this project is not her top priority. To avoid situations like this in the future, you should:

    A. Establish the business analyst's duties well ahead of due dates and tell her you'll be reporting on her performance to her functional manager.

    B. Establish the business analyst's duties well ahead of due dates and tell her you are expecting her to meet these expectations because the customer is counting on the project meeting due dates to save significant costs on their annual mailings.

    C. Negotiate with the business analyst's functional manager during the planning process to establish expectations and request to participate in the business analyst's annual performance review.

    D. Negotiate with the business analyst's functional manager during the planning process to establish expectations and inform the functional manager of the requirements of the project. Agreement from the functional manager will assure the cooperation of the business analyst.

13. The amount of authority a project manager possesses can be related to:

    A. The project manager's communication skills

    B. The organizational structure

    C. The amount of authority the manager of the project manager possesses

    D. The project manager's influencing skills

14. What is one of the advantages of a functional organization?

    A. All employees report to one manager and have a clear chain of command.

    B. All employees report to two or more managers, but project team members show loyalty to functional managers.

    C. The organization is focused on projects and project work.

    D. Teams are collocated.

15. You have been assigned to a project in which the objectives are to direct customer calls to an interactive voice response system before being connected to a live agent. You are in charge of the media communications for this project. You report to the project manager in charge of this project and the VP of marketing, who share responsibility for this project. Which organizational structure do you work in?

    A. Functional organization

    B. Weak matrix organization

    C. Projectized organization

    D. Balanced matrix organization

16. You have been assigned to a project in which the objectives are to expand three miles of the north-south highway through your city by two lanes in each direction. You are in charge of the demolition phase of this project, and you report to the project manager in charge of this project. You have been hired on contract and will be released at the completion of the demolition phase. What type of organizational structure does this represent?

    A. Functional organization

    B. Weak matrix organization

    C. Projectized organization

    D. Balanced matrix organization

17. What are the five project management process groups, in order?

    A. Initiation, Executing, Planning, Controlling, and Closing

    B. Initiation, Controlling, Planning, Executing, and Closing

    C. Initiation, Planning, Controlling, Executing, and Closing

    D. Initiation, Planning, Executing, Controlling, and Closing

18. You have been assigned to a project in which the objectives are to expand three miles of the north-south highway through your city by two lanes in each direction. You are interested in implementing a new project process called Design-Build in order to speed up the project schedule. The idea is that the construction team will work on the first mile of the highway reconstruction at the same time the design team is coming up with plans for the third mile of the reconstruction rather than completing all design before any construction begins. This is an example of:

    A. Managing the projects as a program

    B. Fast tracking

    C. Progressive elaboration

    D. Collocation

19. During which project management process are risk and stakeholder's ability to influence project outcomes the highest at the beginning of the process?

    A. Planning

    B. Executing

    C. Initiation

    D. Controlling

20. You are a project manager working on gathering requirements and establishing estimates for the project. Which process group are you in?

    A. Planning

    B. Executing

    C. Initiation

    D. Controlling

Answers to Review Questions

1. C. The Project Management Institute (PMI) is the industry-recognized standard for project management practices.

2. B. Projects exist to create a unique product or service. The logon screen in this question is not a unique product. A minor change has been requested, indicating this is an ongoing operation function. Some of the criteria for projects are that they are unique, temporary with definitive start and end dates, and considered complete when the project goals are achieved.

3. A. This is a project. The product line is new, which implies this is a unique product—it hasn't been done before. We can discern a definite start and end date by the fact that the new appliances must be ready by the spring catalog release.

4. D. Progressive elaboration is the process of determining the characteristics and features of the product of the project. Progressive elaboration is carried out in steps in detailed fashion.

5. D. A project is considered successful when stakeholder needs and expectations are met or exceeded.

6. B. Conflicts between stakeholders should always be resolved in favor of the customer. This question emphasizes the importance of identifying your stakeholders and their needs as early as possible in the project. We'll discuss this more in later chapters.

7. C. Project management brings together a set of tools and techniques to organize project activities. Project managers are the ones responsible for managing the project processes.

8. D. The triple constraints that drive all projects are time, money, and quality.

9. A. The primary constraint on this project is time because the date absolutely cannot move. The Olympics are scheduled to begin on a certain date, and this can't be changed. The budget is also a constraint because it's set at $12 million, but in this example, it is a secondary constraint. It's important that the project manager understands the priority of the constraints and manages to them.

10. A. Negotiation and influencing skills are needed to convince Jack's boss and come to agreement concerning his assignment.

11. A. Project management processes span industries. A project manager can take these skills across industries and apply them successfully. Technical experience in the industry doesn't hurt, but it's not required. The most important skill any project manager can have is communication skills. Poor communication skills might lead to an unsuccessful conclusion no matter how strong the project manager's other skills are.

12. C. Negotiate with the functional manager to participate in the business analyst's annual performance review.

13. B. The level of authority the project manager has is determined by the organizational structure. For instance, in a functional organization, the project manager has little to no authority, but in a projectized structure, the project manager has full authority.

14. A. An advantage for employees in a functional organization is that they have only one supervisor and a clear chain of command exists.

15. D. Employees in a balanced matrix often report to two or more managers. Functional managers and project managers share authority and responsibility for projects. There is a balance of power between the functional managers and project managers.

16. C. Projectized organizations are focused on the project itself. One issue with this type of structure is determining what to do with project team members when they are not actively involved on the project. One alternative is to release them when they are no longer needed.

17. D. Remember the acronym that sounds like syrup of ipecac: IPECC.

18. B. Fast tracking is starting a new phase before the phase you're working on is completed. This compresses the project schedule, and as a result, the project is completed sooner.

19. C. The Initiation process is where stakeholders have the greatest ability to influence outcomes of the project. Risk is highest during this stage because of the high degree of unknown factors.

20. A. The Planning process is where requirements are fleshed out, stakeholders are identified, and estimates on project costs and time are made.

Chapter 2

Initiating the Project

THE PMP EXAM CONTENT FROM THE PROJECT INITIATION PERFORMANCE DOMAIN COVERED IN THIS CHAPTER INCLUDES:

- ✓ 1. Determining project goals
- ✓ 2. Determining deliverables
- ✓ 3. Determining process outputs
- ✓ 4. Documenting constraints
- ✓ 5. Documenting assumptions

Now that you're fully armed with a detailed overview of project management, you can easily determine if your next assignment really is a project or an ongoing operation. You've also learned some of the basics of good project management techniques and the knowledge areas where you might need specific expertise. We're going to start putting those techniques into practice during the Initiation process. And, as you've probably already guessed, we'll be using some of the general management skills outlined in Chapter 1, "What Is a Project?"

One of the first skills you are going to put to use will be your communication skills. Are you surprised? Of course you're not. It all starts with communication. You can't start defining the project until you've first talked to the project sponsor, key stakeholders, and management personnel. All good project managers have honed their communication skills to a nice sharp edge.

You'll remember from Chapter 1 that Initiation is the first process or phase in a project life cycle. You can think of it as the official project kickoff. Initiation acknowledges that the project, or the next phase in an active project, should begin. Initiation then culminates in the publication of a project charter. (We'll discuss project charters in more depth in Chapter 3, "Creating a Project Charter.")

We will also talk about project Initiation and introduce some of the tasks that make up this process. But before we dive into Initiation, we'll first take a look at what PMI calls the Project Management Knowledge Areas. Knowledge areas are a collection of processes that share similar themes and, therefore, benefit from the expertise of specific knowledge and skills in each of these areas.

At the end of this chapter, we'll introduce a case study that will illustrate the main points of the chapter. We'll take this case study with us from chapter to chapter and begin building a project using each of the skills we learn.

The Project Management Knowledge Areas

According to *A Guide to the PMBOK*, project Initiation, as we've discussed, is the first project management process group in the life cycle of a project. In addition to the project process groups, *A Guide to the PMBOK* classifies the processes that make up each project management process group into nine *Project Management Knowledge Areas*:

- Project Integration Management
- Project Scope Management

- Project Time Management
- Project Cost Management
- Project Quality Management
- Project Human Resource Management
- Project Communications Management
- Project Risk Management
- Project Procurement Management

These groupings, or knowledge areas, bring together processes that have characteristics in common. For example, Project Cost Management involves all aspects of the budgeting process, as you would suspect, such as Resource Planning, Cost Estimating, Cost Budgeting, and Cost Control. These processes belong to different project management process groups, but because they all involve costs and budgeting, they share many characteristics in common.

Let's take a closer look at each area so you really understand how their role works with the process groups. Included in each of the following subsections is a figure that illustrates the knowledge area, the processes that make up each knowledge area, and the project management process groups (or project life cycle phases) that each process belongs to. This will help you to see the big picture in terms of process groups compared to knowledge areas. We'll be discussing each of the processes in the various knowledge areas throughout the book, but for now, let's take a high-level look at each of them.

Exam Spotlight

You will likely find questions regarding the Project Management Knowledge Areas on the exam. To broaden your understanding of the knowledge areas, cross-reference the purposes and the processes that make up each knowledge area with *A Guide to the PMBOK*.

Project Integration Management

Project Integration Management (see Figure 2.1) is comprised of three processes: Project Plan Development, Project Plan Execution, and Integrated Change Control.

The Project Integration Management knowledge area is concerned with coordinating all aspects of the project plan and is highly interactive. Project planning, project execution, and change control occur throughout the project and are repeated continuously while working on the project. Project planning and execution involve weighing the objectives of the project against the alternatives to bring the project to a successful completion. Change control impacts the project plan, which in turn impacts execution, so you can see that these three processes are very tightly linked. The processes in this area, as with all the knowledge areas, also interact with other processes in the remaining knowledge areas.

This process has two tools for assisting with process integration: Earned Value Management and project management software. *Earned value management (EVM)* is a project-integrating methodology used in this knowledge area to integrate the processes and measure project performance through a project's life cycle. We'll further define EVM and talk more about project management software tools in Chapter 7, "Creating the Project Plan."

FIGURE 2.1   Project Integration Management

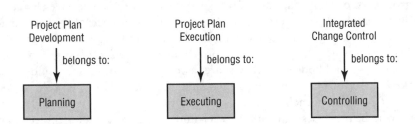

Project Integration Management

Project Plan Development	Project Plan Execution	Integrated Change Control
belongs to:	belongs to:	belongs to:
Planning	Executing	Controlling

Project Scope Management

Project Scope Management (see Figure 2.2) has five processes: Initiation, Scope Planning, Scope Definition, Scope Verification, and Scope Change Control.

Project Scope Management is concerned with defining all of the work of the project. All of the processes involved with the work of the project, and only the work that is required to complete the project, are found in this knowledge area. These processes are highly interactive and occur at least once—and often many times—throughout the project life cycle.

Project Scope Management encompasses both product scope and project scope. *Product scope* concerns the characteristics of the product or service of the project. It's measured against the project requirements. The application area usually dictates the process tools and techniques you'll use to define and manage product scope. *Project scope* involves managing the work of the project and only the work of the project. Project scope is measured against the project plan.

    To ensure a successful project, both product and project scope must be well integrated.

Initiation is the first process within this knowledge area. We'll discuss Initiation in more detail later in this chapter. Scope Planning, Scope Definition, Scope Verification, and Scope Change Control involve:

- Detailing the requirements of the product of the project and the activities that will eventually comprise the project plan

- Verifying those details using measurement techniques
- Controlling changes to these processes

FIGURE 2.2 Project Scope Management

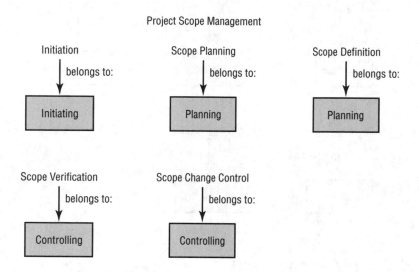

Project Time Management

The *Project Time Management* knowledge area, shown in Figure 2.3, also has five processes: Activity Definition, Activity Sequencing, Activity Duration Estimating, Schedule Development, and Schedule Control.

This knowledge area is concerned with estimating the duration of the project plan activities, devising a project schedule, and monitoring and controlling deviations from the schedule. Collectively, this knowledge area deals with completing the project in a timely manner. Time management is an important aspect of project management, as it concerns keeping the project activities on track and monitoring those activities against the project plan to ensure that the project is completed on time.

In many cases, particularly on small projects, activity sequencing, activity duration estimating, and schedule development are completed as one activity. Only one person is needed to complete these processes for small projects, and they're all worked on at the same time.

FIGURE 2.3 Project Time Management

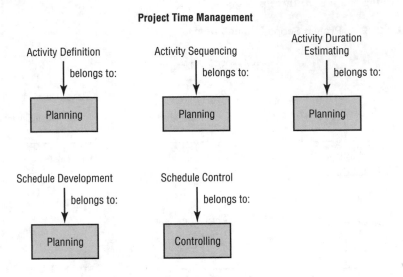

Project Time Management

Activity Definition	Activity Sequencing	Activity Duration Estimating
belongs to:	belongs to:	belongs to:
Planning	Planning	Planning

Schedule Development	Schedule Control
belongs to:	belongs to:
Planning	Controlling

Project Cost Management

As its name implies, the *Project Cost Management* knowledge area centers around costs and budgets. The processes that make up this knowledge area are as follows: Resource Planning, Cost Estimating, Cost Budgeting, and Cost Control. See how they work together in Figure 2.4.

The activities in the Project Cost Management knowledge area establish estimates for costs and resources and keep watch over those costs to ensure that the project stays within the approved budget. This knowledge area is primarily concerned with the costs of resources, but other costs should be considered as well.

Depending on the complexity of the project, these processes might need the involvement of more than one person. For example, the finance person might not have expertise in the Resource Planning area, so the project manager will need to bring in a staff member with those skills to complete the Resource Planning process.

Two techniques are used in this knowledge area to decide among alternatives and improve the project process: life-cycle costing and Value Engineering. The life-cycle costing technique considers a group of costs collectively (such as acquisition, operations, disposal, and so on) when deciding among or comparing alternatives. The Value Engineering technique helps improve project schedules, profits, quality, and resource usage and optimizes life-cycle costs, among others. Some application areas require additional financial analysis to help predict project performance. Techniques such as payback analysis, return on investment, and discounted cash flows are a few of the tools used to accomplish this. We'll discuss these techniques and others in further detail in Chapter 3.

FIGURE 2.4   Project Cost Management

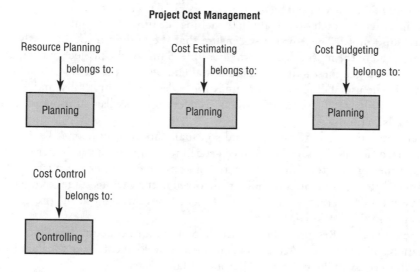

Project Cost Management

Project Quality Management

The *Project Quality Management* knowledge area ensures that the project meets the requirements that the project was undertaken to produce. This knowledge area focuses on product quality as well as on the quality of the project management process used during the project's life cycle. These processes measure overall performance, and monitor project results and compare them to the quality standards set out in the project-planning process to assure that the customer will receive the product or service they thought they purchased.

As you can see from Figure 2.5, Project Quality Management is composed of the following three processes: Quality Planning, Quality Assurance, and Quality Control.

FIGURE 2.5   Project Quality Management

Project Quality Management

Project Human Resource Management

Project Human Resource Management involves all aspects of people management and personal interaction, including leading, coaching, dealing with conflict, performance appraisals, and more. These processes ensure that the human resources assigned to the project are used in the most effective way possible. Some of the project participants whom you'll get to practice these skills on include stakeholders, team members, and customers. Each requires the use of different communication styles, leadership skills, and team-building skills. A good project manager knows when to enact certain skills and communication styles based on the situation.

Projects are unique and temporary and so usually are project teams. Teams are put together based on the skills and resources needed to complete the activities of the project, and many times project team members may not know one another. Because the makeup of each team is different and the stakeholders involved in the various stages of the project may change, you'll use different techniques at different times throughout the project to manage the processes in this knowledge area.

The Project Human Resource Management knowledge area contains the following processes: Organizational Planning, Staff Acquisition, and Team Development. Take a look at Figure 2.6 to see a visual overview of Project Human Resource Management.

FIGURE 2.6   Project Human Resource Management

Project Communications Management

The processes that make up the *Project Communications Management* knowledge area are as follows: Communications Planning, Information Distribution, Performance Reporting, and Administrative Closure.

The processes in the Project Communications Management knowledge area are related to general communication skills, but they encompass much more than an exchange of information. Communication skills are considered general management skills that the project manager utilizes on a daily basis. The processes in the Process Communications Management knowledge area seek to ensure that all project information—including project plans, risk assessments, meeting notes, and more—is collected, documented, archived, and disposed of at the proper time. These processes also ensure that information is distributed and shared with stakeholders, management, and project members at appropriate times. When the project is closed, the information is archived and used as a reference for future projects. This is referred to as *historical information* in several project processes.

Everyone on the project has some involvement with this knowledge area, because all project members will send and or receive project communication throughout the life of the project. It is important that all team members and stakeholders understand how communication affects the project.

Figure 2.7 shows the Project Communications Management process in progress.

FIGURE 2.7   Project Communications Management

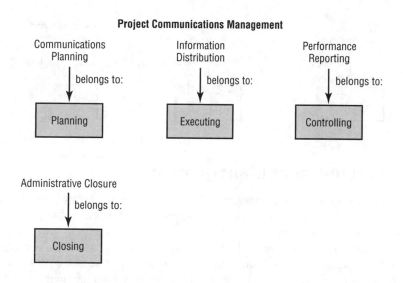

Project Communications Management

Project Risk Management

Project Risk Management, as seen in Figure 2.8, contains six processes: Risk Management Planning, Risk Identification, Qualitative Risk Analysis, Quantitative Risk Analysis, Risk Response Planning, and Risk Monitoring and Control.

Risks include both threats and opportunities. The processes in this knowledge area are concerned with identifying, analyzing, and planning for potential risks that may impact the project, including minimizing their probability and their consequences. They are also used to identify the positive consequences of risk and exploit them to improve project objectives or discover efficiencies that may improve project performance.

Organizations will often combine several of these processes into one step. For example, Risk Identification, Qualitative Risk Analysis, and Quantitative Risk Analysis might be performed at the same time. The important thing about the Project Risk Management knowledge area is that you should strive to identify all the risks and develop responses for those with the greatest consequences to the project objectives.

FIGURE 2.8   Project Risk Management

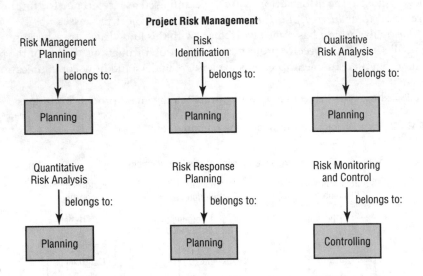

Project Risk Management

Risk Management
Planning

↓ belongs to:

Planning

Risk
Identification

↓ belongs to:

Planning

Qualitative
Risk Analysis

↓ belongs to:

Planning

Quantitative
Risk Analysis

↓ belongs to:

Planning

Risk Response
Planning

↓ belongs to:

Planning

Risk Monitoring
and Control

↓ belongs to:

Controlling

Project Procurement Management

The *Project Procurement Management* knowledge area includes the processes involved with purchasing goods or services from external vendors, contractors, and suppliers. When discussing the Project Procurement Management processes, it's assumed that the discussion is taking place from the perspective of the buyer. As the project manager, you are the buyer purchasing the goods or services from a supplier or contractor, so these processes should be examined from that perspective. Interestingly, the seller may manage their work as a project, particularly when the work is performed on contract, and you as the buyer become a key stakeholder in their project.

The processes in the Project Procurement Management knowledge area, shown in Figure 2.9, are as follows: Procurement Planning, Solicitation Planning, Solicitation, Source Selection, Contract Administration, and Contract Closeout.

The PMP exam will most likely have a question or two regarding the processes that make up a knowledge area. Remember that knowledge areas bring together processes by commonalities, so thinking about the knowledge area itself should tip you off to the processes that belong to it. Projects are executed in process group (life cycle) order, but the knowledge areas allow a project manager to think about groups of processes that require specific skills. This makes the job of assigning resources easier, because team members with specific skills might be able to work on and complete several processes at once.

FIGURE 2.9 Project Procurement Management

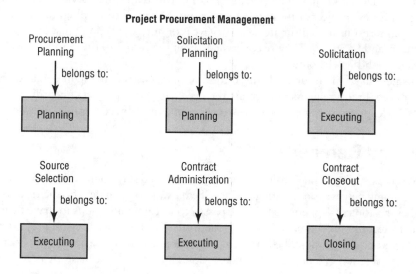

The remainder of this book will deal with processes and process groups as they occur in life cycle order (i.e., Initiation, Planning, Executing, Controlling, and Closing), as this is the way you will encounter and manage them during a project.

Defining the Project Initiation Process

Your company's quarterly meeting is scheduled for today. You take your seat, and each of the department heads gets up and gives their usual "We can do it" rah-rah speech, one after the other. You sit up a little straighter when the CEO takes the stage. He starts out his part of the program pretty much the same way the other department heads did, and before long, you find yourself drifting off. You are mentally reviewing the status of your current project when suddenly your daydreaming trance is shattered. You perk up as you hear the CEO say, "and the new phone system will be installed by Thanksgiving."

Wait a minute. You work in the telecom department and haven't heard a word about this project until today. You also have a funny feeling that you've been elected to manage this project. It's amazing how good communication skills are so important for project managers but not well, we won't go there.

Project *Initiation* is the formal recognition that a project, or the next phase in an existing project, should begin and resources should be committed to the project. Unfortunately, many projects are initiated the way your CEO did in this example. Each of us, at one time or another, has experienced being handed a project with little to no information and told to "make it happen." The new phone system scenario is an excellent example of how *not* to initiate a project.

Taking one step back from Initiation leads you to ask, "How do projects come about in the first place? Do CEOs just make them up like in this example?" Even though your CEO announced this new project at the company meeting with no forewarning, there is no doubt it came about as a result of a legitimate need. Believe it or not, CEOs don't just dream projects up to give you something to do. They're concerned about the future of the company and the needs of the business and its customers.

The business itself might drive the need for a project, customers might demand changes to products, or legal requirements may create the need for a new project. According to *A Guide to the PMBOK*, projects come about as a result of one of six needs or demands.

Needs and Demands

Organizations exist to generate profits or serve the public. To stay competitive, organizations are always examining new ways of creating business, better ways of gaining efficiencies, or better ways to serve their customers. Sometimes laws are passed to force organizations to make their products safer or to protect the environment. Projects result from all of these needs. Most projects will fit one of the six needs or demands described in the following sections. It is those needs and/or demands that dictate the germination of a project. Let's take a closer look at each of these areas.

Market Demand

The demands of the marketplace can drive the need for a project. For example, a bank initiates a project to offer customers the ability to apply for mortgage loans over the Internet due to a drop in interest rates and an increase in demand for refinancing and new home loans.

Business Need

The new phone system talked about earlier that was announced at the quarterly meeting came about as a result of a business need. The CEO, on advice from his staff, was advised that call volumes were maxed on the existing system. Without a new system, customer service response times would suffer, and that would eventually affect the bottom line.

Customer Request

Customer requests run the gamut. Generally speaking, most companies have customers, and their requests can drive new projects. Customers can be internal or external to the organization. Government agencies don't have external customers per se (we're captive customers at any rate), but there are internal customers within departments and across agencies.

Perhaps you work for a company that sells remittance-processing equipment, and you've just landed a contract with a local utility company. This project is driven by the need of the utility company to automate their process or upgrade their existing process. The utility company's request to purchase your equipment and consulting services is the project driver.

Technological Advance

Do you happen to own one of those electronic personal digital assistants? They keep names and addresses handy and usually come with a calendar and a to-do list of some kind. I couldn't live without mine. However, there is always a newer, better version coming to market. The introduction of satellite communications now allows these little devices to connect to the Web or get e-mail almost anywhere in the world. The introduction of satellite communications is an example of a technological advance. Due to this introduction, electronics manufacturers revamped their products to take advantage of this new technology.

Legal Requirement

Private industry and government agencies both generate new projects as a result of laws passed every legislative season. For example, new sales tax laws might require modifications or new programming to the existing sales tax system. The requirement that food labels appear on every package describing the ingredients and the recommended daily allowances of certain vitamins is another example of a project driven by legal requirements.

Social Need

The last need is a result of social demands. For example, perhaps a developing country is experiencing a fast-spreading disease that's infecting large portions of the population. Medical supplies and facilities are needed to vaccinate and cure those infected with the disease. Another example might include cleaning up waste products from the water supply of manufacturing plants prior to putting the water back into a local river or stream to prevent contamination.

Exam Spotlight

Understand the definition of the needs and demands that bring about new projects.

All of these needs and demands represent opportunities, business requirements, or problems that need to be solved. Management must decide how to respond to these needs and demands, which will more often than not initiate new projects.

Project Initiation Process

The Initiation process is part of the Project Scope Management knowledge area. As you've learned, this knowledge area deals with identifying a project, the stakeholders, and the project requirements. The Initiation process lays the groundwork for the Planning process group that follows Initiation. A high percentage of projects fail due to poor planning or no planning. Properly planning your project up front dramatically increases the project's chance for success. Since the Initiation process is the foundation of Planning, the importance of Initiation is self-evident.

The project Initiation process has several inputs: product description, strategic plan, project selection criteria, and historical information. Each of these inputs is processed using tools and techniques to produce the final outputs, one of which is the project charter. Now, we'll examine each of these inputs in a bit more detail.

Product Description

As stated previously, the product description describes the characteristics of the product or service of the project. The product description should be documented and should also include a description of the business need or demand that's driving the reason for the project.

Product descriptions contain less detail in the early phases of a project and more detail as the project progresses, and the details are progressively elaborated. It will contain the greatest amount of detail at the project Execution process.

When a project is performed under contract, typically the buyer of the product or service will provide the product description to the vendor or contractor. The product description can serve as a statement of work when the project is contracted to a vendor. A statement of work describes the product or service in enough detail so that the vendor can accurately price the contract and satisfactorily fulfill the requirements of the project. The statement of work is covered in more detail in Chapter 6, "Establishing Project Planning Controls."

Strategic Plan

Part of the responsibility of a project manager during the Initiation process is to take into consideration the company's strategic plan. Perhaps the strategic plan states that one of the company goals is to build 15 new stores by the end of the next fiscal year. If your project entails installing a new human resources software system, it would make sense to write the requirements for your project with the 15 new stores in mind. Your management team will refer to the strategic plan when choosing which new projects to initiate and which ones to drop, depending on their relationship to the strategic vision of the company.

Project Selection Criteria

Project selection involves making determinations regarding which projects to accept or reject based on criteria such as financial data, sales potential in the marketplace, etc. This subject will be dealt with more thoroughly in Chapter 3.

Historical Information

Historical information can be very useful to project managers and to stakeholders. When you're evaluating new projects, historical information about previous projects of a similar nature can be very handy in determining if the new project should be accepted and initiated. Historical information gathered and documented during an active project is used to assist in determining whether the project should proceed to the next phase. Historical information will help you with Initiation, Scope Definition, Project Plan Development, and Activity Definition, with estimating activities, and more during the project-planning processes. You'll find that historical information is an input to several processes.

Developing a Project Overview

One of the first steps a project manager will take in the Initiation process is to develop a project overview. Some organizations call this a project concept document. The four inputs described in the last section will help to outline the project overview and will be used again when formulating the final project charter.

It should be noted that *A Guide to the PMBOK* holds the view that a project manager is identified and assigned at the completion of the Initiation process. While sometimes that's true, in practice it's common that the project manager is involved at the beginning of the Initiation process and assists with the project overview and information-gathering tasks.

At the completion of the Initiation process, the organization has committed to fund the project and provide the necessary resources to carry it out, or has killed the project. The project has the lowest probability of succeeding during Initiation. That's because no action has been taken regarding project activities. In other words, you haven't actually begun to produce the product of the project. Quite a bit of work will have gone into the project at this stage, but most of it regards the overview of the project and the business justification for the project. The stakeholders have the greatest ability to influence project outcome at this stage because nothing has been cast in stone yet. There is still time for them to negotiate requirements and deliverables. Risk is highest during Initiation, because any number of things can happen between now and the time the project is completed. The project might not be approved, the funding might not be approved, the strategic direction of the company could change and the project no longer fits in with the new vision, the customer could change her mind, etc. This list could become quite lengthy.

Project failure can be controlled and minimized by accurately applying project management techniques to your project and by proper planning.

 Real World Scenario

The Diet Cola Marketing Opportunity

Elizabeth is the project manager for a large soft drink beverage company located in Tallahassee, Florida. One sunny morning, Roger Bruist, the marketing vice president, pays her a visit.

"I asked your boss if it was okay to directly talk to you about this project—she said it would be fine," he starts. "As you've probably heard, we're test-marketing a new diet cola opportunity that we thought would be a big seller. To make a long story short, I had lunch the other day with a friend of mine from the club. He ordered his usual diet cola but requested three slices of lemon with it. I stared at him while he squeezed those lemons into his diet soda and dunked the last rind into the mix. Well, I have to tell you the taste is fabulous!

"We've toyed around with the exact lemon-to-cola mixture in the lab and have come up with what we think is the optimum mix that results in the tastiness factor we're looking for.

"You and I have worked together before, and I know your work is top-notch. What we'd like for you to do is put together a project that test-markets our new soda in three test areas. We want to target markets that utilize a lot of diet soda. We think the best places to target would be Denver, Las Vegas, and the Seattle area.

"We want a project plan that details the distributors we'll send the soda to and how we'll obtain the demographics we're looking for. My department will supply you with the marketing profiles and plans you need to implement in your project plan. We'd also like a page added to the company's website that talks about the new beverage. The project should also include key players from the National Soft Drink Association and have a large, splashy intro on their website as well."

As a project manager, you will often have projects presented to you that are barely past the big-picture stage. Roger has a good idea of how he wants to test-market this new product, but many other processes must come into play here such as planning, budgeting, risk assessment, reporting, and so on. A lot of energy is focused on the vision of the project and the wants and needs of the stakeholders. It's your job to take the vision, examine the needs of all the stakeholders including Roger's, and bring the vision to fruition.

Determining the Project Goals

Several terms are tossed about and sometimes used interchangeably when talking about projects. They are words such as goals, objectives, requirements, and deliverables. Their meanings are sometimes blurred together, but there is some differentiation among these terms. Goals and objectives are the purpose for undertaking the project, and they describe the final result of the project. "Increase warehouse space to house the new product line for distribution" or "Provide faster turnaround times on loan application services" are both examples of objectives. They state the purpose for the project and the desired end result. If we clean these statements up a tad and add some measures and dates, we'll have goals.

Project Goals

Goals describe the *what* it is you're trying to do, accomplish, or produce. Goals should be stated in tangible terms. If your goal is to increase warehouse space, it is better to say the goal is to build four new warehouses. Describing the number of new warehouses to be built is specific and tangible. For that reason, you'll know the project is completed when this goal is met. The goal of offering faster loan approvals might be better stated that the company will provide loan applications over the Internet to increase the speed of the application process by 25 percent by the end of the calendar year. In other words, the purpose for the project is to do something or accomplish something—a goal.

There's no hard and fast rule here. The terms *goal* and *objective* mean the same thing in many organizations. We'll refer to the term *goals* throughout the remainder of this book. The important thing is that you come away understanding what the end purpose of the project is and how to identify when it's been accomplished. Documenting project goals will ensure that you can do just that.

You've probably seen this acronym regarding goal setting a dozen times, but it's worth repeating. Goals should follow the SMART rule:

S—Specific   Goals should be specific and written in clear, concise, and understandable terms.

M—Measurable   Goals should be measurable.

A—Accurate   Goals should be accurate and should describe precisely what's required.

R—Realistic and tangible   Goals that are impossible to accomplish are not realistic and not attainable. Goals must be centered in reality. It's not likely you and I will be sending up rocket ships full of chocolate candies to sell to tourists visiting the moon anytime soon.

T—Time bound   Goals should have a time frame with an end date assigned to them.

Hmm, this all sounds familiar. It seems there are some similarities between goal setting and how we describe and document projects. Let's look at that acronym again from a project perspective:

S—Specific   The project goals are specific and stated in clear, concise, and understandable terms and are documented in the project charter and scope statement. Projects exist to bring about a unique, specific product or service that hasn't existed before.

M—Measurable   The deliverables of the project or project phase are measurable against verifiable outcomes or results.

A—Accurate   The verification and measurement of requirements and deliverables are used to determine accuracy and also to ascertain if the project is on track according to the project plan.

R—Realistic and tangible   Projects are unique and produce tangible products or services. The triple constraints of any project help to define realistic goals and realistic requirements based on the limitations the constraints put on the project.

T—Time bound   Projects are performed in specific time frames, with a definite beginning and definite end date.

Project Requirements

Requirements are not the same as goals and objectives. Requirements are specifications of the goal or deliverables. Requirements help answer the question, "How will we know it's successful?" Requirements are the specifications or necessary prerequisites that make up the product or service you're producing. Let's say you're building those four warehouses. Some of the requirements might be the square footage of each building, the number of loading docks, the location of the warehouses, etc.

Project Deliverables

Deliverables are measurable outcomes, measurable results, or specific items that must be produced to consider the project or project phase completed. Deliverables, like goals, must be specific and verifiable. A manufacturing unit that is part of a larger project might be required to produce widgets with a three-inch diameter. These will in turn be assembled into the final product. This deliverable is specific and measurable. However, if the deliverable was not documented or not communicated to the manager responsible for the manufacturing unit, there could be a disaster waiting to happen. If they deliver two-inch widgets instead of the required three-inch version, it would throw the entire project off schedule, or perhaps cause the project to fail. This could be a career-limiting move for the project manager, because it's the project manager's responsibility to document deliverables and monitor the progress of those deliverables throughout the project or project phase.

A project phase can have multiple deliverables. As in the preceding example, if you are assembling a new product with many parts, each of the parts might be considered independent deliverables.

The bottom line is this: No matter how well you apply your project skills, if the wrong deliverables are produced or the project is managed to the wrong goals, you will have an unsuccessful project on your hands.

Exam Spotlight

Understand the differences between goals, deliverables, and requirements. These are first defined during Initiation and are fine-tuned in more detail during the Planning processes.

Stakeholders

Now you're ready to identify and talk to those stakeholders about the project and get more specifics regarding the goals and deliverables of the project. Your objective at this point is to compile a project overview, or project definition. The overview will have enough information to describe the project, the business requirements, the project's objectives, and how you'll recognize when the project is successfully completed.

Identifying Stakeholders

Think of stakeholders and project participants as a highly polished orchestra. Each participant has a part to play. Some play more than others. And alas, some play their parts better than others. An integral part of project management is getting to know your stakeholders and the parts they play. You'll remember from Chapter 1 that stakeholders are those people or organizations who have a vested interest in the outcome of the project. They have something to either gain or lose as a result of the project and have the ability to influence project results. Stakeholders are officially identified in the Planning process. In practice, key stakeholders will have to be contacted early on to get their input for the project overview, goals, and deliverables.

Identifying key stakeholders should be fairly easy, but once you get beyond the obvious stakeholders, the process can get difficult. Sometimes stakeholders, even key stakeholders, will change throughout the project's life cycle. The key stakeholders on a project might include the project sponsor, the customer (who might be one and the same as the project sponsor), the project manager, project team members, management personnel, contractors, suppliers, etc. Stakeholders can be internal or external to the organization. One way to uncover stakeholders whom you might not have thought about right at the start is to ask known stakeholders if they're aware of anyone else that might be impacted by this project. Ask team members if they're aware of stakeholders who haven't been identified. Stakeholders might also come to the forefront once you start uncovering some of the goals and deliverables of the project.

   Don't forget important stakeholders. That could be a project killer. Leaving out an important stakeholder, or one whose business processes weren't considered during project Initiation and Planning, could spell disaster for your project. Not to mention it could be another one of those career-limiting moves for the project manager.

Understanding Stakeholder Roles

It's important for the project manager to understand each stakeholder's role in the project and their role in the organization. Get to know them and their interests. Determine the relationship structure among the various stakeholders. Start cultivating partnerships with these stakeholders now, as it's going to get pretty cozy during the course of your project. If you establish good working relationships up front and learn a little about their business concerns and needs, it might be easier to negotiate or motivate them later on when you have a pressing issue that needs action. Knowing which stakeholders work well together and which don't can also help you in the future. One stakeholder may have the authority or influence to twist the arm of another, figuratively speaking, of course. Or conversely, you might know of two stakeholders who act like oil and water when put into the same room together. This can be valuable information to keep under your hat for future reference.

Communicating with Stakeholders

Now those finely honed communication skills are going to come in handy. In order to determine the specific goals of your project, you'll want to meet with each of the key stakeholders and document their ideas of the project goals. It's also a good idea at this point to gain an understanding of their needs and concerns regarding the project. Ask them why the project is needed. Ask what business process the project will change, enhance, or replace. Perhaps the existing business processes, and the systems that support them, are so old that little documentation exists for them. Determine if there is a critical business need for this project or if it's a "nice to have," as we say around our office. What will be the result of this project? Will customer service be improved or sales increased? Find out what prevents the stakeholders today from achieving the results they hope the project will accomplish. Ask about the deliverables and how they can be verified and measured. And always ask the stakeholder how they will know that the project was completed successfully.

   One way to help identify project goals is to talk about what is not included in a project. For example, let's say you're working on a highway project to create a new on-ramp from a downtown city street. The goal of this project is to have a new on-ramp constructed and ready for traffic in 18 months from the project start date. Specifically excluded from this project is the demolition of a deteriorating bridge adjacent to the new on-ramp. Make sure you state this in the project overview.

 Remember that the definition of a successful project is one that accomplishes the goals of the project and meets or exceeds stakeholders' expectations. Understand and document those expectations, and you're off to a good start. We'll talk about managing to those expectations in Chapter 9, "Measuring and Controlling Project Performance."

The Project Overview Document

The project overview document is a high-level look at the project goals and deliverables. It serves the purpose of capturing the intended outcome of the project and its deliverables. It provides a brief background of the project and describes the business opportunity the company is attempting to capitalize on. It also describes the business objectives the project should meet. The overview lays the groundwork for future consensus on deliverables and project expectations.

Project overviews are often used as a means to introduce a project to the organization. Since the overview document outlines the high-level project goals, business opportunity, and key deliverables, executive managers can get a "first glance" look at the benefits of the project. This document is a precursor to the project charter and provides just enough information for the management team or project selection committee to make a determination to further investigate the project via a feasibility study, or to initiate the project outright.

Feasibility Studies

Some organizations will require a feasibility study at this point in the project. *Feasibility studies* are undertaken for several reasons. One is to determine if the project is a viable project. A second reason is to determine the probability of the project succeeding. Feasibility studies can also examine the viability of the product of the project. For example, the study might ask, "Will the new lemon-flavored soda be a hit? Or, is it marketable?" The study might also look at the technical issues related to the project and determine if the technology proposed is feasible, reliable, and easily assimilated into the organization's existing technology structure.

The group of people conducting the feasibility study should not be the same ones who will work on the project. Project team members may have built-in biases toward the project and will tend to influence the feasibility outcome toward those biases.

Now that we've fleshed out the project goals and have a high-level view of the deliverables, it's time for the next step. But never fear, we'll be reviewing goals and refining deliverables over the next few chapters. We'll also be using them to help formulate requirements and project estimates. But we're getting ahead of ourselves. We need to constrain this chapter to the topic at hand. Which brings up the next topic—project constraints.

Real World Scenario

The Interactive Voice Response Tax-Filing System

Jason, Sam, and Kate are web programmers working for the Department of Revenue in the State of Bliss. Ron, their manager, approaches them one day with an idea.

"Team, business unit managers are thinking it would be a great idea to offer taxpayers the ability to file their income tax over the telephone. We already offer them the ability to file on the Internet, thanks to all your efforts on that project last year. It's been a fabulous success. No other state has had the success that Bliss has had with our Internet system.

"Kate, I know you've had previous experience with IVR technology, but I'm not sure about you guys, so this is new territory for us. I'd like to hear what each of you thinks about this project."

Jason speaks up first. "I think it's a great idea. You know me, I'm always up for learning new things, especially when it comes to programming. When can we start?"

Sam echoes Jason's comments.

"This technology is pretty sophisticated," Kate says. "Jason and Sam are excellent coders and could work on the programming side of things, but I would have to pick up the telephony piece on my own. After we're up and running, we could go over the telephony portions step by step, so Jason and Sam can help me support it going forward. I'd really like to take on this project. It would be good for the team and good for the department."

Ron thinks for a minute. "Let's not jump right into this. I know you're anxious to get started, but I think a feasibility study is in order. The senior director over the tax business unit doesn't know if this project is cost justified and has some concerns about its life span. A feasibility study will tell us the answers to those questions. It should also help us determine if we're using the right technology to accomplish our goals, and it will outline alternative ways of performing the project that we haven't thought of. I don't want Kate going it alone without first examining all the issues and potential impacts to the organization."

Identifying the Project Constraints

We introduced the triple constraints in Chapter 1: time, budget, and quality. All project managers have to deal with these constraints on almost every project. No project manager I know has ever been given unlimited funding and unlimited time to produce a perfect product. In reality, if we were given unlimited funding and unlimited time, some of us probably wouldn't accomplish much. This is especially true for all of you out there who are the perfectionist types. Just tweak this and then tweak that, it will be perfect by the next iteration—I know because I'm one of you!

Constraints are one of the outputs of the Initiation process. Constraints are anything that either restricts the actions of the project team or dictates the actions of the project team. Constraints put you in a box. (I hope you're not claustrophobic.) As a project manager, you have to manage *to* the project constraints, which sometimes requires creativity. Like most disciplines, project management is as much art as it is science.

Types of Constraints

Constraints can take on many forms and aren't limited to time, budget, and quality. Anything that impedes your project team's ability to perform the work of the project or specifically dictates the way the project should be performed is considered a constraint. Governments are a good example here. Let's say in order to fulfill some of the deliverables of your project you'll have to purchase a large amount of materials and equipment. Procurement processes can be so cumbersome that ordering supplies for a project may literally add months to the project schedule. The procurement process itself becomes a constraint because of the methods and procedures you're required to use to get the materials in house.

Let's take a brief look at some of the common constraints you'll likely encounter on your future projects.

Time Constraints

As I said, time can be a project constraint. This usually comes in the form of an enforced deadline, commonly known as the "make it happen now" scenario. If you are in charge of the company's holiday bash scheduled for December 10, your project is time constrained. Once the invitations are out and the hall has been rented, you can't move the date. All activities on this project are driven by the due date.

Budget Constraints

Budgets are another one of the triple constraints. Budgets limit the project team's ability to obtain resources and might potentially limit the scope of the project. For example, component X cannot be part of this project because the budget doesn't support it.

Quality Constraints

Quality would typically be restricted by the specifications of the product or service. Those three-inch widgets talked about earlier could be considered a quality constraint. Most of the time, if quality is a constraint, one of the other constraints—time or budget—has to have some give. You can't produce high quality on a restricted budget and within a tightly restricted time schedule. Of course, there are exceptions, but only in the movies.

Schedule Constraints

Schedule constraints can cause interesting dilemmas for the project manager. For example, say you're the project manager in charge of building a new football stadium in your city. The construction of the stadium will require the use of cranes—and crane operators—at certain times during the project. If crane operators are not available when your project plan calls for them, you'll have to make schedule adjustments so that the crane operators can come in at the right time.

Technology Constraints

Technology is a marvelous thing. In fact, how did humans survive prior to the invention of computers and cell phones? Technology certainly can be marvelous, but it can also be a project constraint. For example, your project might require the use of brand-new technology that is still so new it hasn't been released on a wide-scale basis. One impact might be that the project will take an additional six months because existing technologies need to be used instead of the new technology.

Directive Constraints

Directives from management can be constraints as well. Your department may have specific policies that management requires for the type of work you're about to undertake. This may add time to the project, so you must consider those policies when identifying project constraints. And, when performing work on contract, the provisions of the contract can be constraints.

Managing Constraints

Constraints, particularly the triple constraints, can be used to help drive out the goals of the project. If it's difficult to discern which constraint is the primary constraint, ask the project sponsor something like this, "Ms. Sponsor, if you could only have one of these two alternatives, which would you choose? The project is delivered on the date you've stated, or the quality is manufactured to the exact specifications you've given." If Ms. Sponsor replies with the quality response, you know your primary constraint is quality. If push comes to shove during the project Planning process, time might have to give because quality cannot.

Be sure to document project constraints. Constraints and assumptions, which we'll talk about in the next section, are used as inputs to other project processes.

You'll want to understand what the primary constraint is on the project. If you assume the primary constraint is budget when in actuality the primary constraint is time, in the immortal words of two-year-olds worldwide, "Uh-oh." Understanding the constraints and which one carries the most importance will help you out later on in the project Planning process with things like scope planning, scheduling, estimating, and project plan development. That's assuming your project gets to the project Planning process. Which brings us to the next topic: project assumptions.

Documenting Your Assumptions

You've probably heard the old saying about the word *assume*, something about what it makes out of "u" and "me." In the case of project management, however, throw this old saying out the window, because it's not true.

It's essential to understand and document the assumptions you're making, and your stakeholders are making, about the project. It's also important to find out as many of the assumptions as you can up front. Projects can fail, sometimes after lots of progress has been made on the project, because an important assumption was forgotten or the assumption was incorrect.

Assumptions are information you presume to be true or real and are progressively elaborated and validated throughout the Planning process. They are an output of the Initiation process and are used as inputs to other processes later in the project, so you'll want to document them.

Let's say you make plans to meet your buddy for lunch on Friday at 11:30 at your favorite spot. When Friday rolls around, you assume he's going to show up, barring any catastrophes between the office and the restaurant. Project assumptions work the same way. For planning purposes, you presume the event or thing you've made the assumptions about is true, real, or certain. For example, you might assume that key resources will be available when needed on the project. Document that assumption. If Nancy is the one and only resource who can perform a specific task at a certain point in the project, document your assumption that Nancy will be available and run it by her manager. If Nancy happens to be on a plane for Helsinki at the time you thought she was going to be working on the project, you could have a real problem on your hands.

Other assumptions could be factors such as vendor delivery times, product availability, contractor availability, the accuracy of the project plan, the assumption that key project members will perform adequately, contract signing dates, project start dates, and project phase start dates. This is not an exhaustive list but should get you thinking in the right direction. As you interview your stakeholders, ask them about their assumptions and add them to your list. Use brainstorming exercises with your team and other project participants to come up with additional assumptions.

Think about some of the factors you normally take for granted when you're trying to identify assumptions. Many times they're the elements everyone expects will be available or will behave in a specific way. Think about factors such as key team member's availability, access to information, access to equipment, management support, vendor reliability, and so on.

Try to validate your assumptions whenever possible. When discussing assumptions with vendors, make them put it in writing. In fact, if the services or goods you're expecting to be delivered by your suppliers are critical to the project, include a clause in the contract to assure a contingency plan in case they fail to perform. For example, if you're expecting 200 PCs to be delivered, configured, and installed by a certain date, require the vendor to pay the cost of rental equipment in the event they can't deliver on the promised due date.

Remember, when assumptions are incorrect or not documented, it could cause problems halfway through the project and might even be a project killer.

The Kitchen Heaven Project Case Study

This chapter introduces a case study that we'll follow throughout the remainder of the book. You'll find an updated case study closing out every chapter. They're designed to show you how a project manager might apply the material covered in the chapter to a real-life project. As happens in real life, not every detail of every process is followed during all projects. Remember that the processes from the *A Guide to the PMBOK* that we'll cover in the remaining chapters are project management guidelines. You will often combine processes during your projects, which allows you to perform several steps at once. The case studies will present situations or processes that you might find during your projects and describe how one project manager resolves them.

Project Case Study: New Kitchen Heaven Retail Store

You are a project manager for Kitchen Heaven, a chain of retail stores specializing in kitchen utensils, cookware, dishes, small appliances, and some gourmet foodstuffs such as bottled sauces and spices. You're fairly new to the position, having been hired to replace a PM who recently retired.

Kitchen Heaven currently owns 49 stores in 34 states and Canada. The world headquarters for Kitchen Heaven is in Denver, Colorado. Counting full-time and part-time employees, the company employs 1500 people, 200 of whom work in the headquarters office.

The company has yearly earnings of $200 million, with average profits on earnings of $30 million. The company is publicly held under the KHVN ticker, and the stock is currently at $17.50/share, with a price-to-earnings ratio of 15.8.

The company's mission statement reads this way: "Great gadgets for people interested in great food."

Recently, the vice president of marketing came to pay you a visit. Dirk Perrier is a very nice man, well dressed, with the formal air that you would suspect a person in his capacity might have. He shakes your hand and gives you a fresh, toothy smile.

"You may not have heard, but we've decided to go forward with our 50th store opening! Sales are up, and our new line of ceramic cookware is a hot seller, no pun intended. I don't know if you're familiar with our store philosophy, so let me take a moment to explain it. We like to place our stores in neighborhoods that are somewhat affluent. We don't seek out the wealthy shoppers, nor do we place our shops in areas where only the wealthy travel. But the plain fact is that most of our shoppers have incomes of over $50,000 a year. We make an effort to place our stores in areas where those folks normally shop.

"Also, unlike some of our competitors who like to maintain a *hoity-toity* store persona, we're more interested in targeting the non-gourmet customer, one who's interested in cooking but won't be making Peking duck. So, the stores are upbeat and convey a little bit of country ambiance—kind of a laid-back feel, if you will.

"Our next store is going to be right here in our home area—Colorado Springs. We have a store in Boulder and one in Denver in the Cherry Creek area, but none down south. Because this is going to be our 50th store, we plan on having a 50th grand-opening celebration, with the kind of surprises and activities you might expect for such a notable opening.

"Our stores generally occupy from 2000 to 4000 square feet of retail space, and we typically use local contractors for the build-out. A store build-out usually takes 120 days from the date the property has been procured until the doors open to the public. I can give you our last opening's project plan so you have a feel for what happens. Your job will be to procure the property, negotiate the lease, procure the shelving and associated store furnishings, get a contractor on the job, and prepare the 50th store festivities. My marketing folks will assist you with that last part.

"You have six months to complete the project. Any questions?"

You take in a deep breath and collect your thoughts. Dirk has just given you a lot of information with hardly a pause in between thoughts. A few initial ideas drift through your head while you're reaching for your notebook.

You work in a functional organization with a separate projectized department responsible for carrying out projects of this nature. You've been with the company long enough to know that Dirk is high up there in the executive ranks and carries the authority and the power to make things happen. Therefore, Dirk is the perfect candidate for project sponsor.

You grab your notebook and start documenting some of the things Dirk talked about, clarifying with him as you write:

- The project goal is to open a new store in Colorado Springs six months from today.

- The store should be located in an affluent area.

- The store will carry the full line of products from utensils to gourmet food items.

- The grand opening will be accompanied by lots of fanfare because this is the 50th store opening.

You have a question or two for Dirk. The first is, "Who are some of the other key stakeholders whom I should speak with?"

"There's Jake Peterson over in Facilities. He's in charge of store furnishings, shelving, things like that—any supplies for the stores that aren't retail products. He can help out with store build-outs, too. He supervised our last eight stores and did a terrific job.

"Ricardo Ramirez heads up our information technology area. Don't tell him I said this, but I'm not very technical myself and don't really know what you're going to need from Ricardo. I do know he takes care of wiring and installing the point-of-sale terminals, but you'll have to get with Ricardo for all the other details."

"Anyone else?" you ask.

"You should also talk to Jill Overstreet, the director in charge of retail products. She can help with the initial store stocking, and once the store is open, her group will take over the ongoing operations. All the district managers report to Jill."

"Great, thanks. Now another question," you say. "Is time the driver on this project? Is there a special reason it has to open...let's see...I'm coming up with the date of February 1st?"

"Yes, we want the store open the first week in February. Early February is when the Garden and Home Show conference hits the Springs area. We'll have a trade show booth there. We know from experience in other areas that our stores generally see a surge in sales during this month as a result of the trade show. It's a great way to get a lot of advertising out there and let folks know where we're located."

"Tell me, Dirk, is there a budget set for this project yet?"

"We haven't set a hard figure," Dirk replies. "But again, from past experience we know it takes anywhere from $1.5 to $2 million to open a new store. And we don't want to forget the big bash at grand opening."

You thank Dirk and tell him you're going to contact Jake, Ricardo, and Jill to ask them a few questions about the project goals.

Dirk concludes with, "Feel free to come to me with questions or concerns at any time."

You document what you've learned so far in your project overview document. You decide to e-mail a summary of your notes to Jake, Ricardo, and Jill for their review before meeting with them personally.

Project Case Study Checklist

   Project Goal: To open a new store in Colorado Springs six months from today.

Demand: Company data concludes that the Kitchen Heaven consumers have incomes of over $50,000 a year. The Colorado Springs area is home to a large number of people with that income. Currently, there is not a Kitchen Heaven there, but there appears to be a demand for one.

Project Sponsor: Dirk Perrier, VP of marketing.

Stakeholders: Jake Peterson, Ricardo Ramirez, and Jill Overstreet.

Organizational Structure: Functional organization with a separate projectized department.

Constraints: Time.

Assumptions:

- A store build-out usually takes 120 days.

- Jill Overstreet will help with the initial store stocking.

- Jake Peterson will provide supplies for the stores that aren't retail products such as store furnishings, shelving, etc. and can help with the store build-out as well.

- Ricardo Ramirez will provide IT details.

- The budget for the project will be anywhere from $1.5 to $2 million.

Summary

This chapter started with a discussion of the nine Project Management Knowledge Areas from *A Guide to the PMBOK*. Knowledge areas bring together the project processes that have things in common. This allows the project manager the opportunity to assign resources with specific skills to multiple project processes. Sometimes these resources can combine project processes and perform them as one activity.

Projects come about as a result of one of six needs or demands, according to *A Guide to the PMBOK*: market demand, business need, customer requests, technological advances, legal requirements, and social needs.

Project Initiation is the first process in a project's life cycle. Initiation is the formal recognition that a project, or project phase, should begin, and it commits the organization to dedicate resources to the project.

The Initiation process has four inputs: product description, strategic plan, project selection criteria, and historical information. These inputs are developed using tools and techniques of the Initiation process to produce the final outputs.

Project managers, according to *A Guide to the PMBOK*, are not identified and assigned until the completion of the Initiation process. In reality, project managers are often identified at the beginning of the Initiation process.

The project goal is the purpose for undertaking the project. Goals should be SMART: specific, measurable, accurate, realistic, and time-bound. Projects can also be defined using the SMART acronym. Interview stakeholders to determine the project goals and begin to understand the deliverables of the project.

Get to know your stakeholders so that you understand the parts they play and how much authority they have. It doesn't hurt to also get familiar with their position in the organization, how much power they have, and how they interact with other stakeholders.

Constraints can restrict or dictate the actions of the project team. Constraints usually involve time, budget, and quality but can also include schedules, technology, and more. Document your constraints as they'll be used as inputs to future project processes.

Throw out that old saying about assumptions and document these as well.

Exam Essentials

Be able to name the nine Project Management Knowledge Areas.   The nine Project Management Knowledge Areas are Project Integration Management, Project Scope Management, Project Time Management, Project Cost Management, Project Quality Management, Project Human Resource Management, Project Communications Management, Project Risk Management, and Project Procurement Management.

Be able to distinguish between the six needs or demands that bring about project creation. The six needs or demands that bring about project creation are market demand, business need, customer requests, technological advances, legal requirements, and social needs.

Be able to denote the project Initiation inputs.   The project Initiation inputs are product description, strategic plan, project selection criteria, and historical information.

Be able to identify the purpose for the project Initiation process.   The purpose of the project Initiation process is to recognize the existence of a new project or project phase and to commit resources to begin the project or project phase.

Be able to define project constraints and assumptions.   Project constraints limit the options of the project team and restrict their actions. Sometimes constraints dictate actions. Time, budget, and quality are the most common constraints. Assumptions are conditions that are presumed to be true or real.

Key Terms

You've learned a lot of new key words in this chapter. PMI has worked hard to develop and define standard project management terms that apply across industries. Here is a list of some of the terms you came across in this chapter:

assumptions	Project Human Resource Management
constraints	Project Integration Management
deliverables	Project Management Knowledge Areas
feasibility studies	Project Procurement Management
goals	Project Quality Management
historical information	Project Risk Management
initiation	project scope
product scope	Project Scope Management
Project Communications Management	Project Time Management
Project Cost Management	requirements

Review Questions

1. The Project Integration Management knowledge area is made up of which of the following processes?

    A. Initiation, Project Plan Development, and Integrated Change Control

    B. Project Plan Development, Project Plan Execution, and Integrated Change Control

    C. Project Plan Development, Initiation, and Scope Planning

    D. Initiation, Scope Planning, and Integrated Change Control

2. When a project is being performed under contract, the product description is provided by which of the following?

    A. The buyer

    B. The project sponsor

    C. The project manager

    D. The contractor

3. You are the project manager for Fun Days vacation packages. Your new project assignment is to head up the Fun Days resort opening in Austin, Texas. You are estimating the duration of the project plan activities, devising the project schedule, and monitoring and controlling deviations from the schedule. Which of the Project Management Knowledge Areas are you working in?

    A. Project Scope Management

    B. Project Quality Management

    C. Project Integration Management

    D. Project Time Management

4. The Project Human Resource Management knowledge area contains which of the following processes?

    A. Staff Acquisition, Team Development, and Resource Planning

    B. Staff Acquisition, Team Development, and Performance Reporting

    C. Organizational Planning, Staff Acquisition, and Team Development

    D. Organization Planning, Team Development, and Resource Planning

5. Your company is going to introduce a new service called Phone Home. This service will allow you to speak the name of the person you want to call into your cellular phone. To call home, you would simply speak the word "home" into the phone, and it will dial that number for you. Your company is taking advantage of the progress that has been made recently with voice recognition software. Initial projections show that market demand is very high for this product. This project came about as a result of which of the following?

   A. Market demand

   B. Customer request

   C. Business need

   D. Technological advance

6. You've been hired as a manager for the Adjustments department of a nationwide bank based in your city. The Adjustments department is responsible for making corrections to customer accounts. This is a large department, with several smaller sections that deal with specific accounts; for example, personal checking or commercial checking. You've received your first set of management reports and can't make heads or tails out of the information. Each section appears to use a different methodology to audit their work and record the data for the management report. You request a project manager from the PMO to come down and get started right away on a project to streamline this process and make the data and reports consistent. This project came about as a result of which of the following?

   A. Technological advance

   B. Business need

   C. Customer request

   D. Legal requirement

7. What are the inputs to the Initiation process?

   A. Product description, strategic plan, project selection criteria, and historical information

   B. Product description, strategic plan, project overview document, and historical information

   C. Strategic plan, project overview document, feasibility study, and historical information

   D. Product description, strategic plan, constraints, and assumptions

8. You work for a large manufacturing plant. You're working on a new project for an overseas product release. This is the company's first experience in the overseas market, and they hope to make a big splash with the introduction of this product. The project entails producing your product in a concentrated formula and packaging it in smaller containers than the U.S. product uses. A new machine is needed in order to mix the first set of ingredients in the concentrated formula. Which of the following is true?

   A. The new machine, the concentrated formula, and the smaller package are all project constraints.

   B. The new machine, the concentrated formula, and the smaller package description must be incorporated into the product description document.

   C. The new machine, the concentrated formula, and the smaller package are all project assumptions.

   D. The new machine, the concentrated formula, and the smaller package are all considered deliverables.

9. You work for a large manufacturing plant. You're in the Initiation process of a new project for an overseas product release. This is the company's first experience in the overseas market, and they hope to make a big splash with the introduction of this product. The project entails producing your product in a concentrated formula and packaging it in smaller containers than the U.S. product uses. A new machine is needed in order to mix the first set of ingredients in the concentrated formula. Which of the following actions should the project manager take?

   A. The project manager should document the project's goals and known deliverables in a high-level overview document and recommend that the project proceed.

   B. The project manager should document the project's goals and known deliverables in a high-level overview document and assume that the project is a go.

   C. The project manager should document the project's goals and known deliverables in a high-level overview document and recommend that a feasibility study be performed.

   D. The project manager should document the project's goals and known deliverables in a high-level overview document and deliver it to the stakeholders.

10. What are the Initiation process outputs?

   A. Project charter, identification and assignment of project manager, constraints, and project overview documents

   B. Project charter, project overview, feasibility study, and constraints

   C. Project charter, identification and assignment of project manager, constraints, and assumptions

   D. Identification and assignment of project manager, project overview, constraints, and assumptions

11. The purpose of the Initiation process is to:

   A. Formally recognize the existence of a project or project phase

   B. Formally recognize the need that brought about the project, be it marketing demand, customer requests, business need, technological advances, or legal requirements

   C. Formally recognize the stakeholders of the project and identify them in the project charter

   D. Formally recognize the project sponsor and document his or her project goals

12. Your nonprofit organization is preparing to host its first annual 5K run/walk in City Park. You worked on a similar project for the organization two years ago when it co-hosted the 10K run through Overland Pass. Which of the Initiation process inputs might be helpful to you on your new project?

   A. The strategic plan, because you'll want to make sure the project reflects the overall strategic direction of the organization.

   B. Historical information on the 10K run project. You might be able to gather helpful project information since this new project is similar in nature.

   C. The product description, which would describe all the details of the run/walk program.

   D. Historical information from the recent blood drive project.

13. Which of the following is true regarding product descriptions?

   A. The product description is an output of the Initiation process. It describes the characteristics of the product or service.

   B. The product description is an output of the Initiation process. It describes the characteristics of the product or service and contains less detail in the early phases of the project.

   C. The product description is an input of the Initiation process. It describes the characteristics of the product or service and contains a lot of detail in the early phases of the project.

   D. The product description is an input of the Initiation process. It describes the characteristics of the product or service.

14. Deliverables can be described as:

   A. The purpose for undertaking the project

   B. The verifiable results of products or services that must be produced to consider the project complete

   C. The specifications regarding the goals of the project that must be produced to consider the project complete

   D. The measurable outcomes of the Scope Definition process

15. You are a project manager working on a new software product your company plans to market to businesses. The project sponsor told you that the project must be completed by September 1. The company plans to demo the new software product at a trade show in late September and therefore needs the project completed in time for the trade show. However, the sponsor has also told you that the budget is fixed at $85,000 and cannot be increased by even $10 due to overall budget cuts this year. You must complete the project within the given time frame and budget. Which of the following is the primary constraint for this project?

A. Budget

B. Quality

C. Time

D. Schedule

16. You are a project manager for a documentary film company. In light of a recent national tragedy, the company president wants to get a new documentary on the rescue efforts of the heroic firefighters to air as soon as possible. She's looking to you to make this documentary the best that's ever been produced in the history of this company. She guarantees you free rein to use whatever resources you need to get this project done quickly. However, the best photographer in the company is currently working on another assignment. Which of the following is true?

A. The primary constraint is time because the president wants the film done quickly. She told you to get it to air as soon as possible.

B. Resources are the primary constraint. Even though the president has given you free rein on resource use, you assume she didn't mean those actively assigned to projects.

C. The schedule is the primary constraint. Even though the president has given you free rein on resource use, you assume she didn't mean those actively assigned to projects. The photographer won't be finished for another three weeks on his current assignment, so schedule adjustments will have to be made.

D. The primary constraint is quality because the president wants this to be the best film ever produced by this company. She's given you free rein to use whatever resources needed to get the job done.

17. What limits the options of the project team?

A. Technology

B. Constraints

C. Deliverables

D. Assumptions

18. Your project depends on a key deliverable from a vendor you've used several times before with great success. You're counting on the delivery to arrive on June 1. This is an example of a

A. Constraint

B. Objective

C. Assumption

D. Goal

19. Halloween is approaching fast. Your market research shows that the little yellow chicks and pink bunny marshmallow candies are the best-selling candy at Easter time, outselling all other types of candies. This prompts the company to introduce a new version of marshmallow candies with Halloween themes this season. Which of the following is true?

    A. This project came about due to customer request, and the primary constraint is time.

    B. This project came about due to market demand, and the primary constraint is time.

    C. This project came about due to market demand, and the primary constraint is quality.

    D. This project came about due to customer request, and the primary constraint is quality.

20. Your company provides answering services for several major catalog retailers. The number of calls coming into the service center per month has continued to increase over the past 18 months. The phone system is approaching the maximum load limits and needs to be upgraded. You've been assigned to head up the upgrade project. Based on the company's experience with the vendor who worked on the last phone upgrade project, you're confident they'll be able to assist you with this project as well. Which of the following is true?

    A. You've made an assumption about vendor availability and expertise. The project came about due to a business need.

    B. Vendor availability and expertise are constraints. The project came about due to a business need.

    C. You've made an assumption about vendor availability and expertise. The project came about due to a market demand.

    D. Vendor availability and expertise are constraints. The project came about due to a market demand.

Answers to Review Questions

1. B. Project Integration Management is made up of Project Plan Development, Project Plan Execution, and Integrated Change Control.

2. A. The buyer provides product descriptions when projects are performed under contract.

3. D. Project Time Management involves the following processes: Activity Definition, Activity Sequencing, Activity Duration Estimating, Schedule Development, and Schedule Control.

4. C. The Project Human Resource Management knowledge area involves managing people and relationships. It includes Organizational Planning, Staff Acquisition, and Team Development. Remember that Resource Planning is part of the Project Cost Management knowledge area, not Project Human Resource Management.

5. D. The correct answer is technological advance. Marketing demand is high for the service, but the service did not come about as a result of customers asking for it; rather, it came to market because of the advances in technology.

6. B. This came about due to a business need. Staff members were spending unproductive hours producing information for the management report that wasn't consistent or meaningful.

7. A. Initiation has four process inputs. Constraints and assumptions are outputs of the Initiation process.

8. D. Deliverables are tangible, verifiable outcomes or items that must be produced in order to complete the project or project phase. These items wouldn't be considered goals, because the goal of the project is to break into the overseas market with a successful product revamped for that audience.

9. C. The most correct answer is to perform a feasibility study. Since this project is taking the company into a new, unknown market, there's lots of potential for error and failure. A feasibility study would help the stakeholders determine if the project is viable and cost effective, and whether it has a high potential for success.

10. C. Project Initiation outputs are the project charter, identification and assignment of the project manager, constraints, and assumptions. Remember for the test that project managers aren't officially assigned until the end of Initiation (as an output) but in reality are oftentimes assigned at the beginning of the Initiation process.

11. A. Initiation formally recognizes the existence of a project. Stakeholders might be identified in the Initiation process, but according to *A Guide to the PMBOK*, they are officially identified during the Planning process.

12. B. Historical information on projects of a similar nature can be very helpful when initiating new projects. They can help in formulating project deliverables and identifying constraints and assumptions, and will be helpful further on in the project Planning process as well.

13. D. Product descriptions are inputs to Initiation and contain less detail in the beginning phases of a project and more detail as the project progresses.

14. B. Deliverables are measurable or verifiable results or specific items that must be produced in order to consider the project complete.

15. C. The primary constraint is time. Since the trade show demos depend on project completion and the trade show is in late September, the date cannot be moved. The budget is the secondary constraint in this example.

16. D. The primary constraint is quality. If you made the assumption as stated in selection B, you assumed incorrectly. Clarify these assumptions with your stakeholders and project sponsors. This applies to option C as well.

17. B. Constraints restrict the actions of the project team.

18. C. This is an example of an assumption. You've used this vendor before and not had any problems. You're assuming there will be no problems with this delivery based on your past experience.

19. B. Market research shows the demand for the candies is extremely high during the Easter season. It's highly likely sales would be high during the Halloween season as well. Time is the constraint as Halloween is driven by a hard date.

20. A. The project came about due to a business need. The phones have to be answered because that's the core business. Upgrading the system to handle more volume is a business need. An assumption has been made regarding vendor availability. Always validate your assumptions.

Chapter

3

Creating a Project Charter

THE PMP EXAM CONTENT FROM THE PROJECT INITIATION PERFORMANCE DOMAIN COVERED IN THIS CHAPTER INCLUDES:

- ✓ 6. Defining strategy
- ✓ 7. Identifying performance criteria
- ✓ 8. Determining resource requirements
- ✓ 9. Defining budget
- ✓ 10. Producing formal documentation

The second half of Chapter 2, "Initiating the Project," started you on the journey into the project life cycle processes, with an introduction to project Initiation. You've already learned how to identify and document the goals of the project, and we talked about project deliverables, constraints, and assumptions. This chapter formally recognizes the launching of the project with the creation of a project charter.

We'll conclude the project Initiation process with this chapter and begin the Planning process in Chapter 4, "Creating the Scope Statement and WBS." We'll discuss one more input to the Initiation process and the tools and techniques of project Initiation, and then finish up the chapter with documenting the project charter. The primary goal of the Initiation process is to produce the project charter.

Using Project Selection Methodologies

Most organizations don't have the luxury of performing every project that's proposed. Even consulting organizations that sell their project management services must pick and choose which projects they want to work on. Selection criteria and methodologies help organizations decide among alternative projects. Project selection methodologies will vary depending on the company, the people serving on the selection committee, the criteria used, and the project. Sometimes selection criteria and methodologies will be purely financial, sometimes purely marketing, and sometimes they'll be based on public perception or political perception. In most cases, the decision is based on a combination of all of these and more.

This section looks at one input to the Initiation process called *project selection criteria*. This is how projects are selected and prioritized. (The other inputs to this process are product description, strategic plan, and historical information, which were covered in Chapter 2.) We'll finish up by looking at one of the two tools and techniques of this process: *project selection methods*. This tool and technique calculates measurable differences between projects and determines the tangible benefits to the company of choosing or not choosing the project. Expert judgment is the remaining tool and technique of this process, and we'll cover that in a later section of this chapter.

Selecting and Prioritizing Projects

Most organizations have a formal, or at least semiformal, process for selecting and prioritizing projects. In my organization, a steering committee is responsible for project review, selection, and prioritization. A *steering committee* is a group of folks comprised of senior managers and sometimes midlevel managers who represent each of the functional areas in the organization.

Here's how our process works. The steering committee requests project ideas from the business staff prior to the beginning of the fiscal year. These project ideas are developed into a project overview, or project concept document, as discussed in Chapter 1, "What is a Project?" These project overview documents contain the project goals, a description of the deliverables, the business justification for the project, a desired implementation date, what the organization stands to gain from implementing the project, a list of the functional business areas affected by the project, and if applicable, a benefit/cost analysis (we'll talk about that in a bit).

A special steering committee meeting is called to review the projects, and a determination is made on each project as to whether it will be included on the upcoming list of projects for the new year. Once the no-go projects have been weeded out, the remaining projects are prioritized according to their importance and benefit to the organization. The projects are documented on an official project list, and progress is reported on the active projects at the regular monthly steering committee meetings.

In theory, it's a great idea. In practice, it works only moderately well. Priorities can and do change throughout the year. New projects come up that weren't originally submitted during the call for projects that must be added to the list. Reprioritization begins anew, and resource alignment and assignments are shuffled. But again, we're getting ahead of ourselves. Just be aware that organizations usually have a process to recognize and screen project requests, accept or reject those requests based on some selection criteria, and prioritize the projects based on some criteria.

Some organizations may use analysis to determine whether or not to pursue a project. Organizations must determine in advance what the criteria will be for selecting projects and who is to be involved in deciding what projects will be selected. Let's look at these issues now.

Needs Analysis

Some organizations require a *needs analysis* or *needs assessment* of projects prior to the beginning of the Initiation process. The purpose of this is to perform a preliminary assessment of the viability of the project, the viability or perhaps marketability of the product or service of the project, and the project's value to the organization. This is usually an informal process and not considered part of the project work itself. Needs analysis is typical for internal service-type projects and for projects that entail new product development. The project concept document can serve as a jumping-off point to perform a needs analysis. Large, complex projects may also require further review via a feasibility study before a decision can be made to accept the project. You will recall that feasibility studies determine the viability of the project and help the company determine if the product or service of the project is marketable, profitable, safe, and doable.

Defining Project Selection Criteria

What are the selection criteria? Funny you should ask. Project selection criteria are an input to the project Initiation process, along with product description, strategic plan, and historical information. According to *A Guide to the PMBOK*, project selection criteria are concerned with the advantages or merits of the product of the project. In other words, selection criteria are concerned with what the product or service of the project will produce and how it will benefit the organization. Selection criteria involve the types of concerns executive managers are typically thinking about. This includes factors like market share, financial benefits, return on investment, customer retention and loyalty, and public perceptions. Selection criteria can be subjective or objective. The criteria for judging project selection could include financial measurements. For example, the selection criteria might dictate that projects must increase profits by a certain percentage in order to be considered. Equally, project selection criteria might include the criteria that an increase in market share or an increase in the public awareness of the company or product will be enjoyed as a result of this project. There aren't any rules for project selection, as the components of selection criteria are up to the company, steering committee, or project review committee to determine.

Power Players

Predetermined selection criteria as mentioned in the preceding section are one aspect of project selection, but so is the individual opinion, and power, of selection committee members. Don't underestimate the importance of the authority, political standing, and individual aspirations of selection committee members. Those committee members who happen to carry a lot of weight in company circles, so to speak, are likely to get their projects approved just on the fact that they are who they are. This is sometimes how project selection works in my organization. How about yours?

Project Selection Methods

Project selection criteria, as we just discussed, is an input to the Initiation process. Project selection methods are tools and techniques used during the Initiation process to measure the project's benefit or value to the organization. Selection criteria differs from selection methods in that selection criteria are concerned with the product of the project and selection methods measure the benefits of the project, or they compare the measurable benefits of one project against another. Selection methods are also used to evaluate and choose between alternative ways of performing the project.

According to *A Guide to the PMBOK*, there are two categories of selection methods: *constrained optimization methods* and *benefit measurement methods*. These selection methods are known as *decision models* and *calculation methods*. Decision models examine different criteria used in making decisions regarding project selection while calculations methods provide a way to calculate the value of the project which is then used in project selection decision making.

Exam Spotlight

You will likely encounter a question or two on project selection methods on the exam. Cross-reference your understanding of benefit measurement methods and constrained methods with the descriptions provided in *A Guide to the PMBOK*.

Constrained Optimization Methods

For the purposes of the exam, all you need to understand about constrained optimization methods is they are mathematical models that use linear, dynamic, integer, nonlinear, and/or multi-objective programming in the form of algorithms—or in other words, a specific set of steps to solve a particular problem. These are complicated mathematical formulas and algorithms that are beyond the scope of this book and require an engineering, statistical, or mathematical background to fully understand. Projects of enormous complexity use techniques such as these to make decisions regarding projects. The vast majority of project selection techniques will use the benefit measurement methods to make project selection decisions.

Benefit Measurement Methods

Benefit measurement methods employ various forms of analysis and comparative approaches to make project decisions. These methods include comparative approaches such as benefit/cost, scoring models, benefit contribution methods that include various cash flow techniques, and economic models. We'll examine several of these methods in this section, starting with benefit/cost.

Benefit/Cost Analysis

One common benefit measurement method is the benefit/cost analysis. This compares the financial benefits to the company of performing the project to the costs of implementing the project. Obviously, a sound project choice is one where the costs to implement or produce the product of the project are less than the financial benefits. How much less is the organization's decision. Some companies are comfortable with a small margin, while others are comfortable with a much larger margin between the two figures.

When examining costs for the benefit/cost analysis, include the costs to produce the product or service, the costs to take the product to market, and ongoing operational support costs. For example, let's say your company is considering writing and marketing a database software product that will allow banks to dissect their customer base, determine which types of customers buy which types of products, and then market more effectively to those customers. Some of the costs you will take into account are:

- The costs to develop the software such as programmer costs, hardware costs, testing costs, etc.

- Marketing costs such as advertising, traveling costs to perform demos at potential customer sites, etc.

- Ongoing costs such as having a customer support staff available during business hours to assist customers with product questions and problems.

Let's say the cost to produce this software plus the ongoing support costs total $5 million. Initial projections look like the demand for this product is high. Over a three-year period, the potential life of the software in its proposed form, projected revenues are $12 million. Taking only the financial information into account, the benefits outweigh the costs of this project. This project should receive a go recommendation.

Projects of significant cost or complexity usually take into account more than one benefit measurement method when making go or no-go decisions or deciding on one project over another. Keep in mind that selection methods can take subjective matter into account as well—the project is a go because it's the new CEO's pet project; nothing else needs to be said.

Scoring Models

Another project selection technique in the benefit measurement category is a *scoring model*, or *weighted scoring model*. My organization uses weighted scoring models to not only choose between projects, but also as a method to choose between competing bids on outsourced projects.

Weighted scoring models are quite simple. The project selection committee decides on the criteria that will be used on the scoring model—for example, profit potential, marketability of the product or service, the ability of the company to quickly and easily produce the product or service, and so on. Each of these criteria is assigned a weight, depending on the importance of the criteria to the project committee. More important criteria should carry a higher weight than the less important criteria.

Then, each project is rated on a scale from 1 to 5 (or some such assignment), with the higher number being the more desirable outcome to the company and the lower number having the opposite effect. This rating is then multiplied by the weight of the criteria factor and added to other weighted criteria scores for a total weighted score. Let's look at an example that brings this together (see Table 3.1).

TABLE 3.1   Weighted Scoring Model

Criteria	Weight	Project A Score*	Project B Score*	Project C Score*
Profit potential	5	5	5	3
Marketability	3	4	3	4
Ease to produce/support	1	4	3	2
Weighted score	—	41	37	29

*5 = highest.

In this example, Project A is the obvious choice.

Cash Flow Analysis Techniques

The remaining benefit measurement methods involve a variety of cash flow analysis techniques, including payback period, discounted cash flows, net present value, and internal rate of return. We'll look at each of these techniques individually and provide you with a crash course on their meanings and calculations.

PAYBACK PERIOD

The *payback period* is the length of time it takes the company to recoup the initial costs of producing the product or service of the project. This method compares the initial investment to the cash inflows expected over the life of the product or service. For example, say the initial investment on a project is $200,000, with expected cash inflows of $25,000 per quarter every quarter for the first two years, and $50,000 per quarter from thereon. The payback period is two years and can be calculated as follows:

Cash inflows = $25,000 × 4 (quarters in a year) = $100,000/year total inflow

Year 1 inflows = $100,000

Year 2 inflows = $100,000

Total = $200,000

Payback is reached in two years.

The fact that inflows are $50,000 per quarter starting in year 3 makes no difference, as payback is reached in two years.

Payback period is the least precise of all the cash flow calculations. That's because payback period does not consider the value of the cash inflows made in later years, commonly called the *time value of money*. For example, if you have a project with a five-year payback period, the cash inflows in year 5 are worth less than they are if you received them today. The next section will explain this idea more fully.

DISCOUNTED CASH FLOWS

As I just stated, money received in the future is worth less than money received today. The reason for that is the time value of money. If I borrowed $2000 from you today and promised to pay it back in three years, you would expect me to pay interest in addition to the original amount borrowed. Okay, if you were a family member or a really close friend maybe you wouldn't, but ordinarily this is the way it works. You would have had the use of the $2000 had you not lent it to me. If you had invested the money (Does this bring back memories of your mom telling you to save your money?), you'd receive a return on that money. Therefore, the future value of the $2000 you lent me today is $2315.25 in three years from now at 5 percent interest per year. Here's the formula for future value calculations:

$FV = PV (1 + i)^n$

In English, this formula says the future value (FV) of the investment equals the present value (PV) times (1 plus the interest rate) times the number of time periods the interest is paid. Let's plug in the numbers:

$FV = 2000 (1.05)^3$

$FV = 2000 (1.157625)$

$FV = \$2315.25$

The *discounted cash flow* technique compares the value of the future cash flows of the project to today's dollars. In order to calculate discounted cash flows, you need to know the value of the investment in today's terms, or the present value (PV). PV is calculated as follows:

$PV = FV \div (1 + i)^n$

This is the reverse of the FV formula talked about earlier. So, if we ask the question, "What is $2315.25 in three years from now worth today given a 5 percent interest rate?" we'd use the preceding formula. Let's try it.

$PV = \$2315.25 \div (1 + .05)^3$

$PV = \$2315.25 \div 1.157625$

$PV = 2000$

$2315.25 in three years from now is worth $2000 today.

Discounted cash flow is calculated just like this for the projects you're comparing for selection purposes or when considering alternative ways of doing the project. Apply the PV formula to the projects you're considering and then compare the discounted cash flows of all the projects against each other to make a selection. Here is an example comparison of two projects using this technique:

Project A is expected to make $100,000 in two years.

Project B is expected to make $120,000 in three years.

If the cost of capital is 12 percent, which project should you choose?

Using the PV formula used previously, calculate each project's worth.

The PV of Project A = $79,719.

The PV of Project B = $85,414.

Project B is the project that will return the highest investment to the company and should be chosen over Project A.

NET PRESENT VALUE

Projects may begin with a company investing some amount of money into the project to complete and accomplish its goals. In return, the company expects to receive revenues, or cash inflows, from the resulting project. *Net present value (NPV)* allows you to calculate an accurate value for the project. The mathematical formula for NPV is complicated, and you do not need to memorize it in that form for the test. However, you do need to know how to calculate NPV for the exam, so I've given you some examples of a less complicated way to perform this calculation in Tables 3.2 and 3.3 using the formulas you've already seen.

Net present value works like discounted cash flows in that you bring the value of future monies received into today's dollars. With NPV, you evaluate the cash inflows using the discounted cash flow technique applied to each period the inflows are expected, instead of in one sum. The total present value of the cash flows is then deducted from your initial investment to determine NPV. NPV assumes that cash inflows are reinvested at the cost of capital.

Here's the rule: If the NPV calculation is greater than zero, accept the project. If the NPV calculation is less than zero, reject the project.

Look at the two project examples in Tables 3.2 and 3.3. Project A and Project B have total cash inflows that are the same at the end of the project, but the amount of inflows at each period differs for each project. We'll stick with a 12 percent cost of capital. Note that the PV calculations were rounded to two decimal places.

TABLE 3.2 Project A

Year	Inflows	PV
1	10,000	8,929
2	15,000	11,958
3	5,000	3,559
Total	30,000	24,446
Less investment	—	24,000
NPV	—	**446**

TABLE 3.3 Project B

Year	Inflows	PV
1	7,000	6,250
2	13,000	10,364
3	10,000	7,118
Total	30,000	23,732
Less investment	—	24,000
NPV	—	**<268>**

Project A has an NPV greater than zero and should be accepted. Project B has an NPV less than zero and should be rejected. When you get a positive value for NPV, it means that the project will earn a return at least equal to or greater than the cost of capital.

Another note on NPV calculations: Projects with high returns early in the project are better projects than projects with lower returns early in the project. In the preceding examples, Project A fits this criteria also.

INTERNAL RATE OF RETURN

The *internal rate of return (IRR)* is the most difficult equation of all the cash flow techniques to calculate that we've discussed. It is a complicated formula and should be performed on a financial calculator or computer. IRR can be figured manually, but it's a trial-and-error approach to get to the answer.

Technically speaking, IRR is the discount rate when the present value of the cash inflows equals the original investment. When choosing between projects or when choosing alternative methods of doing the project, projects with higher IRR values are generally considered better than projects with low IRR values.

Exam Spotlight

For the exam, you need to know three things concerning IRR:

- IRR is the discount rate when NPV equals zero.

- IRR assumes that cash inflows are reinvested at the IRR value.

- You should choose projects with the highest IRR value.

Exam Spotlight

Although *A Guide to the PMBOK* doesn't specifically address these cash flow techniques, you'll likely see exam questions on these topics. They are inferred in *A Guide to the PMBOK* under the "Benefit Measurement Methods" heading.

Applying Project Selection Methods

Now that we've discussed some of the techniques used in the project selection methods tool and technique, let's look at how to apply them when choosing projects or project alternatives. One, two, or several of the benefit measurement methods can be used alone or in combination to come up with a selection decision. Remember that payback period is the least precise of all the cash flow techniques, NPV is the most conservative cash flow technique, and NPV and IRR will generally bring you to the same accept/reject conclusion.

Project selection methods, and particularly the benefit measurement methods, can be used to evaluate multiple projects or a single project. You might be weighing one project against another, or simply considering if the project you're proposing is worth doing. Remember that project selection methods are a tool and technique of Initiation and, this tool and technique covers two broad categories called constrained optimization methods and benefit measurement methods. Both of these together are often called *decision models*.

For the exam, remember that decision models are used as project selection methods (tools and techniques)—not as project selection criteria (input). Also note that the financial benefit measurement methods and the benefit/cost methods can be used for project justification, which we will discuss in Chapter 4. You'll want to refer back to this section when we get to project justification in the next chapter.

Expert Judgment

Expert judgment is the last tool and technique in the Initiation process. The concept behind expert judgment is to rely on individuals, or groups of people, who have training, specialized knowledge, or skills in the areas you're assessing. In the case of project Initiation, expert judgment would be helpful in assessing the inputs to the Initiation process—i.e., product descriptions, strategic plan, project selection criteria, and historical information. For example, as the project manager, you might rely on the expertise of your executive committee to help you understand how the proposed project gels with the strategic plan. Or, you might rely on team members who have participated on similar projects in the past to make recommendations regarding the proposed project.

Expert judgment is a tool and technique used in many other planning processes as well. According to *A Guide to the PMBOK*, experts might be found in other departments within the organization, external or internal consultants, professional and technical associations, or industry groups.

 Real World Scenario

Fun Days Vacation Resorts

Jerry is a project manager for Fun Days Vacation Resorts. He is working on three different project proposals to present to the executive steering committee for review. As part of the information-gathering process, Jerry attends the various resorts pretending to be a guest. This gives him a feel for what Fun Days guests experience on their vacations, and it better prepares him to present project particulars and alternatives.

Jerry has prepared the project overviews for three projects and called upon the experts in marketing to help him out with the projected revenue figures. He works up the numbers and finds the following:

- Project A—payback period = 5 years; IRR = 8 percent

- Project B—payback period = 3.5 years; IRR = 3 percent

- Project C—payback period = 2 years; IRR = 3 percent

Funding exists for only one of the projects. Jerry recommends Project A and predicts this is the project the steering committee will choose since the projects are mutually exclusive.

Jerry's turn to present comes up at the steering committee. Let's listen in on the action.

"And, on top of all the benefits I've just described, Project A provides an IRR of 8 percent, a full 5 percent higher than the other two projects we discussed. I recommend the committee choose Project A."

"Thank you Jerry," Colleen says. "Good presentation." Colleen is the executive chairperson of the steering committee and has the authority to break ties or make final decisions when the committee can't seem to agree.

"However, here at Fun Days we like to have our fun sooner rather than later." Chuckles ensue from the steering committee. They've all heard this before. "I do agree that an 8 percent IRR is a terrific return, but the payback is just too far out into the future. There are too many risks and unknowns for us to take on a project with a payback period this long. As you know, our industry is directly impacted by the health of the economy. Anything can happen in five years' time. I think we're much better off going with Project C. I recommend we accept Project C. Committee members, do you have anything to add?"

Identifying the Project's Initial Requirements

We've got one more stop to make in the Initiation process before we get to the project charter. This section covers project requirements—not like the requirements of the product of the project talked about in Chapter 2. These requirements are resource requirements and budget requirements needed to perform the work of the project. This is the last piece of information you'll gather before writing the project charter.

Most selection committees will want to have some feel for the impact the project will have on the organization in terms of resources and costs. We will delve much deeper into these two topics in Chapter 5, "Resource Planning and Estimating," where we'll talk at length about estimation techniques. For now, let's do an overview of each of these areas.

Defining Resource Requirements

It's forecasted to be a great summer day, one of those perfect hiking or biking kind of days. You and a couple of friends decide a hike is just what you need and think it'd be fun to bring along a light lunch. First, you dig out those old hiking boots you've had since college from the depths of the closet and blow the dust off them. Your feet are protected—now what about that lunch? You poke through the fridge and pull out some aged cheese, a fat bunch of red grapes, a loaf of crusty baguette, and a good bottle of Shiraz. You'll need glasses and a wine opener, too. Next, you pull out that daypack you ordered from that outdoorsy catalog because it looked so cool and you knew it would come in handy one day. Sunscreen and maybe some chocolate sandwich cookies for your friends top off the loaded daypack. You're all set. All you need now is to meet up with the friends, pile into the car, and drive to the trailhead.

If you think of the hike as your project—I'm using the term loosely in this case—the resources can be considered the boots, food, glasses, wine opener, sunscreen, and daypack. Add your friends in the mix and the car to drive you to the trailhead, and you've identified all the resources you're going to need for this project. Oh, a trail map might be handy, too.

Identifying Project Resources

This is exactly how resource identification works on projects. After you've identified the project goals and the project deliverables, you should have a fairly easy time identifying the kinds of resources you're going to need to complete the project. These will vary from project to project. One known resource entity is human resources. All projects will need some human effort and intervention to carry out the project. Also consider items like equipment, materials, hardware, software, telephones, specialized skills, vendors, office space, travel arrangements, contractors, desks, network connections, etc.

Some of these items may sound trivial, but consider the overall impact to the organization when determining what resources are needed. For example, if you're working on a large construction project and need to temporarily house the design team, they will need office furniture, telephones, PCs, design software, and network connections. Telephones and network connections might require new lines, which take time and money to install.

My organization once engaged contractors to work on a project without considering office space, telephone lines, or network connections. The contractors showed up for work as planned and had no place to sit. We set up tables in the hallway for them and had the network team run long cables taped down to the floor out to their PCs on the tables until the project was over. And, they used their own cell phones for telephones. The project manager didn't do an adequate job of determining resource needs for this project. Unfortunately for this project manager, the contractor office space turned out to be an important resource requirement he "didn't think about."

Documenting Skills and Roles

You will also need to detail the types of human resources you're going to need for your project. Does your project require specific skills? If so, note the skills needed. If they cannot be obtained internally, you will have to consider contractor help and factor that into the project costs. Does your project require the help of staff from other areas of the organization? Again, if so, document this. Briefly describe the roles and responsibilities of the key project team members, or the key resources needed for the project. Include this information in the project charter.

At this stage, you don't need every nitty-gritty detail. You're looking for the big hitters that will take time, money, or people with specialized skills to implement. These are the kinds of resources the selection committee will want to know about.

Determining the Initial Budget

Identifying the initial budget is a lot like identifying the initial resource requirements. Again, the selection committee is looking for the major impacts to the organization regarding the costs of performing the project and purchasing necessary equipment or services to carry out project activities. A project budget needs to be established once the project is initiated so that project costs can be attributed directly to it.

The responsibility for determining project costs rests on either the project manager or a finance manager in a functional organization. Sometimes the budget is predetermined by the executive management staff, and you're told what it is and have to work with what you're given. When this happens, you've got a constraint on your hands.

When you are the one responsible for determining the initial budget, there are a couple of places you can look that will help you with estimating project costs. One of the first places to consider is previous projects that were similar in scope to your project. Review the project documents from similar projects and use their total costs to give you a starting place. From there, you can make adjustments to your new budget according to the differences in scope and detail of the new project versus the one you're using as a reference.

You can also talk with key team members, key stakeholders, or others with experience on similar projects and ask them what projects of this type have cost in the past. They're also good folks to run your initial budget figures by before making them public.

Project costs can be broken down into roughly three areas: *human resource costs*, *resource or project costs*, and *administrative costs*. Let's discuss these here.

Human Resource Costs

Human resource, or personnel, costs can be one of your biggest expenses, depending on the kind of project you're working on. Any project that is labor intensive, or requires highly specialized skills or knowledge, will likely have high personnel costs. Research projects, software programming projects, and feasibility studies are some examples of projects that typically have large human resource budgets due to the specialized skills needed to perform the project.

Resource or Project Costs

The project itself will have resource expenses directly related to the project. These are costs that are specific to the project, not the day-to-day operating expenses that we'll cover in a minute. These resource costs might be things like travel expenses related to the project, long-distance phone bills, specialized talent hired for certain portions of the project, vendor fees, equipment purchases, hardware purchases, etc. Again, depending on the kind of project you're working on, resource expenses can be quite high as well. The construction of a new theme hotel on the Las Vegas strip, for example, could run into the tens of millions of dollars in material resources alone, let alone the human resource costs to design, construct, and build the hotel.

Administrative Costs

Administrative costs are the day-to-day costs that keep the organization running, but are not directly related to the project. For example, office equipment, local phone charges, leases (unless office space or building space was leased specifically to house project members, in which case this expense would be a resource expense charged against the project), heat and lights, support personnel, etc.

The project manager will want to identify the major expenses of the project and will have some general thoughts about project costs to share with the selection committee. The project budget will be further defined once adequate estimating can be completed, and at that time, the final project budget can be submitted for approval.

Formalizing and Publishing the Project Charter

We've covered a lot of material before finally getting to this point: formalizing and publishing the project charter. That's because as you've seen, a lot of information goes into the project charter. This document is the foundation for the remaining project activity planning, execution, and control processes.

The *project charter* is the official, written acknowledgment and recognition that a project exists. It's issued by senior management and gives the project manager the authority to assign organizational resources to the work of the project. It describes the business need or demand that the project was initiated to address and includes a description of the product or service of the project. It is usually the first official document of the project once acceptance of the project has been granted. Good project charters that are well documented will address many of the questions your stakeholders are likely to have up front. If your charter is good, you'll avoid a lot of issues early on. If your project is performed under contract, the contract itself can serve as the project charter for the seller.

Pulling the Project Charter Together

In order to create a useful and well-documented project charter, start by including a staple group of components. The project charter should include at least these elements:

- An overview of the project
- Project goals and objectives
- Project deliverables
- Business case or need for the project
- Product description
- Resource and cost estimates
- Feasibility study results if one was performed
- Human resources needed and any special skills required
- Roles and responsibilities of key team members and resources

- List of key stakeholders
- Name of the project manager

Creating the project charter is a matter of incorporating all the information you've gathered so far as outlined earlier in this book, putting it in the document, and then publishing it. Publishing, in this case, simply means distributing a copy of the project charter to the key stakeholders, the customer, the management team, and others who may be involved with the project. Publication can take several forms, including printed format or electronic format distributed via the company e-mail system or on the company's intranet.

The project charter should also describe the preliminary responsibilities of the project manager, project staff, project sponsor, and executive management and their roles in the project. However, we've only touched on roles and responsibilities of key project members, so let's take a closer look at this area and then wrap up with some final notes on project charters.

Project Manager

The project manager is the person who assumes responsibility for the success of the project. The project charter identifies the project manager and describes the authority the project manager has in carrying out the project. The project manager's primary responsibilities are project planning and then executing and managing the work of the project. The oversight of the project charter and the other project-planning documents created later on in the life cycle of the project assures the project manager that everyone knows and understands what's expected of them and what constitutes a successful project.

Project managers are responsible for setting the standards and policies for the projects they work on. As a project manager, it is your job to establish and communicate the project procedures to the project team and stakeholders.

Project managers will identify activities and tasks, resource requirements, project costs, project requirements, performance measures, and more. Communication and documentation must become the project manager's best friends. Keeping stakeholders, the project sponsor, the project team, and all other interested parties informed is "job one," as the famous car manufacturer's ads say.

Exam Spotlight

In some organizations, the project charter might be written by the project manager. Even though this may be common practice, it is not in keeping with *A Guide to the PMBOK* teachings. However, if you (as the project manager) are asked to write the charter, remember that your name should not appear as the author of the project charter document. Since the project charter authorizes the project and authorizes you as the project manager, it doesn't make sense for you to write a document authorizing yourself to manage the project. The author of the charter should be an executive manager in your organization with the power and authority to assign resources to this project. But remember for the exam that the charter is published by a manager external to the project, and one of its primary purposes is to identify the project manager.

Project Sponsor

Have you ever attended a conference or event that was put on by a sponsor? In the information technology field, conferences and seminars are often sponsored by software development companies. The sponsor pays for the event, the facilities, and the goodies, and provides an opportunity for vendors to display their wares. In return, the sponsor comes out looking like a winner. Because they are footing the bill for all this fun, the sponsor gets to call the shots on conference content and they get the prime spots for discussing their particular software solutions. And last but not least, they usually provide the keynote speaker and get to present their information to a captive audience.

Project sponsors are similar to this in that they rally support from stakeholders and the executive management team for the project. The project sponsor is usually an executive in the organization who has the power and authority to make decisions and settle disputes or conflicts regarding the project. The sponsor takes the project to the limelight, so to speak and gets to call the shots regarding project outcomes. The project sponsor is also the one with the big bucks who provides funds for your project. The project sponsor should be named in the project charter and identified as the final authority and decision maker for project issues.

Sponsors are actively involved in the Initiation and Planning phases of the project and tend to have less involvement during the Execution and Controlling phases. It's up to the project manager to keep the project sponsor informed of all project activities, project progress, and any conflicts or issues that arise. The sponsor is the one with the authority to resolve conflict and set priorities when these things can't be dealt with any other way.

Project Champion

The project champion is another strong project supporter. Unlike the sponsor, the project champion doesn't necessarily have a lot of authority or executive powers. The champion helps focus attention on the project from a technical perspective. The project champion is usually someone with a great deal of technical expertise or industry knowledge regarding the project. They can lend credibility to the viability of the project and to the skills and abilities of the key project team members to carry out project activities. Sometimes, the project manager may act as project champion.

The project champion isn't necessarily identified in the project charter. But as a project manager, you'll want to know who this person is, as they're a strong project advocate, and you might need them later on to help rally support for project decisions.

Functional Managers

We covered functional managers in Chapter 2. As a reminder, we'll mention them here again briefly, because project managers must work with and gain the support of functional managers in order to complete the project. Functional managers fulfill the administrative duties of the organization, provide and assign staff members to projects, and conduct performance reviews for their staff. It's a good idea to identify the functional managers who'll be working on project tasks or assigned project responsibilities in the charter.

Project Charter Sign-Off

The project charter isn't complete until you've received sign-off from the project sponsor, senior management, and key stakeholders. Sign-off indicates that the document has been read by those signing it (let's hope so anyway) and that they agree with its contents and are on board with the project. It also involves the major stakeholders right from the beginning and hopefully wins their continued participation in the project going forward. This is important because the charter states the project goals and deliverables, and the time, resources, and costs needed to meet those goals. If someone has a problem with them, now is the time to raise the red flag.

Signing the project charter document is the equivalent of agreeing to and endorsing the project. This doesn't mean that the project charter is set in stone, however. Project charters will change throughout the course of the project. As more details are uncovered and outlined and as the Planning process begins, more project issues will come to light. This is part of the iterative process of project management and is to be expected. The charter will occasionally be revised to reflect these new details, project plans will be revised, and project execution will change to incorporate the new information or direction.

Exam Spotlight

According to *A Guide to the PMBOK*, the project manager is assigned to the project as an output of the Initiation process. The project charter identifies and names the project manager, and the signed project charter gives the project manager the authority to assign resources to the project and move on to the Planning process.

Everyone mentioned here—the project manager, the project sponsor, the project champion, the functional managers, the stakeholders, the clients, and anyone else impacted by the project—should receive a copy of the written project charter. If you've done a good job with the project charter and it's been agreed to and signed off by the project sponsor and stakeholders, you've made your job of producing a scope statement, covered in Chapter 4, much easier.

Project Case Study: New Kitchen Heaven Retail Store

You review your notes and reread the project charter you've prepared for the Kitchen Heaven retail store one last time before looking for Dirk. When you saw him last, he pointed you in the direction of three of the project stakeholders: Jake Peterson, Jill Overstreet, and Ricardo Ramirez. After your meetings with Jake and then Jill, you were better able to refine the project overview and deliverables.

You finally run across Dirk in a hallway near the executive washroom.

"Dirk, I'm glad I caught you. I'd like to go over the project charter with you before the kickoff meeting tomorrow. Do you have a few minutes?"

"Sure," Dirk says to you. "Let's have it."

"The project charter states the project goal, which of course is to open the 50th Kitchen Heaven store in Colorado Springs. I also documented the deliverables, many of which we talked about last time we met.

"When I met with Jake, he confirmed it takes 120 days to do the store build-out. That includes having the shelves set up and in place, ready to stock with inventory."

Dirk asks if Jake told you about his store location idea.

"Yes, Jake gave me a contact name, and I've left her a voicemail. The sooner we can get that lease signed, the better. It takes Jake 120 days to do the build-out, and Jill said she needs two weeks' lead time to order the initial inventory and stock the shelves. That puts us pretty close to our February 1st deadline, counting the time to get the lease papers signed."

"Sounds good so far," Dirk replies. "What else?"

"I included an updated description of the products and services the new store will offer, based on the documentation that was written from the last store opening. Jill reviewed the updates to the description, so we should be in the clear there. The store will include some new lines that we've decided to take on—cookware from famous chefs, that kind of thing.

"The project charter also outlines your role as the project sponsor, my role as project manager, and our expectations of the project staff. Jake has already made contact with a general contractor in the Springs, and he is ready to roll once we've signed the lease."

You add, "I'm using your estimate of $2 million as our initial budget request. Based on projected inflows, I've calculated a payback period of 16 months, with an IRR of 22 percent."

"That's impressive," replies Dirk. "Even better than our Phoenix store. If I recall, the payback period there was just over two years. Let's hope those numbers hold true."

"I think they're reliable figures. Jill showed me her data based on recent store openings in similar-sized cities. And we factored in the economic conditions of the Colorado Springs area. Since they're on a growth pattern, we think the timing is perfect.

"One more thing, Dirk. Since we're including the big bash at grand opening as part of the deliverables, I talked to some of your folks in marketing to get some ideas. They are thinking we should have some great giveaways as door prizes and that we will want to cater in the food. They also thought having some live cooking demonstrations with some local chefs would be a good attraction."

"So what's next?" Dirk asks.

"As you know, the project kickoff is scheduled for tomorrow. What I'll need then is for you to talk about the project and the goals, the commitment you'll need from the management team to support this project, and introduce me as the project manager. I've already forwarded a copy of the project charter to the meeting attendees so that they can review it before the meeting. And, I included a list of the assumptions we've made so far as an appendix to the charter. Lastly, I'll need you to ask everyone present to sign a copy of the project charter."

"Sounds like you've covered everything," Dirk says. "I don't anticipate any problems tomorrow, as everyone is looking forward to this store opening."

Project Case Study Checklist

Payback period calculated at 16 months

IRR calculated at 22 percent

Met with stakeholders to determine high-level list of deliverables:

- Project store opening on February 1

- Build-out of storefront

- Retail product line delivered two weeks prior to grand opening

- Grand-opening party with cooking demos

Created project charter, which contains

- Overview of project goals and objectives

- List of deliverables

- Business case for the project

- Initial completion date of February 1

- Initial budget of $2 million

- Definition of roles of project sponsor and project manager

Kickoff meeting set up to discuss charter and obtain sign-off

Summary

You're well on your way to a successful project. This chapter finished up the Initiation process in this chapter, and the next chapter will begin the Planning process.

You learned about one more input to the Initiation process: project selection criteria. Selection criteria are defined by a selection committee or steering committee to make determinations as to how projects get selected and prioritized.

Project selection methods, on the other hand, are a tool and technique in the Initiation process. Selection methods include decision models in the form of benefit measurement methods and constrained optimization methods. The constrained optimization methods utilize mathematical models. Benefit measurement methods come in the form of benefit/cost analyses, scoring models, and economic analyses. These are primarily comparative approaches. Besides benefit/cost analysis, the most commonly used form of benefit measurement methods is cash flow analysis.

Analysis of cash flows includes payback period, discounted cash flows, net present value (NPV), and internal rate of return (IRR). These last three methods are concerned with the time value of money—or in other words, converting future dollars into today's value. Generally, projects with a shorter payback period are desired over longer payback periods. Projects that have an NPV greater than zero should be accepted. Projects with the highest IRR value are considered a better benefit to the organization than projects with low IRR values.

Expert judgment is considered a tool and technique of Initiation. Experts usually have specialized knowledge or skills and can include staff from other departments in the company, external or internal consultants, and members of professional and technical associations or industry groups.

Initial project requirements should be included in the project charter. Resources, personnel, budgets, and costs should be outlined to give the selection committee some overall idea of project costs.

The project charter is the official acknowledgment and recognition that the project exists. It appoints the project manager and outlines their authority. It contains an overview of the project and the project's goals and objectives. The charter should be signed by the project sponsor, stakeholders, and other key management members and then published and distributed to all interested parties.

The case study project charter will include all the elements talked about in this chapter. It's a formalized document that represents the issues you've mentioned here to Dirk. Recall that a charter is the document that authorizes the project to go forward. As such, it has to be comprehensive and must include details such as the project goals and deliverables, resource needs, the business need for the product of the project, the project sponsor, roles and responsibilities of other project members, projected budget, and other items that are relevant to managers who must authorize and endorse the project.

Exam Essentials

Be able to define decision models. Decision models are project selection methods that are a tool and technique in the Initiation process. Decision models include benefit measurement methods and constrained optimization methods.

Be able to describe and calculate payback period.   Payback period is the amount of time it will take the company to recoup its initial investment in the product of the project. It's calculated by adding up the expected cash inflows and comparing them to the initial investment to determine how many periods it takes for the cash inflows to equal the initial investment.

Be able to denote the decision criteria for NPV and IRR.   Projects with an NPV greater than zero should be accepted, and those with an NPV less than zero should be rejected. Projects with high IRR values should be accepted over projects with lower IRR values. IRR is the discount rate when NPV is equal to zero, and IRR assumes reinvestment at the IRR rate.

Be able to describe the importance of the project charter.   The project charter is the document that officially recognizes and acknowledges that a project exists. It dedicates the organization's resources to the project, names the project manager, and describes the goals and deliverables of the project.

Be able to describe the importance of sign-off of the project charter.   Sign-off assures all parties have read the charter, agree to its contents, and endorse the project. Participation early on by the key stakeholders will likely ensure their participation in the project as it progresses.

Key Terms

You've learned a lot of new key words in this chapter. PMI has worked hard to develop and define standard project management terms that apply across industries. Here is a list of some of the terms you came across in this chapter:

administrative costs	needs analysis or needs assessment
benefit measurement methods	net present value (NPV)
constrained optimization methods	payback period
discounted cash flow	project charter
expert judgment	resource or project costs
feasibility study	scoring model or weighted scoring model
human resource costs	selection criteria
internal rate of return (IRR)	steering committee

Review Questions

1. What are the tools and techniques used in the Initiation process?

    A. Project selection criteria, historical information, and expert judgment

    B. Project selection methods, historical information, and expert judgment

    C. Project selection criteria and expert judgment

    D. Project selection methods and expert judgment

2. Comparative methods, scoring methods, and economic and cash flow analysis are all part of which of the following?

    A. Benefit measurement methods, which are a tool and technique in Initiation

    B. Constrained optimization methods, which are a tool and technique in Initiation

    C. Benefit measurement methods, which are an input to Initiation

    D. Decision models, which are an output of Initiation

3. You are the project manager for the Late Night Smooth Jazz Club chain, with stores in 12 states. Smooth Jazz is considering opening a new club in Arizona or Nevada. You have derived the following information:

    Project Arizona: Payback period is 18 months, and the NPV is <250>.

    Project Nevada: Payback period is 24 months, and the NPV is 300.

    Which project would you recommend to the selection committee?

    A. Project Arizona, because the payback period is shorter than Project Nevada.

    B. Project Nevada, because its NPV is a positive number.

    C. Project Arizona because its NPV is a negative number.

    D. Project Nevada, because its NPV is a higher number than Project Arizona's NPV.

4. You are the project manager for the Late Night Smooth Jazz Club chain, with stores in 12 states. Smooth Jazz is considering opening a new club in Kansas City or Spokane. You have derived the following information:

    Project Kansas City: The payback period is 27 months, and the IRR is 35 percent.

    Project Spokane: The payback period is 25 months, and the IRR is 32 percent.

    Which project should you recommend to the selection committee?

    A. Project Spokane, because the payback period is shortest.

    B. Project Kansas City, because the IRR is highest.

    C. Project Spokane, because the IRR is lowest.

    D. Project Kansas City, because the payback period is longest.

5. Which of the following is true regarding NPV?

   A. NPV assumes reinvestment at the cost of capital.

   B. NPV decisions should be made based on the highest value for all of the selections.

   C. NPV assumes reinvestment at the prevailing rate.

   D. NPV assumes reinvestment at the NPV rate.

6. You are the project manager for Insomniacs International. Since you don't sleep much, you get a lot of project work done. You're considering recommending a project that costs $575,000; expected inflows are $25,000 per quarter for the first two years, and then $75,000 per quarter thereafter. What is the payback period?

   A. 40 months

   B. 38 months

   C. 39 months

   D. 41 months

7. Which of the following is true regarding IRR?

   A. IRR assumes reinvestment at the cost of capital.

   B. IRR is the discount rate when NPV is greater than zero.

   C. IRR is a constrained optimization method.

   D. IRR is the discount rate when NPV is equal to zero.

8. Mathematical models using linear, dynamic, integer, or algorithm models are considered:

   A. Project selection criteria

   B. A form of expert judgment

   C. Project selection methods

   D. A form of historical information

9. You are the newly appointed project manager for a pharmaceutical company. Your company has asked you to head up a project to research a new children's medication. You've identified the lab equipment you'll need, the software needed to perform analysis and measurements, and the skill level and types of the technicians and researchers for this project. Which of the following is true?

   A. The project manager and resources have been identified as part of the outputs of the Initiation process, and this information can be found in the project charter.

   B. The resources and project manager have been identified as an input to the project Initiation phase. Further information is needed to produce the project charter, which will include the resources and the project manager.

   C. The project manager and resources have been identified as part of the project selection process. The selection committee requires resource information to make a final decision.

   D. The resources and project manager have been identified as a result of a tool and technique in the Initiation process.

10. Your selection committee meets on a semiannual basis. They've determined that projects must meet or exceed a specific profit limit in order to be accepted and prioritized on the project list. Which of the following is true?

    A. The selection committee has defined project selection criteria, which are a tool and technique of Initiation.

    B. The selection committee has defined project selection methods, which are a tool and technique of Initiation.

    C. The selection committee has defined project selection methods, which are an input to Initiation.

    D. The selection committee has defined project selection criteria, which are an input to Initiation.

11. What are the Initiation process outputs?

    A. Project charter, historical information, and project manager identification and assignment

    B. Project charter, project manager identification and assignment, constraints, and assumptions

    C. Project charter, historical information, constraints, and assumptions

    D. Project charter, constraints, and assumptions

12. Ruby is an administrative assistant with another department. Her manager has agreed to loan Ruby's services to you on a part-time basis during your current project. Ruby is putting together the cost projections you've gathered so far. You want to include these costs in the project charter. Ruby is formatting this information for you into a spreadsheet package and is printing copies. Which of the following is true?

    A. All of the costs, including Ruby's time, are charged to the project.

    B. All of the costs Ruby is typing into the spreadsheet are project costs. Ruby's time is not directly related to the project and should not be included.

    C. The project costs, including Ruby's time, should be included in the project charter.

    D. The project costs, excluding Ruby's time, should be considered project constraints.

13. Your project selection committee used a weighted scoring model and found that Project B, with a score of 54, should be chosen over the other competing projects. Which of the following is true?

    A. Weighted scoring models are a benefit measurement method, which is a tool and technique in the Initiation process.

    B. Weighted scoring models are a constrained optimization method, which is an output of the Initiation process.

    C. Weighted scoring models are a constrained optimization method, which is a tool and technique in the Initiation process.

    D. Weighted scoring models are a benefit measurement method, which is an output of the Initiation process.

14. Your selection committee is debating between two projects. Project A has a payback period of 18 months. Project B has a cost of $125,000, with expected cash inflows of $50,000 the first year and $25,000 per quarter after that. Which project should you recommend?

    A. Either Project A or Project B, because the payback periods are equal.

    B. Project A, because Project B's payback period is 21 months.

    C. Project A, because Project B's payback period is 24 months.

    D. Project A, because Project B's payback period is 20 months.

15. Which of the following is true?

    A. Discounted cash flow analysis is the least precise of the cash flow techniques, because it does not consider the time value of money.

    B. NPV is the least precise of the cash flow analysis techniques, because it assumes reinvestment at the discount rate.

    C. Payback period is the least precise of the cash flow analysis techniques, because it does not consider the time value of money.

    D. IRR is the least precise of the cash flow analysis techniques, because it assumes reinvestment at the cost of capital.

16. Project selection criteria might include:

    A. Benefit measurement methods

    B. Constrained optimization analysis

    C. NPV calculations

    D. Potential market share or increased public perception

17. You are a project manager for Zippy Tees. Your selection committee has just chosen a project you recommended for implementation. Your project is to manufacture a line of miniature stuffed bears that will be attached to your company's trendy T-shirts. The bears will be wearing the same T-shirt design as the shirt they're attached to. Your project sponsor thinks you've really impressed the big boss and wants you to skip to the manufacturing process right away. What is your response?

    A. Agree with the project sponsor because they are your boss, and they have a lot of authority and power in the company.

    B. Require that a preliminary budget be established and a resource list be put together to alert other managers of the requirements of this project. This should be published and signed by the other managers who are impacted by this project.

    C. To require a project charter be published and signed off on by all stakeholders before proceeding.

    D. To require a project charter be written to include the resources needed, the budget, and the project manager's authority. The project manager is the only one who needs to see this document, as other documents will be distributed later that contain the same details as the charter.

18. Which of the following is true regarding the project charter?

    A. The project charter should be published under the name of a manager external to the project.

    B. The project charter should be published under the project sponsor's name.

    C. The project charter should be published under the name of the project manager.

    D. The project charter should be published under the name of the project champion.

19. You are the project manager for Zippy Tees. Your company has decided to outsource the manufacturing of miniature bears to be attached to your trendy T-shirts. Which of the following is true?

    A. A good product description is all that's required. The project manager will supply this to the vendor.

    B. The contract can serve as the project charter. The product description will be included in the contract.

    C. The project manager should write the project charter, because the project manager will be managing the vendor portion of this project as well.

    D. The vendor should write the project charter, because they are responsible for manufacturing the bears.

20. The project charter:

    A. Includes a product description, describes the business need of the project, and is published by the project manager.

    B. Includes a product description, describes the business need of the project, and is published by the project sponsor.

    C. Includes the contract when the project is performed by a vendor and is published by a manager external to the project.

    D. Includes a product description, describes the business need of the project, and is published by a manager external to the project.

Answers to Review Questions

1. D. The tools and techniques in the Initiation process are project selection methods and expert judgment.

2. A. Benefit measurement methods include comparative methods, scoring models, and cash flow analysis, which are all part of the project selection method tools and techniques in Initiation.

3. B. Projects with NPV greater than zero should be given an accept recommendation.

4. B. Projects with the highest IRR value are favored over projects with lower IRR values.

5. A. Net present value (NPV) assumes reinvestment is made at the cost of capital.

6. C. Year 1 and 2 inflows are each $100,000 for a total of $200,000. Year 3 inflows are an additional $300,000. Add one more quarter to this total and the $575,000 is reached in three years and three months, or 39 months.

7. D. IRR assumes reinvestment at the IRR rate and is the discount rate when NPV is equal to zero.

8. C. Mathematical models are part of the constrained optimization methods used as a project selection method technique.

9. A. Initiation outputs include the project charter and identification and assignment of the project manager. Resource needs are detailed in the project charter.

10. D. Project selection criteria can be objective or subjective. Selection criteria are an input to the Initiation process. Project selection methods use decision models to assist with project selection and are a tool and technique of the Initiation process.

11. B. Outputs to Initiation include the project charter, project manager identification and assignment (even though this might be stated in the charter, this is still a specific output of Initiation), constraints, and assumptions.

12. B. Project costs are those costs directly related to the project. Ruby is part-time on the project and works for the organization, not the project manager. Therefore, her time is not counted in the initial budget projections.

13. A. Benefit measurement methods include comparative methods and scoring models, among others, to make project selections.

14. B. Project B has a payback period of 21 months. $50,000 is received in the first 12 months, with another $75,000 coming in over each of the next three quarters, or nine months.

15. C. Payback period does not consider the time value of money and is therefore the least precise of all the cash flow analysis techniques.

16. D. Project selection criteria include subjective information such as potential market share. Objective material can be considered in project selection criteria, but the other answers listed here are specific project selection methods.

17. C. The project should be kicked off with a project charter outlining the project goals, deliverables, resources, budget, and roles and responsibilities of the project team. This ensures that everyone is working from the same assumptions and with the same goals in mind.

18. A. According to *A Guide to the PMBOK*, the project charter should be published by a manager external to the project but with sufficient power and authority to carry it off.

19. B. When a project is performed under contract, the contract can serve as the project charter. Project charters always include product descriptions.

20. D. Project charters, according to *A Guide to the PMBOK*, must at least include the product description and the business need for the product or service of the project. Charters are published by managers external to the project according to *A Guide to the PMBOK*, but in practice, they are often published by the project sponsor.

Creating the Scope Statement and WBS

THE PMP EXAM CONTENT FROM THE PROJECT PLANNING PERFORMANCE DOMAIN COVERED IN THIS CHAPTER INCLUDES:

- ✓ 1. Refining a project
- ✓ 2. Creating a WBS

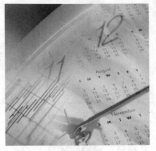

Great job! You've successfully completed the project Initiation process and published the project charter. The project is officially under way. Stakeholders have been informed, there is management buy-in on the project, the project manager has been assigned, and the project goals and deliverables have been identified. A solid foundation for the Planning process is in place.

In this chapter, we will begin the Planning process of the project. In fact, we will continue discussing the Planning processes through Chapter 7, "Creating the Project Plan." Planning is a significant activity in any project and, if done correctly, will go a long way toward ensuring project success.

This chapter begins with the Scope Planning process. This process will take you through one more look at project goals and deliverables. You'll use the project charter you created in the last chapter—plus some other inputs—and then apply the tools and techniques of this process to come up with the scope statement and the scope management plan. From there, you're off to the Scope Definition process, where you'll begin to break down the work of the project via a work breakdown structure (WBS), the primary output of this process. This chapter wraps up with a short discussion of the Communications Planning process.

We've talked a lot about documentation so far, and we will discuss it more in this chapter. Documentation is something you will do throughout the remainder of the project, and the Communications Planning process details how to collect information, how to store it, and when and how to distribute it to stakeholders.

Scoping Out the Project

Scope Planning is the first process in the Planning process group. The primary purpose of Scope Planning is to progressively elaborate and document the work of the project (cleverly called *project scope*) and to produce two documents: the scope statement and the scope management plan, each of which are the final outputs of this process. We'll discuss both of these outputs plus a third Scope Planning output—supporting details—in just a bit. For now let's concentrate on the inputs to this process, which will help you get started elaborating the work of the project.

Exam Spotlight

According to *A Guide to the PMBOK*, page 55, "Scope Planning is the process of progressively elaborating and documenting the project work (project scope) that produces the product of the project." Understand this concept for the exam.

Scope Planning Inputs

Even though I've discussed the inputs to the Scope Planning process in various chapters in this book already, I haven't specifically defined them as inputs to Scope Planning. It's important for you to see how these inputs work together and serve as the starting point for documenting the work of the project. It's difficult to document the project scope if you don't first understand the purpose for the project, the product or service you're trying to produce, and the constraints and assumptions you're working under. That brings us to the inputs to the Scope Planning process, which are:

- Product description
- Project charter
- Project constraints
- Project assumptions

I discussed the product description in detail in Chapter 2, "Initiating the Process," but you'll remember that the product description includes the product requirements and describes the characteristics of the product or service of the project, also known as the product design. The product requirements are a result of customer needs, and the product design must incorporate and match the product requirements. You'll recall from Chapter 3, "Creating a Project Charter," that the project charter outlines the project goals and objectives. We'll examine the project goals and objectives later in this process in order to progressively elaborate project scope, which is the goal of this process.

We covered constraints in several of the previous chapters as well. Remember that constraints either restrict or dictate the actions of the project team. Assumptions—the last input to this process—are those things you believe to be true. They were documented as part of the Initiation process.

Now that we've refreshed your memory on the definitions of these inputs, let's examine the tools and techniques used in Scope Planning.

Scope Planning Tools and Techniques

We have already discussed two of the tools and techniques of Scope Planning: benefit/cost analysis and expert judgment. Remember from Chapter 3 that benefit/cost analysis (also called cost benefit analysis) compares the costs of the project to the expected benefits to determine the best choice among projects or the best alternative method of performing the work of the project. Benefit/cost analysis might include cash flow analysis and economic analysis. In Scope Planning, benefit/cost analysis is used to determine various project and/or product alternatives. These techniques determine the profitability and viability of the project and/or product alternatives and may also be used as selection criteria, as discussed in the last chapter. Return on investment (ROI) is a benefit/cost technique that's used in Scope Planning to compare one alternative to another. ROI measures how effectively the investment in each project alternative is at generating profit or savings.

Expert judgment is relying on people or groups with specific skills, knowledge, or training to help assess the process inputs. One expert you can count on in this process is the executive manager who wrote the project charter. They can clarify questions you may have about the project goals as well as the product description. Stakeholders or other project managers with previous experience on projects similar to yours can help you assess the constraints and assumptions as you further elaborate project scope. Two techniques remain for the Scope Planning process: product analysis and alternatives identification. We'll examine these two techniques next.

Product Analysis

Product analysis goes hand in hand with the product description. Product analysis is simply a deeper understanding of the product or service of the project. According to *A Guide to the PMBOK*, this goes further than product description in that product analysis might include performing value analysis, function analysis, systems-engineering techniques, or value-engineering techniques to further define the product or service.

Exam Spotlight

It's beyond the scope of this book to go into the various analysis techniques used in product analysis. For exam purposes, remember that product analysis is a tool and technique of Scope Planning and memorize the list of analysis techniques that might be performed in this process.

Alternatives Identification

Alternatives identification is a technique used to discover different methods or ways of accomplishing the project. For example, brainstorming might be used to discover alternative ways of implementing one of the project objectives. Perhaps the project's budget doesn't allow for a portion of the project that the stakeholders really think needs to be included. Brainstorming might uncover an alternative that would allow the needed portion to be accomplished.

Let's assume you have your inputs at hand and have used the tools and techniques described to analyze these inputs. Now you're ready to document them in the scope statement.

Why Do You Need a Scope Statement?

The purpose of the *scope statement* is to document the project goals, deliverables, and requirements so that they can be used as a baseline for future project decisions. The scope statement is an agreement between the project and the project customer that states precisely what the work of the project will produce. Simply put, the scope statement tells everyone concerned with the project exactly what they're going to get when the work is finished. If questions arise during the course of the project regarding deliverables or requirements, you can refer back to the agreed-upon scope statement for clarification.

You've already accomplished a lot of work regarding the scope statement just by producing the project charter. The charter is used as an input to the scope statement and already contains the project goals and major project deliverables as discussed. If the project charter was written well and the goals and deliverables are complete, it's simply a matter of transferring the goals and deliverables information from the charter to the scope statement.

Exam Spotlight

Understand that the purpose of the scope statement according to *A Guide to the PMBOK* is to provide a basis for future project decisions and to provide all the stakeholders with a foundational understanding of project scope.

The scope statement is the baseline for the project, as mentioned earlier. This means if questions arise or changes are proposed later in the project, they can be compared to what's documented in the scope statement. Making change decisions is easier when the original deliverables and requirements are well documented. The criteria outlined in the scope statement will also be used to determine if the project was completed successfully. Hopefully you're seeing the importance of documenting project scope.

Scope Statement Components

According to *A Guide to the PMBOK*, the scope statement should include all of the following: project justification, project's product, project deliverables, and project objectives. If details surrounding these are spelled out in other documents, you don't have to re-enter all the information into the scope statement. Simply reference the other document in the scope statement so that readers know where to find it. Let's take a look at each of the elements in the project scope.

Project Justification

The project justification describes the business need of the project. If the business need—or business case—was written as part of the project charter, reference it in the scope statement. Project justification also includes the cost benefit and cash flow analysis used to determine the projected profitability of the project. See Chapter 3 for details on these techniques.

Project's Product

The project's product is the product description talked about in Chapter 3 and referenced earlier in this chapter. If the product description is contained in the project charter, you can reference the project charter in the scope statement. Chances are very good you'll be using a word processing system of some sort to write these documents. An even better idea is to copy and paste the information from the project charter into the scope statement. It won't hurt anything to have it in both places and will make reading the scope statement easier.

Project Deliverables

A Guide to the PMBOK describes project deliverables as the major deliverables of a project and all the subcomponents that make up the deliverables. The completion of these deliverables signals project completion. For example, your project goal or objective might be to produce a new bottle of beer for the holidays. One major deliverable is the holiday cartons to hold the bottles. The subcomponents to produce this major deliverable might be the carton design, photographs, color choices, and so on.

Documenting *All* of the Deliverables

One of the project manager's primary goals is to accurately document the deliverables and requirements of the project and then manage the project so that they are produced according to the agreed-upon criteria. Deliverables describe the components of the goals and objectives in a quantifiable way. Requirements are the specifications of the deliverables.

The project manager should use the project charter as a starting point for identifying project deliverables, but in the charter, it's possible that only some of the deliverables will be documented. Remember that the charter was written by a manager external to the project, and it was the first take at defining the project objectives and deliverables. As the project manager, it's your job to make certain *all* the deliverables are identified and documented in the scope statement. That's because the scope statement (not the project charter) serves as the agreement among stakeholders—including the customer of the project—regarding what project objectives and deliverables will be produced in order to meet and satisfy the requirements of the project.

Interview the stakeholders, other project managers, project team members, customers, management staff, industry experts, and any other experts who can help you identify all the deliverables of the project. Depending on the size of the project, you might be able to accomplish this in a group setting using simple brainstorming techniques, whereas large complex projects may have scope statements for each deliverable of the project. Remember that the scope statement is progressively elaborated into finer detail and is used later on to help decompose the work of the project into smaller tasks and activities. But for now, we'll focus on decomposing the deliverables into requirements.

Project Objectives

Objectives, according to *A Guide to the PMBOK*, are quantifiable criteria used to measure project success. At the very least, the quantifiable criteria must include schedule, cost, and quality measures. These may sound familiar. That's because these criteria are the same as the triple constraints—time, cost, and quality. In the case of project objectives, these elements are used as measurements to determine project satisfaction and successful completion. Costs are typically stated in monetary units (U.S. dollars, Euro dollars, and so on) and should be specific.

Schedules are typically stated in time measurements, and I recommend sticking with a consistent measurement throughout your project. If you use hours, state all schedule-related topics in hours. We'll discuss quality and quality measurements in Chapter 6, "Establishing Project Planning Controls," and Chapter 9, "Measuring and Controlling Project Performance."

Remember from Chapter 3 that objectives and goals are specific, measurable, and timely. Continuing with the holiday beer example, the objective of this project would be properly stated as follows: "Beer Buddies, Inc. will produce two million cases of holiday beer to be shipped to our distributors by October 30 at a cost of $1.5 million or less."

The objective criteria in this statement are clearly stated, and fulfillment of the project objective can be easily measured. Stakeholders will know the objective is met when the two million cases are produced and shipped by the due date within the budget constraint.

Critical Success Factors

Deliverables and objectives are sometimes referred to as *critical success factors*. Critical success factors are those elements that must be completed in order for the project to be considered complete. For example, if you're building a bridge, one of the deliverables might be to produce a specific number of trusses that will be used to help support the bridge. Without the trusses, the bridge can't be completed; in fact, the bridge might not stand without them. The trusses, in this case, are a critical success factor. Not all deliverables are necessarily critical success factors, but many of them will fall into this category and should be documented as such.

Project Requirements

After all the deliverables are identified, the project manager needs to discover and document all of the requirements of the project. Requirements describe the characteristics of the deliverable. Requirements might include things like dimensions, ease of use, color, specific ingredients, and so on. For example, if one of our deliverables is a blue cube that will become part of another component, the requirements might state the dimensions, material composition, texture, and so on.

Again, the project manager needs to pull those communications skills out of her tool bag and use them to interview stakeholders, customers, project team members, and business process owners about the project requirements. While the project manager is responsible for making certain the requirements are documented, it doesn't mean this task must be performed by the project manager. The project manager can enlist the help of business analysts or requirements analysts to conduct the interviews and document the requirements. The project manager then reviews the requirements and incorporates them into the project documentation and project plan.

Business process owners are those people who are experts in their particular area of the business. They are invaluable resources to the project manager. They are usually the midlevel managers and line managers who still have their fingers in the day-to-day portion of the business. For example, it takes many experts in various areas to produce and market a great bottle of beer. There are machinists whose specialty is regulating and keeping the stainless steel and copper drums in top working order. There are chemists who daily check and adjust the secret formulas brewing in the vats. Graphic artists must develop colorful and interesting labels and cartons to attract the attention of those thirsty patrons. And of course, those great TV commercials advertising the tasty brew are produced by yet another set of business experts. These are the kinds of people you'll interview and ask to assist you in identifying requirements.

Getting the business process owners and stakeholders (who could be one and the same, depending on the project) together in a meeting room and brainstorming the requirements can produce terrific results. Depending on the size of the project, this isn't always possible, but the idea holds true. Interview your stakeholders and business experts to get at the requirements and then document them in the scope statement.

You can use the same techniques to determine requirements as you did to determine deliverables. There are several techniques discussed in the "Risk Planning" section of Chapter 6 that you can use during the Scope Planning process as well to identify deliverables and requirements.

Exam Spotlight

Even though *A Guide to the PMBOK* does not go into great detail about project requirements, you may find a question or two on this topic. Since requirements are closely linked to deliverables, it makes sense to document them in the scope statement.

Other Considerations

It's important that the project objectives, deliverables, and requirements are clearly and concisely stated in the scope statement so there are no misunderstandings later on. "Producing a special run of holiday beer" is not the same as "Producing two million cases of holiday beer by October 30." The former statement can be interpreted different ways by the project sponsor and project manager. You'd have to put real effort into misunderstanding the latter statement.

As stated earlier, the scope statement should contain a comprehensive listing of all the project requirements. This is important because this document forms the basis for agreement between the stakeholders and project team from this point forward. You'll want to be certain you have not missed anything when writing the scope statement. Run the draft by some of the key stakeholders and project team members before publishing it to see if they think anything is missing. You're going to use this document to determine if the project has been successfully completed by comparing what's been delivered to what's described here, so be sure you've covered everything.

Approving and Publishing the Scope Statement

Just like the project charter, the scope statement should be published and distributed to the stakeholders, key management personnel, and project team members. You will also want a formal sign-off procedure for the scope statement. When stakeholders sign off and agree to the scope statement, they're agreeing to the deliverables and requirements of the project. And, as with the project charter, their agreement and endorsement of the project requirements and deliverables will likely sustain their participation and cooperation throughout the rest of the project. That doesn't mean they'll agree to everything as the project progresses, but it does mean the stakeholders are informed and will likely remain active project participants.

Exclusions from Scope

The following statement may seem obvious, but we'll note it anyway: Objectives, deliverables, and requirements not specifically included in the scope statement are explicitly excluded from the project. Your scope statement could have a section for exclusions so that everyone knows in advance what isn't going to be included in the project.

Supporting Detail

Supporting detail is an output of the Scope Planning process and directly references the information you've assembled for the scope statement. Supporting detail should be documented and should include the project constraints, assumptions, and any other information not specifically documented in the scope statement. You could list the deliverables and requirements that are excluded from the project here, unless they were already noted in the scope statement. This document, like the scope statement, will be referenced in future Planning processes, so keep it handy.

 Real World Scenario

Mountain Streams Services

Maria Sanchez is the CEO of Mountain Streams Services. She recently accepted a prestigious industry award on behalf of the company. Maria knows that without the dedication and support of her employees, Mountain Streams Services wouldn't have achieved this great milestone.

Maria wants to host a reception for the employees and their guests in recognition of all their hard work and contributions to the company. Maria has appointed you to arrange the reception.

The reception is scheduled for April 12, and Maria has given you a budget of $125 per person. The company employs 200 people. The reception should be semiformal.

You've documented the deliverables as follows:

- Location selection

- Food and beverage menu

- Invitations

- Entertainment

- Insurance coverage

- Decorations

- Photographer

- Agenda

In addition to the deliverables, you want to go over the following requirements with Maria to be certain you both are in agreement:

- The location should be somewhere in the downtown area.

- Employees are encouraged to bring one guest, but no children.

- There will be an open bar paid for by Maria.

- The agenda will include a speech by Maria, followed by the distribution of bonus checks to every employee. This is to be kept secret until the reception.

- The decorations should include gold-trimmed fountain pens with the company logo at every place setting for the attendees to keep.

Once you've documented all the particulars, you ask to speak with Maria to go over this scope statement and get her agreement before proceeding with the project plan and task assignments.

We're making progress. We've covered two of the three Scope Planning process outputs: the scope statement and supporting detail. All the deliverables and requirements have now been documented, along with measurable or quantifiable criteria for each. Stakeholders have approved and signed off on them, and the scope statement has been published and distributed.

 Like other project-planning documents, the scope statement is not cast in stone. Progressive elaboration of the deliverables and requirements will likely bring about changes to the scope statement.

The scope statement can and probably will change as the project progresses. Changes to the project scope should be documented and the scope statement modified to incorporate these changes. Changes are managed according to the scope management plan, which is the last output of this process. We'll discuss this plan in the next section.

Publishing the Scope Management Plan

Change is inevitable. One thing you and I know for certain is that changes are going to occur on your next project. Change isn't something to be dreaded, but it is something to be managed. The *scope management plan* helps the project manager do just that. This plan is an important supplementary document to the project plan, as it describes how changes to the project scope will be incorporated into the project. It also defines the process of how to go about requesting a change.

The scope management plan should be written and distributed at roughly the same time the scope statement is published. If you get the scope management plan in the hands of the stakeholders early on, it will hopefully eliminate questions about scope changes later in the project.

Exam Spotlight

The purpose of the scope management plan, according to *A Guide to the PMBOK*, is to describe how scope changes will be managed and incorporated into the project. This includes analyzing the reliability and stability of the project scope. In other words, the scope management plan examines and documents the likelihood that scope change will occur (meaning changes to goals, deliverables, or requirements).

The scope management plan answers the questions, "Are a lot of changes expected?", "How dramatic will the changes be?", and "How frequently will changes occur?" The answers to these questions are determined by the complexity of the project you're working on. The example of the employee reception at the end of the last section probably won't have a lot of change, because the project is small and the deliverables and requirements are simple and very clear. The scope management plan for that project would make such a statement.

The Scope Management Change Process

According to *A Guide to the PMBOK*, the scope management change process can be formal or informal. I would agree that for small, uncomplicated projects with one or two stakeholders, an informal broad-based process will work well. Large or complex projects should always have a detailed scope management plan. In either case, it's been my experience whether the process is formal or informal, all change requests should be put in writing. Stakeholders and project managers can sometimes have foggy memories. And what you think you said might not be what the stakeholder heard, and vice versa. Documenting the change request eliminates these issues.

Hmm, have we talked about documentation?

Documenting Change Requests

All changes should be requested in writing on a formal change request form, and the impact of the changes should be noted. Changes will usually impact one, if not all, of the triple constraints. But for now, all you need to know is the kind of change requested and have a high-level understanding of its impact on time, cost, or quality. These changes should be logged and tracked throughout the course of the project. Some changes will not be approved but might need to be incorporated into the next product release or project. If you log and file these change requests with the project information, they will help you define the requirements for the next project. In a later chapter, we'll discuss the process for change approval and communication of the change.

According to *A Guide to the PMBOK*, the scope management plan should spell out how changes will be identified and how they will be classified. If you require project team members and stakeholders to identify changes in writing, for example, the scope management plan should document the procedure for requesting the changes and how to obtain a change request form. The project itself, or perhaps your organizational procedures, will dictate how changes are classified. I recommend using a simple three- or four-tier system. An example of change classifications are:

- Required
- Important
- Non-critical
- Nice to have but not essential.

Provide a space on the change request form for the requestor to indicate the classification of the change. The classification is one of the criteria used to determine whether the change should be incorporated into the project. We'll talk more about how changes are approved or denied (this is called *change control*) in Chapter 10, "Controlling Change."

Exam Spotlight

According *A Guide to the PMBOK,* page 56, identification and classification of scope change is essential when product characteristics are still being elaborated.

For the exam, remember that the scope management plan is a document that identifies how project scope will be managed and how changes will be incorporated into the project. It assesses the probability of scope changes, their frequency, and their impact. Formalizing this process for large or complex projects is highly recommended.

Formulating the Scope Definition

Now we're getting to the meat of the project Planning process. We've identified and documented all the project deliverables and requirements, and we're ready to further break these down into project work. In the *Scope Definition* process, the project deliverables are broken down into smaller, manageable components so that you can eventually plan project tasks and activities.

Exam Spotlight

The subdividing of deliverables into smaller components is the purpose of the Scope Definition process. *A Guide to the PMBOK* calls this *decomposition*.

This breaking-down or decomposing process will accomplish several things for you, one of which is improving estimates. It's easier to estimate the costs, time, and resources needed for individual work components than it is to estimate them for a whole body of work or deliverable. Using smaller components also makes it easier to assign performance measures and controls. These give you a baseline to compare against throughout the project or phase. And finally, assigning resources and responsibility for the components of work makes better sense, as several resources with different skills might be needed to complete one deliverable. Breaking them down assures that assignment, and the responsibility for that assignment, goes to the proper parties. We'll discuss decomposition in more detail in the next section.

The Scope Definition process has five inputs that we've already covered elsewhere:

- Scope statement
- Project constraints
- Assumptions
- Other Planning process outputs
- Historical information.

The tools and techniques of Scope Definition are the work breakdown structure templates and decomposition. These tools work together to create the work breakdown structure (WBS), which we'll look at next.

Creating the Work Breakdown Structure

Have you ever mapped out a family tree? A *work breakdown structure (WBS)* is very similar to a family tree. It maps out the deliverables of the project, with subdeliverables and activities stemming from each major deliverable in a tree or chart format. *A Guide to the PMBOK*, pages 59 and 60, describes a WBS this way: "A WBS is a deliverable-oriented grouping of project components that organizes and defines the total scope of the project; work not included in the WBS is outside the scope of the project." Simply put, a WBS is a deliverable-oriented hierarchy that defines the work of the project and only the work of the project. Like the scope statement, the WBS serves as a foundational agreement among the stakeholders and project team members regarding project scope.

Exam Spotlight

Know the definition and purpose of a WBS.

The WBS will be used throughout many of the remaining Planning processes and is an important part of project planning. As you probably have concluded, everything we've done so far builds on the previous step. The project charter outlines the project goals and major deliverables. The scope statement further refines these deliverables into an exhaustive list. Now, that comprehensive list of deliverables is going to be used to build the framework of the WBS.

 The importance and accuracy of the work you've done up to this point can't be stressed enough. Your WBS will only be as accurate as your list of deliverables. The deliverables will become the groupings that will form the higher levels of the WBS from which activities will be derived.

The WBS should detail the full scope of work needed to complete the project. This breakdown will smooth the way for estimating project cost and time, scheduling resources, and determining quality controls later in the Planning process. Project progress will be based on the estimates and measurements assigned to the WBS segments. So again, accuracy and completeness are required when composing your WBS.

Decomposing the Deliverables

Decomposition is one of the tools you'll use when preparing your WBS. This process involves breaking down the deliverables into components distinct enough to support all the project management process groups (with the exception of Initiation). The idea here is to break down the deliverables to a point where you can easily plan, execute, control, and close out the project deliverables. Decomposition in the Scope Definition process typically pertains to breaking deliverables down into smaller deliverables, or component deliverables. Decomposing the deliverables to the activity level occurs in the Activity Definition process. We'll cover that process in Chapter 5, "Resource Planning and Estimating."

As stated earlier, it's easier to estimate resources and costs, assign performance measures and controls, and assign resources when deliverables are broken into smaller components. According to *A Guide to the PMBOK*, this is a four-step process:

1. Step one includes identifying all the major project deliverables. This step was completed when you wrote the scope statement. *A Guide to the PMBOK* makes a point of noting that the deliverables should be defined according to the way the work of the project is organized. One way to organize a project is by project phases. The phases are your first level of decomposition, followed by the deliverables. For example, let's say you work in the construction industry. The project phases used in your industry might include project initiation, planning, design, build, installation, and turnover. A feasibility study might be a deliverable under the project initiation phase and blueprints might be a deliverable under the planning phase, and so on. Also note that *A Guide to the PMBOK* says that project management should be identified in this step as one of the deliverables.

2. Step two includes determining adequate estimates for cost and duration. If adequate estimates cannot be made at this level of detail, you need to decompose the deliverable further until you can make adequate estimates. (That's step three.) Not all deliverables will have the same levels of decomposition. In the construction example, a feasibility study is the deliverable in the project initiation phase. There are only two levels of decomposition needed to describe this deliverable in enough detail to make adequate cost and duration estimates. Other deliverables may require several levels of decomposition to get to a point where adequate estimates can be made. It's possible that some deliverables on very large or complex projects may not be easily decomposed at this point in the project Planning process, especially if the deliverable is scheduled for production late in the project plan. If that's the case, decomposition will come later when the deliverables are defined for each of the sub-projects that make up the larger project.

3. Step three involves identifying each of the individual components that make up the deliverable. *A Guide to the PMBOK* calls these *constituent components*. These components, like the deliverables and requirements, should be defined in tangible, verifiable terms so that performance and successful completion (or delivery) are easily measured and verified. Each component you identify in step three needs cost and duration estimates assigned. That means you'll repeat step two of this process for each constituent component you identify. This step is only needed when it's determined that adequate cost and duration estimates cannot be made at step one; that is, the major deliverables need further decomposition in order to determine adequate cost and duration estimates.

4. Step four is a verification step. Examine the decomposition to determine if all the components are clear and complete. Determine if each component listed is absolutely necessary to fulfill the requirements of the deliverable. Also determine if you can easily schedule, estimate, budget, and assign each component. If you cannot do this easily, you need to further decompose the components until you can.

The components you've identified can now be plugged into the WBS. This all sounds like a lot of work. I won't kid you—it is, but it's essential to proper scope definition. If you don't perform the Scope Definition process adequately and accurately, you might end up setting yourself up for a failed project at worst, or for lots of project changes, delayed schedules, and increased costs at best. Not to mention all those team members who'll throw up their hands when you go back to them for the third or fourth time to ask that they do work they've already completed. I know you won't let this happen, so let's move on to documenting the WBS.

Constructing the WBS

There is no "right" way to construct a WBS. In practice, the chart structure is used quite often. (This structure resembles an organization chart.) But a WBS could be composed in outline form as well. The choice is yours.

The organization of the content in the WBS is consistent no matter which form you use. Its content is defined by a series of levels that reflect the components you decomposed earlier. These levels are often in sequential order, but they don't have to be. The sequential ordering of those levels takes place in a later step, although in practice, you'll probably combine these steps. We'll look at the levels of a WBS next.

Understanding the Various WBS Levels

Although the project manager is free to determine the number of levels in the WBS based on the complexity of the project, the highest level of the WBS, level one, is considered the project itself. This is followed by the deliverables, which might be followed by more deliverables, which may be followed by activities, and so on. Each of these breakouts is called a *level* in the WBS, with the project itself as level one, the deliverables as level two, components in level three, and so on.

Exam Spotlight

Page 60 of *A Guide to the PMBOK* says, "Each descending level [of the WBS] represents an increasingly detailed description of the project deliverables."

The easiest way to describe this process is with an example. Let's suppose you work for a software company that publishes children's games. You're the project manager for the new Billy Bob's Bassoon game, which teaches children about music, musical rhythm, and beginning sight reading. The first level of your WBS is the project name; it appears at the top of the WBS, as shown in Figure 4.1.

The next level should describe the major deliverables for the project. In this example, some of the deliverables might be requirements definition, design specifications, and programming. This isn't an exhaustive list of deliverables; in practice, you would go on to place all of your major deliverables into the WBS as level two content. For illustration purposes, just look at a slice of the WBS for this project. Figure 4.1 shows the WBS with level one and level two detail added.

FIGURE 4.1 WBS levels one and two

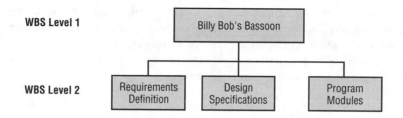

Level three content might be the constituent deliverables that are further broken out from the major deliverables of level two, or it might be activities that contribute to the deliverable. The Billy Bob's Bassoon example shows further deliverables as level three content. See Figure 4.2 for an illustration of the WBS so far.

FIGURE 4.2 WBS levels one, two, and three

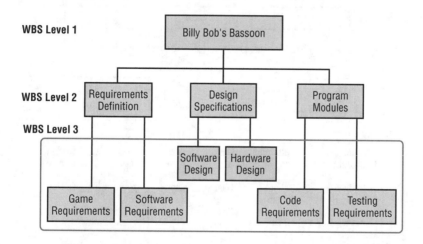

The goal here is to eventually break the work out to the point where responsibility and accountability can be assigned to a specific person or team of people for each unit of work. The higher levels of the WBS contain the deliverables. An easy way to differentiate between deliverables and activities later in the WBS is to use nouns as the deliverable descriptors and verbs as activity descriptors. Reaching way back to my grade school English, I recall that a noun is a person, place, or thing. In this example, the deliverables in level two and level three are described using nouns. The activity level, level four in the example in Figure 4.3, is described using verbs, or action words. Some of the verbs used in level four are *define*, *design*, *determine*, etc. There are many more activities that would go with these deliverables, but for the sake of illustration, we've listed just a few for each deliverable to give you an idea of how the WBS is constructed.

You can see from these illustrations how a poor scope definition or inadequate list of deliverables will lead to a poorly constructed WBS. Not only will this make the WBS look sickly, but the project itself will suffer and might even succumb to the dreaded premature project demise. The final cost of the project will be higher than estimated, and lots of rework (translate as late nights and weekends) will be needed to account for the missing work not listed on the WBS. You can construct a good WBS and maintain a healthy project by taking the time to document all the deliverables during the Scope Planning process.

FIGURE 4.3   WBS levels one, two, three, and four

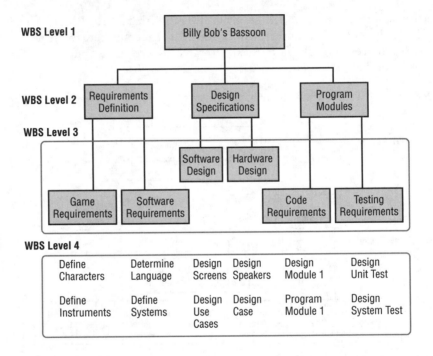

Work breakdown structures can be constructed using WBS templates or the WBS from a similar completed project. A bit earlier, we mentioned that WBS templates are a tool and technique in the Scope Definition process. While every project is unique, many companies and industries repeat the same kind of projects over and over. The deliverables are similar from project to project, and they generally follow a consistent path. The WBS templates can be used in a case like this as a tool to simplify the WBS process, saving the project manager time.

Large, complex projects are often composed of several subprojects that collectively make up the main project. The WBS for a project such as this would show the subprojects as level two detail. These subprojects would then list their major deliverables as level three content, perhaps more deliverables as level four, activities as level five, and so on.

Unique WBS Identifiers

Each element at each level of the WBS is generally assigned a unique identifier according to *A Guide to the PMBOK*. This unique identifier is typically a number, and it's used to sum and track the costs and resources associated with the WBS elements. These numbers are usually associated with the corporation's financial system chart of accounts, which are used to track costs by category. Collectively, these numeric identifiers are known as the *code of accounts*. The unique identifiers for the requirements definition branch of the WBS might look something like this:

10 Requirements Definition

    10-1 Game Requirements

        10-1-1 Define Characters

        10-1-2 Define Instruments

    10-2 Software Requirements

        10-2-1 Determine Language

        10-2-2 Define Systems

 Real World Scenario

The Lincoln Street Office Building

Flagship International has just purchased a new building to house their growing staff. They consider themselves very lucky to have won the bid on the property located in a prime section of the downtown area. The building is a historic building and is in need of some repairs and upgrades to make it suitable for office space. Constructing the renovations will require special handling and care as outlined in the *Historical Society Building Revisions Guide*.

Alfredo Magginetti is the project manager assigned to the renovation project. Alfredo has already gathered the deliverables for this project. In so doing, he's discovered that he will not be able to manage all the work himself. He will need several subproject managers working on individual deliverables, all reporting to him. Alfredo calls a meeting with the other project managers to deliver the WBS. Let's eavesdrop on the meeting.

"As you all know, we're planning to move into the Lincoln Street building by November 1st. There is quite a bit of work to do between now and then, and I'm enlisting each of you to manage a segment of this project. Take a look at this WBS."

A portion of the WBS Alfredo constructed looks like this:

Lincoln Street Building Renovation

    1.0 Facility Safety

        1.1 Sprinkler System

1.2 Elevators

1.3 Emergency Evacuation Plans

2.0 Asbestos Abatement

2.1 Inspection and Identification

2.2 Plans for Removal

3.0 Office Space

3.1 Building Floor Plans

3.2 Plans for Office Space Allocation

3.3 Plans for Break Room Facilities

3.4 Plans for Employee Workout Room

Alfredo continues, "I'm going to manage the Facility Safety project. Adrian, I'd like you to take the Asbestos Abatement project, and Orlando, you're responsible for the Office Space project."

"Alfredo," Adrian says. "Asbestos abatement is going to take contractors and specialized equipment. We don't have staff to do these tasks."

"I understand. You'll need to take charge of securing the contractor to handle this. Your responsibility will be to manage the contractor and keep them on schedule," Alfredo answers.

Orlando reminds Alfredo that he's missed a deliverable on the WBS. "Part of the Office Space project needs to include the network communications and telecommunications equipment rooms. I don't see that on here."

"Good point, Orlando," Alfredo says. "The level three and four elements of this WBS are not complete. Each of you has been assigned to the subproject level, level two. Your first assignment is to meet back here in two weeks with your WBS broken down to the activity level for each of your projects. And I'd like to see some ideas about the staff assignments you'd make at the activity level and how long you think these activities will take. We'll refine those after we meet next."

Defining Work Packages

As mentioned, the project manager is free to determine the number of levels in the WBS based on the complexity of the project. You need to include enough levels to accurately estimate project time and costs but not so many levels that it's difficult to distinguish between the activities. Regardless of the number of levels in a WBS, the lowest level in a WBS is called a *work package*.

Work packages are the activities or components that can be easily assigned to one person, or team of people, with clear accountability and responsibility for completing the assignment. Assignments are easily made at the work package level; however, assignments can be made at any level in the WBS, as in the Lincoln Street Office Building scenario. The work package level is where time estimates, cost estimates, and resource estimates are determined.

Including Activities

There is some controversy among project managers over whether activities should be listed on the WBS. There isn't a rule in *A Guide to the PMBOK* regarding this; it's up to the project manager to determine how far to break the deliverables down and whether to include activities. In practice, I often include activities on my work breakdown structure, as it facilitates other Planning processes later on. In this case, the activities are the work package level. However, you should realize that large, complex projects will not likely list activities on the WBS. And for the exam, remember that you will decompose activities during the Activity Definition process.

Work Packages as Subprojects

Work package levels on large projects can represent subprojects that are further decomposed into their own work breakdown structures. They may also consist of project work that will be completed by a vendor, another organization, or another department in your organization. If you're giving project work to another department in your organization, you'll assign the work packages to individual managers, who will in turn break them down into activities during the Activity Definition process later in the Planning process.

If you're assigning work packages to external vendors, activities will not be listed on the WBS either. For example, perhaps one of the deliverables in your project is special packaging, and a vendor is responsible for completing this work. The vendor will likely treat this deliverable as a project within their own organization and break the work down to the activity level. However, for your project, it's a deliverable listed at the work package level of the WBS.

This may seem self-evident, but work elements not shown on the WBS are not included in the project. The same holds true for the scope statement—if the deliverable isn't noted there, it isn't part of the project.

WBS Dictionary

The *WBS dictionary*, according to *A Guide to the PMBOK*, is where work component descriptions are documented. It contains a description of the work package level and the details regarding the activities within the work package. Information such as costs, budgets, schedule dates, resource assignments, and activity descriptions are found in the WBS dictionary.

Noting Milestones

There's one last topic I should mention regarding the WBS. Some project managers choose to note milestones on their WBS. A milestone is a major accomplishment in a project. The completion of a deliverable could be a milestone, for example. Milestones are like checkpoints along the way in the project to help determine progress. In most cases, the higher levels of the WBS can be flagged as milestones. The higher levels indicate major accomplishments on the project. For example, Asbestos Abatement in the Lincoln Street Office Building example is a major accomplishment that could be considered a milestone. The project would not be considered successful or complete if this milestone was not met. Sometimes critical activities can be flagged as milestones as well. We'll talk more about milestones in Chapter 7, "Creating the Project Plan."

Scope Statement Updates

Many times, you'll find when you're creating the WBS that deliverables might need further definition or refining. As you work through the decomposition process, you might discover new deliverables that weren't thought of during the Scope Planning process. The scope statement should be updated to reflect these changes. Be certain to notify the stakeholders of the update. Scope statement updates are the last output of the Scope Definition process and allow you to do just that.

The Communications Planning Process

We've talked a good deal about documentation so far, and this topic will continue to come up throughout the remainder of the book. Keeping good documentation should become the motto of all good project managers. "Is that documented?" should be an ever-present question on the mind of the project manager. Documentation can save your bacon, so to speak, later in the project. Documentation is only one side of the equation though—communication is the other. You and your stakeholders need to know who gets what information and when.

The *Communications Planning* process involves determining the communication needs of the stakeholders by defining the types of information needed and the format for communicating the information.

Communication Planning Inputs

Communications requirements is the first input of the Communications Planning process. All of the information requirements of the project stakeholders are represented by this input. According to *A Guide to the PMBOK*, in order to determine communications requirements, you'll want to examine project organization and stakeholder relationships; all the departments and disciplines involved on the project; the number of people associated with the project and their location; and any external needs that organizations like the media, government, or industry groups may have that require communication updates. This input requires an analysis of the information to make certain you're communicating information that's valuable to the stakeholders.

The second input to this process is communications technology. This examines the methods (or technology) used to communicate the information to, from, and among the stakeholders. Methods of communicating can take many forms such as written, spoken, e-mail, formal status reports, meetings, online databases, online schedules, and so on. This input examines the technology elements that may affect project communications. You should consider several factors before deciding what methods you'll choose to transfer information.

The timing of the information or need for updates is the first factor. The availability of the technology you're planning on using to communicate project information is important as well. Do you need to procure new technology or systems, or are there systems already in place that will work? Staff experience with the technology is another factor. Are the project team members and stakeholders experienced at using this technology, or will you need to train them? Finally, consider the duration of the project. Will the technology you're choosing work throughout the life of the project or will it have to be upgraded or updated at some point?

The answers to these questions should be documented in the communications management plan. We'll cover that next.

Communications Management Plan

All projects require sound communication plans, but not all projects will have the same types of communication or the same methods for distributing the information. The *communications management plan*, which is the only output of the Communications Planning process, documents the types of information needs the stakeholders have, when the information should be distributed, and how the information will be delivered.

The type of information you will typically communicate includes project status, scope statements and scope statement updates, project baseline information, risks, action items, performance measures, project acceptance, and so on. We'll cover all of these topics in greater detail in the remaining chapters of this book. What's important to know now is that the information needs of the stakeholders should be determined early on in the Planning process so that as you and your team develop more project planning documents, you already know who should receive copies of them and how they should be delivered.

The information that will be shared with stakeholders and the distribution methods are based on the needs of the stakeholders, the project complexity, and the organizational policies. Some communications may be informal—a chat by the water cooler, for instance—while other communications are written and a copy is filed with the project files.

Exam Spotlight

The communications management plan documents how to collect, store, file, and make corrections or updates to previously published material. It also contains a list of the information that will be distributed, the timing of the communication, and the distribution structure, and it describes how stakeholders can access project information between publication dates.

You might consider setting up an intranet site for your project and posting the appropriate project documentation there for the stakeholders to access any time they wish. If you use this method, make sure to document it in the communications management plan and notify your stakeholders when updates or new communication is posted.

Chapter 8, "Developing the Project Team," discusses communication methods in more depth.

Project Case Study: New Kitchen Heaven Retail Store

You're just finishing your phone conversation with Jill, and you see Dirk headed toward your office. The realtor has found a great location, and you and Jill have set up a time to take a tour later this week.

Dirk walks in, crosses his arms over his chest, and stands next to your desk with an "I'm here for answers" look.

"I thought I'd drop by and see if you have signed a lease and gotten Jake started on that build-out yet," says Dirk.

"I just got off the phone with Jill," you reply. "We set up a time to tour a location the end of this week."

"What's been the holdup?" Dirk asks. "I thought we'd be ready to start the build-out about now."

"I've been working on the project plans."

"Project plans," Dirk interrupts. "We already have a plan. That charter thing you drew up last week spelled things out pretty clearly."

"The charter was the project kickoff, and I agree it did include all the deliverables. However, it's not detailed enough to start mapping out the project plans. I wrote a scope statement that further details the project deliverables and other project information. I've already forwarded that to you. I've also drawn up a work breakdown structure with all the deliverables shown in a tree structure that I'd like to go over with you before showing it to the project team."

"We aren't building trees; we're building a new store. I don't understand why you're wasting all this time planning. We all know what the goals are."

"Dirk," you reply. "If we put the right amount of effort and time into the planning stage, the execution stage should go pretty smoothly. Planning is probably one of the most important things we can do on this project. If we don't plan correctly, we might miss something very important that could delay the store opening. That date is pretty firm, I thought."

"Yes, the date is firm. But I don't see how we could miss anything. You and I have met several times, and I know you've met with Jill and Jake. They're the other key players on this."

"You're right. I have met with Jill and Jake. And that's a perfect example of why we need to plan. When I met with Jill, she told me how all the store's data is communicated via a satellite network connection on a nightly basis. That means we need to involve the IT group."

You glance down at your notes. "Ricardo Ramirez heads up IT. I spoke with him last week about his deliverables, and I've included his group as a subproject on the work breakdown structure."

"Oh," Dirk replies. "I forgot about IT. You're right, that's an important part of the project, and we can't leave them out. Okay, I'm beginning to see why you're taking planning seriously. Let's have a look at this work breakdown structure."

You hand Dirk a copy of the WBS. A partial version is shown here.

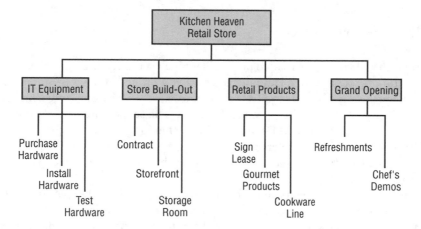

Project Case Study Checklist

Interviewed project stakeholders and business process owners for further definition of deliverables

Created project scope statement, which includes:

- Project justification—the business need.

- Project product—the product description.

- Project deliverables—clear and concise deliverables.

- Project objectives—including constraints. Objectives are specific, measurable, and timely.

Decomposed deliverables into a WBS

WBS includes:

- Level one is the project.

- Level two is subprojects or deliverables.

- Level three is deliverables or activities.

- Remaining levels are activities.

- Last level of WBS is the work package level, where time and cost estimates can be defined in the next process.

Summary

This chapter started you on the road to project Planning via the Scope Planning process and the Scope Definition process. Scope Planning is where you produce the scope statement, which describes the project goals, deliverables, and requirements. The scope statement forms the baseline you'll use to weigh future project decisions. The scope statement must contain an exhaustive list of project deliverables that will be used in future Planning processes. Measurement criteria (which primarily refers to project objectives) agreed upon by the stakeholders and project manager are associated with these deliverables and documented in the scope statement to track project progress.

The deliverables, requirements, and measurement criteria should be spelled out clearly and concisely in the scope statement to avoid any misunderstandings later in the project. Formal acceptance of the scope statement is required by the stakeholders and project manager. Acceptance is usually accompanied by sign-offs on the document indicating that it has been read and that the signing party agrees with the deliverables and requirements of the project.

The purpose of the scope management plan is to analyze the reliability and stability of the project scope. The scope management plan documents the process to manage the project scope and changes to the scope.

The Scope Definition process is concerned with decomposition and the production of a work breakdown structure (WBS). Decomposition is breaking down deliverables into manageable pieces of work, which might be further broken down into activities.

A WBS is a deliverable-oriented group of project essentials. The highest levels of the WBS are described using nouns, and the lowest levels are described with verbs. Each element in the WBS has its own set of objectives and deliverables that must be met in order to fulfill the deliverables of the next highest level, and ultimately the project itself. In this way, the WBS validates the completeness of the work.

The lowest level of the WBS is known as work packages. This breakdown allows the project manager to determine cost estimates, time estimates, resource assignments, and quality controls.

Exam Essentials

Be able to name the Scope Planning outputs.   The outputs of the Scope Planning process are the scope statement, supporting detail, and the scope management plan.

Understand the purpose of the scope statement.   The scope statement serves as a baseline for future project decisions and a common understanding of project scope. The project objectives and deliverables and their quantifiable measurements are documented in the scope statement and are used by the project manager and the stakeholders to determine if the project was completed successfully.

Be able to name the Scope Definition tools and techniques and outputs.   The tools and techniques from the Scope Definition process are decomposition and WBS templates. Decomposition is breaking the deliverables down into workable, manageable units of work. The outputs of the Scope Definition process are the work breakdown structure (WBS) and scope statement updates.

Be able to describe the purpose of the scope management plan.   The scope management plan describes how scope changes will be handled during the project and how to request changes. It details how likely it is that scope changes will occur, their frequency, and their impact.

Be able to define a WBS and its components.   The WBS is a deliverables-oriented hierarchy. It uses the deliverables from the scope statement or similar documents and decomposes them into logical, manageable units of work. Level one is the project level, level two is the major deliverable level or subproject level, and so on. The lowest level of any WBS is called a work package.

Be able to describe the purpose of the communications management plan.   The communications management plan determines the communication needs of the stakeholders. It documents what information will be distributed, how it will be distributed, to whom, and the timing of the distribution. It also documents how to collect, store, file, and make corrections to previously published material.

Key Terms

Before you take the exam, be certain you are familiar with the following terms:

alternatives identification	Scope Definition
code of accounts	scope management plan
communications management plan	Scope Planning
Communications Planning	scope statement
constituent components	supporting detail
critical success factors	WBS dictionary
decomposition	work breakdown structure (WBS)
product analysis	work package

Review Questions

1. You are a project manager for Laredo Pioneer's Traveling Rodeo Show. You're heading up a project to promote a new line of souvenirs to be sold at the shows. You need to gather the inputs to write the scope statement. Which of the following do you need to gather?

    A. Project charter, product description, assumptions, and constraints

    B. Project charter, product analysis, and cost benefit analysis

    C. Product description, product analysis, and project charter

    D. Product description, assumptions, constraints, and product analysis

2. You are a project manager for Laredo Pioneer's Traveling Rodeo Show. You're heading up a project to promote a new line of souvenirs to be sold at the shows. You're ready to write the scope statement. Which of the following should the scope statement contain?

    A. Project justification, benefit/cost analysis, project deliverables, and product analysis

    B. Product analysis, project's product, and project deliverables

    C. Project justification, project's product, project deliverables, and project objectives

    D. Product analysis, project deliverables, benefit/cost analysis, and project objectives

3. Which of the following is true regarding the scope statement?

    A. The scope statement describes how to make changes to the project scope.

    B. The scope statement describes project deliverables and serves as a baseline for future project decisions.

    C. The scope statement assesses the stability of the project scope and is a baseline for future project decisions.

    D. The scope statement assesses the reliability of the project scope and describes the frequency of changes and their impacts.

4. You are a project manager for an agricultural supply company. You have just completed and obtained sign-off on the scope statement for your new Natural Bug Busters project. A key stakeholder has informed you that a deliverable is missing from the scope statement. This deliverable is a critical success factor. Which of the following actions should you take?

    A. Inform the stakeholder that work not stated in the scope statement is excluded from the project.

    B. Modify the scope statement to reflect the new deliverable.

    C. Inform the stakeholder that this deliverable can be included in the next project since sign-off has already been obtained.

    D. Modify the scope statement after an approved change request has been received from the stakeholder.

5. You are a project manager responsible for the construction of a new office complex. You are taking over for a project manager who recently left the company. The prior project manager completed the project charter and the scope statement for this project. In your interviews with some key stakeholders, you conclude that the scope statement was poorly constructed. Which of the following statement do you know is *not* true?

A. It will be difficult to assess future project decisions from this scope statement.

B. It will be difficult to decompose the deliverables from this scope statement.

C. It will be difficult to assess cost and time estimates from this scope statement.

D. It will be difficult to create an accurate WBS from this scope statement.

6. You are a project manager responsible for the construction of a new office complex. You are taking over for a project manager who recently left the company. The prior project manager completed the scope statement and scope management plan for this project. In your interviews with some key stakeholders, you conclude which of the following?

A. They understand that the scope statement assesses the stability of the project scope and outlines how to incorporate scope changes into the project.

B. They understand that the scope management plan assesses the stability of the project scope and outlines how to incorporate scope changes into the project.

C. They understand that the scope management plan is deliverable-oriented, and cost estimates can be easily derived from it.

D. They understand that the scope statement is deliverables-oriented, and cost estimates can be easily derived from it.

7. Which of the following statements about decomposition is *not* true?

A. Decomposition is an output of the Scope Definition process.

B. Decomposition is a tool and technique of the Scope Definition process.

C. Decomposition is used to create a WBS.

D. Decomposition subdivides the major deliverables into smaller components.

8. Your company has asked you to be the project manager for the product introduction of their new DeskTop Rock media system. You recently published a document that establishes the scope baseline. Which of the following is true?

A. This is the scope statement, which is an output of the Scope Planning process.

B. This is the scope statement, which is an output of the Scope Definition process.

C. This is the scope statement, which is a tool and technique of the Scope Definition process.

D. This is the scope management plan, which is an output of the Scope Definition process.

9. You are a project manager for a new Information Technology project. Your organization requires you to organize the project according to standard project phases common to programming projects (project management, requirements gathering, detail design, code, test, and implement). Once requirements are gathered, the major deliverables of the project will be finalized. You're in the Scope Definition process, and you know that which of the following statements is true?

    A. Each of the major deliverables will have different levels of decomposition.

    B. The project phases should not be part of the decomposition process.

    C. Each of the major deliverables will have the same levels of decomposition.

    D. The levels of decomposition are the same for projects within an industry when the organization uses standard project phases to organize the project.

10. Your company has asked you to be the project manager for the product introduction of their new DeskTop Rock media system. You recently published the scope statement and the supporting detail. Which of the following is *not* contained in the supporting detail?

    A. Constraints

    B. Other project information not noted in the scope statement

    C. Code of accounts

    D. Assumptions

11. You are a project manager for Giraffe Enterprises. You've recently taken over for a project manager who lied about his PMI certification and was subsequently fired. Unfortunately, he did a poor job of Scope Definition. You know if you don't correct this, one of the following could happen:

    A. The stakeholders will require overtime from the project team to keep the project on schedule.

    B. The WBS will adversely affect the deliverable breakdowns, and costs will increase.

    C. The scope management plan will require changes.

    D. The project costs could increase, there might be rework, and schedule delays may result.

12. Which of the following does *not* describe a reason for Scope Definition?

    A. To subdivide project deliverables into smaller components

    B. To assess the stability of the project scope

    C. To facilitate time and cost estimates

    D. To facilitate responsibility and assignment

13. Which of the following statements does *not* correctly describe constituent components?

    A. Constituent components are a further decomposition of the project deliverables.

    B. Step two of decomposition should be repeated for each constituent component that's been identified.

    C. Constituent components should be tangible and verifiable and should be organized in terms of how the work of the project will be organized.

    D. Identification of constituent components should occur concurrently with the identification of major deliverables.

14. Your company, Kick That Ball Sports, has appointed you project manager for their new Cricket product line introduction. This is a national effort, and all the retail stores across the country need to have the new products on the shelves before the media advertising blitz begins. The product line involves three new products, some with multiple deliverables. You are ready to create the WBS. Which of the following is true?

    A. The WBS should include the three new products and the advertising campaign as level two deliverables.

    B. The WBS should include the three new products as level two deliverables.

    C. The WBS should include the three new products as level two deliverables and the advertising campaign as a level three deliverable.

    D. The WBS should include the three new products and the advertising campaign as level three deliverables.

15. You are working on a communications management plan for your project. You examine characteristics like the project organization and stakeholder relationships, the different departments involved on the project, the number of people associated with the project and where they work, and the government reporting needs you have because of the nature of this project. Which of the following does this question describe?

    A. Communications skills

    B. Communications technology

    C. Stakeholder analysis

    D. Communications requirements

16. Which of the following statements is *not* true regarding the WBS?

    A. The WBS is a deliverables-oriented grouping of project deliverables and elements.

    B. The WBS defines and organizes the work of the project in a hierarchical form.

    C. The WBS provides a framework for the work of the project, and work not shown on the WBS is not included in the project.

    D. The WBS defines all the deliverables of the project, but the activities level should not be listed on the WBS.

17. You are the project manager for Lucky Stars nightclubs. They specialize in live country and western band performances. Your newest project is in the Planning process. You've published the scope statement and scope management plan. The document that describes who will receive copies of this information as well as future project information, how it should be distributed, and how the information should be stored and filed is which of the following?

    A. Scope management plan

    B. Communications management plan

    C. Information distribution plan

    D. Project charter

18. You are the project manager for Lucky Stars nightclubs. They specialize in live country and western band performances. Your newest project is in the Planning process. You are working on the WBS. The finance manager has given you a numbering system to assign to the WBS. Which of the following is true?

   A. The numbering system is a unique identifier known as the code of accounts, which is used to track the costs of the WBS elements.

   B. The numbering system is a unique identifier known as the WBS dictionary, which is used to track the descriptions of individual work elements.

   C. The numbering system is a unique identifier known as the code of accounts, which is used to track time and resource assignments for individual work elements.

   D. The numbering system is a unique identifier known as the WBS dictionary, which is used to assign quality control codes to the individual work elements.

19. You've constructed the WBS for your recent project. Level two assignments have been made, and you've requested that the subproject managers report back to you in three weeks with each of their individual WBSs constructed. Which statement is *not* true?

   A. The work package level facilitates resource assignments.

   B. The work package level is the lowest level in the WBS.

   C. The work package level defines the agreed-upon deliverables.

   D. The work package level facilitates cost and time estimates.

20. The grouping of project elements by deliverables is known as what?

   A. The code of accounts

   B. The work package

   C. The work breakdown structure

   D. The work breakdown dictionary

Answers to Review Questions

1. **A.** The inputs of the Scope Planning process are product description, project charter, constraints, and assumptions.

2. **C.** According to *A Guide to the PMBOK*, the scope statement includes all of the following: project justification, project's product, project deliverables, and project objectives.

3. **B.** The scope statement describes the project deliverables, requirements, and objectives. It serves as a baseline for future project decisions.

4. **D.** The scope statement will change throughout the project as change requests are received and approved. Project managers must be certain to seek out all deliverables before publishing the scope statement to prevent situations like this.

5. **C.** Cost estimates, time estimates, and quality controls are derived from the WBS in the Scope Definition process, not from the scope statement, which is an output of the Scope Planning process.

6. **B.** The scope management plan assesses the stability and reliability of the project scope and addresses how frequently scope changes will occur and what their impacts might be. The scope management plan outlines the method for requesting changes to the project scope and for incorporating those changes into the project.

7. **A.** Decomposition subdivides the major deliverables into smaller components. It is a tool and technique of Scope Definition, along with WBS templates, and this process is used to create a WBS.

8. **A.** The scope statement establishes the baseline for the project. The scope statement is an output of the Scope Planning process.

9. **A.** Deliverables will have different levels of decomposition, depending on the complexity of the deliverable.

10. **C.** The code of accounts is assigned to the elements in the WBS.

11. **D.** Selection A might seem like a correct answer, but selection D is a more correct answer. We don't have enough information to determine if stakeholders will require overtime. We do know that poor Scope Definition may lead to cost increases, rework, schedule delays, and poor morale.

12. **B.** The scope management plan assesses the stability of the project scope.

13. **D.** Identification of constituent components occurs after a decision is made that adequate cost and duration estimates cannot be determined from the major deliverables.

14. A.   Level one of the WBS is the project itself. There are three new products plus the advertising campaign. Each of these is a subproject under level one.

15. D.   Communications requirements—an input to the Communications Planning process—considers things like project organization and stakeholder relationships, all the departments and disciplines involved on the project, the number of people associated with the project and their location, and any external needs like the media, government, or industry organizations that may require communication updates.

16. D.   It is up to the project manager to determine how many levels to detail on the WBS. Small projects can easily show activities on the WBS.

17. B.   The communications management plan documents what information will be distributed, how it will be distributed, to whom, and the timing of the distribution. It also documents how to collect, store, file, and make corrections to previously published material.

18. A.   Each element in the WBS is assigned a unique identifier. These are collectively known as the code of accounts. Typically, these codes are associated with a corporate chart of accounts and are used to track the costs of the individual work elements in the WBS.

19. C.   The work package level is the lowest level in the WBS and facilitates resource assignment and cost and time estimates. The agreed-upon deliverables in selection C would be higher levels in the WBS.

20. C.   The WBS is the deliverables-oriented hierarchy of project work.

Resource Planning and Estimating

THE PMP EXAM CONTENT FROM THE PROJECT PLANNING PERFORMANCE DOMAIN COVERED IN THIS CHAPTER INCLUDES:

- ✓ 3. Developing a resource management plan
- ✓ 4. Refining time and cost estimates

Hold on to your hats! We're going to cover a lot of material in this chapter, but it will go fast, I promise. We'll start out with a section on Resource Planning, Organizational Planning, and Staff Acquisition. These particular processes are straightforward, so we'll just touch on the important points for each of these topics. Be sure to study the inputs, tools and techniques, and outputs for each of these processes so you understand which ones go with which process. Many of them are self-explanatory.

Although it isn't mentioned in *A Guide to the PMBOK,* it's a good idea to pull the information from the combined outputs of all of these processes into a resource plan. For organizational and planning purposes, I find it works well to have all of the information from these processes in one location.

We'll spend the majority of our time in this chapter looking at the time and cost estimating techniques found in the Cost Estimating process. You'll likely find several exam questions on the tools and techniques of this process, so make sure to spend plenty of time understanding and memorizing them.

Resource Planning

All projects require resources, from the smallest project to the largest. The term *resources* in this case does not mean just people; it means all the physical resources required to complete the project. This includes people, equipment, supplies, materials, software, hardware—the list goes on depending on the project you're working on. *Resource Planning* is the process of determining what physical resources are needed, and in what quantity, to perform project activities.

A Guide to the PMBOK notes that Resource Planning should be closely coordinated with the Cost Estimating process. That's because resources—whether people or material—are typically the largest expense you'll have on any project. The physical resource expenses combined with the human resource expenses will probably consume the majority of the costs you'll encounter on any project. Identifying the resources becomes a critical component of the project planning process so that later on, estimates—and ultimately the project budget—can be accurately derived. The purpose of the Resource Planning process is to identify and document the resource requirements for the project. You'll look at the inputs and tools and techniques that will help you document these requirements next.

Resource Planning Inputs

The Resource Planning process has several inputs you are already familiar with, including the work breakdown structure (WBS), historical information, and the scope statement. The WBS is the primary input to this process, because it identifies the deliverables of the project and the processes that will need resources in order to accomplish the work of the project. This is the first place you should start when identifying project resources. Don't forget the scope statement as an input, because the project justification, objectives, and deliverables are detailed there. The project objectives and justification might give you some insight into resource needs. The three remaining inputs of the Resource Planning process are new:

- Resource pool description
- Organizational policies
- Activity duration estimates

Resource Pool

The *resource pool description* lists the types of resources that might be needed for the project. For example, if you are working on a project that requires the use of specialized equipment during the course of the project, the resource pool description should contain the details concerning this resource and the specific knowledge or skills needed to use the equipment. The same is true for human resources. Suppose you need an expert in thermodynamics in one or several phases of your project. The resource pool description should list this specific resource requirement.

The resource pool description will vary throughout the Planning processes and should be updated as more project information becomes known and is documented. For example, early on in the project you might know that you'll need several skilled laborers for the project. So at this point, "skilled laborers in large numbers" is listed in your resource pool description. As the work of the project is decomposed and other Planning processes are performed, these resources can be further defined as "two welders, four electricians, and four plumbers," for example. List all the materials, equipment, skills, or special talents you might need during any part of your project in the resource pool description.

Organizational Policies

Organizational policies regarding materials purchases, hiring processes, leases, vendor relationships, and so on should be taken into consideration when performing Resource Planning. Don't confuse this input with the Organizational Planning process, discussed in the next section. Organizational policies in this case are merely how the company handles obtaining supplies and resources. Are there policies and procedures in place that should be followed regarding renting or purchasing supplies and equipment? If so, take note of these procedures and adhere to them when ordering supplies, hiring staff, and so on.

Activity Duration Estimates

Activity duration estimates are a quantifiable estimate of the number of work periods needed to complete the activities listed on the WBS or the subproject WBS. They are an output of the Activity Duration Estimating process. We'll cover this process in more detail a little later in this chapter.

Documenting Resource Requirements

The goal of the Resource Planning process is to document the *resource requirements*. The tools and techniques that will help you get to the resource requirements include expert judgment, which we talked about in Chapter 3, "Creating a Project Charter," alternatives identification, covered in Chapter 4, "Creating the Scope Statement and WBS," and project management software. Project management software is a helpful tool during this process, because many programs available today will help you define resource availability, allocate their time, and estimate costs based on resource rates.

Resource requirements are the only output of the Resource Planning process. The resource requirements are listed in a document that contains a detailed description of the kinds of resources needed for the project and the quantity needed of each resource. Resource needs and resource quantity should always be identified for each element in the work package level of the WBS. Lower-level WBS resource requirements can be summarized or listed to determine resource requirement at the higher levels of the WBS.

Staffing requirements are a subset of resource requirements. (Remember that the resource requirements document lists the details for all the resources required for the project, not just staffing resources.) The staffing requirements list should identify the kinds of skills required, the competency levels, and the individuals or groups who might provide these skills to the project. The staffing requirements list should also document the time frames during the project when these skills will be needed. For example, the thermodynamics expert might be needed only during the design phase, so be certain to note in the resource requirements document where and when on the WBS this expert is needed.

A strange thing happens here. Resource requirements become an input to other Planning processes. But so do staffing requirements, which are a subset of resource requirements. This is the only process where an output is split into two pieces and each piece becomes an input to other processes.

Developing an Organizational Plan

The Organizational Planning process focuses on the human resources aspect of project planning. Its purpose is to document the roles and responsibilities of individuals or groups for various project elements and then document the reporting relationships for each. Reporting relationships can be assigned to groups as well as to individuals, and the groups or individuals may be internal or external to the organization or a combination of both. Communications Planning goes hand in hand with Organizational Planning, because the organizational structure affects the way communications are carried out among project participants and the project interfaces.

Organizational Planning has three inputs: project interfaces, staffing requirements, and constraints. We covered staffing requirements in the last section and don't need to add anything here. We've also covered constraints in previous chapters, but there is some new information to introduce regarding constraints that we'll look at after we define project interfaces.

Project Interfaces

A *Guide to the PMBOK* identifies three categories of project interfaces:

- Organizational interfaces
- Technical interfaces
- Interpersonal interfaces

Each of these defines the type of reporting relationships that exist among the different categories.

Organizational interfaces deal with the types of reporting relationships that exist within an organization's structure, be it functional, matrix, or projectized. Chapter 1 dealt with organizational structures if you need a refresher. The reporting relationships in the organization might be formal or informal, and as the project manager, you should take these into consideration when outlining the project plan. These are typically the most difficult project interfaces to deal with.

Reporting relationships are also important for *technical interfaces*, which deal with the reporting relationships that exist within the technical areas of an organization. You should consider the technical interfaces, both within the project phases and between the project phases during the handoff from phase to phase.

Interpersonal interfaces deal with the reporting relationships that exist among project team members and among other project participants. All projects fall into the interpersonal interfaces and organizational interfaces categories. Whether technical interfaces affect the project depends on the project itself.

Exam Spotlight

Make sure you understand the definitions of the three project interfaces for the exam.

Constraints

The topic of constraints seems to come up a lot, so you probably remember that constraints are things that limit the options available to the project team. These typically involve time, costs, or quality. However, there are a few new constraints regarding project team organizations that you should know about:

Organizational structures   Organizational structures can be a constraint. For example, a strong matrix organization provides the project manager with much more authority and power than the weak matrix organization. Functional organizations typically do not empower their project managers with the proper authority to carry out a project. If you work in a functional organization as I do, it's important to be aware that you'll likely face power struggles with other managers and in some cases, a flat-out lack of cooperation. Don't tell them I said this, but functional managers tend to be territorial and aren't likely to give up control easily. The best advice I have for you in this case is to:

- Establish open communications early on in the project.
- Include all the functional managers with key roles in important decisions.
- Get the support of your project sponsor to empower you (as the project manager) with as much authority as possible. It's important that the sponsor makes it clear to the other managers that he expects their cooperation on project activities.

Collective bargaining agreements   Collective bargaining agreements are actually contractual obligations of the organization. Collective bargaining is typically associated with unions and organized employee associations. Other organized employee associations or groups may require specialized reporting relationships as well—especially if they involve contractual obligations. You will not likely be involved in the negotiations of collective bargaining agreements, but if you have an opportunity to voice opinions regarding employee duties or agreements that would be helpful to your project or future projects, by all means take it.

Team preferences   Preferences of the project management team might be a constraint. Success with certain organizational structures in the past might lead team members to prefer one type of team or organizational structure over another. Since you are the project manager, you typically have a significant amount of influence over the team members and the type of team structure you'll use for the project. Use your influence and authority to keep the consequences of this constraint to a minimum by negotiating (or choosing) team members and team structures that are best suited to the project.

Staffing assignments   The organization of the project team will likely be influenced by the skills, specialized knowledge, and competencies of the individual project team members who will serve on the team. The work of the project will be influenced by the skills of the individuals assigned to the activities. For example, perhaps your project requires a microbiologist and there's only one person on staff in your organization who can fulfill this role. However, the microbiologist on staff has limited experience in the activity you need them for. Since their competency is limited, you need to allow for more time on the project for this person to perform the needed research to get their competency level up to par. Another workaround for this constraint is to consider hiring someone from outside the organization to fulfill this role, but that's not always an option given the project budget or schedule. This constraint is called expected staff assignments.

Organizational Planning Tools and Techniques

Organizational Planning has four tools and techniques:

Templates *Templates* are tools that help define reporting relationships. Organizations usually perform projects that are similar in nature, whereby one project resembles other projects the organization has worked on in the past. Templates can be used from previous projects to show the reporting relationships among project team members.

Human resources practices *Human resource practices* provide the project management team with guidelines, policies, and procedures related to organization roles and responsibilities, including how-tos on management policies.

Organizational theory The project management team should have an understanding of *organizational theory* as it relates to the organizational structure the project is operating within. For example, if you work in a projectized organization, understanding the theories regarding this structure will help you better understand roles, responsibilities, and the reporting structures of the organization and the project team members.

Stakeholder analysis *Stakeholder analysis* includes identifying the project stakeholders, their needs, and the methods you'll use to make certain their needs are met. On most projects, stakeholders will come and go as the project moves throughout its life cycle. One phase of a project may involve many more stakeholders than another. For this reason, pay particular attention to the methods you'll use to satisfy their needs, because one method may work well in one project phase but not so well in another.

Now let's put the inputs and tools and techniques to use to produce the various outputs of this process.

Assigning Resources

The outputs of the Organizational Planning process are concerned with identifying resources, documenting their responsibilities, and determining when and how they come on and off the project. The outputs of this process include roles and responsibilities assignment, staffing management plan, the organization chart, and supporting detail. We'll look at each of these next.

Exam Spotlight

Make sure you understand the Organizational Planning process for the exam. You may encounter questions regarding the organizational, technical, and interpersonal project interfaces; the organizational structure, collective bargaining agreements, project management team preferences, and expected staff assignments constraints; and the roles and responsibilities assignment output in particular.

Roles and Responsibilities Assignment

Project roles in the context of the roles and responsibilities assignment refer to the project manager, the project team members, and the stakeholders. Responsibilities refer to what duties these project roles will fulfill and who decides what. Don't forget to include yourself as project manager in this list, because your role and responsibilities for the project are generally critical to the overall success of the project.

According to *A Guide to the PMBOK*, the roles and responsibilities for this process are closely tied to the project scope definition. Because the WBS also describes project scope, there is a link between the WBS and the roles and responsibilities as well, even though this isn't specifically stated in *A Guide to the PMBOK*. Since project scope (outlined in the scope statement) identifies all the work of the project, each element of work should have a corresponding role and responsibility assignment.

Many times a project manager will use a *Responsibility Assignment Matrix (RAM)* to graphically display this information. A RAM is usually depicted as a chart with resource names listed in each row (for example, programmers, testers, trainers, etc.) and project phases or WBS elements listed as the columns. Indicators in the intersections show where the resources are needed. However, the level of detail is up to you. One RAM might be developed showing only project phases. Another RAM may show level two WBS elements for a complex project, with more RAMs subsequently produced for the additional WBS levels. Or a RAM might be constructed with level three elements only. Table 5.1 shows a sample portion of a RAM for a software development team. In this example, the RAM shows the level of accountability each of the participants has on the project. For example, programmers are required to participate in the design and testing phases. However, programmers are the group responsible for completing the design phase (represented by the "R" in the matrix) and ensuring its success whereas the testers participate in the design phase but are not the folks primarily responsible for the outcomes. You can come up with your own legends to depict the level of accountability, responsibility, and participation with a matrix like this. It's a great tool because it shows at a glance not only where a person is working but what that person's responsibility level is on the project.

TABLE 5.1 Sample RAM

	Design Phase	**Testing Phase**	**Implementation Phase**
Programmers	R	P	
Testers	P	R	
Trainers		P	R

Legend: R = responsible for outcomes and phase success, P = participate in the phase

Staffing Management Plan

The staffing management plan documents how and when people resources are introduced to the project and later released. Again, the level and amount of detail contained in this plan are up to you. It can be formal or informal, and it can contain lots of detail or only high-level detail. The staffing management plan is a subsidiary plan to the project plan.

A Guide to the PMBOK points out that attention should be given to how you'll release project team members at the end of their assignment. You should have reassignment procedures in place to move folks onto other projects or back to assignments they had prior to the project. This reduces overall project costs, because you won't have a tendency to simply keep them busy between assignments or until the end of their scheduled end date if they complete their activities early. Having these procedures in place will also improve morale, because everyone will be clear about how reassignment will occur. This should reduce anxiety about their opportunity for employment at the conclusion of the project or their assignment.

Many staffing management plans make use of a *resource histogram*. This is usually drawn in chart form, with project time along the horizontal axis and hours needed along the vertical axis. The following example histogram shows the hours needed for an asphalt crew on a construction project:

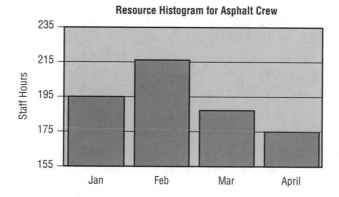

Resource Histogram for Asphalt Crew

Organization Chart

The organization chart is just like the org charts you've seen dozens of times before. It shows the reporting relationships of the project members in graphical form. An *organizational breakdown structure (OBS),* a special type of organization chart, relates WBS elements—usually the work package level for very large projects—to the organizational unit that's responsible for completing the work.

Supporting Detail

Information that further describes the organization and the impacts to the organizational units due to work requests is considered *supporting detail*. This information varies depending on the project size and the industry—or application area—in which the project is being performed. Job descriptions (in some organizations these are called position descriptions) and training needs are examples of information gathered for this output.

This process ensures that roles and responsibilities are clearly outlined and that reporting structures are documented and communicated to all project participants. This process is completed early on in the project-planning process and should be reviewed regularly throughout the project to assure accuracy. Document changes are needed as project circumstances change.

Exam Spotlight

Understand the difference between the Resource Planning process and the Organizational Planning process for the exam. Resource Planning includes identifying all the resources needed for the project (including human, materials, equipment, and so on) and in what quantity. The Organizational Planning process primarily involves identifying and documenting the roles and responsibilities of the project stakeholders and their reporting relationships.

Acquiring Staff

The *Staff Acquisition* process involves attaining and assigning human resources to the project. Project staff may come from inside the company, or from outside the company in the form of full-time employees hired specifically for the project, or as contract help. In any case, it's your job as the project manager to ensure that resources are available and skilled in the project activities they're assigned to.

The Staff Acquisition process inputs are as follows: the staffing management plan that was produced as an output to Organizational Planning, the staffing pool description, and recruitment practices.

Recruitment practices are a matter of making certain you consult any organizational procedures or policies currently in place when hiring and assigning staff. Organizational policies that dictate recruitment practices are constraints. We'll look at the staffing pool description in more depth next.

Staffing Pool Description

Some project activities may require special skills or knowledge in order to be completed. The *staffing pool description* involves taking this information into account as well as considering personal interests, characteristics, and availability of potential team members before making assignments. For example, consider the previous experience of the staff member you're thinking of assigning to a specific activity. Have they performed this function before? Do they have the experience necessary for the level of complexity this project activity calls for? Are they competent and proficient at these skills?

Personal interests and personal characteristics play a big role as well. If the person you're thinking of just isn't interested in the project, they aren't likely to perform at their best. If you can, think about assigning someone else in a case like this. Unfortunately, some people just don't play well with others. When you're assigning staff, if at all possible, don't put the only two people in the whole company who can't get along together on the same project. If the staff member you need has a skill no one else has or they can perform a function like no one else can, you might not have a choice. In this case, you'll have to employ other techniques to keep the team cohesive and working well together despite the not-so-friendly characteristics of the vital team member.

One final consideration: Check on the availability of key team members. If the team member you must have for the activity scheduled in February is on her honeymoon, you probably aren't going to win the toss.

Negotiating for Team Members

Negotiation, preassignment, and procurement are tools and techniques of the Staff Acquisition process. As the project manager, you will use the negotiation technique a lot. You'll have to negotiate with functional managers and other organizational department managers—and sometimes with the vendor to get some of their best people—for resources for your project and for the timing of those resources.

Availability is one part of the equation. You'll have to work with the functional manager to ensure that the staff member is available when the schedule says they're needed.

The second part of the equation is the competency level of the staff member they're assigning to your project. I remember hearing someone say once that availability is not a skill set. Be wary of functional managers who are willing to offer up certain individuals "any time" while others are "never available." Be certain your negotiations include discussions about the skills and personal characteristics of the team members you're asking for.

Preassignment happens when the project is put out for bid and specific team members are promised as part of the proposal, or when internal project team members are promised and assigned as a condition of the project. When staff members are promised as part of the project proposal—particularly on internal projects—they should be identified in the project charter.

Procurement is another tool and technique of the Staff Acquisition process. It involves hiring individuals or teams of people for certain project activities, either as full-time employees or as contract help during the course of the project or project phase or for specific project activities. Procurement is usually required when the organization does not have employees available to work on the project with the required skills and competencies.

 Chapter 6, "Establishing Project Planning Controls," talks more about the procurement planning process.

Assigning Project Staff

After determining the staffing pool description, reviewing recruitment practices, and negotiating for staff, project team members are assigned to project activities, and a project team directory is published listing the names of all project team members and stakeholders. The resulting outputs of the Staff Acquisition process are the assignment of project staff and the project team directory.

Now that you know what the project activities are and what resources are needed to perform these activities, you'll need to perform time and cost estimates for these activities. You're working toward the development of the project schedule where you determine the actual start and stop dates for activities, but you have several processes to complete before you get there.

 Real World Scenario

The Only Candidate

"Hey, did you hear?" your friend Story asks. "Roger has been assigned to the project team."

"Over my dead body," you reply, pushing away from your computer screen. You head straight for the project manager's office and don't wait for a response from Story.

Ann seats the phone into the cradle just as you walk through the door. Fortunately for you, Ann's door is always open and she welcomes drop-ins.

"Seems like something is on your mind," Ann says. "What can I help with?"

"Story just told me that Roger has been assigned to the project team. I can't work with Roger. He's arrogant and doesn't respect anyone's work but his own. He belittles me in front of others, and I don't deserve that. I write good code copy, and I don't need Roger looking over my shoulder. I want to be on this team, but not if Roger is part of it."

Ann thinks for a minute and replies, "I want you to have the opportunity to work on this project; it's a great opportunity for you. But there isn't anyone else who can work on the analysis phase of this project except Roger. He's the only one left who has a solid understanding of the mainframe legacy code. Unfortunately, those old programs were never documented well, and they've evolved over the years into programs on top of programs. Without Roger's expertise of the existing system, we'd blow the budget and time estimates already established for this project. What would you say to a meeting with you and Roger and me to talk about these issues and see if we can't work this out?"

Time Estimating Techniques

Estimating the duration of project activities first involves identifying the activities in the Activity Definition process and then sequencing them in the correct order in the Activity Sequencing process. Then, time estimates are assigned in the Activity Duration Estimating process. The time estimates are baseline measurements used to track project activities to ensure the project is completed on time. In order to determine accurate duration estimates, the Activity Definition process must be completed first. From there, you may either sequence the activities or estimate the activities. In practice, it makes the most sense to define the activities, sequence them in the correct order, and then estimate them. We'll describe each of these processes in this section, as they are closely related and many times performed at the same time.

Activity Definition, Activity Sequencing, Activity Duration Estimating, and Schedule Development are separate processes, each with inputs, tools and techniques, and outputs. In practice, especially for small- to medium-sized projects, these processes are condensed into one process or step. We'll take a look at each of the activity-related processes now. Chapter 7, "Creating the Project Plan," describes the Schedule Development process.

Understanding the Activity Definition Process

The *Activity Definition* process is a further breakdown of the work package elements of the WBS. It documents the specific activities needed to fulfill the deliverables detailed on the WBS. This process is especially necessary when you are working with large projects where the original WBS only goes to level two or level three elements and the work package level describes deliverables or subdeliverables. At this point, the work package level is then assigned to subproject managers to further break down and identify individual activities.

In practice, when you're working on a small project or projects that aren't that complex, Activity Definition might be accomplished during the construction of the WBS and the activities themselves become the work package level.

This process produces an output called an *activity list,* which is an extension of the WBS. The activity list should contain all the activities of the project, with a description of each activity so that team members understand what the work is and how it is to be completed. Once the activity list is completed, the WBS might need to be updated. Work breakdown structure updates is the second output in the Activity Definition process.

Exam Spotlight

The PMP exam may have a question or two regarding the activity list or WBS updates.

The inputs to the Activity Definition process are:

- WBS
- Scope statement
- Historical information

- Constraints
- Assumptions
- Expert judgment

The tools and techniques of the Activity Definition process are decomposition and templates, and the remaining output of this process is supporting detail. You should be familiar with these inputs and tools and techniques from previous discussions.

Understanding the Activity Sequencing Process

You've identified the activities, and now you need to sequence them in a logical order and find out if dependencies exist among the activities. The interactivity of logical relationships must be sequenced correctly in order to facilitate the development of a realistic, achievable project schedule in a later process.

Consider a classic example. Let's say you're going to paint your house, but unfortunately, it's fallen into a little disrepair. The old paint is peeling and chipping and will need to be scraped before a coat of primer can be sprayed on the house. After the primer dries, then the painting can commence. In this example, the primer activity depends on the scraping. You can't—okay, *you shouldn't*—prime the house before scraping off the peeling paint. The painting activity depends on the primer activity in the same way. You really shouldn't start painting until the primer has dried.

During *Activity Sequencing*, you will use a host of inputs and tools and techniques to produce the final outputs, a project network diagram, and activity list updates. We're going to look at three of the inputs, and we'll examine all of the tools and techniques needed for this process. The remaining inputs are:

- An activity list, which is an output of the Activity Definition process just discussed
- Product description
- Milestones

Dependencies

Dependencies are just as described in the house-painting example; that is, you can't paint until the scraping and priming activities are completed. The three inputs to Activity Sequencing are:

- Mandatory dependencies
- Discretionary dependencies
- External dependencies

As you've probably guessed, *A Guide to the PMBOK* defines dependencies differently depending on their characteristics. Let's look at each of these in more detail.

Mandatory Dependencies

Mandatory dependencies, also known as *hard logic* or *hard dependencies*, are defined by the type of work being performed. The scraping, primer, painting sequences are examples of mandatory dependencies. The nature of the work itself dictates the order the activities should be performed in. Activities with physical limitations are a tell-tale sign that you have a mandatory dependency on your hands.

Discretionary Dependencies

Discretionary dependencies are defined by the project management team. Discretionary dependencies are also known as *preferred logic, soft logic,* or *preferential logic.* These are usually process- or procedure-driven, or "best practices" techniques based on past experience. For example, past experience on house-painting projects has shown that all trim work should be hand-painted, while the bulk of the main painting work should be done with a sprayer.

External Dependencies

External dependencies are, well, external to the project. The weather forecast might be an external dependency in the painting example, because you wouldn't want to start painting prior to a rain storm. This may seem obvious, but *A Guide to the PMBOK* points out that even though the dependency is external to the project (and therefore a non-project activity), it impacts project activities. For example, perhaps your project is researching and marketing a new drug. The FDA must approve the drug before your company can market it. This is not a project activity but the project cannot move forward until approval occurs. That means FDA approval is an external dependency.

Once you've identified the dependencies and assembled all the other inputs for the Activity Sequencing process, you'll take this information and produce a diagram—or schematic display—of the project activities. The project network diagram shows the dependencies—or logical relationships—that exist among the activities. You can use one of several tools and techniques to produce this output. Let's examine each in detail.

Precedence Diagramming Method (PDM)

The *precedence diagramming method (PDM)* is what most project management software programs use to do Activity Sequencing today. Precedence diagrams connect activities with arrows that show dependencies between the activities. This method is also called *activity on node (AON).*

The activity information is written on the nodes, with arrows connecting the nodes, or dependent activities. The nodes are usually shown as boxes or rectangles, and you are free to put as much information about the activity on the node as you'd like. The minimum information that should be displayed on the node is the activity name. Sometimes the nodes are displayed with activity name, activity number, start and stop dates, due dates, slack time, and so on. (We'll cover slack time in Chapter 7.) For the exam, remember that the PDM uses only one time estimate to determine duration.

The following graphic shows a PDM—or AON—of the house-painting example.

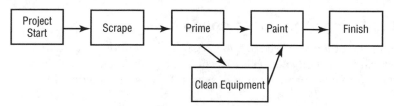

The PDM is further defined by four types of *logical relationships*. *A Guide to the PMBOK* also calls these *dependencies* or *precedence relationships*. You may already be familiar with these if you've used Microsoft Project or some other similar project management software program. The four dependencies, or logical relationships, are as follows:

Finish-to-start (FS)   The finish-to-start relationship is the most frequently used dependency. This relationship says that the independent—or *from* activity—must finish before the dependent—or *to* activity—can start.

Start-to-finish (SF)   The start-to-finish relationship says that the independent activity must start before the dependent activity can finish. This dependency is seldom used.

Finish-to-finish (FF)   This finish-to-finish relationship says that the independent activity must finish before the dependent activity finishes.

Start-to-start (SS)   I think you're getting the hang of this. The start-to-start relationship says that the independent activity must start before the dependent activity can start.

Keep these dependencies in mind when constructing your project network diagram. Remember that finish-to-start is the most commonly used dependency in the PDM method. This is also the dependency type you should employ when you're using project management software to diagram your activities. Using the other dependencies in most project management software programs will likely produce unpredictable results.

Arrow Diagramming Method (ADM)

The *arrow diagramming method (ADM)* is visually the opposite of the PDM. The arrow diagramming method places activities on the arrows, which are connected to dependent activities with nodes. This method is also called *activity on arrow (AOA)*. This technique isn't used nearly as often as PDM, but there are some industries that prefer the ADM diagramming method to the PDM method. For the record, note that AOA allows for more than one time estimate to determine duration and uses only the finish-to-start dependency.

And there's one more unique note about ADM to tuck away: Sometimes dummy activities must be plugged into the diagram to accurately display the dependencies.

The following example shows the AOA method applied to the house-painting example:

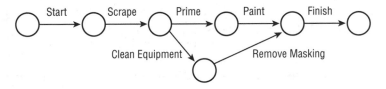

Conditional Diagramming Methods

The most important thing you need to know regarding *conditional diagramming methods* such as the Graphical Evaluation and Review Technique (GERT) and System Dynamics models is that they allow for nonsequential activities such as loops and conditional branches. Loops are situations where activities must be repeated such as a test; and branches allow for conditional situations. For example, an inspection detects an error that requires a new set of activities that may need to be repeated until resolved. Repeating the new set of activities until the situation is resolved is a loop condition. PDM and ADM do not allow loops or conditional branches. We will cover the GERT technique more in depth in Chapter 7.

Network Templates

Network templates are like the templates we've talked about in other processes. Perhaps the project you're working on is similar to a project that's been completed in the past. You can use a previous project network diagram as a template for the current project.

Exam Spotlight

I recommend you memorize the following graphic to help you remember the tools and techniques of the Activity Sequencing process and their characteristics for the exam.

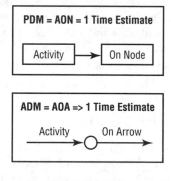

This may look a little strange, but I think it will work for you now that you understand what each of these diagramming methods is about. This is information you need to know for the exam. If this graphic isn't useful for you, come up with your own mnemonic or sample that will help you remember which of these is which. Don't say I didn't warn you.

Activity Sequencing Outputs

The outputs of Activity Sequencing are the project network diagram and activity list updates. We've just spent a good deal of time describing the different types of project network diagrams you can construct using PDM or ADM techniques. Project network diagrams (one of the outputs of this process) are actually the PDM, ADM, and conditional diagramming methods just talked about. This is a little odd in that these three diagrams are both tools and techniques and project network diagrams (the output).

Project network diagrams can be generated on a computer, or you can manually draw them out by hand. ADMs are a little easier to draw manually. Like the WBS, these diagrams may contain all the project details or may contain only summary-level details, depending on the complexity of the project. *A Guide to the PMBOK* calls these summary-level activities *hammocks*. Think of hammocks as a group of related activities rolled up into a summary heading that describes the activities likely contained in that grouping.

Keep in mind that the construction of these network diagrams might bring activities to light that you missed when defining your activity list, or it might make you break an activity down into two activities in places where you thought one activity might work. If this is the case, you will produce activity list updates based on this new information. Activity list updates are the other output of the Activity Sequencing process.

We're sailing right along. One more activity process remains, and then we've completed the time estimating segment of this chapter.

Exam Spotlight

You'll likely find that the Activity Sequencing process gets a lot of coverage on the exam. Be certain you understand its inputs and tools and techniques well. Then again, remember the exam is randomly generated from a pool of questions, so don't ever concentrate all your memorization efforts on only one or two processes.

Estimating Activity Durations

The *Activity Duration Estimating* process takes the activities defined in the WBS (project scope), the activity list, and required resources and assesses the number of work periods needed to complete these activities. Work periods are usually expressed in hours or days. However, larger projects might express duration in weeks or months. Work periods are the duration estimates, and they become inputs to the project schedule in a later process.

When you're estimating activity duration, you are estimating the length of time the activity will take to complete, including any elapsed time needed from the beginning to the ending of the activity.

For example, let's look at the house-painting project. You estimate that it will take three days, including drying time, to prime the house. Now, let's say priming is scheduled to begin on Saturday, but your crew doesn't work on Sunday. The activity duration in this case is four days, which includes the three days to prime and dry plus the Sunday the crew doesn't work. Most project management software programs will handle this kind of situation automatically.

Progressive elaboration comes into play during this process also. Estimates typically start out at a fairly high level, and as more and more details are known about the deliverables and their associated activities, the estimates become more accurate. The inputs to this process include:

- Activity list
- Constraints
- Assumptions

- Resource requirements
- Resource capabilities
- Historical information
- Identified risks

The only two inputs we haven't talked about before are resource capabilities and identified risks.

Resource capabilities are what you would expect: They're a description of the capabilities of the human and material resources you're assigning to the activity.

Identified *risks* are the result of a process we haven't talked about yet called *Risk Identification*. Risks can impact duration estimates and should be taken into consideration by the team when establishing duration estimates. Risks that are very likely to occur or have significant impact to the project if they do occur are of particular importance to this process, because they're the ones most likely to impact activity duration estimates. We'll talk more about risks in Chapter 6. For now let's get right to the tools and techniques of Activity Duration Estimating.

Activity Duration Estimating is performed using the following tools and techniques:

- Expert judgment
- Analogous estimating
- Quantitatively based durations
- Reserve time (contingency)

Exam Spotlight

A Guide to the PMBOK states that you can also use the tools and techniques of Activity Duration Estimating to determine overall project duration. *However* (this is the key word), calculating overall project duration is more appropriately done as an output of the Schedule Development process.

Expert Judgment

Activities are most accurately estimated by the staff members who will perform the activities. In this case, *expert judgment* is used by team members because of their experience with similar activities in the past. You should be careful with these estimates, though, as they are subject to bias and aren't based on any scientific means. Your experts should consider that resource levels, resource productivity, resource capability, risks, and other factors can impact estimates. It's good practice to combine expert judgment with historical information and use as many experts as you can.

Analogous Estimating

Analogous estimating, also called *top-down estimating*, is a form of expert judgment. With this technique, you will use the actual duration of a similar activity completed on a previous project to determine the duration of the current activity—provided the information was documented and stored with the project information on the previous project. This technique is most useful when the previous activities you're comparing are truly similar to the activity you're estimating and don't just appear to be similar. And you want the folks who are working on the estimate to have experience with these activities so they can provide reasonable estimates. This technique is especially helpful when detailed information about the project is not available such as in the early phases of the project.

Top-down estimating techniques are also used to estimate total project duration. The best way to think about top-down techniques is to look at the estimate as a whole. Think about being on a mountaintop where you can see the whole picture as one rather than all the individual items that make up the picture.

For instance, let's go back to the house-painting example. You would compare a previous house-painting project to the current house-painting project, where the houses are of similar size and the paint you're using is the same quality. The first house-painting project can be used to estimate the project duration for the second house-painting project because of the similarities in the project.

Top-down techniques are useful when you're early on in the project-planning process and are only just beginning to flesh out all the details of the project. Sometimes during the project selection process, the selection committee may want an idea of the project's duration. You can derive a project estimate at this stage by using top-down techniques.

Quantitatively Based Durations

The best way to describe the meaning of quantitatively based durations is with an example. Suppose you are working on a company-wide network upgrade project. This requires you to run new cable to the switches on every floor in the building. Quantitatively based durations can be used to determine activity duration estimates by taking a known element—in this case, the amount of cable needed—and multiplying it by the amount of time it takes to install a unit of cable to come up with an estimate. In other words, suppose you have 10,000 meters of new cable to run. You know from past experience it takes one hour to install 100 meters. Using this measurement, you can make a quantitatively based estimate for this activity of 100 hours to run the new cable. Therefore, the cable activity duration estimate is 100 hours.

Reserve Time (Contingency)

Reserve time—also called *buffer* or *contingency time* in *A Guide to the PMBOK*— means adding a portion of time to the activity to account for schedule risk. You might choose to add a percentage of time or a set number of work periods to the activity or the overall schedule. For example, you know it will take 100 hours to run new cable based on the quantitative estimate you came up with earlier. You also know that sometimes you hit problem areas when running the cable. To make sure you don't impact the project schedule, you build in a reserve time of 10 percent of your original estimate to account for the problems you might encounter. This brings your activity duration estimate to 110 hours for this activity.

Activity Duration Estimating Outputs

Everything we've talked about up to this point has brought us to the primary output of this process: the activity duration estimates. The inputs and tools and techniques are used to establish these estimates. As we said in the opening of this section, activity duration estimates are an estimate of the required work periods needed to complete the activity. This is a quantitative measure usually expressed in hours, weeks, days, or months.

One thing to note about your final estimates as an output to this process is they should contain a range of possible results. For example, in the cable-running example, you would state the activity duration estimates as "100 hours 10 hours," to show that the actual duration will take at least 90 hours and may go as long as 110 hours.

The other two outputs of Activity Duration Estimating include basis of estimates and activity list updates. Basis of estimates requires that you document the assumptions you used when deriving the estimates.

 Real World Scenario

Desert State University (DSU)

DSU has hired a contract agency to create their new registration website. The website will allow students in good academic standing to register for classes over the Internet. You have been appointed the project manager for the DSU side of this project. You'll be working with Henry Lu from Websites International to complete this project.

Henry has given you an activity list and asked for time estimates that he can plug into the project plan.

Your first stop is Jim Mahoney's desk. He's the expert on the mainframe registration system and will be writing the interface programs to accept registration data from the new website. Jim will also create the download that the Internet program will use to verify students' academic standing. Jim has created other programs just like this in the past. His expertise and judgment are very reliable.

The next stop is Gloria Stillwater. She's the new team leader over the testing group. Gloria has been with DSU for only one month. Since she has no experience working with DSU data and staff members, she tells you she'll get back to you within a week with estimates for the testing activities. She plans to read through the project binders of some similar projects and base her estimates against the historical information on similar projects. She'll run the estimates by her lead tester before giving them to you.

Jim Mahoney's estimates are an example of using the tool and technique of expert judgment to derive activity duration estimates. The estimates expected from Gloria Stillwater will be derived using the historical information tool and technique (implied by the research she's going to do into past similar projects) and expert judgment, because she's involving her lead tester to verify the estimates.

Cost Estimating Techniques

You now have an exhaustive breakdown of project activities, and you have some pretty good duration estimates. Now the question that's forever on the mind of the executive management staff: How much is it going to cost? The purpose of the Cost Estimating process is to answer that question.

Every project has a budget, and part of completing a project successfully is completing it within the approved budget. Sometimes project managers are not responsible for the budget portion of the project. This function is assigned instead to a functional manager who is responsible for tracking and reporting all the project costs. I believe project managers will have more and more responsibility in this area as the project management discipline evolves. Keep in mind that if you, as the project manager, don't have responsibility for the project budget, your performance evaluation for the project should not include budget or cost measurements.

Accuracy in Cost Estimating

As with time estimates, the WBS is the key to determining accurate cost estimates. The *Cost Estimating* process develops a cost estimate for the resources required for each activity outlined in the WBS. This includes weighing alternative options and examining trade-offs.

For example, many times software development projects take on a life of their own. The requested project completion dates are unrealistic; however, the project team commits to completing the project on time and on budget anyway. How do they do this? By cutting things like design, analysis, and documentation. In the end, the project might get completed on time and on budget, but was it really? The costs associated with the extended support period due to a lack of design and documentation and the hours needed by the software programmers to fix the reported bugs aren't included in the original cost of the project (but they should have been). Therefore, the costs actually exceed what was budgeted. You should examine trade-offs such as these when determining cost estimates.

When you are determining cost estimates, be certain to include all the costs of the project over its entire life cycle. Include warranty periods and ongoing costs in your estimates. As in the preceding example, software projects often have warranty periods that guarantee bug fixes or problem resolution within a certain time frame. This is a legitimate cost that should be included in your estimates.

Don't confuse pricing with Cost Estimating. If you are working for a company that performs consulting services on contract, for example, the price you will charge for your services is not the same thing as the costs to perform the project. The costs are centered on the resources needed to produce the product or service of the project. The price your company might charge for the service includes not only these costs, but a profit margin as well.

Cost Estimating Inputs

You are already familiar with most of the Cost Estimating inputs. Two that you haven't seen before are the resource rates and the chart of accounts.

Resource rates are the unit cost of the resources you're considering. If you're hiring contract Java coders, their unit cost might be $135 per hour. To determine the estimate, you multiply the number of hours needed—which was estimated during the Activity Duration Estimating process—by the number of resources needed. If your project requires certain materials or equipment, use the unit cost to calculate the appropriate estimate. When unit costs are not known, you might need to estimate them as well.

Be certain to estimate all the resources you're going to need for the project. This includes staff wages, contractor costs if applicable, materials, supplies, equipment, hardware, software tools, design tools, and so on.

A *chart of accounts* is the coding system used by the finance department to record transactions in the company's general ledger. The chart of accounts is where the project costs will be tracked. They are typically recorded by category such as equipment, supplies, personnel costs, and so on. The code of accounts we talked about in association with the WBS comes from the chart of accounts.

Cost Estimating Tools

Cost Estimating has five tools and techniques used to derive estimates:

- Analogous estimating
- Parametric modeling
- Bottom-up estimating
- Computerized tools
- Other Cost Estimating methods

We'll look at each of these next.

Analogous Estimating

We talked about Analogous Estimating in the time estimating section earlier in this chapter. The information relayed there applies to Cost Estimating as well. Remember that analogous estimating is a top-down estimating technique and is a form of expert judgment. It is a less costly technique than the others we'll look at and also less accurate.

Parametric Modeling

Parametric modeling is a mathematical model that uses parameters—or project characteristics—to forecast project costs. The idea here is to find a parameter—or multiple parameters—that changes proportionately with project costs and then plug that into the model to come up with a total project cost. In order to use this technique, there must be a pattern that exists in the work so that you can use an estimate from that work element to derive the total project estimate.

For example, you might know from past experience that it costs $275 per square foot to build an office building. The $275 becomes the parameter that you use in the parametric model to come up with an estimate of total project cost. If you're using multiple parameters, each parameter is also assigned a weight that is included in the calculations. This allows for cost estimates to be calculated simultaneously.

Parametric modeling is similar to analogous estimating, because it estimates the cost of the entire project (top-down). This method's costs and accuracy can vary depending on the information available to develop the model. Parametric modeling is more accurate when historical information is used to help construct the model and when the parameters are easily quantified and the model is scalable.

Bottom-Up Estimating

The *bottom-up estimating* technique is the opposite of top-down estimating. Here you estimate every activity or work item individually and then roll up that estimate, or add them all together, to come up with a total project estimate. This is a very accurate means of estimating, provided that the estimates at the work package level are accurate. However, it takes a considerable amount of time to perform bottom-up estimating, because every work package must be assessed and estimated accurately to be included in the bottom-up calculation. The smaller and more detailed the activity, the greater the accuracy and cost of this technique.

You wouldn't choose this technique to provide a cost estimate for the project in the Initiation stage if one were requested, because you don't have enough information at that stage to use the bottom-up technique. Instead, use the top-down estimation technique when a project cost estimate is needed early on in the project selection stage.

Computerized Tools

Project management software can be a useful tool in Cost Estimating, as are spreadsheet programs. Using software like Microsoft Project can make the job of Cost Estimating easy and fast.

Other Cost Estimating Methods

Analogous estimating, parametric modeling, bottom-up estimating, and computerized tools are the primary methods you'll use to calculate cost estimates. You may also use other techniques or methods. For example, when your project is performed under contract or you need to procure resources under contract, you might analyze vendor bids to determine cost estimates for these activities. Make certain to document the Cost Estimating method you used in the supporting detail output of this process.

Exam Spotlight

Make sure you're familiar with all the cost estimating tools and techniques, their benefits, and under what conditions you use them for the exam.

Documenting the Cost Estimates

Obviously, one of the outputs of the Cost Estimating process is the cost estimates. These are quantitative amounts—usually stated in monetary units—that reflect the cost of the resources needed to complete the project activities. The tools and techniques we just described help you derive these estimates.

Supporting detail and the cost management plan are the remaining two Cost Estimating outputs. Supporting detail is just as you've seen in other processes. Any information that supports how the estimates were developed, what assumptions were made during the Cost Estimating process, and any other details you think need to be documented go here. According to *A Guide to the PMBOK*, the supporting detail should include the following:

- A description of the work that was estimated. (The WBS is a good source for this as the full scope of work is documented there.)

- A description of how the estimate was developed or the basis for the estimate.

- A description of the assumptions made about the estimates or the method used to determine them.

- A range of possible results. Like the time estimates, the cost estimates should be stated within ranges such as "$500 ± $75."

Cost variances will occur and estimates will be refined as you get further into your project. As you've probably suspected, there is a plan that defines how these cost variances should be managed. That plan is called the *cost management plan* and is the last output of the Cost Estimating process. Your cost management plan should define how changes to cost estimates or changes in resource unit costs will be reflected in the project budget. Changes or variances with a significant impact should be communicated to the project sponsor and stakeholders. In addition, the cost management plan should define how and when this notification process works. And like some of the other management plans we've discussed to date, the cost management plan is also a subsidiary plan of the project plan.

Cost Estimating uses several techniques to make an accurate assessment of the project costs. In practice, using a combination of techniques is your best bet to come up with the most reliable cost estimates. The Cost Estimating output will become an input to the Cost Budgeting process, which allows you to establish a baseline for project costs to track against.

Project Case Study: New Kitchen Heaven Retail Store

"Thanks everyone for your timely responses. I'll look over the activity lists and estimates you've assigned and start working on the project plan." The meeting adjourns, and you head back to your office to review the estimates and resource assignments. You'd like to get the project schedule constructed soon and go over it with Dirk. This information is the first cut at the project schedule.

Ricardo Ramirez from the IT department has outlined his activity list and estimates. He reminds you that data is sent from each store over a T1 connection, not over satellite as Jill told you originally. Ricardo's estimates are as follows. He's also taken the trouble to write them in sequential order:

1. Procure the T1 connection. This takes 30 to 45 days and will have ongoing costs of $300 per month. This can be done concurrently with the other activities listed here. Ricardo will handle this activity.

2. Run Ethernet cable throughout the building. This activity depends on the lease being signed and must finish before the build-out can start. The estimated time to complete is 16 hours using quantitatively based estimates. Ricardo has one person on staff who can complete this specialized activity. His first available date is October 5.

3. Purchase the router, switch, server, and rack for the equipment room and four point-of-service terminals. The estimated costs are $17,000. Delivery time is two weeks. Ricardo will do this activity.

4. Install the router and test the connection. Testing depends on the T1 installation at demarcation. The time estimate to install is eight hours. Ricardo's staff will do this activity.

5. Install the switch. Based on past experience, the time estimate to install is two hours. Ricardo's staff will do this activity.

6. Install the server and test. The testing depends on the T1 connection installation. Based on past experience, the time estimate to install is six hours. Ricardo's staff will do this activity.

7. The web team will add the new store location and phone number to the lookup function on the Internet site. The time estimate is eight hours. Ricardo will assign his applications-programming manager to this activity. This activity depends on the lease being signed.

Jake and Jill have each written similar lists with estimates and resource assignments. You begin to align all the activities in sequential order and discover a problem. Jill needs 7 days to stock shelves and train employees, meaning that the build-out must be finished by January 24. Build-out takes approximately 120 days and therefore must start by September 20. The problem is that Ricardo's Ethernet cable expert isn't available until October 5, and he needs two days to complete the cabling. This pushes out the build-out start date by almost two weeks, which means the project completion date, or store-opening date, is delayed by two weeks.

After gathering more information from Ricardo, you head to Dirk's office.

"So, Dirk," you conclude after filling him in on all the details. "We have two options. Hire a contractor to perform the cable run since Ricardo's person isn't available, or push the store opening out by two weeks."

Dirk asks, "How much will the contractor charge to run the cable, and are they available within the time frame you need?"

"Yes, they are available, and I've already requested Ricardo book the week of September 17 to hold this option open for us. They've quoted a price of $10,000."

"Okay, let's bring in the contractor. $10,000 isn't going to break the budget at this point. How is that planning coming anyway? Signed a lease yet?"

"Yes, we've signed the lease. Jake has been meeting with Gomez construction on the build-out. We've used Gomez on three out of the last five new stores and have had good luck with them."

Project Case Study Checklist

Activity Definition

Activity Sequencing

Activity Duration Estimating

- Expert judgment

- Quantitatively based estimates

Cost Estimating

- Other Cost Estimating methods—vendor bids

Summary

The Resource Planning process considers all the resources needed and the quantity of resources needed to perform project activities. This information is tied to the WBS elements and is detailed in the resource requirements document.

Staffing requirements are a subset of the resource requirements output. Staffing requirements are concerned with the human resource aspect of the resource plan and detail special skills or knowledge that might be needed for a project activity.

Organizational planning identifies and assigns roles and responsibilities and reporting relationships. Many times the roles and responsibilities assignments are depicted in a Responsibility Assignment Matrix (RAM). The staffing management plan describes how and when project team members will be brought on and off the project and is an output of the Organizational Planning process.

The Staff Acquisition process details staff assignments and publishes the project team directory.

Duration estimates are produced as a result of the Activity Duration Estimating process. Prior to this process, activities must be identified and sequenced in logical order. Activity

Sequencing is performed using PDM, which is an activity on node (AON) method, or using ADM, which is an activity on arrow (AOA) method, or with conditional diagramming or network templates. ADM is seldom used today.

Activity duration estimates document the number of work periods needed for each activity, including their elapsed time. Analogous estimating—also called top-down estimating—is one way to determine activity duration estimates. Top-down techniques can also be used to estimate project durations and total project costs. Quantitatively based durations multiply a known element—like the quantity of materials needed—by the time it takes to install or complete one unit of materials. The result is a total estimate for the activity. Reserve time takes schedule risk into consideration by adding an additional percentage of time or another work period to the estimate just in case you run into trouble.

The Cost Estimating process determines how much the project resources will cost, which is usually stated in dollars. The cost management plan outlines how costs will be managed throughout the project. Analogous estimating is one technique that can be used to determine cost estimates. Another estimating technique is parametric modeling. This is a mathematical model that forecasts project costs. Bottom-up estimating can be used for project cost estimates. This involves estimating the cost of each work package and then rolling these up to come up with a total cost.

Exam Essentials

Be able to identify the tools and techniques of Activity Sequencing.   The tools and techniques of Activity Sequencing are the precedence diagramming method (PDM), the arrow diagramming method (ADM), the conditional diagramming method, and network templates.

Be able to discuss the difference between PDM and ADM.   PDM uses activity on node (AON) diagrams, and ADM uses activity on arrow (AOA) diagrams.

Be able to name the tools and techniques of Activity Duration Estimating.   The tools and techniques of Activity Duration Estimating are expert judgment, analogous estimating, quantitatively based durations, and reserve time.

Be able to identify the tools and techniques of Cost Estimating.   The tools and techniques of Cost Estimating are analogous estimating, parametric modeling, bottom-up estimating, computerized tools, and other Cost Estimating methods.

Be able to define the difference between analogous estimating and bottom-up estimating.   Analogous estimating is a top-down technique that uses expert judgment and historical information. Bottom-up estimating performs estimates for each work item and rolls them up to a total.

Key Terms

Before you take the exam, be certain you are familiar with the following terms:

Activity Definition	parametric modeling
Activity duration estimates	preassignment
Activity Duration Estimating	precedence diagramming method (PDM)
Activity list	precedence relationships
Activity on arrow (AOA)	preferential logic
Activity on node (AON)	preferred logic
Activity Sequencing	procurement
analogous estimating	reserve time
arrow diagramming method (ADM)	resource capabilities
Bottom-up estimating	resource histogram
Buffer	Resource Planning
chart of accounts	resource pool description
contingency time	resource rates
Cost Estimating	resource requirements
dependencies	resources
discretionary dependencies	Responsibility Assignment Matrix (RAM)
external dependencies	Risk Identification
hammocks	risks
hard dependencies	soft logic
hard logic	Staff Acquisition
interpersonal interfaces	staffing pool description
logical relationships	staffing requirements
mandatory dependencies	technical interfaces

Review Questions

1. Which of the following statements is true regarding the Resource Planning process?

   A. Resource Planning involves the human resource aspect of planning only, and its output is staffing requirements.

   B. Resource Planning involves the human resource aspect of planning only, and its output is resource requirements.

   C. Resource Planning encompasses all the physical resources needed for the project, and its output is staffing requirements.

   D. Resource Planning encompasses all the physical resources needed for the project, and its output is resource requirements.

2. Sally is a project manager working on the Resource Planning process. She should consider all of the following when developing the resource requirements output except:

   A. WBS

   B. Supply purchase policies

   C. Resource rates

   D. Special knowledge and talents

3. Which of the following are constraints that you might find during the Organizational Planning process?

   A. Organizational structure, expected staff assignments, collective bargaining agreements, and project management team preferences

   B. Organizational structure, organizational interfaces, technical interfaces, and interpersonal interfaces

   C. Organizational interfaces, expected staff assignments, collective bargaining agreements, and project management team preferences

   D. Organizational interfaces, technical interfaces, and interpersonal interfaces

4. You are the project manager for a scheduled version release of your company's software tracking product. You have linked the WBS and project scope definition, and you have assigned roles and responsibilities. You might want to display the roles and responsibilities in which of the following?

   A. RDM

   B. PDM

   C. AOA

   D. RAM

5. Which of the following is true regarding the staffing management plan?

    A. It details the resource requirements and the quantity of resources needed for project activities. It is an output of the Resource Planning process.

    B. It details how and when staff resources will be brought on and off the project. It is an output of the Organizational Planning process.

    C. It details how and when staff resources will be brought on and off the project. It is an output of the Resource Planning process.

    D. It details the resource requirements and the quantity of resources needed for project activities. It is an output of the Organizational Planning process.

6. All of the following statements describe the activity list except:

    A. The activity list is an extension of the WBS.

    B. The activity list includes all activities of the project.

    C. The activity list describes the WBS updates.

    D. The activity list includes a description of project activities.

7. You are the project manager for Design Your Website, Inc. Your company is designing the web-site for a national grocery store chain. You have your activity list in hand and are ready to diagram the activity dependencies using the PDM technique. You know that:

    A. PDM uses AON diagramming methods.

    B. PDM uses AOA diagramming methods.

    C. PDM uses ADM diagramming methods.

    D. PDM uses PDM diagramming methods.

8. You are the project manager for Design Your Website, Inc. Your company is designing the website for a national grocery store chain. You have your activity list in hand and several time estimates for each activity and are ready to diagram the activity dependencies. You should use which of the following?

    A. PDM techniques

    B. PDM or ADM techniques

    C. AON techniques

    D. ADM techniques

9. All of the following statements are true regarding the tools and techniques of Activity Sequencing except:

    A. GERT uses analogous methods.

    B. GERT allows for loops.

    C. GERT is a conditional diagramming method.

    D. GERT allows for conditional branches.

10. Which of the following statements is true regarding the risks with high probability or impact as part of the identified risks input of the Activity Duration Estimating process? Choose the best answer.

    A. Risks with high probability and impact increase the activity duration estimates.

    B. Risks with high probability and impact decrease the activity duration estimates.

    C. Risks with high probability and impact have no affect on the activity duration estimates.

    D. Risks with high probability and impact are the ones most likely to impact activity duration estimates.

11. This subsidiary output deals with the competency levels of individuals (or groups of people) who will be assigned to the project activities. This document or list should identify the kinds of skills required and the individuals or groups who might provide these skills to the project and the time frames during the project when these skills will be needed. Which of the following answers best describes this output?

    A. Staffing requirements

    B. Resource requirements

    C. Resource management plan

    D. Activity list updates

12. As project manager, you know that all of the following statements are true concerning analogous estimating techniques except:

    A. Analogous estimating is a quantitatively based estimating technique.

    B. Analogous estimating is a top-down estimating technique.

    C. Analogous estimating is a tool and technique of Activity Duration Estimating and Cost Estimating.

    D. Analogous estimating is a form of expert judgment.

13. You have been hired as a contract project manager for Grapevine Vineyards. Grapevine wants you to design an Internet wine club for their customers. Customers must preregister before being allowed to order wine over the Internet so that legal age can be established. You know that the module to verify preregistration must be written and tested using data from Grapevine's existing database. This new module cannot be tested until the data from the existing system is loaded. This is an example of which of the following?

    A. Preferential logic

    B. Soft logic

    C. Discretionary dependency

    D. Hard logic

14. You have been hired as a contract project manger for Grapevine Vineyards. Grapevine wants you to design an Internet wine club for their customers. One of the activities for this project is the installation and testing of several new servers. You know from past experience it takes about 16 hours per server to accomplish this task. Since you're installing 10 new servers, you estimate this activity to take 160 hours. Which of the estimating techniques have you used?

   A. Analogous estimating

   B. Bottom-up estimating

   C. Quantitatively based durations

   D. Reserve time

15. Your project sponsor has requested a cost estimate for the project. She would like the cost estimate to be as accurate as possible, because this might be her one and only chance to secure the budget for this project due to recent cuts in special projects. You decide to use:

   A. Analogous estimating techniques

   B. Bottom-up estimating techniques

   C. Top-down estimating techniques

   D. Expert judgment techniques

16. All of the following statements accurately describe reassignment plans except:

   A. A reassignment plan is part of the Organizational Planning process.

   B. A reassignment plan reduces costs, because resources are reassigned as soon as their activities are finished and they aren't allowed to linger on the project simply to fill up time.

   C. A reassignment plan improves morale because resources know their next assignment prior to the conclusion of their activity or scheduled end date on the project.

   D. A reassignment plan is part of the staffing management plan.

17. All of the following are true regarding parametric modeling except:

   A. Parametric modeling is a form of top-down estimating.

   B. Parametric modeling is a mathematical model.

   C. Parametric modeling is a tool used to estimate project costs.

   D. Parametric modeling is a tool used to estimate project time.

18. Your project's primary constraint is quality. In order to make certain the project team members don't feel too pressed for time and to avoid schedule risk, you decide to use which of the following activity estimating tools?

   A. Expert judgment

   B. Quantitatively based durations

   C. Reserve time

   D. Analogous estimating

19. When your project network diagram contains only summary-level activities due to the complexity of the project, what is that called according to *A Guide to the PMBOK*? Choose the best answer.

    A. Nodes

    B. Hammocks

    C. Arrows

    D. Hanger

20. Which logical relationship does the PDM use most often?

    A. Start-to-finish

    B. Start-to-start

    C. Finish-to-finish

    D. Finish-to-start

Answers to Review Questions

1. D. Resource Planning is the process that determines all the physical resources needed for the project and what quantities of resources are needed. The output is resource requirements.

2. C. Resource rates are an input to Cost Estimating. Supply purchase policies would be found in the organizational policies input, which the project manager should consider when writing the resource requirements.

3. A. Constraints can be anything that limits the option of the project team. Organizational structure, collective bargaining agreements, preferences of the project management team, and expected staff assignments are all constraints that might be encountered during this process.

4. D. The Responsibility Assignment Matrix (RAM) links project roles and responsibilities with project activities.

5. B. The staffing management plan details how and when human resources will be added to and taken off the project. It is an output of Organizational Planning.

6. C. The activity list is produced as an extension of the WBS and includes all the project activities, with descriptions of the activities. The activity list and the WBS updates are outputs to the Activity Definition process.

7. A. Precedence diagramming methods are also known as activity on node (AON) diagramming methods.

8. D. PDM uses one time estimate to determine duration, while ADM can use more than one time estimate.

9. A. GERT is a conditional diagramming method that allows for loops and conditional branches.

10. D. Risks with high probability and impact are the ones most likely to impact activity duration estimates. Their effects should be considered when estimating activities. While most risks generally will add time to the activity estimate, this isn't always true in every case. The estimate might remain the same even when the effects of the risk are considered. In some cases, particularly when the risk is an opportunity, the risk might actually decrease the activity estimate.

11. A. Staffing requirements are a subset of resource requirements. Resource requirements describe the types of resources needed and the quantity of resources needed for the work package level of the WBS. Staffing requirements take this one step further and document the kinds of skills required and the time frames during which these skills are needed.

12. A. Analogous estimating is not a quantitatively based technique. It is a top-down estimating technique that considers previous similar activities when calculating estimates.

13. D.   This is an example of a mandatory dependency, also known as hard logic. Mandatory dependencies are inherent in the nature of the work. Discretionary dependencies, also called preferred logic, preferential logic, and soft logic, are defined by the project management team.

14. C.   Quantitatively based durations multiply a known element—like the quantity of materials needed—by the time it takes to install or complete one unit of materials. The result is a total estimate for the activity. In this case, 10 servers multiplied by 16 hours per server gives you a 160-hour total duration estimate.

15. B.   Bottom-up techniques are the most time-consuming and the most accurate estimates you can use. With bottom-up estimating, each work item is estimated and rolled up to a project total.

16. C.   A reassignment plan reduces costs because resources don't linger on the project, simply because they're filling time between assignments or waiting for their scheduled end date. It improves morale because anxiety about future employment is reduced. It is part of the staffing management plan, which is an output of the Organizational Planning process.

17. D.   Parametric modeling is a Cost Estimating technique.

18. C.   Reserve time takes schedule risk into consideration and adds a percentage of time or additional work periods to the estimate to prevent schedule delays.

19. B.   Hammocks are the term *A Guide to the PMBOK* calls summary-level activities on project network diagrams.

20. D.   Finish-to-start (FS) is the most commonly used logical relationship in PDM and most project management software packages.

Chapter 6

Establishing Project Planning Controls

THE PMP EXAM CONTENT FROM THE PROJECT PLANNING PERFORMANCE DOMAIN COVERED IN THIS CHAPTER INCLUDES:

✓ 5. Establishing project controls

Each of the project Planning processes we've discussed so far, along with what we'll cover here and in Chapter 7, "Creating the Project Plan," will culminate in the final output of the project Planning process, which is the project plan. The Execution and Controlling process groups depend on the project plan to measure and track project performance. In order to measure performance, several more plans need to be put into place, including a quality plan, a risk response plan, and a procurement plan. We'll cover each of these in the upcoming sections of this chapter.

We have a lot of material to cover in this chapter, including several processes on risk management. This chapter covers Quality Planning, Risk Management Planning, Risk Identification, Qualitative Risk Analysis, Quantitative Risk Analysis, Risk Response Planning, Solicitation Planning, and Procurement Planning.

Identifying Quality Standards

Quality is one of the triple constraints found in all projects. It's the third leg to the successful completion of a project and more typically defines whether stakeholder expectations were met. Being on time and on budget is one thing; if you deliver the wrong product or an inferior product, on time and on budget suddenly don't mean much. Remember those career-limiting moves we talked about in a previous chapter? This could be one of them if you don't plan and monitor quality properly on your project.

The *Quality Planning* process is concerned with targeting quality standards that are relevant to the project at hand and devising a plan to meet and satisfy those standards. The quality management plan is the primary output of this process. It describes how the quality policy will be implemented by the project management team during the course of the project. Everything discussed in this section, including the inputs and tools and techniques of this process, will be used to help develop the quality management plan.

> **Exam Spotlight**
>
> The Quality Management knowledge area, which includes the Quality Planning, Quality Assurance, and Quality Control processes, involves the quality management of the project as well as the quality aspects of the product or service the project was undertaken to produce. We'll discuss Quality Assurance and Quality Control in later chapters.

Quality Inputs

The Quality Planning process has several inputs: quality policy, scope statement, product description, standards and regulations, and other process outputs. We'll look at two of these inputs now: quality policy, and standards and regulations.

Quality Policy

The quality policy is a guideline published by executive management that describes what quality policies should be adopted for projects the company undertakes. It's up to the project manager to understand this policy and incorporate any predetermined company guidelines into the quality plan. If a quality policy does not exist, it's up to the project management team to create one for the project.

Standards and Regulations

As with the quality policy, the project manager should consider any standards or regulations that exist concerning the work of the project when writing the quality plan. A *standard* is defined by *A Guide to the PMBOK* as something that's approved by a recognized body and that employs rules, guidelines, or characteristics that should be followed. For example, the Americans with Disabilities Act (ADA) has established standards for web page designers that outline alternative viewing options of web pages for people with disabilities. PMI guidelines regarding project management are another example of standards.

Standards aren't mandatory, but it's a good idea to follow them. If your project creates a software product that ignores standard protocols, your customers won't be able to use it.

Standards can be set by the organization, by independent bodies or organizations such as the International Organization for Standardization (ISO), and so on.

A regulation is mandatory. *Regulations* are almost always imposed by governments or institutions like the American Medical Association. However, organizations may have their own self-imposed regulations that you should be aware of as well. Regulations require strict adherence, particularly in the case of government-imposed regulations, or stiff penalties and fines could result—maybe even jail time if the offense is serious enough. Hmm, might be tough to practice project management from behind bars—not a recommended career move.

If possible, it's a good idea to include information from the quality policy and any standards and regulations that affect the project in the quality management plan. If it's not possible to include this information in the quality management plan, then at least make reference to the information and where it can be found. It's the project manager's responsibility to be certain all stakeholders are aware of and understand the policy issues and standards or regulations that might impact the project.

Since we covered the remaining inputs to Quality Planning such as scope statement, product description, and other process outputs in previous chapters, let's move on to the tools used in Quality Planning.

One note regarding the "other process outputs": Contracts might have certain provisions for quality requirements that you should account for in the quality management plan. This will be discovered during the Procurement Planning process. In this case, the "other process output" from Procurement Planning becomes an input to Quality Planning.

Quality Planning Tools

Quality Planning has five tools and techniques used to help construct the quality management plan. Make sure you understand each of these tools and techniques and its purpose for the exam. Let's take a look.

Benefit/Cost Analysis

You've seen the benefit/cost analysis technique before in other Planning processes. In the case of quality management, you'll want to consider the trade-offs of the cost of quality. It's cheaper and more efficient to prevent defects in the first place than to have to spend time and money fixing them later. According to *A Guide to the PMBOK*, the benefits of meeting quality requirements are as follows:

- Stakeholder satisfaction is increased.

- Costs are lower.

- Productivity is higher.

- There is less rework.

A Guide to the PMBOK notes that the primary cost of meeting quality requirements for a project are the expenses incurred while performing project quality management activities.

Benchmarking

Benchmarking is a process of comparing previous similar activities to the current project activities to provide a standard to measure performance against. This comparison will also help you derive ideas for quality improvements on the current project. For example, if your current printer can produce 8 pages per minute and you're considering a new printer that produces 14 pages per minute, the benchmark is 8 pages per minute.

Flowcharting

Flowcharts are diagrams that show the logical steps that must be performed in order to accomplish an objective. They can also show how the individual elements of a system interrelate. Flowcharting can help identify where quality problems might occur on the project. This is important because it allows the project team the opportunity to develop alternative approaches for dealing with anticipated quality problems identified with this tool and technique. In the case of quality management planning, two types of flowcharts are commonly used: cause-and-effect diagrams and system or process flowcharts.

Cause-and-effect diagrams show the relationship between the effects of problems and their causes. This diagram depicts every potential cause and subcause of a problem and the effect that each proposed solution will have on the problem. This diagram is also called a fishbone diagram, or Ishikawa diagram after its developer Kaoru Ishikawa. Figure 6.1 shows an example cause-and-effect diagram.

FIGURE 6.1   Cause-and-effect diagram

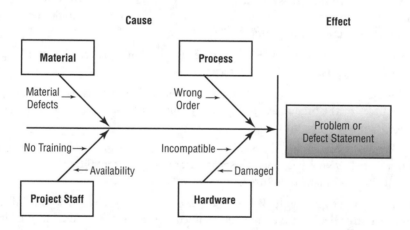

The system or process flowchart shows the logical steps needed to accomplish an objective and the interrelation of individual elements of a system. This flowchart is probably the one you're most familiar with. It's usually constructed with rectangles and parallelograms that step through a logical sequence and allow for "Yes" and "No" branches (or some similar type of decision).

Design of Experiments

Design of experiments is a statistical technique that identifies the elements—or variables—that will have the greatest effect on overall project outcomes. This technique is used most often concerning the product of the project but can also be applied to project management processes to examine trade-offs. This process designs and sets up experiments to determine the ideal solution for a problem using a limited number of sample cases.

Cost of Quality

The *cost of quality* is the total cost to produce the product or service of the project according to the quality standards. These costs include all the work necessary to meet the product requirements whether the work was planned or unplanned. It also includes the costs of work performed due to nonconforming quality requirements.

There are three costs associated with the cost of quality:

- Prevention costs
- Appraisal costs
- Failure costs, which consist of internal and external costs

Prevention Costs   Prevention means keeping defects out of the hands of customers. *Prevention costs* are the costs associated with satisfying customer requirements by producing a product without defects. These costs are manifested early on in the process and include things like quality planning, training, design review, and contractor and supplier costs.

Appraisal Costs   *Appraisal costs* are the costs expended to examine the product or process and make certain the requirements are being met. Appraisal costs might include costs associated with things like inspections and testing.

Failure Costs   *Failure costs* are what it costs when things don't go according to plan. There are two types of failure costs: internal and external.

Internal failure costs result when customer requirements are not satisfied while the product is still in the control of the organization. Internal failure costs may include corrective action, rework, scrapping, and downtime.

External failure costs occur when the product has reached the customer and they determine that their requirements have not been met. Costs associated with external failure costs may include inspections at the customer site, returns, and customer service costs.

Cost of quality is a topic you'll likely encounter on the exam. This section will discuss some of the pioneers in this field. Quality must be planned into the project, not inspected in after the fact to make certain the product or service meets stakeholders' expectations.

Three people in particular are responsible for the rise of the quality management movement and the theories behind the cost of quality: Philip B. Crosby, Joseph M. Juran, and W. Edwards Deming. Each of these men developed steps or points that led to commonly accepted quality processes that we use today. We'll also look at a quality technique called the Kaizen Approach that originated in Japan.

Philip B. Crosby

Philip B. Crosby devised the *zero defects* practice, which means, basically, do it right the first time. (Didn't your dad used to tell you this?) Crosby says that costs will increase when quality planning isn't performed up front, which means you'll have to engage in rework, thus affecting productivity. Prevention is the key to Crosby's theory. If you prevent the defect from occurring in the first place, costs are lower, conformance to requirements is easily met, and the cost measurement for quality becomes the cost of nonconformance rather than the cost of rework.

Joseph M. Juran

Joseph M. Juran is noted for his *fitness for use* premise. Simply put, this means the stakeholders' and customers' expectations are met or exceeded. This says that conformance to specifications—meaning the product of the project that was produced is what the project set out to produce—is met or exceeded. Fitness for use specifically reflects the customers' or stakeholders' view of quality and answers the following questions:

"Did the product or service produced meet the quality expectation?"

"Did it satisfy a real need?"

"Is it reliable and safe?"

Juran also proposed that there could be grades of quality. However, you should not confuse grade with quality. Low quality is usually not an acceptable condition; however, low grade might be. For example, your new Dad's Dollars Credit Card software tracking system might be of high quality, meaning there are no bugs and the product performs as advertised, but of low grade, meaning there are few features. You'll almost always want to strive for high quality, regardless of the acceptable grade level.

W. Edwards Deming

W. Edwards Deming suggested that as much as 85 percent of the cost of quality is a management problem. Once the quality issue has hit the floor, or the worker level, the workers have little control. For example, if you're constructing a new highway and the management team that bid on the project proposed using inferior-grade asphalt, the workers laying the asphalt have little control over its quality. They're at the mercy of the management team that purchased the supplies.

Deming also proposed that workers cannot figure out quality on their own, and thus cannot perform at their best. He believed that workers need to be shown what acceptable quality is, and that they need to be made to understand that quality and continuous improvement are necessary elements of any organization—or project in your case.

Kaizen Approach

The Kaizen approach is a quality technique from Japan. In fact, *Kaizen* means continuous improvement in Japanese. With this technique, all project team members and managers should be constantly watching for quality improvement opportunities. The Kaizen approach states that you should improve the quality of the people first, then the quality of the products or service.

Exam Spotlight

Understand each of these men's theories on the cost of quality for the exam. Here's a key to help you remember:

- Crosby = zero defects and prevention or rework results

- Juran = fitness for use, conformance

- Deming = quality is a management problem

- Kaizen = continuous improvement

Quality Planning Outputs

Quality Planning uses many techniques to determine the areas of quality improvement that can be implemented, controlled, and measured throughout the rest of the project, as you've seen. These are recorded in the primary output of this process, which is called the quality management plan. The *quality management plan* describes how the project management team will enact the quality policy. It also documents the resources needed to carry out the quality plan, the responsibilities of the project team in implementing quality, and all the processes and procedures the project team and organization should use to satisfy quality requirements.

The quality management plan is written by the project manager in cooperation with the project staff. You then assign quality actions to the activities listed on the work breakdown structure (WBS) based on the quality plan requirements. Isn't that WBS a handy thing? The quality plan should document the quality actions associated with the WBS activities. Later in the Quality Control process, measurements will be taken to determine if the quality to date is on track with the quality standards outlined in the quality management plan.

Operational Definitions

Operational definitions describe what is being measured and how it will be measured by the Quality Control process. For example, let's say you're managing the opening of a new restaurant in July of next year. Perhaps one of the deliverables is the procurement of flatware for 500 place settings. The operational definition in this case might include the date the flatware must be delivered and a counting or inventory process to ensure you received what you ordered. Operational definitions are sometimes called *metrics*.

Checklists

If you're like me, you start your day at the office with a big to-do list that has so many items on it you won't be able to finish them all. Nevertheless, you faithfully write the list every day and check off the things that you accomplish throughout the day. *Checklists* are like this in that they provide a means to determine if the required steps in a process have been followed. As each step is completed, it's checked off the list. Checklists can be activity-specific or industry-specific, and might be very complex or easy to follow. Sometimes, organizations may have standard checklists they use for projects. You might also be able to obtain checklists from professional associations.

Remember that checklists are an output of the Quality Planning process but are a tool and technique of the Risk Identification process, and are an input to the Quality Control process. Many times, outputs of one process become inputs to another, so that isn't unusual. However, I believe this is the only case where an input/output is also a tool and technique in another process.

Inputs to Other Processes

Quality Planning finishes up its outputs with inputs to other processes. In the process of identifying Quality Planning measurements and controls, you might be alerted to other Planning processes that need to be tweaked in order to comply with the new information you've discovered.

Quality is an important planning and measuring tool. You'll revisit quality during the Execution and Controlling processes, where you get into quality measurements and controls. But for now, let's move on to defining project risks.

 Real World Scenario

Candy Works

Juliette Walters is a contract project manager for Candy Works. They've introduced a new line of hard candy drops in various exotic flavors: caffe latte, hot buttered popcorn, and jalapeño spice, just to name a few.

Juliette is writing the quality management plan for this project. After interviewing stakeholders and key team members, she's found several quality factors of importance to the organization. Quality will be measured by

Candy size   Each piece should measure 3 mm.

Appearance   No visible cracks or breaks should appear in the candy.

Flavor   Flavor must be distinguishable when taste tested.

Number produced   9000 pieces per week is the production target. The current machine has been benchmarked at 9200 candies per week.

Intensity of color   There should be no opaqueness in the darker colors.

Wrappers   Properly fitting wrappers cover the candies, folding over twice in back, and twisted on each side. There is a different wrapper for each flavor of candy, which must be matched exactly.

The candy is cooked and then pulled into a long cylinder shape roughly 6 feet long and 2 feet in diameter. This cylinder is fed into the machine that molds and cuts the candy into drops. The cylinders vary a little in size, because they're hand-stretched by expert candy makers prior to feeding them into the drop maker machine. As a result, the end of one flavor batch—the caffe latte flavor—and the beginning of the next batch—the hot buttered popcorn flavor—merge. This means the drops that fall into the collection bins are intermingled during the last run of the first flavor batch. In other words, the last bin of the caffe latte flavor run has some hot buttered popcorn drops mixed in. And, there isn't a way to separate the drops once they've hit the bin. From here, the drops go on to the candy-wrapping machine, where brightly colored wrappers are matched to the candy flavor. According to the quality plan, hot buttered popcorn drops cannot be wrapped as caffe latte drops. Juliette ponders what to do.

As she tosses and turns that night thinking about the problem, it occurs to her to present this problem as an opportunity to the company rather than as a problem. In order to keep production in the 9000 candies per week category, the machines can't be stopped every time a new batch is introduced. So Juliette comes up with the idea to wrap candies from the intermixed bins with wrappers that say "Mystery Flavor." This way, production keeps pace with the plan, and the wrapper/flavor quality problem is mitigated.

Risk Planning

Every one of us takes risks on a daily basis. Just getting out of bed in the morning is a risk. You might stub your toe in the dark on the way to the light switch or trip over the dog and break a leg. These things don't usually happen, but the possibility exists. The same is true for your project. Risk exists on all projects, and the potential that a particular risk will occur depends on the nature of the risk.

Risk, like much of the information gathered during other Planning processes, changes as the project progresses and should be monitored throughout the project. As you get close to a risk event, that's the time to reassess your original assumptions about the risk and your plans to deal with the risk and to make any adjustments as required.

Not all risks are bad. Risks can present opportunities as well as threats to the project. All risks have causes, and if the risk event occurs during the project, there are consequences as a result of that risk. Those consequences will likely impact one or more of the triple constraints, and you'll need to know if the consequences have positive or negative impacts.

The Risk Management knowledge area encompasses several risk processes. We'll examine most of them in this chapter. The idea behind this knowledge area is that you identify all the risks and then evaluate and quantify the risks to come up with a plan to deal with or avert them. The first step is the Risk Management Planning process. Here, you determine the approach you'll use for risk management activities and document your plans for them in a risk management plan. Let's look at that process now.

Risk Management Planning

Risks come about for many reasons. Some are internal to the project, and some are external. The project environment, the planning process, the project management process, inadequate resources, and so on can all contribute to risk. Some risks you'll know about in advance and plan for during this process; others will occur unannounced during the project. The *Risk Management Planning* process determines how you'll plan for risks on your project.

Exam Spotlight

A Guide to the PMBOK states on page 129 that the Risk Management Planning process is an important foundation for all the risk processes that follow "...to ensure that the level, type, and visibility of risk management are commensurate with both the risk and importance of the project to the organization." Understand this concept for the exam.

Risks associated with the project generally concern the project objectives, which in turn impact time, costs, or quality, or any combination of the three. As you might have guessed, the project charter is the first input to this process, since it spells out your project objectives. The other inputs to this process include

- Organization's risk management policies
- Defined roles and responsibilities
- Stakeholder risk tolerances
- Template for the organization's risk management plan
- WBS

Most of these inputs are self-explanatory, so we won't spend a great deal of time on them. Organization's risk management policies are any policies your organization might have that you should consider when planning for risks. Defined roles and responsibilities outline what authority levels the stakeholders and/or project manager have for making decisions regarding risk planning. (Do consider that these decisions can affect other planning processes.) Your organization may have pre-existing templates that you can use during this process. These templates should be updated on a regular basis.

One consideration to take into account when assessing risk is risk tolerance. Stakeholder risk tolerance is one of the inputs in the Risk Management Planning process. Organizations and stakeholders, as well as individuals, all have different tolerances for risk. One organization might believe that the risk of a potential 17 percent cost overrun is high, while another might think it's low. However, either one of these organizations may decide to accept the risk if they believe it's in balance with the potential rewards. It's important for the project manager to understand the tolerance level the organization and the stakeholders have for risk before evaluating and ranking risk.

There is only one tool and technique of this process: planning meetings. Obviously, what happens here is meetings are held with project team members, stakeholders, functional managers, and others who may have involvement in the risk management process to contribute to the risk management plan.

Risk Management Plan

The purpose of the Risk Management Planning process is to create a *risk management plan*, which describes how you will define, monitor, and control risks throughout the project. The risk management plan becomes part of the project plan at the conclusion of the Planning process. The risk management plan is the only output of this process. The risk management plan details how risk management processes (including Risk Identification, Qualitative Risk Analysis, Quantitative Risk Analysis, Risk Response Planning, and Risk Monitoring and Control) will be implemented, monitored, and controlled throughout the life of the project. It details how you will manage risks but does not attempt to define responses to individual risks. The risk response plan describes in detail the individual risk responses. We'll talk about that a little later in this chapter.

According to *A Guide to the PMBOK*, the risk management plan might include the following elements:

- Methodology
- Roles and responsibilities
- Budgeting
- Timing
- Scoring and interpretation
- Thresholds
- Reporting formats
- Tracking

Methodology is a description of the methodology you'll use to perform risk management. Roles and responsibilities describe the team of people who are responsible for managing the identified risks and their responses. These teams might not be the same as the project team. Risk analysis should be unbiased, which may not be possible when project team members are involved.

The budget for risk management is included in the plan as well. Qualitative and quantitative scoring interpretation methods should be documented and describe the type and timing of the analysis you'll use in risk planning. Thresholds for risk describe the risk tolerance levels of the organization and the stakeholders. It describes the threshold criteria for risk that will require action and defines who will take the action and in what manner. Thresholds are also used to measure the effectiveness of the project team at executing risk response plans. Reporting formats should describe the content of the risk response plan and the format of this document. (We'll talk more about the risk response plan later in this chapter.) Reporting formats also detail how risk management information will be maintained, updated, and reported to project participants.

Tracking includes a description of how you'll document the history of the risk activities for the current project and how the risk processes will be audited. You can reference this information when you're performing risk planning processes later in the current project or on future projects. This information is also helpful for lessons learned, which we'll cover in Chapter 11, "Closing Out the Project."

 It's very important to spend time developing the risk management plan, because it's an input to every other risk-planning process. It is also an input to the Risk Monitoring and Control process, which we'll cover in Chapter 10, "Controlling Change."

Identifying Potential Risk

The *Risk Identification* process involves identifying all the risks that might impact the project, documenting them, and documenting their characteristics. Risk Identification is an iterative process that continually builds on itself. You can include project team members, stakeholders, subject matter experts, users, and anyone else who you think may help in the Risk Identification process. Perhaps in the first round of Risk Identification, you include just the project team, and then you bring in the stakeholders or risk management team to further flesh out risks during the second round of identification.

Risks may or may not adversely affect the project. Some risks have positive consequences, while others have negative consequences. However, all risk events and their consequences should be identified. Here's a partial list to get you thinking about where risk may be found:

- Budgets/funding
- Schedules
- Scope or requirements changes
- Project plan
- Project management processes
- Technical issues
- Personnel issues
- Hardware
- Contracts
- Political concerns
- Business risk
- Legal risk
- Environmental risk

This is by no means an exhaustive list. Realize that risk is lurking almost anywhere on your project. It's your job to discover all the possible risks using the tools and techniques of this process and to document these risks.

Risk Identification Inputs

The inputs to the Risk Identification process include:

- The risk management plan
- Project Planning outputs
- Risk categories
- Historical information

We've already discussed the risk management plan and several of the "project planning outputs." They include the project charter, the WBS, your cost and time (or schedule) estimates, assumptions and constraints, and the procurement plan. We'll discuss the procurement plan later in this chapter. This section focuses on the risk categories and historical information.

Risk Categories

The risk categories input, according to *A Guide to the PMBOK*, states that project risks should be identified and organized into risk categories. These categories may include:

- Technical, quality, or performance risks
- Project management risks
- Organizational risks
- External risks

Risk categories may reflect the type of industry or application area in which the project exists. For example, Information Technology projects will likely have many risks that fall into the technical category whereas construction projects may be more subject to risks that fall into the external risks category. A description of each of the categories is shown next.

Technical/quality/performance risks   Technical, quality, or performance risks include risks associated with unproven technology, complex technology, or changes to technology anticipated during the course of the project. Performance risks may include unrealistic performance goals. Perhaps one of the project deliverables concerns a component manufactured to specific performance standards that have never been achieved. That's a performance risk.

Project management risks   The project management risk category includes improper schedule and resource planning, poor project planning, and improper or poor project management disciplines.

Organizational risks   The organizational risk category can include resource conflicts due to multiple projects occurring at the same time in the organization; scope, time, and cost objectives that are unrealistic given the organization's resources or structure; and lack of funding for the project or diverting funds from this project to other projects.

External risks   The external risk category includes those things external to the project such as new laws or regulations, labor issues, weather, changes in ownership, and foreign policy for projects performed in other countries. Catastrophic risks—known as *force majeure*—are usually outside the scope of risk management planning and instead require disaster recovery techniques. Force majeure includes events like earthquakes, meteorites, volcanoes, floods, civil unrest, terrorism, and so on.

Historical Information

The historical information input refers to previous project experiences via the project files and/or published information like commercial databases or academic research that might exist for your application areas. Project team knowledge is another form of historical information.

Tools and Techniques Used to Identify Risk

The Risk Identification process is undertaken using five tools and techniques:

- Documentation reviews
- Information-gathering techniques
- Checklists
- Assumptions analysis
- Diagramming techniques

Documentation reviews involve reviewing project plans, assumptions, and historical information from a total project perspective as well as at the individual deliverables or activities level. This review helps the project team identify risks associated with the project objectives. Let's look at the remaining tools and techniques of this process starting with information gathering.

Information Gathering

Information gathering encompasses several techniques, including brainstorming, the Delphi technique, interviewing, and strength and weakness analysis. Let's take a quick look at each of these techniques.

Brainstorming

Brainstorming is probably the most often used technique of Risk Identification. You've probably used this technique many times for many purposes. Brainstorming involves getting subject matter experts, team members, risk management team members, and anyone else who might benefit the process in a room and asking them to start identifying possible risk events. The trick here is that one person's idea might spawn another idea, and so on, so that by the end of the session you've identified all the possible risks.

Delphi Technique

The *Delphi technique* is a lot like brainstorming, only the people participating in the meeting don't necessarily know each other. In fact, the people participating in this technique don't all have to be located in the same place and can participate anonymously. You can use e-mail to facilitate the Delphi technique very easily.

What you do is assemble your experts, both from inside and outside the company, and ask them via a questionnaire to identify potential risks. They in turn send their responses back to you (or to the facilitator of this process). All the responses are organized by content and sent back to the Delphi members for further input, additions, or comments. The participants then send their comments back one more time, and a final list of risks is compiled by the facilitator.

The Delphi technique is a great tool that allows consensus to be reached very quickly. It also helps prevent one person from unduly influencing the others in the group and thus prevents bias in the outcome because the participants are usually anonymous and don't necessarily know how others in the group responded.

Nominal Group Technique

Another technique that is similar to the Delphi technique is the *nominal group technique*. It isn't a named tool and technique of this process but is a technique you might find useful and that you may find on the exam.

This technique requires the participants to be together in the same room. Each participant has paper and pencil in front of them, and they are asked to write down what risks they think the project faces. Sticky-backed notes are a good way to do this. Each piece of paper should contain only one risk. The papers are given to the facilitator, who sticks them up to the wall or a white board. The panel is then asked to review all the risks posted on the board; rank them and prioritize them, in writing; and submit the ranking to the facilitator. Once this is done, you should have a complete list of risks.

Interviewing

Interviews are question-and-answer sessions held with others, including other project managers, subject matter experts, stakeholders, customers, the management team, project team members, and users. These folks provide you with possible risks based on their past experiences with similar projects.

This technique involves interviewing those folks with previous experience on projects similar to yours, or those with specialized knowledge or industry expertise. Ask them to tell you about any risks that they've experienced or that they think may happen on your project. Show them the WBS and your list of assumptions to help get them started thinking in the right direction.

Strengths, Weaknesses, Opportunities, and Threats (SWOT)

Strengths, weaknesses, opportunities, and threats (also known as SWOT analysis) examines each of these viewpoints regarding the project itself, project management processes, resources, the organization, and so on, and helps broaden your perspective of where to look for risks.

Exam Spotlight

Understand the difference between the various information-gathering techniques for the exam.

Checklists

Checklists used during Risk Identification are usually developed based on historical information and previous project team experience. If you typically work on projects that are similar in nature, begin to compile a list of risks. You can then convert this to a checklist that will allow you to identify risks on future projects quickly and easily. However, don't rely solely on checklists for Risk Identification because you might miss important risks.

Assumptions Analysis

Assumptions analysis is a matter of validating the assumptions you identified and documented during the course of the project Planning processes. Assumptions should be accurate, complete, and consistent. Examine all your assumptions for these qualities. Assumptions are also used as a jumping-off point to further identify risks.

Diagramming Techniques

Cause-and-effect diagrams and system or process flowcharts are usable in the Risk Identification process as well as in the Quality Planning process. We discussed these diagramming techniques earlier in this chapter.

A third diagramming technique used during Risk Identification is called *influence diagrams*. According to *A Guide to the PMBOK*, influence diagrams typically show the casual influences among project variables, the timing or time order of events, and the relationships among other project variables and their outcomes.

Each of these techniques provides a way for you to help identify project risks. It's important that you identify all the risks early on. The better job you do of identifying the project's risks at the Planning stage, the better your risk response plan will look. Risk Identification is not an area of project Planning that you should skip.

Risk Identification Outputs

The outputs of the Risk Identification process include risks, triggers, and inputs to other processes. This process has culminated in the identification of project risks. While *A Guide to the PMBOK* doesn't specifically mention it in this process, you should understand that all risks should be documented, tracked, reviewed, and managed throughout the project.

Risks

Risks are all the potential events and their subsequent consequences that could occur, as discussed in this section. Once you've identified all the potential risks, you might want to log them in a risk database or tracking system to organize them and keep a close eye on their status. This can easily be done in spreadsheet format or whatever means you choose. List the risks and assign each risk a tracking number. This gives you a means to track the risks, their occurrence, and the responses implemented. We'll talk more about risk databases in the Risk Monitoring and Control process in Chapter 10.

Triggers

If you've ever suffered from a hay fever attack, you can't mistake the itchy, runny nose and scratchy throat that can come on suddenly and send you into a sneezing frenzy. Risk symptoms, also known as *triggers*, work the same way. Be on the alert for symptoms that might signal a risk event is about to occur.

For example, if you're planning an outdoor gathering and rain clouds start rolling in from the north on the morning of the activity, you probably have a risk event waiting to happen. A key team member hinting about job hunting is a warning sign that they may be thinking of leaving, which in turn can cause schedule delays, increased costs, etc. This is another example of a trigger.

Inputs to Other Processes

Inputs to other processes may occur as a result of the risks you've identified and can include schedule updates, modifications to the WBS, cost revisions, and other process updates.

Qualitative Risk Analysis

Qualitative Risk Analysis involves determining what consequences the identified risks will have on the project objectives and the probability they'll occur. It also puts the risks in priority order according to their effect on the project objectives.

Qualitative Risk Analysis should be performed throughout the project, and this process should guide you in developing a risk response plan. Using Qualitative Risk Analysis methods allows you to determine the probability a risk will occur and to evaluate its consequences. According to *A Guide to the PMBOK*, this process helps correct biases in the project plan.

Qualitative Inputs

Qualitative Risk Analysis has seven inputs:

- Risk management plan
- Identified risks
- Project status
- Project type
- Data precision
- Scales of probability and impact
- Assumptions

You should already have an understanding of the risk management plan, identified risks, and assumptions inputs. We'll briefly cover the remaining four in this section.

Project status   Project status refers to examining the life cycle phase the project is currently in. As you progress through the project, changes occur and new risks may come to light, or previously identified risks may take on new consequences.

Project type   Project type refers to the complexity of the project and whether you and the team have had experience with projects of this kind. If you're working on a project that is similar in size and scope to others you've worked on, you'll have a much better understanding of the probability of the occurrence of risk events and their consequences. However, if you're working on a new project that's particularly complex or you're using new, bleeding edge technology, you will have little information on the probability of risk events. Therefore, this project type will have more uncertainty than a project similar to one you've worked on before.

Data precision   Data precision is concerned with the reliability of the data used to identify and describe risks and the level of understanding regarding their consequences.

Scales of probability and impact   Scales of probability and impact are used to determine and measure risk probability and the effect of the risk on the project objectives. These scales are predetermined either by the organization or by the project team prior to performing the Qualitative Risk Analysis process. It makes more sense to discuss these scales in the tools and techniques section, because that's where you're going to use them to assign risk ratings. I'll remind you when we get there that these scales are the inputs to this process. Let's get to the tools and techniques discussion next.

Risk Probability Analysis

The Qualitative Risk Analysis tools and techniques are primarily concerned with discovering the probability of a risk event and determining the impact (or consequences) the risk will have if it does occur. The outputs of this process will prioritize the risks you've scored here using these tools and techniques to determine which ones should receive further Risk Response Planning. All of the information you gather regarding risks and probability needs to be as accurate as possible. It's also important that you gather unbiased information so that you don't unintentionally overlook risks with great potential or consequences.

The purpose of this process is to determine risk event probability and risk impact. You'll use the tools and techniques of this process to establish risk scores, which is a way of categorizing the probability and risk impact. The tools and techniques of the Qualitative Risk Analysis process include:

- Risk probability and impact
- Probability/impact risk rating matrix
- Project assumptions testing
- Data precision ranking

Risk Probability and Impact

This tool and technique assigns probability to the risk events you've identified and determines the effect their consequences have on the project objectives. Analyzing risks in this way allows you to determine which risks require the most aggressive management.

During Qualitative Risk Analysis, you simply assign a high, medium, or low value—or some similar combination—to the risk. For example, maybe you've identified the departure of a key team member as a potential risk for the project. Depending on how familiar you are with the situation, you may know that this probability is very likely and the consequences would have significant impact. If so, assign a high probability to this risk. If the key team member is happy with the company and wouldn't dream of leaving save for extreme circumstances, assign this risk a low probability.

These assignments include the probability of the risk occurring and the severity of the impact should it occur. The next technique—probability/impact risk rating matrix—deals with this issue more fully.

Probability/Impact Risk Rating Matrix

A probability/impact (PI) matrix assigns an overall risk rating classification to each of the project's identified risks. This classification is usually expressed as high, medium, or low. According to *A Guide to the PMBOK*, high risks are considered a red condition, medium risks are considered a yellow condition, and low risks are considered a green condition. This type of ranking is known as an *ordinal scale* because the values are rank ordered from high to low. (In practice, ordinal values may also include ranking by position. In other words, the risks are listed in rank order as the first, the second, the third, and so on.)

The PI matrix is determined by multiplying two values: the probability value times the risk impact value. The probability value comes from the probability scale, and the risk impact value comes from the risk impact scale. Both of these scales are considered the "scales of probability and impact" input talked about earlier in this section.

Assessing probability and risk impact is typically accomplished using expert judgment and interviewing techniques. In addition, some of the tools and techniques outlined in the Risk Identification process like brainstorming, interviewing, and the Delphi technique can be used during this process to determine probability and impact.

We'll look at the probability and risk impact scales in more detail and then pull it all together with a final discussion of the PI matrix values.

Probability Scale

Probability is the likelihood that an event will occur. The classic example is flipping a coin. There is a .50 probability of getting heads and a .50 probability of getting tails on the flip. One thing to note is that the probability that an event will occur plus the probability that the event will not occur always equals 1.0. In this coin-flipping example, there is a .50 chance that you'll get heads on the flip. There is also, therefore, a .50 chance you will not get heads on the flip. The two responses added together equal 1.0. *Probability scales* are always expressed as a number between 0.0—which means there is no probability of the event occurring—and 1.0—which means there is 100 percent certainty the risk will occur.

Determining risk probability can be difficult, because it's most commonly accomplished using expert judgment. In non-PMP terms, this means you're guessing (or asking other experts to guess) at the probability a risk event will occur. Granted, you're basing your guess on past experiences with similar projects or risk events, but no two risk events (or projects) are ever the same. It's best to fully develop the criteria for determining probability and get as many experts involved as you can. Carefully weigh their responses to come up with the best probability scale and probability values possible. If you choose, you could develop a probability matrix similar to the risk impact matrix discussed in the next section to assist you and the team in determining probability.

Risk Impact Scales

The severity of the risk impact, called an *impact scale*, is assigned an ordinal value or a *cardinal scale* value. Cardinal scales or values are actual numeric values assigned to the risk. Cardinal scales are expressed as values between 0.0 and 1.0 and may be stated in equal or unequal increments.

The idea behind both probability scales and impact scales is to develop predefined measurements that describe what value to place on a risk event. (The predefined criteria will determine what cardinal value to assign to the impact that you'll plug into the probability/impact matrix shortly.) Your organization may already have risk impacts and probability scales developed. If not, determine the criteria for them and develop your own risk impact ratings early on in the project.

Now let's look at an example matrix. You have identified a risk event that could impact project costs, and your experts believe costs could increase by as much as nine percent. According to the risk impact rating matrix in Table 6.1, this risk carries a medium impact, with a value of 0.40. Hold onto that number, because you're going to plug it into the PI matrix—along with the probability value—to determine an overall risk value next.

TABLE 6.1   Risk Impacts Rating Matrix

Objectives	Low-Low	Low	Medium	High	High-High
	0.05	0.20	0.40	0.60	0.80
Cost	No significant impact	Less than 6% increase	7–12% increase	13–18% increase	More than 18% increase
Time	No significant impact	Less than 6% increase	7–12% increase	13–18% increase	More than 18% increase
Quality	No significant impact	Few components impacted	Significant impact requiring customer approval to proceed	Unacceptable quality	Product not usable

Determining the Probability/Impact Matrix Values

The purpose of the PI matrix is to assign an overall risk rating of high, medium, or low to each risk. This is derived by multiplying the probability value by the risk impact value, as stated earlier.

Remember that the probability value and risk impact value are derived from the input to this process called scales of probability and impact.

Going back to the previous example, your team has identified a risk event that could increase costs to your project. The team has determined that there is a 0.2 probability of this risk event occurring, and the risk impact matrix shows a 0.4 impact should the event occur. If you multiply the probability by the impact, you come up with an overall risk score of 0.08. The formula looks like this:

0.2 probability × 0.4 impact = 0.08 overall risk score

Now you need to determine whether 0.08 is a high, medium, or low rating. Table 6.2 shows a sample PI matrix. The values for this matrix and the overall ratings are determined prior to the start of this process, usually by the same team of experts who are developing the scales of probability and impact.

TABLE 6.2   Sample PI Matrix

Probability	Risk Scores*				
.8	.04	.16	*.32*	*.48*	*.64*
.6	.03	.12	.24	*.36*	*.48*
.4	.02	.08	.16	.24	*.32*
.2	.01	.04	.08	.12	.16

*The legend for the PI matrix is as follows: no formatting = low assignment; bold = medium assignment; bold italics = high assignment.

First look at the probability column. Your risk event has a probability of .2. Now follow that row until you find the risk score of .08. According to your PI matrix values, a score of 0.08 for a probability value of 0.2 falls in the low threshold, so this risk is assigned a low value.

The values assigned to the risks determine how Risk Response Planning is carried out for the risks later during the risk-planning processes. Obviously, risks with high probability and high impact are going to need further analysis and formal responses. Keep in mind that *A Guide to the PMBOK* states that the PI matrix can be developed using cardinal or ordinal scales.

A further example of the PI risk rating matrix is shown in the "Screen Scrapers, Inc." sidebar later in this section.

Project Assumptions Testing

The important thing to note about the project assumptions testing tool and technique is that all assumptions are tested against two facts, according to *A Guide to the PMBOK*:

- The strength of the assumption or the validity of the assumption
- The consequences that may impact the project if the assumption turns out to be false

All assumptions that are false should be evaluated and scored just like the risks you identified and scored earlier in this section.

Data Precision Ranking

Data precision ranking involves determining the usefulness of the data gathered to evaluate risk. The data must be unbiased and accurate. According to *A Guide to the PMBOK*, data precision ranking looks at:

- The quality of the data used
- The availability of data regarding the risks
- How well the risk is understood
- The reliability and integrity of the data

 Real World Scenario

Screen Scrapers, Inc.

Screen Scrapers is a software-manufacturing company that produces a software product that looks at your mainframe screens, commonly called *green screens*, and converts them to browser-based screens. The browser-based screens look like any other Windows-compatible screens with buttons, scroll bars, and drop-down lists.

Screen Scrapers devised this product for companies that use mainframe programs to update and store data, because many of the entry-level workers beginning their careers today are not familiar with green screens. They're cumbersome and difficult to learn, and no consistency exists from screen to screen or program to program. An F5 key in one program might mean go back one page, while an F5 key in another program might mean clear the screen. New users are easily confused, make a lot of mistakes, and have to write tablets full of notes on how to navigate all the screens.

Your company has purchased the Screen Scraper product and has appointed you the project manager over the installation. There are lots of issues to address on this project, and you've made great headway. You're now at the risk identification and quantification stage. You decide to use the Delphi technique to assist you in identifying risk and assigning probability and impact rankings. There are some experts available in your company who can serve on the Delphi panel, as well as some folks in industry organizations you belong to outside the company.

You assemble the group, and set up a summary of the project and send it out via e-mail, requesting responses to your questions about risk. After the first pass, you compile the list of risks as follows (this list is an example and isn't exhaustive as your list will be project-specific):

- Vendor viability—will they stay in business?
- Vendor responsiveness with problems after implementation

- Software compatibility risks with existing systems

- Hardware compatibility risk

- Connection to the mainframe risk

- Training IT staff members to maintain the product

You send this list back to the Delphi members and ask them to assign a probability of high-high, high, medium, low, or low-low and an impact level of 0.0–1.0 to each risk. The Delphi members assign probability based on a probability scale designed by the risk management team.

The values of the probability scale are as follows:

- High-high = 0.8

- High = 0.6

- Medium = 0.4

- Low = 0.2

- Low-low = 0.05

The PI matrix index shows the probability assignment thresholds listed in Table 6.3 (following this sidebar). The table is populated by multiplying the risk event probability times the impact values of 0.05, 0.2, 0.4, 0.6, and 0.8. The table is read based on the probability of the risk occurring. For example, if the risk event has a 0.8 probability of occurring and the risk score is 0.16, the risk would receive an overall medium rating.

The completed risk list and their rankings that you received from the Delphi members looks like Table 6.4 (following this sidebar).

Based on the PI matrix thresholds, the project risks are assigned the following overall probabilities:

- Vendor viability = high

- Vendor responsiveness = low

- Software compatibility = medium

- Hardware compatibility = medium

- Mainframe connection = high

- Training = low

TABLE 6.3   PI Matrix for Screen Scrapers, Inc.

Probability	Risk Scores*				
.8	**.04**	**.16**	*.32*	**.48**	*.64*
.6	**.03**	**.12**	.24	*.36*	*.48*
.4	.02	**.08**	.16	.24	*.32*
.2	.01	.04	.08	.12	.16

*The legend for the PI matrix is as follows: no formatting = low assignment; **bold** = medium assignment; ***bold italics*** = high assignment.

TABLE 6.4   Risk Impacts Rating Matrix for Screen Scrapers, Inc.

Risk	Probability	Impact	Risk Scores
Vendor viability	.4	.8	.32
Vendor responsiveness	.2	.5	.10
Software compatibility	.4	.4	.16
Hardware compatibility	.4	.3	.12
Mainframe connection	.8	.8	.64
Training	.2	.3	.06

*The legend for the PI matrix is as follows: no formatting = low assignment; bold = medium assignment; bold italics = high assignment.

Risk Ranking

The goal of the Qualitative Risk Analysis process is to rank the risks and determine which ones need further analysis and eventually, risk response plans. The outputs of this process include:

- Overall risk ranking for the project
- List of prioritized risks
- List of risks for additional analysis and management
- Trends in Qualitative Risk Analysis results

Overall Risk Ranking for the Project

This output assigns an overall risk ranking for the project by comparing the list of risks and their overall rankings to other similar projects. (Remember that you determined the overall risk ratings by using the PI matrix.) You can use the overall risk scores of the current project as a gauge to determine if it has more or less risk than projects of similar size and scope. Overall risk score comparisons are also used to help determine if further analysis should be performed regarding the project and to make go or no-go decisions about the project or project phase. For example, suppose the project you're considering has an overall risk score that's significantly higher than a previous project of a similar nature. You'll want to determine why the risk is higher for this project, and you should also consider doing further benefit/cost analysis and revisiting some of the project justification techniques to determine if the project is worth pursuing considering its high risk rating. A relatively high risk score usually indicates that you need to assign more resources to the high-risk areas. It can also indicate that the project should be canceled.

List of Prioritized Risks

As the title implies, the risks you've identified and scored during this process are now listed in priority order. Priority is determined using the risk scores and other criteria, which might include the timing of the risk event (Is a risk response needed immediately or in the future?), the WBS level impacted, and so on. According to *A Guide to the PMBOK*, risks that affect quality, schedule, cost, or functionality can be evaluated independently with their own individual rating scales.

List of Risks for Additional Analysis and Management

This output examines the risks and their scores to determine which ones should receive further analysis, including Quantitative Risk Analysis. Those risks with scores of high, for example, probably need further review and action by the risk management team.

Quantifying Risk

Quantitative Risk Analysis evaluates the impacts of risk and quantifies the risk exposure of the project by assigning numeric probabilities to each risk and their impacts on project objectives. This is accomplished using techniques like Monte Carlo analysis and decision analysis. To paraphrase *A Guide to the PMBOK*, page 137, the purpose of this process is to perform the following:

- Determine the probability of achieving the project objectives.
- Quantify risk exposure for the project and determine the size of cost and schedule contingency reserves.
- Identify risks that need the most attention by quantifying their contribution to overall project risk.
- Identify realistic and achievable schedule, cost, or scope targets.

Quantitative Risk Analysis—like Qualitative Risk Analysis—examines each risk and its potential impact on the project objectives. You may choose to use both of these processes to assess risk or only one of them, depending on the complexity of the project and the organizational policy regarding risk planning. If you use both the qualitative and quantitative processes, the Qualitative Risk Analysis process must precede the Quantitative Risk Analysis process.

We have already covered all the inputs to the Quantitative Risk Analysis process in previous sections or chapters. They are as follows:

- Risk management plan
- Identified risks
- List of prioritized risks
- List of risks for additional analysis and management
- Historical information
- Expert judgment
- Other planning outputs

We'll take a look at the tools and techniques of this process next, which include:

- Interviewing
- Sensitivity analysis
- Decision tree analysis
- Simulation

Interviewing

This technique is like the interviewing technique talked about in Risk Identification. Project team members, stakeholders, and subject matter experts are prime candidates for risk interviews. Ask them about their experiences on past projects and about working with the types of technology or processes you'll use during this project.

Make certain you document how the interviewees decided upon the risk ranges, the criteria they used to place risks in certain categories, and the results of the interview. This will help you later in developing risk responses as well.

Exam Spotlight

For the exam, you should know that there are several types of probability distributions that are useful in determining and displaying risk information. The type of distribution you use determines the type of information you should gather during the interviewing process.

It's beyond the scope of this book to delve into probability distributions and calculations, so I'll point out a few things you should remember for the exam regarding them.

Continuous probability distributions are commonly used in Quantitative Risk Analysis. According to *A Guide to the PMBOK*, continuous probability distributions include normal and log normal distributions, triangular, beta, and uniform types. Distributions are graphically displayed and represent both the probability and the consequences of the risk to the project.

Also remember that triangular distributions use estimates based on pessimistic, most likely, and optimistic values. This means that during your interviews, you'll gather three pieces of information from your experts: the least likely (optimistic) estimate, the most likely estimate, and the high (pessimistic) estimate. Then you'll use these to quantify risk for each WBS element. (There is more information on this estimating technique in Chapter 7.)

Normal and log normal distributions use mean and standard deviations to quantify risk, which also require gathering the optimistic, most likely, and pessimistic estimates.

Sensitivity Analysis

Sensitivity analysis is a quantitative method of analyzing the potential impact of risk events on the project and determining which risk event (or events) has the greatest potential for impact. Sensitivity analysis can also be used to determine stakeholder risk tolerance levels.

Decision Tree Analysis

Unfortunately, this isn't a tree outside your office door that produces "Yes" and "No" leaves that you can pick to help you make a decision. Decision trees are diagrams that show the sequence of interrelated decisions and the expected results of choosing one alternative over the other. Typically, more than one choice or option is available when you're faced with a decision, or, in this case, potential outcomes from a risk event. The available choices are depicted in a tree form starting at the left with the risk decision and branching out to the right with possible outcomes. Decision trees are usually used for risk events associated with time or cost.

Figure 6.2 shows a sample decision tree using expected value (EV) as one of its inputs.

FIGURE 6.2   Decision tree

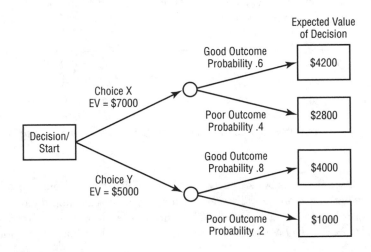

Expected value is the anticipated impact of the decision. This example shows expected value in dollars. The expected value of the decision is a result of the probability of the risk event multiplied by the impact. Impact is shown in dollars in this example. The squares represent decisions to be made, and the circles represent the points where risk events may occur.

The decision with an expected value of $4200 is the correct decision to make, as the resulting outcome has the greatest value.

Simulation

Monte Carlo Analysis is a simulation technique that helps you quantify risks associated with the project as a whole. The identified risks and their potential impacts to the project objectives are examined from the perspective of the whole project. Monte Carlo Analysis is used to determine potential outcomes by simulating the project over and over multiple times. Monte Carlo Analysis can also be used during the Schedule Development process.

Simulation techniques are used to predict schedule or cost risks. Schedule simulations are usually performed using the precedence diagramming method, while cost simulation typically uses the WBS as its basis.

Quantitative Risk Analysis Outputs

The outputs of the Quantitative Risk Analysis process are as follows:

Prioritized lists of quantified risks   The prioritized list in this process is similar to the list produced during the Qualitative Risk Analysis process. The list of risks includes those that present the greatest risk or threat to the project and their impacts. It also lists those risks with the greatest opportunities to the project.

Project risks include both threats and opportunities to the project's objectives, and their consequences can have either positive or negative effects.

Probabilistic analysis of the project   Probabilistic analysis of the project is the forecasted results of the project schedule and costs as a result of the outcomes of risk analysis. These results include projected completion dates and costs, along with a confidence level associated with each. Confidence levels describe the level of confidence placed on the result. For example, suppose the projected schedule completion date is July 12 and the confidence level is .85. This says that you believe the project will finish on or before July 12 and that you have an 85 percent level of confidence that this date is accurate.

Probability of achieving the cost and time objectives   Using the tools and techniques of Quantitative Risk Analysis allows you to assign a probability of achieving the cost and time objectives of the project. This output documents those probabilities and as such, requires a thorough understanding of the current project objectives and knowledge of the risks.

Trends in Quantitative Risk Analysis results Trends in Quantitative Risk Analysis will likely appear as you repeat the risk analysis processes. This information is useful as you progress, making those risks with the greatest threat to the project more evident, which allows you the opportunity to perform further analysis or go on to develop risk response plans.

Exam Spotlight

Understand the differences between the Qualitative Risk Analysis and Quantitative Risk Analysis processes for the exam.

Risk Response Planning

Risk Response Planning is a process of deciding what actions to take to reduce threats and take advantage of the opportunities discovered during the risk analysis processes. This process also includes assigning departments or individual staff members the responsibility of carrying out the risk response plans you'll outline in this process. The more effective your risk response plans are, the better your chances for a successful project; well developed and well-written risk response plans will decrease overall project risk.

Generally, you'll want to develop risk response plans for those risks with a combination of high probability of occurrence and significant impact to the project. Developing risk response plans for risks of low severity or insignificant impact is not efficient.

Several strategies are used in this process to reduce or control risk. It's important that you choose the right strategy for each risk, so that the risk and its impacts are dealt with effectively. After deciding on which strategy to use, you'll develop an action plan to put this strategy into play should the risk event occur. You may also choose to designate a secondary or backup strategy.

Exam Spotlight

The severity of the risk will dictate the level of risk response planning that should be done. For example, a risk with low severity wouldn't warrant the time it takes to develop a detailed risk response plan. Risk responses should be cost effective—if the cost of the response is more than the consequences of the risk, you might want to examine a different risk response. Risk responses should also be timely, agreed to by all the project stakeholders, and assigned to an individual who is responsible for monitoring and carrying out the risk response plan if needed.

There are eleven inputs to this process, most of which we've covered elsewhere or are fairly straightforward. They are:

- Risk management plan
- List of prioritized risks
- Risk ranking of the project
- Prioritized list of quantified risks
- Probabilistic analysis of the project
- Probability of achieving the cost and time objectives
- List of potential responses
- Risk thresholds
- Risk owners
- Common risk causes
- Trends in qualitative and quantitative risk analysis results

The tools and techniques of this process include the following strategies:

- Avoidance
- Transference
- Mitigation
- Acceptance

Let's look at each of these tools and techniques in detail.

Avoidance

Risk *avoidance* involves avoiding the risk altogether, eliminating the cause of the risk event, or changing the project plan to protect the project objectives from the risk event. Let's say you're going to take a car trip from your home to a point 800 miles away. You know—because your friends who just took the same trip told you—that there is a long stretch of construction on one of the highways you're planning on using. To avoid the risk of delay, you plan the trip around the construction work and use another highway for that stretch of driving. In this way, you change your plans, avoid the risk of getting held up in construction traffic, and arrive at your destination on time.

With risk avoidance, you essentially eradicate the risk by eliminating its cause. Here's another example: Suppose your project was kicked off without adequate scope definition and requirements gathering. You run a high probability of experiencing scope creep—ever-changing requirements—as the project progresses, thus impacting the project schedule. You can avoid this risk by adequately documenting the project scope and requirements during the Planning process and taking steps to monitor and control changes to scope so it doesn't get out of hand.

Risks that occur early in the project might easily be avoided by improving communications, refining requirements, assigning additional resources to project activities, refining the project scope to avoid risk events, and so on.

Transference

The idea behind risk *transference* is to transfer the risk and the consequences of that risk to a third party. The risk hasn't gone away, but the responsibility for the management of that risk now rests with another party. Most companies aren't willing to take on someone else's risk without a little cash thrown in for good measure. This strategy will impact the project budget and should be included in the cost estimate exercises if you know you're going to use it.

Transfer of risk can occur in many forms but is most effective when dealing with financial risks. Insurance is one form of risk transfer. You are probably familiar with how insurance works. As an example, you purchase car insurance so that if you come upon an obstacle in the road and there is no way to avoid hitting it, the cost to repair the damage to the car is paid by the insurance company. Okay, minus the deductible and all the calculations for the age of the car, the mileage, the color and make of the car, the weather conditions the day you were driving—but we digress.

Another method of risk transfer is contracting. Contracting transfers specific risks to the vendor, depending on the work required by the contract. The vendor accepts the responsibility for the cost of failure. Again, this doesn't come without a price. Contractors charge for their services, and depending on the type of contract you negotiate, the cost might be quite high. For example, in a fixed-price contract, which we'll talk more about in the Procurement Planning section, the vendor (or seller) increases the cost of the contract to compensate for the level of risk they're accepting. A cost reimbursable contract however, leaves the majority of the risk with you, the buyer. However, this type of contract may reduce costs if there are project changes midway through the project.

Keep in mind that contracting isn't a cure-all. You might just be swapping one risk for another. For example, say you hire a driver to go with you on your road trip and their job is to do all the driving. If the driver becomes ill or in some way can't fulfill their obligation, you aren't going to get to your destination on time. You've placed the risks associated with the drive on the contract driver; however, you've taken on a risk of delay due to nonperformance, which means you've just swapped one risk for another. You'll have to weigh your options in cases like this and determine which side of the risk coin your organization can more readily accept.

Other forms of transference include warranties, guarantees, and performance bonds.

Mitigation

Risk *mitigation* attempts to reduce the probability of a risk event and its impacts to an acceptable level. This strategy is a lot like defensive driving. You see an obstacle in the road ahead, survey your options, and take the necessary steps to avoid the obstacle and proceed safely on your journey.

Seeing the obstacle ahead (identifying risk) allows you to reduce the threat by planning ways around it or planning ways to reduce its impact if the risk does occur (mitigation strategies).

According to *A Guide to the PMBOK*, the purpose of mitigation is to reduce the probability that a risk will occur and reduce the impact of the risk to a level where you can accept the risk and its outcomes. It's easier to take actions early on that will reduce the probability of a risk or its consequences than it is to fix the damage once it's occurred.

Acceptance

Acceptance means that you won't make any plans to try to avoid or mitigate the risk. You're willing to accept the consequences of the risk should it occur. Avoidance may also mean the project team was unable to come up with an adequate response strategy and must accept the risk and its consequences.

Let's revisit the road trip example. You could plan the trip using the original route and just accept the risk of running into construction. If you get to that point and you're delayed, you'll just accept it. This is called passive acceptance. You could also go ahead and make plans to take an alternate route, but not enact those plans until you actually reach the construction and know for certain that it is going to impede your progress. This is called active acceptance and may involve developing a contingency plan.

Contingency Planning

Contingency planning involves planning alternatives to deal with the risks should they occur. This is different than mitigation planning in that mitigation looks to reduce the probability of the risk and its impact, whereas contingency planning doesn't necessarily attempt to reduce the probability of a risk event or its impacts. Contingency planning says the risk may very well occur and we better have plans in place to deal with it.

Contingency comes into play when the risk event occurs. This implies you need to plan for your contingencies well in advance of the threat. After the risks have been identified and quantified, contingency plans should be developed and kept at the ready.

Contingency allowances or reserves are a common contingency response. *Contingency reserves* include project funds that are held in reserve to offset any unavoidable threats that might occur to project scope, schedule, cost overruns, or quality. It also includes reserving time and resources to account for risks.

Fallback plans, according to *A Guide to the PMBOK*, should be developed for risks with high impact or for risks with identified strategies that may not be the most effective.

In practice, you'll find that identifying risks, quantifying risks, and developing responses for potential threats may happen simultaneously. In any case, you don't want to be taken by surprise, and that's the point of the risk processes. If you know about potential risks early on, you can very often mitigate or avoid them altogether.

Risk Response Planning Outputs

Risk Response Planning has several outputs:

Risk response plan

Residual risks

Secondary risks

Contractual agreements

Contingency reserve amounts needed

Inputs to other processes

Inputs to a revised project plan

The last four of these outputs are self-explanatory. Remember that you might need to revisit other Planning processes after performing Risk Response Planning to modify project plans as a result of risk responses.

Now let's examine the first three outputs of the Risk Response Planning process.

Risk Response Plan

The *risk response plan* describes the actions you'll take should the identified risks occur. According to *A Guide to the PMBOK*, the risk response plan is also known as the *risk register*. It should include all the identified risks, descriptions of the risks, and the area of the project in which the impact will occur. The risk detail should also describe the causes of risk and how they'll impact the project objectives. The department or staff members responsible for risk management are documented here. All of the results of the qualitative and quantitative processes and the details regarding risk strategies (acceptance, avoidance, and so on) are documented here as well.

The meat of this plan contains the responses to risks, whether one of the risk strategies or a detailed action plan. All of the responses should document the time and cost needed to implement the response.

The contingency plans, reserves, and fallback plans are part of the risk response plan as well.

Residual Risks

A *residual risk* is a leftover risk so to speak. After you've implemented a risk response strategy—say mitigation, for example—some minor risk may still remain. The contingency reserve is set up to handle situations like this.

Secondary Risks

Secondary risks are risks that come about as a result of implementing a risk response. The example given previously where you transferred risk by hiring a driver to take you to your destination but they became ill along the way is an example of a secondary risk. Their illness delayed your arrival time, which is risk directly caused by hiring the driver or implementing a risk response. When planning for risk, identify and plan responses for secondary risks that could occur as well.

Risks exist on all projects, and risk planning is an important part of the project Planning process. Just the act of identifying risks and planning responses can decrease their impact if they occur. Don't take the "What I don't know won't hurt me" approach to risk planning. This is definitely a case where not knowing something can be devastating. Risks that are easily identified and have planned responses aren't likely to kill projects or your career. Risks that you should have known about but ignored could end up costing the organization thousands or millions of dollars, causing schedule delays, or ultimately killing the project. There could be a personal cost as well, as cost and schedule overruns due to poor planning on your part are not easily explained on your resume.

Understanding Procurement Planning

Procurement Planning is a process of identifying what goods or services you're going to purchase from outside of the organization. Part of what you'll accomplish in this process is determining whether you should purchase the goods or services, and if so, how much and when. Keep in mind that we're discussing the Procurement Planning process from the buyer's perspective, as this is the approach used in *A Guide to the PMBOK*.

You need to perform each process in the Project Procurement Management knowledge area (beginning with Procurement Planning and ending with Contract Closeout) for each product or service that you're buying outside of the organization. Obviously, if you're procuring all your resources from within the organization, the only process you'll perform in this knowledge area is the Procurement Planning process.

Sometimes, your entire project will be procured from a vendor. In cases like these, the vendor will have a project manager assigned to the project. Your organization may choose to have an internal project manager assigned as well to act as the conduit between your company and the vendor and to provide information and monitor your organization's deliverables. When this happens, the vendor or contracting company is responsible for fulfilling all of the project management processes as part of the contract. In the case of an outsourced project, the seller—also known as the vendor, supplier, or contractor—manages the project, and the buyer becomes the stakeholder.

Procurement Planning has several inputs including:

- Scope statement
- Product description
- Procurement resources
- Market conditions
- Other planning outputs
- Constraints
- Assumptions

We've covered some of them before, and the ones we haven't looked at are self-explanatory. I recommend you study the inputs to this process on your own. The exam focuses primarily on the tools and techniques and outputs of this process. We'll look at two of the tools and techniques now: make or buy analysis and contract type selection. Expert judgment is also a tool and technique in this process, but we've already covered that ground.

Make or Buy Analysis

The main decision you're trying to get to in *make or buy analysis* is whether it's more cost-effective to buy the products and services or more cost-effective for the organization to produce the goods and services needed for the project.

Costs should include both direct costs—in other words, the actual cost to purchase the product or service—and indirect costs such as the salary of the manager overseeing the purchase process or ongoing maintenance costs.

Other considerations in make or buy analysis might include things like capacity issues, skills, availability, and trade secrets. Strict control might be needed for a certain process, and thus the process cannot be outsourced. Perhaps your organization has the skills in-house to complete the project, but their current project list is so backlogged that they can't get to the new project for months, so you need to bring in a vendor.

Make or buy analysis is considered a general management technique and concludes with the decision to do one or the other.

Contract Type Selection

A *contract* is a compulsory agreement between two or more parties and is used to acquire products or services from outside the organization. Contracts can be made between two or more parties, and money is typically exchanged for goods or services. Contracts are also enforceable by law and require an offer and an acceptance.

There are different types of contracts for different purposes. *A Guide to the PMBOK* divides contracts into three categories. Within each category are different types of contracts. We'll look at each. There may be an exam question or two regarding contract types, so spend some time getting familiar with them.

Fixed Price or Lump Sum Contracts

Fixed price contracts set a specific, firm price for the goods or services rendered. The buyer and seller agree on a well-defined deliverable for a set price. In this kind of contract, the biggest risk is borne by the seller. The seller—or contractor—must take great strides to assure they've covered their costs and will make a comfortable profit on the transaction. The seller assumes the risks of increasing costs, nonperformance, or other problems. However, to counter these unforeseen risks, the seller builds in the cost of the risk to the contract price.

Fixed price contracts can be disastrous for both the buyer and the seller if the scope of the project is not well-defined or the scope changes dramatically. It's important to have accurate, well-defined deliverables when you're using this type of contract. Conversely, fixed price contracts are relatively safe for both buyer and seller when the original scope is well-defined and remains unchanged. They typically reap only small profits for the seller and force the contractor to work productively and efficiently. This type of contract also minimizes cost and quality uncertainty.

Fixed price plus incentive contracts are another type of fixed price contract. The difference here is that the contract includes an incentive—or bonus—for early completion or for some other agreed-upon performance criteria that's exceeded according to contract specifications. The criteria for early completion, or other performance enhancements, must be spelled out in the contract so both parties understand the terms and conditions.

Another thing to note with fixed price plus incentive contracts is that some of the risk is borne by the buyer as opposed to the firm fixed price contract, where most all of the risk is borne by the seller. The buyer takes some risk, albeit minimal, by offering the incentive to get the work done earlier, etc. For example, the buyer really would like the product delivered 30 days prior to when the seller thinks they can deliver, so the buyer assumes the risk for the early delivery via the incentive.

Cost Reimbursable Contracts

Cost reimbursable contracts are as the name implies. The allowable costs—allowable is defined by the contract—associated with producing the goods or services are charged to the buyer. All the costs the seller takes on during the project are charged back to the buyer; thus the seller is reimbursed.

Cost reimbursable contracts carry the highest risk to the buyer, because the total costs are uncertain. As problems arise, the buyer has to shell out even more money to correct the problems. However, the advantage to the buyer with this type of contract is that scope changes are easy to make and can be made as often as you wish—but it will cost you.

Cost reimbursable contracts are risky for the buyer and have a lot of uncertainty associated with them. There is little incentive for the contractor to work efficiently or be productive. This type of contract protects the contractor's profit, because increasing costs are passed back to the buyer rather than taken out of profits, as would be the case with a fixed price contract. Be certain to audit your statements when using a contract like this, so that charges from some other project the vendor is working on don't accidentally end up on your bill.

Cost reimbursable contracts are used most often when there is a lot of uncertainty regarding the project scope such as for cutting-edge projects, and research and development. They also used for projects with that have large investments early in the project life Let's discuss the two kinds of cost reimbursable contracts: cost plus fixed fee and cost plus incentive fee contracts.

Cost Plus Fixed Fee

The first type of cost reimbursable contract is *cost plus fixed fee (CPFF)*. CPFF contracts charge back all allowable project costs to the seller and include a fixed fee upon completion of the contract. This is how the seller makes money on the deal, because the fixed fee portion is the seller's profit. The fee is always firm in this kind of contract, but the costs are variable. The seller doesn't necessarily have a lot of motivation to control costs with this type of contract, as you can imagine. And the only motivation to complete the project is driven by the fixed fee portion of the contract.

Cost Plus Incentive Fee

The next category of cost reimbursable contract is *cost plus incentive fee*. This is the type of contract in which the buyer reimburses the seller for the seller's allowable costs and includes an incentive for exceeding the performance criteria laid out in the contract. An incentive fee actually encourages better cost performance by the seller, and there is a possibility of shared savings between the seller and buyer if performance criteria are exceeded. The qualification for exceeded performance must be written into the contract and agreed to by both parties as does the definition of allowable costs; the seller can possibly lose the incentive fee if agreed-to targets are not achieved.

There is moderate risk for the buyer under the cost plus incentive fee contract, and, if well-written, it can be more beneficial for both the seller and buyer than a cost reimbursable contract.

Time and Materials (T&M) Contracts

Time and materials (T&M) contracts are a cross between the fixed price and cost reimbursable contract. The full amount of the material costs is not known at the time the contract is awarded. This resembles a cost reimbursable contract, because the costs will continue to grow during the contract's life and are reimbursable to the contractor.

Unit rates may be used in a time and materials contract to preset the rates of certain elements or portions of the project. For example, a contracting agency might charge you $135 per hour for a Java programmer, or a leasing company may charge you $2000 per month for the hardware you're renting during the testing phase of your project. These rates are preset and agreed upon by the buyer and seller ahead of time and resemble a fixed price contract.

Exam Spotlight

Understand the difference between a fixed price contract and a cost reimbursable contract for the exam. Also know when each type of contract should be used and which party bears the most risk under each type of contract.

Procurement Planning Outputs

There are only two outputs in the Procurement Planning process. The first is the *procurement management plan*. We've seen a lot of other outputs with the wording, "___ management plan," so you're probably already ahead of me on this one. But hold the phone—let's make sure we touch on the important points. The second output of Procurement Planning is the statement of work.

Procurement Management Plan

The procurement management plan details how the procurement process will be managed. It includes the following information:

- The types of contract to use
- The authority of the project team
- How the procurement process will be integrated with other project processes
- Where to find standard procurement documents (provided your organization uses standard documents)
- How many vendors or contractors are involved and how they'll be managed
- How the procurement process will be coordinated with other project processes such as performance reporting and scheduling

The procurement management plan, like all the other management plans, becomes a part of the project plan document that we'll talk about in Chapter 7.

Statement of Work

A *statement of work (SOW)* contains the details of the procurement item in clear, concise terms. It includes

- The project objectives
- A description of the work of the project
- Concise specifications of the product or services required
- A project schedule

The SOW may be prepared by either the buyer or the seller. Buyers might prepare the SOW and give it to the sellers, who, in turn, rewrite it so that they can price the work out properly. If the buyer does not know how to prepare a SOW, or the seller would be better at creating the SOW due to their expertise concerning the product or service, the seller may prepare it and then give it to the buyer to review.

The seller uses the SOW to determine whether they are able to produce the goods or services as specified in the SOW. In addition, it wouldn't hurt to include a copy of the WBS with the SOW. Any information the seller can use to properly price the goods or services helps both sides understand what's needed and how it will be provided.

Projects may require some or all of the work of the project to be provided by a vendor. The Procurement Planning process determines if goods or services should be procured from outside of the organization—and if so, describes what will be outsourced and what kind of contract to use, and documents the information in the SOW and procurement management plan.

Solicitation Planning

Solicitation Planning is the last process covered in this chapter. (I hear you cheering out there!) The purpose of *Solicitation Planning* is to prepare the documents you'll use in the Solicitation process. The inputs to this process are the procurement management plan, the statement of work, and other planning outputs. We've covered all these inputs previously.

The tools and techniques of solicitation planning are standard forms and expert judgment. Standard forms are a tool used to facilitate the procurement process. These are forms that are standardized for your organization and for the types of goods or services typically procured by the organization. Your organization may or may not have standard forms. They are usually found in organizations that write a lot of contracts and procure a significant number of goods and services.

The three outputs of the Solicitation Planning process are procurement documents, evaluation criteria, and statement of work updates. SOW updates are self-explanatory, so let's take a quick look at the first two outputs.

Procurement Documents

Procurement documents are used to solicit vendors to bid on your procurement needs. You're probably familiar with some of the titles of procurement documents. They might be called request for proposal (RFP), request for information (RFI), invitation for bid (IFB), request for quotation (RFQ), and so on.

Procurement documents should clearly state the description of the work requested, they could include the SOW, and they should explain how vendors should respond. Any special provisions or contractual needs should be spelled out as well. For example, many organizations have data concerning personal information like Social Security numbers and the company's financial data on their systems. The vendor will have access to this private information, and in order to ensure they maintain confidentiality, you should require they sign a nondisclosure agreement.

A few terms are used during this process—usually interchangeably—that you should be aware of. When your decision is going to be made primarily on price, the terms *bid* and *quotation* are used, as in IFB or RFQ. When considerations other than price, such as technology or specific approaches to the project are the deciding factor, the term *proposal* is used, as in RFP. As stated, these terms are used interchangeably, even though they have specific meanings in *A Guide to the PMBOK*. In my organization, all solicitation requests are submitted as RFPs, even though our primary deciding factor is price.

Evaluation Criteria

Evaluation criteria are the remaining output of the Solicition Planning process. This term refers to the method your organization will use to choose a vendor from among the proposals you receive. In some cases, price may be the only criteria. The vendor that submits the lowest bid will win the contract.

Other projects may require more extensive criteria. In this case, scoring models might be used as well as rating models, or purely subjective methods of selection might be utilized. An example weighted scoring method was described in Chapter 3, "Creating a Project Charter," in the "Describing Project Selection Methods" section. This method can easily be used to score vendor proposals. Sometimes, the evaluation criteria are made public in the procurement process so that vendors know exactly what you're looking for.

There are pros and cons to this approach. If the organization typically makes known the evaluation criteria, you'll find that almost all the vendors that bid on the project meet every criteria you've outlined (in writing that is). When it comes time to perform the contract however, you may discover some surprises. The vendor might have done a great job of writing up the bid based on your criteria but in reality they don't know how to put the criteria into practice. On the other hand, having all the criteria publicly known beforehand gives ground to great discussion points and discovery later on in the Source Selection process.

Project Case Study: New Kitchen Heaven Retail Store

Ricardo knocks on your office door and asks if you have a few minutes to talk. "Of course," you reply, and he takes a seat on one of the comfy chairs at the conference table. You have a feeling this might take a while.

"I think you should know that I'm concerned about the availability of the T1 line. I've already put in the call to get us on the list because, as I said last week, there's a 30- to 45-day lead time on these orders."

"We're only midway through the Planning process. Do you need to order the T1 so soon? We don't even know the store location yet," you say.

"Even though they say lead time is 30 to 45 days, I've waited as much as five or six months to get a T1 installed in the past. I know we're really pushing for the early February store opening, so I thought I'd get the ball rolling now. What I need from you is the location address, and I'll need that pretty quick."

"We're narrowing down the choices between a couple of properties, so I should have that for you within the next couple of weeks. Is that soon enough?"

"The sooner the better," Ricardo replies.

"Great. I'm glad you stopped by, Ricardo. I wanted to talk with you about risk anyway, and you led us right into the discussion. Let me ask you, what probability would you assign to the T1 line installation happening six months from now?"

"I'd say the probability for six months is low. It's more likely that if there is a delay, it would be within a three- to four-month time frame."

"If they didn't get to it for six months, would it be a showstopper? In other words, is there some other way we could transfer Jill's data until the T1 did get installed?"

"Sure, there are other methods we could use. Jill won't want to do that for very long, but there are workarounds available."

"Good. Now, what about the risk for contractor availability and hardware availability and delivery schedules?" you ask.

You and Ricardo go on to discuss the risks associated with the IT tasks. Later, you ask Jill and Jake the same kinds of questions and compile a list of risks. In addition, you review the project information for the Atlanta store opening, as it's very similar in size and scope to this store. You add those risks to your list as well. You divide some of the risks into the following categories: IT, Facilities, and Retail. A sample portion of your list appears as follows, with overall assignments made based on Qualitative Risk Analysis and the PI matrix:

Category/Risk: IT

- T1 line availability and installation. Risk score: Low

- Contractor availability for Ethernet installation. Risk score: Medium

- POS and server hardware availability. Risk score: Medium

Category/Risk: Facilities

- Desirable location in the right price range. Risk score: High

- Contractor availability for build-out. Risk score: Low

- Availability of fixtures and shelving. Risk score: Low

Category/Risk: Retail

- Product availability. Risk score: Medium

- Shipment dates for product. Risk score: Medium

After examining the risks, you decide that response plans should be developed for the last two items listed under the IT source, the first item under Facilities, and both of the risks listed under Retail.

Ricardo has already mitigated the T1 connection and installation risk by signing up several months ahead of when the installation is needed. The contractor availability can be handled with a contingency plan that specifies a backup contractor should the first choice not be available. For the POS terminals and hardware, you decide to use the transfer strategy. As part of the contract, you'll require these vendors to deliver on time, and if they cannot, they'll be required to provide and pay for rental equipment until they can get your gear delivered.

The Facilities risk and Retail risks will be handled with a combination of acceptance, contingency plans, and mitigation.

You've calculated the expected value for several potential risk events. Two of them are detailed here.

Desirable location has an expected value of $780,000. The probability of choosing an incorrect or less-than-desirable location is 60 percent. The potential loss in sales is the difference between a high-producing store that generates $2.5 million in sales per year versus an average store that generates $1.2 million in sales per year.

The expected value of the product availability event is $50,000. The probability of the event occurring is 40 percent. The potential loss in sales is $125,000 for not opening the store in conjunction with the Garden and Home Show.

Kitchen Heaven has a file drawer full of standard forms, as they've opened several retail stores each year for the last three years. You'll use these standard forms to secure the contracts with the vendors and order the retail items.

Project Case Study Checklist

Risk Management Planning

Risk Identification

- Documentation reviews

- Information-gathering techniques

Qualitative Risk Analysis

- Risk probability and impact

- Probability/impact risk rating

- List of prioritized risks

Quantitative Risk Analysis

- Interviewing

- Expected value

Risk Response Planning

- Avoidance, transference, mitigation, and acceptance strategies

- Risk response plan

Procurement Planning

- Standard forms

Solicitation Planning

- Procurement documents

Summary

Congratulations! You've completed another fun-filled, action-packed chapter. We covered a lot of material in this chapter, starting with Quality Planning and risk-related planning, and ending up with Procurement and Solicitation Planning.

Quality Planning targets the quality standards that are relevant to your project. You need to consider the cost of quality when considering stakeholder needs. Three men led to the rise of the cost of quality theories. Crosby is known for his zero defects theory, Juran for the fitness for use theory, and Deming for contributing 85 percent of cost of quality to the management team. The Kaizen approach says that people should be improved first, then the quality of the products or services.

Flowcharting is a tool and technique in Quality Planning that diagrams the logical steps that must be performed to accomplish your objective. Cause-and-effect diagrams show the relationship between the effects of quality problems and their causes. Design of experiments is an analytical technique that determines what variables have the greatest effect on the project outcomes.

The quality management plan outlines how the project team will enact the quality policy.

Risk is inherent in all projects. The Risk Management Planning process determines how you will plan for risks on your project. Its only output is the risk management plan, which details how you will manage risks.

The Risk Identification process seeks to identify and document the project risks using brainstorming, the Delphi technique, interviewing, and checklists.

Qualitative Risk Analysis and Quantitative Risk Analysis involve evaluating risks and assigning probability and impact factors to the risks. Many tools and techniques are used during these processes, including risk probability and impact, probability/impact risk rating matrix, interviewing, sensitivity analysis, decision tree analysis, and simulation.

A probability/impact risk rating matrix uses the combination of the probability score multiplied by the impact value to determine the risk score and assignment. The threshold of risk based on high, medium, and low tolerances is determined by comparing the risk score based on the probability level to the PI matrix.

Monte Carlo simulation is a technique used to quantify schedule or cost risks. Decision trees graphically display decisions and their various choices and outcomes.

The Risk Response Planning process is the last risk-planning process and culminates with the risk response plan. The risk response plan details the strategies you'll use to respond to risk and assigns individuals to manage each risk response. Risk response strategies include avoidance, mitigation, acceptance, and transfer. Insurance and contracting are examples of transferring risk.

Contingency planning involves planning alternatives to deal with risk events should they occur. Part of the risk management plan should detail the contingency plans for high-probability, high-impact risk events.

Procurement Planning involves performing analysis to determine if the goods and services needed to perform the project should be procured from a vendor or produced internally. Several types of contracts are considered during procurement. The risk impact with fixed price contracts typically rests on the seller, while the risk impact with cost reimbursable contracts rests on the buyer.

The procurement management plan details how the procurement process will be managed during the course of the project. Solicitation Planning is a matter of preparing the documents you'll use in the Solicitation process during the Executing process of the project.

Exam Essentials

Be able to identify what produces increased stakeholder satisfaction, lower costs, higher productivity, and less rework.   These are the benefits of meeting quality requirements and are discovered during benefit/cost analysis in Quality Planning.

Be able to name the purpose of Risk Identification.   The purpose of the Risk Identification process is to identify all risks that may impact the project, document them, and identify their characteristics.

Be able to define the purpose of Qualitative Risk Analysis.   Qualitative Risk Analysis determines the impact the identified risks will have on the project and the probability they'll occur, and puts the risks in priority order according to their effect on the project objectives.

Be able to define the purpose of the risk response plan.   The risk response plan describes the actions to take should the identified risks occur. It should include all the identified risks, a description of the risks, how they'll impact the project objectives, and the people assigned to manage the risk responses.

Be able to name the purpose for the Procurement Planning process.   The purpose of the Procurement Planning process is to identify which project needs should be obtained from outside the organization.

Be able to identify the contract types and their usage.   Use fixed price contracts for well-defined projects with a high value to the company, and use cost reimbursable contracts for projects with uncertainty and large investments early in the project life. Time and materials contracts are a cross between fixed and cost reimbursable contracts.

Key Terms

Before you take the exam, be certain you are familiar with the following terms:

acceptance	influence diagrams
appraisal costs	Kaizen
avoidance	make or buy analysis
benchmarking	metrics
brainstorming	mitigation
cardinal scale	nominal group technique
cause-and-effect diagrams	operational definitions
checklists	ordinal scale
contingency planning	prevention costs
contingency reserves	probability
contract	probability scales
cost of quality	procurement documents
cost plus fixed fee (CPFF)	procurement management plan
cost plus incentive fee	Procurement Planning
cost reimbursable contracts	Qualitative Risk Analysis
Delphi technique	quality management plan
design of experiments	Quality Planning
failure costs	Quantitative Risk Analysis
fitness for use	regulations
fixed price contracts	residual risk
fixed price plus incentive contracts	Risk Identification
flowcharts	risk management plan
force majeure	Risk Management Planning
impact scale	risk register

risk response plan

Risk Response Planning

secondary risks

Solicitation Planning

standard

statement of work (SOW)

time and materials (T&M) contracts

transference

triggers

zero defects

Review Questions

1. When considering benefit/cost analysis trade-offs during the Quality Planning process, you know that all of the following statements are true except for which one? Choose the least correct answer.

    A. Benefit/cost analysis examines the quality requirements that must be managed most aggressively to meet the quality standards of the product of the project.

    B. Meeting quality requirements will help improve productivity.

    C. The primary cost of meeting quality requirements is the expense of performing project quality management activities.

    D. The primary benefit of meeting quality requirements is less rework.

2. Three people are responsible for establishing cost of quality theories. Crosby and Juran are two them, and their theories respectively are:

    A. Grades of quality, fitness for use

    B. Fitness for use, zero defects

    C. Zero defects, fitness for use

    D. Cost of quality, zero defects

3. The theory that 85 percent of the cost of quality is a management problem is attributed to:

    A. Deming

    B. Kaizen

    C. Juran

    D. Crosby

4. All of the following are benefits of meeting quality requirements except

    A. An increase in stakeholder satisfaction

    B. Less rework

    C. Low turnover

    D. Higher productivity

5. You are a project manager for Fountain of Youth Spring Water bottlers. You are installing a new accounting system and have identified several problems and their causes. You decide to use which of the following flowcharts to diagram the problems' causes and effects?

    A. Decision tree diagram

    B. Fishbone diagram

    C. Benchmark diagram

    D. Simulation tree diagram

6. The process of assessing the probability and consequences of identified risks to the project objectives, assigning an overall risk ranking to the project, and creating a list of prioritized risks describes which of the following processes?

A. Quantitative Risk Analysis

B. Risk Identification

C. Qualitative Risk Analysis

D. Risk Management Planning

7. Each of the following statements is true regarding the risk management plan except:

A. The risk management plan is an output of the Risk Management Planning process.

B. The risk management plan includes a description of the responses to risks and triggers.

C. The risk management plan includes thresholds, scoring and interpretation methods, responsible parties, and budgets.

D. The risk management plan is an input to all the remaining risk-planning processes.

8. You are using the interviewing technique of the Quantitative Risk Analysis process. You intend to use normal and log normal distributions. All of the following statements are true regarding this question except:

A. Interviewing techniques are used to quantify the probability and impact of the risks on project objectives.

B. Normal and log normal distributions use mean and standard deviation to quantify risks.

C. Common distributions represent the probability or risk to the project objective.

D. Triangular distributions rely on optimistic, pessimistic, and most likely estimates to quantify risks.

9. Which of the following processes assesses the likelihood of risk occurrences and their consequences using numeric probability assignments?

A. Qualitative Risk Analysis

B. Risk Identification

C. Quantitative Risk Analysis

D. Risk Response Planning

10. You are the project manager for a new website for the local zoo. You need to perform Qualitative Risk Analysis. When you've completed this process, you'll produce all of the following outputs except:

A. Overall risk ranking for the project

B. List of prioritized risks

C. Inputs to other processes

D. List of risks for additional analysis and management

11. You've identified a risk event on your current project that if it occurs, could save $100,000 in project costs. Which of the following is true based on this statement? Choose the best answer.

    A. This is a risk event that should be accepted, because the rewards outweigh the threat to the project.

    B. This risk event is an opportunity to the project.

    C. This risk event is a threat to the project.

    D. There is not enough information to determine if this risk event is a threat to the project.

12. Which of the following tools and techniques shows the impacts of one decision over another as well as the probability and cost of each risk along a logical path?

    A. Simulation

    B. Decision tree

    C. Probability/impact risk matrix

    D. Sensitivity analysis

13. Which of the following describes the cost of quality associated with scrapping, rework, and downtime?

    A. Internal failure costs

    B. External failure costs

    C. Prevention costs

    D. Appraisal costs

14. Your hardware vendor left you voicemail saying that a potential snowstorm in the Midwest might prevent your equipment from arriving on time. She wanted to give you a heads-up and asked that you return the call. Which of the following statements is true?

    A. This is a secondary risk, which is an output of Risk Response Planning.

    B. This is a contingency plan, which is an output of Risk Response Planning.

    C. This is a risk, which is an output of Risk Identification.

    D. This is a trigger, which is an output of Risk Identification.

15. You are constructing a probability/impact risk rating matrix for your project. Which of the following statements is true?

    A. The PI matrix multiplies the risk's probability by the cost of the impact to determine an expected value of the risk event.

    B. The PI matrix multiplies the risk's probability scales—which fall between 0.0 and 1.0— and the risk's impact scales to determine a risk score.

    C. The PI matrix multiplies the risk's probability by the expected value of the risk event to determine the risk impact and assign a risk score based on a predetermined threshold.

    D. The PI matrix multiplies the risk's probability scales and the risk's impact scales— which fall between 0.0 and 1.0—to determine a risk score.

16. All of the following strategies are tools and techniques of Risk Response Planning used to reduce or control risk except:

    A. Mitigation

    B. Simulation

    C. Avoidance

    D. Acceptance

17. Your hardware vendor left you voicemail saying that a snowstorm in the Midwest will prevent your equipment from arriving on time. You identified a risk response for this risk and have arranged for a local company to lease you the needed equipment until yours arrives. This is an example of which risk response strategy?

    A. Transference

    B. Acceptance

    C. Mitigation

    D. Avoidance

18. You are the project manager for an upcoming outdoor concert event. You're working on the procurement plan for the computer software program that will control the lighting and screen projections during the concert. You're comparing the cost of purchasing a software product to the cost of your company programmers writing a custom software program. You are engaged in which of the following?

    A. Procurement planning

    B. Sensitivity analysis

    C. Transference of risk

    D. Make or buy analysis

19. You are the project manager for an outdoor concert event scheduled for one year from today. You're working on the procurement plan for the computer software program that will control the lighting and screen projections during the concert. You've decided to contract with a professional services company that specializes in writing custom software programs. You want to minimize the risk to the organization, so you'll opt for which contract type?

    A. Fixed price plus incentive

    B. Cost plus fixed fee

    C. Fixed price

    D. Cost plus incentive

20. You are the project manager for Heart of Texas casual clothing company. They're introducing a new line of clothing called Black Sheep Ranch Wear. You will outsource the production of this clothing line to a vendor. The vendor has requested a SOW. All of the following statements are true except:

A. The SOW contains a description of the new clothing line.

B. As the purchaser, you are required to write the SOW.

C. The SOW contains the objectives of the project.

D. The vendor requires a SOW to determine if they can produce the clothing line given the very detailed specifications of this project.

Answers to Review Questions

1. A. Benefit/cost analysis examines all the quality requirements, not just the quality requirements that need the most attention.

2. C. Philip Crosby devised the zero defects theory, meaning do it right the first time. Proper Quality Planning leads to less rework and higher productivity. Joseph Juran's fitness for use says that stakeholders' and customers' expectations are met or exceeded.

3. A. W. Edwards Deming conjectured that the cost of quality is a management problem 85 percent of the time and that once the problem trickles down to the workers, it is outside their control.

4. C. The benefits of meeting quality requirements are increased stakeholder satisfaction, lower costs, higher productivity, and less rework.

5. B. The cause-and-effect flowcharts—also called fishbone diagrams or Ishikawa diagrams—show the relationship between the causes and effects of quality problems.

6. C. The purpose of Qualitative Risk Analysis is to determine what impact the identified risks will have on the project and the probability they'll occur. It also puts risks in priority order according to their effect on the project objectives and assigns an overall risk ranking for the project.

7. B. The risk management plan details how risk management processes will be implemented, monitored, and controlled throughout the life of the project. The risk management plan does not include responses to risks or triggers. Responses to risks are detailed in the Risk Response Planning process.

8. C. Distributions represent both the probability and impact of the risk to the project objectives.

9. C. Quantitative Risk Analysis analyzes the probability of risks and their consequences using numeric probability assignments. Qualitative Risk Analysis may use numeric probability analysis, but *A Guide to the PMBOK* distinguishes between these two processes by stating that Quantitative Risk Analysis analyzes probability numerically. The Quantitative Risk Analysis process evaluates risk impacts and assesses the range of possible project results.

10. C. Inputs to other processes are an output of Risk Identification and Risk Response Planning. The other output of Qualitative Risk Analysis not listed here is trends in Qualitative Risk Analysis results.

11. B. Risks are either threats or opportunities to the project objectives. This risk event is an opportunity that should be exploited.

12. B. Decision trees allow you to show the sequence of choices and their outcomes in a tree form, starting with the decision or risk event at the left and each option branching out from there to the right. This is a tool and technique of the Quantitative Risk Analysis process.

13. A. Internal failure costs are costs associated with not meeting the customer's expectations while you still had control over the product. This results in rework, scrapping, and downtime.

14. D. The best answer is D. Triggers are also called risk symptoms, which are an output of Risk Identification. Triggers are warning signs of an impending risk.

15. B. The PI matrix multiplies the probability—determined with the risk's probability scales—which fall between 0.0 and 1.0, and impact—determined with impact scales—to determine a risk score and assign a high, medium, or low designation to the risk based on a predetermined threshold.

16. B. The tools and techniques of Risk Response Planning are avoidance, transference, mitigation, and acceptance.

17. C. Mitigation tries to reduce the impact of a risk event should it occur. Making plans to arrange for the leased equipment reduces the consequences of the risk.

18. D. Make or buy analysis is determining whether it's more cost-effective to purchase the goods or services needed for the project or more cost-effective for the organization to produce them internally.

19. C. Fixed price contracts have the highest risk to the seller and the least amount of risk to the buyer. However, the price the vendor charges for the product or service will compensate for the amount of risk they're taking on.

20. B. The SOW can be written by either the buyer or the seller. Sometimes the buyer will write the SOW, and the seller may modify it and send it back to the buyer for verification and approval.

Chapter 7

Creating the Project Plan

THE PMP EXAM CONTENT FROM THE
PROJECT PLANNING PERFORMANCE
DOMAIN COVERED IN THIS CHAPTER
INCLUDES:

- ✓ 5. Establishing Project Controls
- ✓ 6. Developing a project plan
- ✓ 7. Obtaining plan approval

The Planning process group has more processes than any other process group. As a result, a lot of time and effort goes into the Planning process of any project. You'll find on some projects that you spend as much time planning the project as you do executing and controlling the project. This isn't a bad thing. The better planning you do up front, the more likely you'll have a successful project.

Speaking of planning...the Planning, Executing, and Controlling process groups together account for almost 70 percent of the PMP exam questions, so *plan* on spending about the same percentage of your study time on these areas.

We'll spend this chapter wrapping up the remaining Planning processes and conclude with a discussion of the Project Plan Development process. This process takes the outputs of other Planning processes and creates a project plan that's used throughout the project Executing and project Controlling processes to track project performance. All other processes in the Planning process group have to be completed before working on the Project Plan Development process. We'll cover Schedule Development and Cost Budgeting in this chapter as well and begin the Executing process group in the next chapter.

Developing the Project Schedule

The *Schedule Development* process is the heart of the Planning process group. This is where you lay out the schedule for your project tasks, determine their start and finish dates, and finalize activity sequences and durations. This process, along with Activity Duration Estimating and Cost Estimating, is repeated several times before you actually come up with the project schedule. You'll learn later in this section that project management software comes in very handy during this process. In fact, it is one of the tools and techniques of this process.

Although there are no exam questions regarding the order that processes are performed in, it might help to understand that Schedule Development cannot be performed until all of the following core processes of project Planning are completed: Scope Planning, Scope Definition, Resource Planning, Activity Definition, Activity Sequencing, Activity Duration Estimating, Risk Management Planning, and Cost Estimating. Schedule Development must be completed prior to the Cost Budgeting process, which we'll cover later in this chapter. The Schedule Development and Cost Budgeting processes then feed the final Planning process, Project Plan Development. Don't neglect the facilitating processes when planning your project. These include: Quality Planning, Organizational Planning, Staff Acquisition, Procurement Planning, Solicitation Planning, Communication Planning, Risk Identification, Qualitative Risk Analysis, Quantitative Risk Analysis, and Risk Response Planning. Even though these are not core processes and don't directly feed into the Project Plan Development process, in many cases project failure may be attributed to the lack of attention given to these processes. Many of these facilitating processes, particularly the risk processes, Communication Planning, and Quality Planning processes, have a direct bearing on project success. Make certain you include the time and cost of the activities associated with the facilitating processes in your overall project plan as well.

We've got a lot of material to cover in this process. We'll start out with the inputs that are new to the Schedule Development process; then follow up with an in-depth discussion of the tools and techniques of the process. These techniques will help you get to the primary output of this process, which is the project schedule.

Schedule Development Inputs

Schedule Development has 10 inputs, 6 of which are outputs from previous Planning processes. They are as follows:

- Project network diagrams
- Activity duration estimates
- Resource requirements
- Resource pool description
- Constraints
- Calendars
- Assumptions
- Leads and lags
- Risk management plan
- Activity attributes

You can see how important it is to perform all of the Planning processes accurately, because the information you derive from almost every process in the Planning group is used somewhere else in Planning, many of them in this process alone or in the other process groups. Your project schedule will reflect the information you know at this point in time. If you have incorrectly estimated activity durations or didn't identify the right dependencies, for example, the inputs to this process will be distorted and your project schedule will not be correct. It's definitely worth the investment of time to correctly plan your project and come up with accurate outputs for each of the Planning processes.

We're going to revisit resource pool description and constraints and discuss three of the inputs to the Schedule Development process that are new: calendars, leads and lags, and activity attributes. A short description of each is given next.

Resource Pool Description

Resource pool description is an input to the Resource Planning process which we covered in Chapter 5, "Resource Planning and Estimating." The resource pool lists the types of resources needed for the project, including materials, equipment, human resources, skills, or special talents. It's important to know what resources are needed and when they're available for the Schedule Development process; the resource pool description gives you this information.

Constraints

Of course you remember that constraints are with you throughout the life of the project. The most important constraints to consider in the Schedule Development process are time constraints. According to *A Guide to the PMBOK*, the time constraints in this process fall into two categories: imposed dates, and key events or major milestones.

Imposed dates are used to restrict the start or finish date of activities. The two most common constraints used to restrict dates are enforced by most computerized project management software programs. They are "start no earlier than" and "finish no later than" constraints. For example, let's go way back to Chapter 5's house-painting example. The painting activity cannot start until the primer has dried. If the primer takes 24 hours to dry and is scheduled to be completed on Wednesday, this implies the painting activity can *start no earlier than* Thursday. This is an example of an imposed date.

Key events or milestones refer to the completion of specific deliverables by a specific date. Stakeholders, customers, or management staff may request certain deliverables be completed or delivered by specific dates. Once you've agreed to those dates (even if the agreement is only verbal), it's often cast in stone and very difficult to change. These dates, therefore, become constraints.

Be careful of the delivery dates you commit to your stakeholders or customers. You may think you're simply discussing the matter or throwing out ideas, while the stakeholder may take what you've said as fact. Once the stakeholder believes the deliverable or activity will be completed by a specific date, there's almost no convincing them that the date needs changing.

Calendars

Calendars are divided into two types: project calendars and resource calendars. *Project calendars* concern all the resources involved in the project and specify the working periods for those resources. For example, if your project work will be completed during normal working hours, the project calendar shows work periods from Monday through Friday between the hours of 8 A.M. and 5 P.M.

Resource calendars look at a particular resource or groups of resources and their availability. Perhaps your project calls for a marketing resource, and the person assigned to the marketing activities is on an extended vacation in October. The resource calendar would show this person's vacation schedule.

Leads and Lags

Leads and lags are related to Activity Sequencing. Remember that Activity Sequencing puts tasks in logical order and determines if there are dependencies that exist among the activities.

You then take these tasks and develop a network diagram from them. (We discussed this in Chapter 5 if you need a quick review.)

Lags require the dependent activity to have time added either to the start date or to the finish date of the activity. *Leads*, conversely, require time to be subtracted from the start date or the finish date of the dependent activity. Lead time is not used as often as lag time.

Let's revisit the house-painting example to put all this in perspective. In order to paint, you first need to scrape the peeling paint and then prime. However, you can't begin painting until the primer has dried, so you shouldn't schedule priming for Monday and painting for Tuesday if you need the primer to dry on Tuesday. Therefore, the priming activity requires lag time, so you need to add time to the end of this activity to allow for the drying time needed before you can start painting.

Lead time works just the opposite. Suppose, for this example, you could start priming before the scraping is finished. Maybe there are areas on the house that don't require scraping, so you don't really need to wait until the scraping activity finishes to begin the priming activity. Priming in this example has lead time subtracted from the beginning of the activity so that this activity begins prior to the finish of the previous activity.

Activity Attributes

Activity attributes are the characteristics of the activity. These might include a description of where the work of the activity will take place, who will perform the activity, and whether the activity is a summary-level activity—level two or three on the WBS perhaps—or a detailed activity with particular specifications.

Understanding the Tools and Techniques of Schedule Development

The two primary outputs of Schedule Development are the project schedule and the schedule management plan. You can employ several tools and techniques in order to produce these outputs. The tools and techniques you choose will depend on the complexity of the project. For the exam, however, you'll need to know them all.

There are six tools and techniques used in Schedule Development:

- Mathematical analysis
- Duration compression
- Simulation
- Resource-leveling heuristics
- Project management software
- Coding structure

A lot of information is packed into some of these tools and techniques, and you should dedicate study time to each of them for the exam. The first tool and technique, mathematical analysis, includes several techniques, each of which are thoroughly covered on the exam. So, let's get to it!

Mathematical Analysis

Mathematical analysis involves calculating early and late start dates and early and late finish dates for project activities. These calculations are performed without taking resource limitations into consideration, so the dates you end up with are theoretical. What you're attempting to establish at this point is the time periods within which the activities can be scheduled. Resource limitations and other constraints will be taken into consideration when you get to the outputs of this process.

Mathematical analysis includes three commonly known techniques:

- Critical Path Method (CPM)
- Graphical Evaluation and Review Technique (GERT)
- Program Evaluation and Review Technique (PERT)

CPM and PERT are very similar network-planning methods, and in some organizations, CPM and PERT are used synonymously. We'll examine each of these techniques momentarily. Keep in mind that CPM and PERT are methods to determine schedule durations without regard to resource availability.

Critical Path Method

Critical Path Method (CPM) calculates the earliest start date, earliest finish date, latest start date, and latest finish date for each activity. This method relies on sequential networks (one activity occurs before the next, or a series of activities occurring concurrently are completed before the next series of activities, and so on) and on a single duration estimate for each activity.

The *critical path (CP)* on any project is the longest full path. Any project activity with a float time that equals zero is considered a critical path task.

Float time is also called *slack time*, and you'll see these terms used interchangeably. There are two types of slack: total slack and free slack. *Total slack* is the amount of time you can delay the start of a task without delaying the ending of the project. *Free slack* is the amount of time you can delay the start of a task without delaying the start of a successor task.

In this section, you'll calculate the CP for a sample project and illustrate how all the dates, the CP, and the float times are derived.

GATHERING ACTIVITY AND DEPENDENCY INFORMATION

Let's say you are the project manager for a new software project. The company you are working for is venturing into the movie rental business over the Web. You need to devise a software system that tracks all the information related to rentals and also supplies the management team with reports that will help them make good business decisions. For purposes of illustration, I'm showing only a limited portion of the tasks that you would have on a project like this.

You'll start this example by plugging information into Table 7.1 (later in this section) from the processes you've already completed. The list of activities comes from the work package level of the WBS and the activity list compiled during the Activity Definition process. The durations for each activity are listed in the column by that title and were derived during the Activity Duration Estimating process. The duration times are listed in days.

The Dependency column lists the activities that require a previous activity to finish before the current activity can start. You're using only finish-to-start relationships. For example, you'll see that activity number 2 and activity number 4 each depend on activity 1 to finish before they can begin. The dependency information came from the Activity Sequencing process. Now, you'll proceed to calculating the dates.

CALCULATING DATES

Project Deliverables is the first activity and, obviously, where the project starts. This activity begins on April 1. Project Deliverables has a 12-day duration. So take April 1 and add 12 days to this to come up with an early finish date of April 12. Watch out, because you need to count day one, or April 1, as a full workday. The simplest way to do this calculation is to take the early start date, add the duration, and subtract one. Therefore, the early finish date for the first activity is April 12. By the way, we are ignoring weekends and holidays for this example. Activity 2 depends on activity 1, so it cannot start until activity 1 has finished. Its earliest start date is April 13. Add the duration to this date minus one to come up with the finish date.

You'll notice that activity 4 depends on activity 1 finishing, so its earliest start date is also April 13. Continue to calculate the remaining early start and early finish dates in the same manner. This calculation is called a *forward pass*.

To calculate the late start and late finish dates, you begin with the last activity. The late finish for activity 9 is July 10. Since the duration is only one day, July 10 is also the late start date. You know that activity 8 must finish before activity 9 can begin, so activity 8's late finish date, July 9, is one day prior to activity 9's late start date, July 10. Subtract the duration of activity 8 (three days) from July 9 and add one to get the late start date of July 7. You're performing the opposite calculation that you did for the forward pass. This calculation is called a *backward pass*, as you might have guessed. Continue calculating the late start and late finish through activity 4.

Activity 3 adds a new twist. Here's how it works. Activity 7 cannot begin until activity 3 and activity 6 are completed. No other activity depends on the completion of activity 3. If activity 7's late start date is June 29, activity 3's late finish date must be June 28. June 28 less eight days plus one gives you a late start date of June 21. Activity 3 depends on activity 2, so activity 2 must be completed prior to beginning activity 3. Calculate these dates just like you did for activities 9 through 4.

Activity 1 still remains. Activity 4 cannot start until activity 1 is completed. If activity 4's late start date is April 13, the late finish date for activity 1 must be April 12. Subtract the duration of activity 1 and add one to come up with a late start date of April 1. Alternatively, the forward pass and backward pass can be calculated by saying the first task starts on day zero and then adding the duration to this. As an example, activity number 1's early start date is April 1, which is day zero. Add 12 days to day zero and you come up with an early finish date of April 12.

The calculation for float/slack time is determined by subtracting the early start date from the late start date. If the float time equals zero, the activity is on the critical path.

CALCULATING THE CRITICAL PATH

To determine the CP duration of the project, add up the duration of every activity with zero float. You should come up with 101 days, because you're adding the duration for all activities, except for activity 2 and activity 3. A critical path task is any task that cannot be changed without impacting the project end date. By definition, these are all tasks with zero float.

TABLE 7.1 CPM Calculation

Activity Number	Activity Description	Dependency	Duration	Early Start	Early Finish	Late Start	Late Finish	Float/ Slack
1	Project Deliverables	—	12	4/1	4/12	4/1	4/12	0
2	Procure Hardware	1	2	4/13	4/14	6/19	6/20	68
3	Test Hardware	2	8	4/15	4/22	6/21	6/28	68
4	Procure Software Tools	1	10	4/13	4/22	4/13	4/22	0
5	Write Programs	4	45	4/23	6/6	4/23	6/6	0
6	Test and Debug	5	22	6/7	6/28	6/7	6/28	0
7	Install	3, 6	8	6/29	7/6	6/29	7/6	0
8	Training	7	3	7/7	7/9	7/7	7/9	0
9	Acceptance	8	1	7/10	7/10	7/10	7/10	0

Another way to determine the critical path is by looking at the network diagram. If the duration is included with the information on the node, or if start and end dates are given, you simply calculate the duration and then add up the duration of the longest path in the diagram to determine the CP. However, this method is not as accurate as what's described in Table 7.1.

Figure 7.1 shows the same project in diagram form. Duration is printed in the top-right corner of each node. Add up the duration of each path to determine which one is the critical path.

Remember that CP is always the path with the longest duration. In Figure 7.1, path 1-2-3-7-8-9 equals 34 days. Path 1-4-5-6-7-8-9 equals 101 days; therefore this path is the critical path.

FIGURE 7.1   Critical path diagram

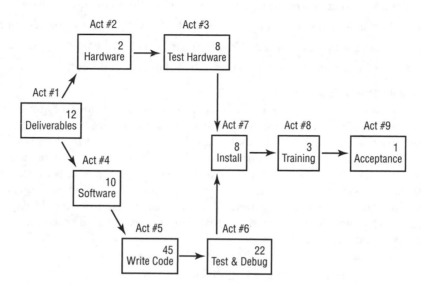

Graphical Evaluation and Review Technique

The only thing you need to understand about the *Graphical Evaluation and Review Technique (GERT)* for the exam is that GERT allows for conditional branching and looping, and probabilistic treatment. GERT allows you to loop back through a process or perform branching to show alternatives. For example, the software project in the CPM example might require unit testing of individual modules before the entire program can be tested, and each module must pass its unit test. If the unit test fails, GERT allows you to depict a looping condition so that you can come back through unit testing and then progress to the next activity once the unit test is passed. Probabilistic treatment simply means an activity may be performed more than once, it may not be performed at all, or it might only partially be performed.

Program Evaluation and Review Technique

The *Program Evaluation and Review Technique (PERT)* was developed in the 1950s by the United States Navy. They were working on one of the most complex engineering projects in history at the time—the Polaris Missile Program—and needed a way to manage the project and forecast the project schedule with a high degree of reliability. PERT was developed to do just that.

EXPECTED VALUE

PERT and CPM are similar techniques. The difference is CPM uses the most likely duration to determine project duration, while PERT uses what's called expected value (or the weighted average) to determine project duration. *Expected value* is calculated using three time estimates for activity duration instead of one and then finding the weighted average of the three time estimates. If you take this one step further and determine the standard deviation of each activity, you can assign a confidence factor to your project estimates. Without getting too heavily involved in the mathematics of probability, understand that for data that fits a bell curve, which is what you're about to calculate with the PERT technique, the following is true:

- Work will finish within plus or minus three standard deviations 99.73 percent of the time.
- Work will finish within plus or minus two standard deviations 95.44 percent of the time.
- Work will finish within plus or minus one standard deviation 68.26 percent of the time.

CALCULATING EXPECTED VALUE

The three time estimates used to calculate expected value are the optimistic estimate, the pessimistic estimate, and the most likely estimate. Going back to the software example, let's find out what these three time estimates might look like for the activity called Write Programs. You get these estimates by asking the lead programmer, or key team member, to estimate the optimistic, pessimistic, and most likely duration for the activity based on their past experience. Other historical information could be used to determine these estimates as well. Say in this case that you're given 38 days for the optimistic time, 57 days for the pessimistic, and 45 days for the most likely. (45 days was derived from the Activity Duration Estimating process and is the estimate you used to calculate CPM.)

The formula to calculate expected value is as follows:

(optimistic + pessimistic + (4 most likely)) ÷ 6

The expected value for the Write Programs activity is as follows:

(38 + 57 + (4 × 45)) ÷ 6 = 45.83

The formula for standard deviation, which helps you determine confidence level, is as follows:

(pessimistic − optimistic) ÷ 6

The standard deviation for your activity is as follows:

(57 − 38) ÷ 6 = 3.17

You could say the following given the information you now have:

- There is a 68.26 percent chance that the Write Programs activity will be completed between 42.66 days and 49 days.
- There is a 95.44 percent chance that the Write Programs activity will be completed between 39.49 days and 52.17 days.

You calculated the range of dates for the 68.26 percent chance by adding and subtracting one standard deviation, 3.17, from the expected value, 45.83. The 95.44 percent chance was calculated by multiplying the standard deviation times 2, which equals 6.34, and adding and subtracting that result from the expected value to come up with the least number of days and the most number of days it will take to finish the activity. Generally speaking, two standard deviations, or 95.44 percent, is a close enough estimate for most purposes.

NOTE   The higher the standard deviation is for an activity, the higher the risk. Since standard deviation measures the difference between the pessimistic and the optimistic times, a greater spread between the two, which results in a higher number, indicates a greater risk. Conversely, a low standard deviation means less risk.

DETERMINING DATE RANGES FOR PROJECT DURATION

Let's bring your table of activities back and plug in the expected values and the standard deviation for each (please see Table 7.2).

TABLE 7.2   PERT Calculation

Activity Number	Activity Description	Optimistic	Pessimistic	Most Likely	Expected Value	Standard Deviation	SD Squared
1	Project Deliverables	10	14	12	12.00	0.67	0.45
2	Procure Hardware	—	—	—	—	—	—
3	Test Hardware	—	—	—	—	—	—
4	Procure Software Tools	8	14	10	10.33	1.00	1.0
5	Write Programs	38	57	45	45.83	3.17	10.05
6	Test and Debug	20	30	22	23.00	1.67	2.79
7	Install	5	10	8	7.83	0.83	0.69
8	Training	3	3	3	3.00	0	0
9	Acceptance	1	1	1	1.00	0	0
Totals for CP tasks					**102.99**		**14.98**

Now let's look at the total project duration using PERT and the standard deviation to determine a range of dates for project duration. You should add only the tasks that are on the critical path. Remember from the CPM example that tasks 2 and 3 are not on the critical path, so their expected value and standard deviation calculations have been left blank in this table. When you add all the remaining tasks, the total expected value duration is 102.99 days, or 103 days rounded to the nearest day.

Your next logical conclusion might be to add the Standard Deviation column to get the standard deviation for the project. Unfortunately, you cannot add up the standard deviations, because you will come out with a number that is much too high. Totaling the standard deviations assumes that all of the tasks will run over schedule, and that's not likely. It is likely that a few tasks will run over, but not every one of them. So now you're probably wondering how to calculate the magic number.

You might have noticed an extra column at the right called SD Squared. This is the standard deviation squared—or for those of you with math phobias out there, the standard deviation multiplied by itself.

Once you have calculated the standard deviation squared for each activity, add up the squares, for a total of 14.98. There's one more step and you're done. Take the square root of 14.98 (you'll need a calculator) to come up with 3.87. This is the standard deviation you will use to determine your range of projected completion dates. Here's a recap of these last few calculations:

Total expected value = 103.00

Sum of SD Squared = 14.98

Square root of SD Squared = 3.87

You can now make the following predictions regarding your project:

- There is a 68.26 percent chance that the project will be completed between 99.13 days and 106.87 days.

- There is a 95.44 percent chance that the project will be completed between 95.26 days and 110.74 days.

PERT is not used very often today. When it is, it's used for very large, highly complex projects. However, PERT is a useful technique to determine project duration when your activity durations are uncertain. It's also useful for calculating the duration for individual tasks in your schedule that may be very complex or risky. You might decide to use PERT for a handful of the activities, those with the highest amount of risk for example, and use other techniques to determine duration for the remaining activities.

Exam Spotlight

For the exam, I recommend that you know one standard deviation gives you a 68 percent (rounded) probability and two standard deviations gives you a 95 percent (rounded) probability. Also know how to calculate the range of project duration dates based on the expected value and standard deviation calculation. You probably don't need to memorize how to calculate the standard deviation, because I believe most of the questions give you this information. You should, however, memorize the PERT formula and know how it works. It wouldn't hurt to go ahead and memorize the standard deviation formula as well—you never know what might show up on the exam.

Duration Compression

Duration compression is a form of mathematical analysis that's used to shorten the project schedule without changing the project scope. Compression is simply shortening the project schedule to accomplish all the activities sooner than estimated.

Schedule compression might happen when the project end date has been predetermined or if after performing the CPM or PERT techniques, you discover that the project is going to take longer than the original promised date. In the CPM example, you calculated the end date to be July 10. What if the project was undertaken and a July 2 date was promised? That's when you'll need to employ one of two duration compression techniques called crashing and fast tracking.

Crashing

Crashing is a compression technique that looks at cost and schedule trade-offs. One of the things you might do to crash the schedule is add resources—from either inside or outside the organization—to the critical path tasks. It wouldn't help you to add resources to non-critical path tasks, as these tasks don't impact the schedule end date anyway because they have float time. You might also limit or reduce the project requirements. Ask stakeholders if the features or functions are "nice to have" or necessary. You might also try changing the sequence of tasks. This sometimes shortens the schedule, but isn't always possible.

Be certain to check the critical path when you've used the crashing technique, because crashing might have changed the critical path. Also consider that crashing doesn't always come up with a reasonable result. It often increases the costs of the project as well. The idea with crashing is to try to gain the greatest amount of schedule compression with the least amount of cost.

Fast Tracking

We talked about fast tracking in Chapter 1, "What Is a Project?" *Fast tracking* is starting two tasks at the same time that were previously scheduled to start sequentially. Fast tracking can increase project risk and might cause the project team to have to rework tasks. For example, fast tracking is often performed in object-oriented programming. The programmers might begin writing code on several modules at once, out of sequential order, and prior to the completion of the design phase.

Simulation

Simulation uses different sets of activity assumptions to produce multiple project durations. *Monte Carlo Analysis* is a simulation technique that we discussed in the Quantitative Risk Analysis process. In the Schedule Development process, Monte Carlo Analysis uses a range of probable activity durations for each activity, which are then used to calculate a range of probable duration results for the project itself. Monte Carlo runs the possible activity durations and schedule projections many, many times to come up with the schedule projections and their probability, critical path duration estimates, and float time.

What-if analysis is another simulation technique that allows you to examine the project schedule under different circumstances. For example, you might want to know what the possible project durations are if a major deliverable is delayed. Using simulation, you can determine schedule impacts under a variety of circumstances and prepare response plans or contingency plans to account for those situations.

Exam Spotlight

For the exam, remember that Monte Carlo is a simulation technique that shows the probability of all the possible project completion dates.

Resource Leveling Heuristics

Earlier, I said that mathematical analysis (CPM, GERT, and PERT) does not consider resource availability. Now that you have a schedule of activities, it's time to plug in resources for those activities and adjust the schedule according to any resource constraints you discover.

Remember that you identified resources and acquired staff during the Resource Planning and Staff Acquisition processes, which we discussed in Chapter 5. Skill sets, previous experience, availability, and personal interests were documented during these processes, and staff was assigned to the project. Staff members were not assigned directly to tasks at that point—just to the project itself. Organizational development described roles and responsibilities as they related to scope definition and produced the staffing management plan, which describes how to bring resources on and off the project.

Now during Schedule Development, resources are assigned to specific activities. Usually, you'll find that your initial schedule has periods of time with more activities than you have resources to work on them. You will also find that it isn't always possible to assign 100 percent of your team members' time to tasks. Sometimes your schedule will show a team member who is over-allocated, meaning they're assigned to more work than they can physically perform in the given time period. Other times, they might not be assigned enough work to keep them busy during the time period. This problem is easy to fix. You can assign under-allocated resources to multiple tasks to keep them busy.

Resource Assignments

Having over-allocated resources is a little more difficult problem to resolve. *Resource leveling—*also called *resource-based method*—attempts to smooth out the resource assignments to get tasks completed without overloading the individual while trying to keep the project on schedule. This typically takes the form of allocating resources to critical path tasks first.

There are several ways the project manager can accomplish resource leveling. You might delay the start of a task to match the availability of a key team member. Or you might adjust the resource assignments so that more tasks are given to team members who are under-allocated. You could require the resources to work mandatory overtime—that one always goes over well! Perhaps you can split some tasks so that the team member with the pertinent knowledge or skill performs the critical part of the task and the noncritical part of the task is given to a less skilled team member. All of these methods are forms of resource leveling.

Generally speaking, resource leveling of over-allocated team members extends the project end date. If you're under a date constraint, you'll have to go back and rework the schedule after assigning resources to keep the project on track with the committed completion date. This might include moving key resources off of non-critical tasks and assigning them to critical path tasks or adjusting assignments as previously mentioned. Reallocating those team members with slack time to critical path tasks to keep them on schedule is another option. Don't forget, fast tracking is an option to keep the project on schedule also.

Reverse Resource Allocation Scheduling

Reverse resource allocation scheduling is a technique used when key resources—like a thermo-dynamic expert, for example—are required at a specific point in the project, and they are the only resource, or resources, available to perform these activities. This technique requires the resources to be scheduled in reverse order, that is, from the end date of the project rather than the beginning, in order to assign this key resource at the correct time.

Critical Chain Method

Critical chain method is a relatively new contribution to the project management world. It's a technique that allows you to consider limited or restricted resources when modifying the project schedule. This method typically schedules high-risk tasks early in the project so that problems can be identified and addressed right away. It allows for combining several tasks into one task when one resource is assigned to all the tasks. In a nutshell, critical chain is a technique that's designed to help you manage the uncertainties of a project.

 Real World Scenario

Sunny Surgeons, Inc.

Kate Newman is a project manager for Sunny Surgeons, Inc. Sunny Surgeons is a software company that produces software for hand-held display devices for the medical profession. The software allows surgeons to keep notes regarding patients, upcoming surgeries, and ideas about new medicines and techniques to research. Kate's latest project is to write an enhanced version of the patient-tracking program with system integration capabilities to a well-known desktop software product used by the medical industry.

There has been some recent turnover in the programming department. Fortunately, Stephen, the senior programmer who led the development effort on the original version of the patient tracker, still works for Sunny. His expertise with hand-held technologies as well as his knowledge of the desktop software product make him an invaluable resource for this project.

Kate discovered a problem during the development of the project schedule. Stephen is over-allocated for three key activities. Kate decides to see what his take is on the situation before deciding what to do.

Stephen, the eternal optimist programmer who loves his job and does all but sleep in his office at night, says he can easily complete all the activities and that Kate shouldn't give it a second thought. He also suggests to Kate that Karen Wong, a junior programmer on his team, worked on the last project with him and might be able to handle the noncritical path task on her own, with a little direction from Stephen.

Kate thinks better of the idea of over-allocating her key project resource, even if he does think he can do the entire thing single-handed. She decides to try some resource leveling to see what that turns up.

Kate discovers that rearranging the order of activities, along with assigning Karen to handle the noncritical path activity, might be a possible solution. However, this scenario lengthens the project by a total of eight days. Since Kate knows the primary constraint on this project is quality, she's fairly sure she can get buy-off from the project sponsor and stakeholders on the increased schedule date. She can also sell the resource-leveled schedule as a low-risk option as opposed to assigning Stephen to all the activities and keeping the project end date the same. Over-allocating resources can cause burnout and stress-related illnesses, which will ultimately have a negative impact on the project schedule.

Project Management Software

Given the examples you've worked through on Schedule Development and resource leveling, you probably already have concluded how much project management software might help you with these processes. Project management software automates the mathematical calculations and performs resource-leveling functions for you. Obviously, you can then print the schedule that's been produced for final approval and ongoing updates. It's common practice to e-mail updated schedules with project notes so that stakeholders know what activities are completed and which ones remain to be done.

It's beyond the scope of this book to go into all the various software programs available to project managers. Suffice it to say that project management software ranges from the very simple to the very complex. The level of sophistication and the types of project management techniques that you're involved with will determine which software product you should choose. Many project managers I know have had great success with Microsoft Project software and use it exclusively. It contains a robust set of features and reporting tools that will serve most projects well.

Don't forget that you are the project manager, and your good judgment should never be usurped by the recommendation of a software product. Your finely tuned skills and experience will tell you if relationship issues between team members might cause bigger problems than what the resource-leveling function indicates. Constraints and stakeholder expectations are difficult for a software package to factor in. Rely on your expertise when in doubt. If you don't have the experience yet to make knowledge-based decisions, seek out another project manager or a senior stakeholder, manager, or team member and ask them to confirm if you're on the right track. Project management software is a wonderful tool, but it is not a substitute for sound project management practices or experience.

Coding Structure

Coding structure is a tool and technique that refers to the ability to sort activities based on attributes you assign to the activities. These attributes include things like WBS classifications, project phases, the type of activity, responsibility assignment, and so on.

Producing the Schedule Development Outputs

The Schedule Development process has four outputs:

- Project schedule
- Supporting detail
- Schedule management plan
- Resource requirements updates

The two primary outputs from this process that will carry forward throughout the rest of the project are the project schedule and the schedule management plan. We'll start with the project schedule output first.

Project Schedule

The purpose of the Schedule Development process is to determine the start and finish dates for each of the project activities. One of the primary outputs of this process is the *project schedule*, which details this information as well as the resource assignments. However, depending on the size and complexity of your project or your organization's culture, the resource assignments may not be completed until the Project Plan Development process is performed. If that's the case, the project schedule is considered preliminary until the resources are assigned to the activities.

In *A Guide to the PMBOK* terms, the project schedule is considered preliminary until resources are assigned. In reality, beware that once you've published the project schedule (even though it's in a preliminary state) some stakeholders may regard this as the actual schedule and expect you to manage to the dates shown.

The project schedule should be approved and signed off by stakeholders and functional managers. This assures you that they have read the schedule, understand the dates and resource commitments, and will likely cooperate. You'll also need to obtain confirmation that resources will be available as outlined in the schedule when you're working in a functional organization. The schedule cannot be finalized until you receive approval and commitment for the resource assignments outlined in the schedule. Approval and finalization of the schedule should be completed prior to the end of the Project Plan Development process.

Once the schedule is approved, it will become your baseline for the remainder of the project. Project progress and task completion will be monitored and tracked against the project schedule to determine if the project is on course as planned.

The schedule can be displayed in a variety of ways, some of which are variations on what you've already seen. Network diagrams, like the ones discussed in Chapter 5, will work as schedule diagrams when you add the start and finish dates to each activity. These diagrams usually show the activity dependencies and critical path. Figure 7.2 shows a sample portion of a network diagram highlighting the programming activities.

FIGURE 7.2 Network diagram with activity dates

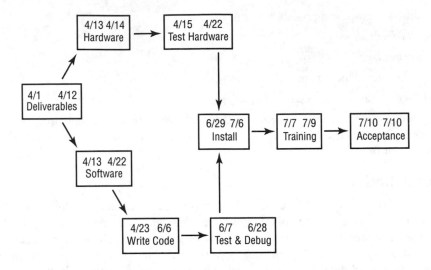

Gantt charts are easy to read and commonly used to display schedule activities. Depending on the software you're using to produce the Gantt chart, it might also show activity sequences, activity start and end dates, resource assignments, activity dependencies, and the critical path. Figure 7.3 is a simple example that plots various activities against time. These activities do not relate to the activities in the tables or other figures shown so far. Gantt charts are also known as *bar charts*.

FIGURE 7.3 Gantt chart

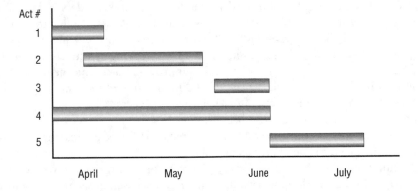

Milestone charts are another way to depict schedule information. *Milestones* mark the completion of major deliverables or some other key event in the project. For example, approval and sign-off on project deliverables might be considered a milestone. Other examples might be completion of a prototype, system testing, contract approval, and so on.

Milestone charts might show the key events and their start or completion dates in a bar chart form similar to a Gantt chart. Or they can be written in a simple table format with milestones listed in the rows and expected schedule dates in one column and actual completion dates in another, as in the following example. As the milestones are met, the Actual Date column is filled in. This information can be included with the project status reports.

Milestone	Scheduled Date	Actual Date
Sign off on deliverables	4/12	4/12
Sign off on hardware test	4/22	4/25
Programming completed	6/06	
Testing completed	6/28	
Acceptance and sign-off	7/10	
Project closeout	7/10	

Supporting Detail

The minimum amount of information in the supporting detail output is the project constraints and assumptions. Other information that should be documented but doesn't necessarily fit into the other categories would get documented here. Always err on the side of too much documentation, rather than not enough.

You will have to be the judge of what other information to include here, as it will depend on the nature of the project. *A Guide to the PMBOK* suggests that you might include resource histograms. There is an example resource histogram in Chapter 5 if you need to review. Resource histograms typically display hours needed on one axis and period of time (days, weeks, months, years) on the other axis. You might also include alternative schedules or contingency schedule reserves in this section.

Schedule Management Plan

The schedule management plan should be published and distributed along with your other project-planning documents. Like other management plan outputs, the schedule management plan describes how schedule changes will be managed and is an important part of your overall project plan.

Resource Requirements Updates

Resource requirements are an output of the Resource Planning process. As a result of scheduling activities and leveling resources, you may have to make adjustments to the resource requirements document. As I've noted during some of the other Planning processes, project planning and project management are an iterative process. Rarely is anything cast in cement. You will continue to revisit processes throughout the project to refine and adjust. Eventually, processes do get put to bed. You wouldn't want to come back to the Planning process at the conclusion of the project, for example, but keep in mind that the Planning, Executing, and Controlling process groups are iterative, and it's not unusual to have to revise processes within these process groups as you progress on the project.

In practice, Activity Definition, Activity Sequencing, Activity Duration Estimating, and Schedule Development are easily completed at the same time with the aid of good project management software. Gantt charts, critical path, PERT charts, resource allocation, activity dependencies, what-if analysis, and various reports are easily produced after plugging in your scheduling information to most project management software tools. Regardless of your methods, be certain to obtain sign-off of the project schedule and provide your stakeholders and project sponsor with regular updates. And keep your schedule handy—there will likely be changes and modifications as you go.

Establishing the Cost Budget Baseline

Our next process on the road to Project Plan Development is to determine the cost baseline, which is the only output of the Cost Budgeting process. The *Cost Budgeting* process assigns cost estimates to activities and is used to measure the variance and performance of the project throughout the remaining process groups. Thus, it serves as a baseline for cost measurements, as the *cost baseline* is now the expected cost for the project. Remember that costs are tied to the financial system through the chart of accounts—or code of accounts—and are assigned to project activities at the work package level of the WBS.

The budget will be used as a plan for allocating costs to project activities. The Schedule Development and Cost Estimating processes must be completed prior to working on Cost Budgeting because their outputs become the inputs to this process. The inputs for Cost Budgeting are cost estimates (an output of the Cost Estimating process), the WBS (an output of the Scope Definition process), the risk management plan (an output of the Risk Management Planning process), and the project schedule (an output of the Schedule Development process).

The same tools and techniques discussed for the Cost Estimating process in Chapter 5 are used in the Cost Budgeting process. A quick reminder of those tools and techniques won't hurt:

Analogous estimating   Analogous estimating is a top-down technique that uses historical information to determine estimates and is a form of expert judgment.

Parametric modeling   Parametric modeling is a mathematical model used to estimate project costs.

Bottom-up estimating   Bottom-up estimating involves estimating the individual costs of each activity and then rolling them up to come up with a total project cost.

Computerized tools   Computerized tools are used to perform the preceding estimating techniques automatically.

The cost baseline (the output of Cost Budgeting) can be displayed graphically, with time increments on one axis against dollars expended on the other axis, as shown in Figure 7.4. The costs shown on this graph are cumulative costs, meaning that what you spent this period is added to what was spent last period and then charted. Many variations of this graph exist showing dollars budgeted against dollars expended to date and so on. Cost budgets can be displayed using this type of graph as well by plotting the sum of the estimated costs excepted per period.

FIGURE 7.4   Cost baseline

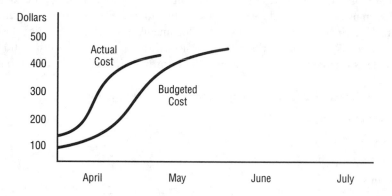

Exam Spotlight

For the exam, remember that cost baselines are displayed as an S-curve. The reason for this is that project spending starts out slowly, gradually increases over the project's life until it reaches a peak, and then tapers off again as the project wraps up. Large projects are difficult to graph in this manner, because the timescale isn't wide enough to accurately show fluctuations in spending. There are other methods that more accurately graph costs that we'll look at in the Cost Control process.

The cost baseline budget should contain all the costs for all of the expected work on the project. You would have identified most of these costs in the Cost Estimating process. Schedule Development might have uncovered additional activities that need to be added to the budget as well, so don't forget to add them to your budget.

The cost baseline budget should also contain appropriations for risk response. We covered several categories and tools of Risk Response Planning in Chapter 6, "Establishing Project Planning Controls," including avoidance, mitigation, insurance, and contingency plans. Some of the budget should be allocated to each of the techniques that you identified in your risk management plan. Additionally, you'll want to set aside money for contingency reserves. This is for the unforeseen, unplanned risks that may occur. Even with all of the time and effort you spend on planning, unexpected things do crop up. Better to have the money set aside and not need it than to need it and not have it.

The cost baseline is the only output of the Cost Budgeting process. We'll revisit the cost baseline when we talk about the Cost Control process and examine different ways to measure costs.

Developing the Project Plan

You've finally made it to Project Plan Development. All the work you've done up to this point culminates in this final Planning process.

Project Plan Development takes the outputs from all the other Planning processes and brings them together in a concise, logical format. This might end up being one main document with reference to other pertinent documents, or several documents organized in a logical fashion. The project plan, which is an output of this process, is used throughout the Executing and Controlling processes for decision making and guiding project performance based on the details outlined in the project plan.

Project Plan Development has five inputs that you've seen before:

- Other planning outputs
- Historical information
- Organizational policies
- Constraints
- Assumptions

Other planning outputs are all of the outputs of the processes in the Planning process group. *A Guide to the PMBOK* points out that organizational policies should be consulted when developing your project plan and might include things like quality management, personnel administration, and financial controls.

Tools and Techniques

The tools and techniques of Project Plan Development are all new and they are:

- Project planning methodology
- Stakeholder skills and knowledge
- Project management information system (PMIS)
- Earned value management (EVM)

We'll describe each of these now.

Project Planning Methodology

We've been explaining and employing *project planning methodology* since the beginning of the first chapter. This is simply a formal, structured technique that the project manager uses to help develop the project plan. For example, some organizations have project management offices with standardized forms, templates, and processes that project managers can use to facilitate the Planning process. Most of these structured techniques involve using what *A Guide to the PMBOK* calls *hard* tools like Microsoft Project software, and or *soft* tools like paper templates or facilitated meetings.

For example, my organization has a project management office (PMO) that provides templates and forms for the Planning process (soft tools) and also requires the use of project management software (hard tools) to schedule project activities and assign resources and costs. The PMO also provides assistance and guidance in completing the templates for project managers who work in functional departments that fall outside the scope of the PMO's authority (soft tools).

For complex projects, Monte Carlo Analysis is a project planning methodology that can be used during this process as well. Since Planning is such an iterative process, Monte Carlo comes in handy when you're looking at schedule risks, project durations, and the like.

Stakeholder Skills and Knowledge

Yes, stakeholders have skills and knowledge that might be helpful to the project manager during project Planning. Believe it or not—and I'm positive you are not one of these types—there are project managers who think stakeholders have no business helping with any aspect of the project Planning, Executing, or Controlling process groups. I'm not certain how you would end up with a successful project (as defined by meeting or exceeding stakeholder expectations) when stakeholders have not been included in the Planning process or other project process groups. Don't let this happen to you. As the project manager, one of your most important jobs is to create an open, communicative atmosphere so that stakeholders contribute to the process.

It's important that stakeholders participate in the project Planning processes and sign off on the final project plan. This assures you that stakeholders agree to, or at least know, the details regarding project activities, duration, activity costs, risks, and budgets, and how each of these things impacts the project scope and their own departments and resources. Stakeholders usually have less of a say in how the project is executed and controlled, because the objectives and scope are firmly defined by then. This makes their cooperation and participation in the Planning processes even more important. Do everything you can to ensure that stakeholders take the project seriously and actively solicit their input during Project Plan Development.

Project Management Information System (PMIS)

Project management information system (PMIS) is an information system that stores all the information related to your project. It allows you to gather information, incorporate it with other project information, and produce reports for distribution to stakeholders and team members. The information system is used from the beginning of the project through closeout. Keep in mind that the information system could be a software product or a combination of software and a manual system.

As the project manager, you need to be certain that you're managing the project, and not just managing the project management information system. It's easy to get caught up in the software features and in the processes and planning logic and not pay attention to the project itself. Be certain that the project is where your attention is and not just the software or information system you're using to manage the software.

Earned Value Management (EVM)

Earned value management (EVM) is concerned with measuring and reporting on the progress of the project. It incorporates the project schedule, scope, and resources as a whole to determine if variances exist in the project. Earned value analysis is a technique used to calculate performance measures that we'll explore in more detail in Chapter 9, "Measuring and Controlling Project Performance."

Project Plan Development Outputs

This brings you to the outputs of the Project Plan Development process, which are the project plan and supporting detail. Let's talk a little bit more about each of these.

Project Plan

The *project plan* is the approved, formal, documented plan that's used to guide you throughout the project Executing process group. It's the map that tells you where you're going and how to perform the activities of the project plan during the Project Plan Execution process. It serves several purposes, the most important of which is tracking and measuring project performance through the Executing and Controlling phases and making future project decisions. The project plan is critical in all communications you'll have from here forward with the stakeholders, management, and customers. The project plan also documents all project planning assumptions, all project planning decisions, and important management reviews needed.

The project plan encompasses everything we've talked about up to now and is represented in a formal document, or collection of documents. This document contains the project scope statement, deliverables, assumptions, risks, WBS, milestones, activity schedule, resources, and more. It becomes the baseline you'll use to measure and track progress against. It's also used to help you control the components that tend to stray from the original plan, so you can get them back in line.

The project plan is used as a communication and information tool for stakeholders, team members, and the management team. They will use the project plan to review and gauge progress as well.

Exam Spotlight

A Guide to the PMBOK makes a point of differentiating the project performance measurement baselines from the project plan. The project plan is the document, or assortment of documents, that constitutes what the project is, what the project will deliver, and how all the processes will be managed. There will be changes to the project plan throughout the remaining process groups, and the document, or documents, need to be updated to reflect those changes.

The performance measurement baselines are the management controls in place that should change only infrequently. Examples of the performance measurement baselines we've looked at so far are Cost Budgeting baselines and schedule baselines. The project plan itself also becomes a baseline. If changes in scope or schedule do occur after Planning is complete, there's a formalized process that you should go through to implement the changes, which we'll cover in a Chapter 10, "Controlling Change."

Supporting Detail

You've seen the supporting detail output before. The supporting detail for the Project Plan Development process includes any information not previously included in the other project Planning processes. Technical information such as design specifications might be included here as well. Chapter 6 talked about standards and policies. If they're applicable to the project, you could include the standards here or reference where they might be found. Again you're back to your project management mantra: "Document, document, document." If you cannot find any other logical place to put information that you know should be included with the project, put it in supporting detail. Last but not least, don't forget to include assumptions and constraints that were discovered during this phase of the Planning process.

Don't forget that sign-off is an important part of this process. Your last step in the Planning process group is obtaining sign-off of the project plan from stakeholders, the sponsor, and the management team.

Project Case Study: New Kitchen Heaven Retail Store

You've spent a couple of days working on the project schedule in Microsoft Project 2000, clarifying tasks and activities with Jake, Ricardo, and Jill. You decide that a Gantt chart will work excellently for reporting status for this project. A portion of your first draft of the Gantt chart shows the following at the end of the project:

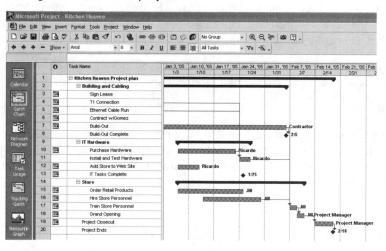

The detail behind the Gantt chart snapshot is as follows. This is a limited amount of detail for example purposes:

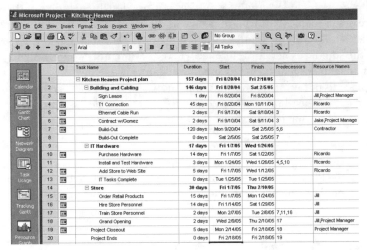

		O	Task Name	Duration	Start	Finish	Predecessors	Resource Names
	1		⊟ Kitchen Heaven Project plan	157 days	Fri 8/20/04	Fri 2/18/05		
	2		⊟ Building and Cabling	146 days	Fri 8/20/04	Sat 2/5/05		
	3	▦	Sign Lease	1 day	Fri 8/20/04	Fri 8/20/04		Jill,Project Manager
	4	▦	T1 Connection	45 days	Fri 8/20/04	Mon 10/11/04		Ricardo
	5	▦	Ethernet Cable Run	2 days	Fri 9/17/04	Sat 9/18/04	3	Ricardo
	6	▦	Contract w/Gomez	2 days	Fri 9/10/04	Sat 9/11/04	3	Jake,Project Manage
	7	▦	Build-Out	120 days	Mon 9/20/04	Sat 2/5/05	5,6	Contractor
	8		Build-Out Complete	0 days	Sat 2/5/05	Sat 2/5/05	7	
	9		⊟ IT Hardware	17 days	Fri 1/7/05	Wed 1/26/05		
	10	▦	Purchase Hardware	14 days	Fri 1/7/05	Sat 1/22/05		Ricardo
	11	▦	Install and Test Hardware	3 days	Mon 1/24/05	Wed 1/26/05	4,5,10	Ricardo
	12	▦	Add Store to Web Site	5 days	Fri 1/7/05	Wed 1/12/05		Ricardo
	13	▦	IT Tasks Complete	0 days	Tue 1/25/05	Tue 1/25/05		
	14		⊟ Store	30 days	Fri 1/7/05	Thu 2/10/05		
	15	▦	Order Retail Products	15 days	Fri 1/7/05	Mon 1/24/05		Jill
	16	▦	Hire Store Personnel	14 days	Fri 1/14/05	Sat 1/29/05		Jill
	17	▦	Train Store Personnel	2 days	Mon 2/7/05	Tue 2/8/05	7,11,16	Jill
	18	▦	Grand Opening	2 days	Wed 2/9/05	Thu 2/10/05	17	Jill,Project Manager
	19	▦	Project Closeout	5 days	Mon 2/14/05	Fri 2/18/05	18	Project Manager
	20		Project Ends	0 days	Fri 2/18/05	Fri 2/18/05	19	

You stare intensely at the problem you see on the screen. The Grand Opening task (number 18) is scheduled to occur nine days later than when you need it! Grand opening must happen February 1 and 2, not February 9 and 10 as the schedule shows. You trace the problem back and see that Grand Opening depends on Train Store Personnel, which itself depends on several other tasks including Hire Store Personnel, Install and Test Hardware, and Build-out. Digging deeper, build-out can't begin until the Ethernet cable is run throughout the building. Ricardo already set up the time with the contractor to run the cable September 17. This date cannot move, which means build-out cannot start any sooner than September 20.

You pick up the phone and dial Jake's number. "Jake," you say into the receiver. "I'm working on the project schedule, and I have some issues with the Gomez activity."

"Shoot," Jake says.

"Gomez Construction can't start work until the Ethernet cable is run. I've already confirmed with Ricardo that there is no negotiation on this. Ricardo is hiring a contractor for this activity, and the earliest they can start is September 17. It takes them two days to run the cable, which puts the start date for build-out at September 20."

"That's three days," Jake says.

"Gomez doesn't work on Sundays so the soonest the build-out can start is the following Monday."

"Right," Jake replies. "What's the problem with the September 20th date?"

"Jill wants to have the build-out finished prior to hiring the store personnel. During the last store opening, those activities overlapped, and she said it was unmanageable. She wants to hire folks and have them stock the shelves in preparation for store opening but doesn't want contractors in there while they're doing it. A September 19 start date for Gomez puts us at a finish date of February 5, which is too late, regardless of the problem with Jill. Hence, my question, is 120 days to finish a build-out a firm estimate?"

"Always—I've got this down to a science. Gomez has worked with me on enough of these build-outs that we can come within just a couple of days of this estimate either way," Jake says.

You pick up your schedule detail and continue. "I've scheduled Gomez's resource calendar as you told me originally. Gomez doesn't work Sundays and neither do we. Their holidays are Labor Day, a couple of days at Thanksgiving, Christmas, and New Year's, but this puts us too far out on the schedule. I know Dirk won't go for a later date; he's firm on the February 1 opening."

"I can't change the 120 days. Sounds like you have a problem."

"I need to crash the schedule," you say. "What would the chances be of Gomez agreeing to split the build-out tasks? We could hire a second contractor to come in and work alongside Gomez's crew to speed up this task. That would shorten the duration to 100 days, which means we could meet the February 1 date."

"Won't happen. I know Gomez. They're a big outfit and have all their own crews. We typically work with them exclusively. If I brought another contractor into the picture, I might have a hard time negotiating any kind of favors with them later if we get into a bind."

"Alright," you say. "How about this? I'm making some changes to the resource calendar while we're talking. What if we authorize Gomez's crew to work six 10-hour days, which still leaves them with Sundays off, and we ask them to work Labor Day and take only one day at each of the other holidays instead of two?"

The detail showing these changes is as follows:

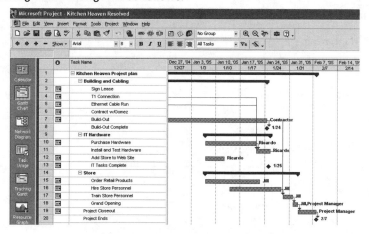

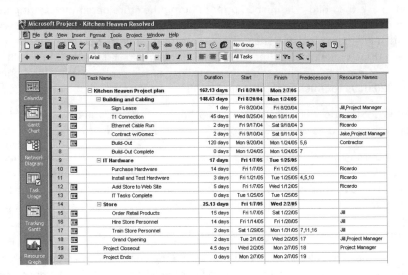

"I think Gomez would go for that. You realize it's going to cost you?"

"Project management is all about trade-offs. We can't move the start date, so chances are the budget might take a hit to accommodate schedule changes or risk. Fortunately, I'm just now wrapping up the final cost budget baseline, so if you can get me the increased cost from Gomez soon, I'd appreciate it. This change will keep us on track and resolve Jill's issues too."

"I don't think Gomez's crew will mind the overtime during the holiday season. Everyone can use a little extra cash at that time of year, it seems. I'll have the figures for you in a day or two."

Project Case Study Checklist

Developing project schedule

- Calendars

- Lead and lag time

- Critical path

Duration compression

- Crashing

Utilizing project management software

Producing project schedule

- Milestones

- Gantt chart

- Resource leveling

Cost baseline

Finalized project plan

Summary

Great job, you've made it through the entire Planning process. We covered three processes in this chapter: Schedule Development, Cost Budgeting, and Project Plan Development.

Schedule Development is the process in which you assign beginning and ending dates to tasks and determine their duration. You can use several methods to do this, including CPM, GERT, and PERT. The CPM calculates early start, early finish, late start, and late finish dates. It also determines float time. All tasks with zero float are critical path tasks. The critical path is the longest path in the project.

GERT allows for conditional branching and looping; CPM and PERT do not.

PERT calculates a weighted average estimate for each activity by using the optimistic, pessimistic, and most likely times and then determines variances, or standard deviations, to come up with a total project duration within a given confidence range. 68.26 percent of the time, work will finish within plus or minus one standard deviation. 95.44 percent of the time, work will finish within plus or minus two standard deviations.

Schedules sometimes need to be compressed to meet promised dates or to shorten the schedule times. Crashing looks at cost and schedule trade-offs. Adding resources to critical path tasks and limiting or reducing the project requirements or scope are ways to crash the schedule. Fast tracking involves beginning two tasks that were originally scheduled to start one after the other at the same time. Fast tracking increases project risk.

Monte Carlo Analysis can be used in the Schedule Development process to determine multiple, probable project durations.

Resource leveling attempts to smooth out the schedule and properly allocate resources to critical path tasks. This may require updates to the resource management plan.

The project schedule details the activities in graphical form through the use of network diagrams with dates, Gantt charts, milestone charts, or time-scaled network diagrams.

The schedule management plan details how the project schedule will be managed and how changes will be incorporated into the project schedule.

The Cost Budgeting baseline will be used throughout the project to measure project expenditures, variance, and project performance. The cost baseline is graphically displayed as an S-curve.

Project Plan Development is the last process in the Planning process group. The project plan is used as a guideline throughout the project Executing and Controlling processes to help make future project decisions. It's also used to measure and track project performance. The project plan might be one document or several documents stored together in an organized, logical format.

Exam Essentials

Be able to calculate the critical path.   The critical path is the activities whose durations add up to the longest full path utilizing the forward pass, backward pass, and float calculations.

Be able to define a critical path task.   A critical path task is a project activity with zero float.

Be able to describe and calculate PERT duration estimates.   This is a weighted average technique that uses three estimates: optimistic, pessimistic, and most likely. The formula is as follows: (optimistic + pessimistic + (4 × most likely)) ÷ 6.

Be able to name the duration compression techniques.   The duration compression techniques are crashing and fast tracking.

Be able to describe the cost baseline.   The cost baseline is the expected cost of the project and is used to measure performance. It's displayed as an S-curve.

Key Terms

Before you take the exam, be certain you are familiar with the following terms:

backward pass	milestone charts
bar charts	milestones
cost baseline	Monte Carlo Analysis
Cost Budgeting	Program Evaluation and Review Technique (PERT)
crashing	project calendars
critical chain method	project plan
critical path (CP)	Project Plan Development
Critical Path Method (CPM)	project planning methodology
duration compression	project schedule
fast tracking	resource calendars
float time	resource leveling
forward pass	resource-based method
Gantt charts	reverse resource allocation scheduling
Graphical Evaluation and Review Technique (GERT)	Schedule Development
lags	simulation
leads	slack time

Review Questions

1. The project schedule is used to determine all of the following except:

   A. Cost estimates

   B. Activity start dates

   C. Float times

   D. Activity end dates

2. You are a project manager for Picture Shades, Inc. They manufacture window shades for hotel chains that have replicas of Renaissance-era paintings on the inside of the shades. Picture Shades is taking their product to the home market, and you're managing the new project. They will offer their products at retail stores as well as on their website. You're developing the project schedule for this undertaking and have determined the critical path. Which of the following statements is true?

   A. You calculated the most likely start date and most likely finish dates, float time, and weighted average estimates.

   B. You calculated the activity dependency, and the optimistic and pessimistic activity duration estimates.

   C. You calculated the early and late start dates, the early and late finish dates, and float times for all activities.

   D. You calculated the optimistic, pessimistic, and most likely duration times and the float times for all activities.

3. You are a project manager for Picture Shades, Inc. They manufacture window shades for hotel chains that have replicas of Renaissance-era paintings on the inside of the shades. Picture Shades is taking their product to the home market, and you're managing the new project. They will offer their products at retail stores as well as on their website. You're developing the project schedule for this undertaking. Looking at the following graph, which path is the critical path?

   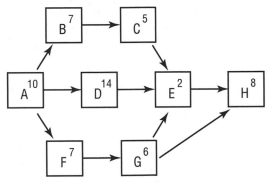

   A. A-B-C-E-H

   B. A-D-E-H

   C. A-F-G-H

   D. A-F-G-E-H

4. Use the following graphic to answer this question. If the duration of activity B was changed to 10 days and the duration of activity G was changed to 9 days, which path is the critical path?

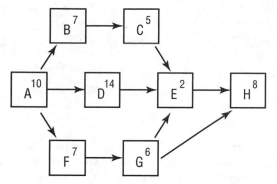

    A. A-B-C-E-H

    B. A-D-E-H

    C. A-F-G-H

    D. A-F-G-E-H

5. Which of the following statements is true regarding the critical path?

    A. It should never be compressed.

    B. It allows for looping and branching.

    C. The critical path technique is the same as PERT.

    D. It's the duration of all tasks with zero float.

6. All of the following are tools and techniques of the Schedule Development process except:

    A. CPM

    B. EVM

    C. GERT

    D. PERT

7. You are a project manager for a new software development project. You have a few activities that require specialized testing. The testing might need to be repeated more than once. Which of the following do you choose?

    A. The Graphical Evaluation and Review Technique, because it allows for conditional branching and looping for the testing activity.

    B. The Critical Path Method, because it allows for float time to be calculated for the testing activity.

    C. The Program Evaluation and Review Technique, because it allows for conditional branching and looping for the testing activity.

    D. The Program Evaluation and Review Technique, because it allows for a weighted average distribution, which will even out the time needed for the testing activity.

8. You are a project manager for Move It Now trucking company. Your company specializes in moving household goods across the city or across the country. Your project involves upgrading the nationwide computer network for the company. Your lead engineer has given you the following estimates for a critical path activity: 60 days most likely, 72 days pessimistic, 48 days optimistic. What is the expected value, or weighted average?

   A. 54

   B. 66

   C. 60

   D. 30

9. You are a project manager for Move It Now trucking company. Your company specializes in moving household goods across the city or across the country. Your project involves upgrading the nationwide computer network for the company. Your lead engineer has given you the following estimates for a critical path activity: 60 days most likely, 72 days pessimistic, 48 days optimistic. What is the standard deviation?

   A. 22

   B. 20

   C. 2

   D. 4

10. If you know expected value is 500 and the standard deviation is 12, you can say with approximately a 95 percent confidence rating which of the following?

    A. The activity will take between 488 and 512 days.

    B. The activity will take between 464 and 536 days.

    C. The activity will take between 494 and 506 days.

    D. The activity will take between 476 and 524 days.

11. If your expected value is 110 and the standard deviation is 12, which of the following is true?

    A. There is approximately a 99 percent chance of completing this activity between 86 and 134 days.

    B. There is approximately a 68 percent chance of completing this activity between 98 and 122 days.

    C. There is approximately a 95 percent chance of completing this activity between 98 and 122 days.

    D. There is approximately a 75 percent chance of completing this activity between 86 and 134 days.

12. You are the project manager working on a research project for a new drug treatment. Your preliminary project schedule runs past the due date for a federal grant application. The manager of the R&D department has agreed to release two resources to work on your project in order to meet the federal grant application date. This is an example of:

    A. Crashing

    B. Fast tracking

    C. Resource leveling

    D. Adjusting the resource calendar

13. You are the project manager working on a research project for a new drug treatment. Your preliminary project schedule runs past the due date for a federal grant application. You adjust the schedule and find that two activities previously scheduled to start sequentially can be started at the same time. This is an example of:

    A. Crashing

    B. Fast tracking

    C. Resource leveling

    D. Adjusting the resource calendar

14. You are the project manager for Rivera Gourmet Adventure Vacations. Rivera combines the wonderful tastes of great gourmet food with outdoor adventure activities. Your project involves installing a new human resources software system. Jason, the database analyst working on this project, is over-allocated. Which of the following statements is true?

    A. You should use resource requirements updates to determine availability and smooth out resource over-allocation.

    B. You should use crashing to resource-level the critical path tasks.

    C. You should use resource-leveling heuristics to smooth out resource assignments.

    D. You should use fast tracking to resource-level the critical path tasks.

15. What is one of the problems with project management software?

    A. The project manager manages the software instead of the project.

    B. Project duration calculations are sometimes approximate.

    C. You cannot override the project management software decisions regarding schedules.

    D. It's expensive and difficult to use.

16. Obtaining formal project plan approval and sign-off is important for all of the following reasons except:

    A. Stakeholders are able to recommend a project planning methodology to follow throughout the remaining process groups.

    B. Stakeholders are aware of the project details, which makes them more likely to participate in future project decisions.

    C. Stakeholders will be more likely to cooperate.

    D. Stakeholders are aware of the specific details regarding project schedules, budgets, and risks.

17. Which of the following are the tools and techniques of the Cost Budgeting process?

    A. Project management information system, analogous estimating, bottom-up estimating, and mathematical analysis

    B. Analogous estimating, bottom-up estimating, mathematical analysis, and computerized tools

    C. Project management software, analogous estimating, bottom-up estimating, and parametric modeling

    D. Analogous estimating, bottom-up estimating, parametric modeling, and computerized tools

18. You are the project manager for a custom home-building construction company. You are working on the model home project for the upcoming Show Homes Tour. The model home includes Internet connections in every room and talking appliances. You are working on the cost budget for this project. All of the following statements are true except:

    A. This process assigns cost estimates to project activities, including risks and contingency plans.

    B. The cost baseline will be used to measure variances and future project performance.

    C. This process assigns cost estimates for expected future period operating costs.

    D. The cost baseline is the expected cost for the project.

19. Which of the following is displayed as an S-curve?

    A. Gantt

    B. Cost baseline

    C. Critical path

    D. PERT

20. All of the following statements are true regarding the project plan except:

    A. Some of project plan's inputs are outputs from other Planning processes.

    B. The project plan is used to guide the project Executing and Controlling processes and is the baseline used to measure project performance.

    C. The project plan consists of one or more documents that should be formally approved and signed by stakeholders.

    D. The project plan contains things like the WBS, project schedule, and resource assignments.

Answers to Review Questions

1. **A.** The project schedule determines the start and ending dates of activities, determines float times, generally shows resource assignments, and details the activity sequences and durations.

2. **C.** The CPM calculates a single early and late start date and a single early and late finish date for each activity. Once these dates are known, float time is calculated for each activity to determine the critical path. The other answers contain elements of PERT calculations.

3. **B.** The only information you have for this example is activity duration, therefore the critical path is the path with the longest duration. Path A-D-E-H with a duration of 34 days is the critical path.

4. **D.** The only information you have for this example is activity duration, so you must calculate the critical path based on the durations given. The duration of A-B-C-E-H increased by 3 days for a total of 35 days. The duration of A-F-G-H and A-F-G-E-H each increased by 3 days. A-F-G-E-H totals 36 days and becomes the new critical path.

5. **D.** The critical path is calculated by adding together the durations of all the tasks with zero float. The critical path can be compressed using crashing techniques.

6. **B.** EVM is earned value management, which is a tool and technique of the Project Plan Development process.

7. **A.** GERT is the only Schedule Development tool that allows for conditional branching and looping.

8. **C.** The calculation for PERT is the sum of optimistic time plus pessimistic time plus four times the most likely time divided by 6. The calculation for this example is as follows: $(48 + 72 + (4 \times 60)) \div 6 = 60$.

9. **D.** The standard deviation is calculated by subtracting the optimistic time from the pessimistic time and dividing the result by 6. The calculation for this example looks as follows: $(72 - 48) \div 6 = 4$

10. **D.** There is a 95 percent probability that the work will finish within plus or minus two standard deviations. The expected value is 500, and the standard deviation times 2 is 24, so the activity will take between 476 and 524 days.

11. **B.** A 68 percent probability is calculated using plus or minus one standard deviation, a 95 percent probability uses plus or minus two standard deviations, and a 99 percent probability uses plus or minus three standard deviations.

12. **A.** Crashing the schedule includes things like adding resources to the critical path tasks or limiting project requirements.

13. **B.** Fast tracking is starting two tasks at the same time that were previously scheduled to start one after the other.

14. C. Resource-leveling heuristics attempt to smooth out resource assignments by splitting tasks, assigning under-allocated team members to more tasks, or delaying the start of tasks to match team members' availability.

15. A. Project management software is a very useful tool for the project manager, and it automates project scheduling allowing for what-if analysis and easy changes. But if you focus too much on the tool and ignore the project, the tool becomes a distraction.

16. A. Stakeholders ordinarily will not have much say in the project planning methodology used by the project manager. The methodology employed is usually determined by either the organization, the project office, or the project manager.

17. D. Cost Budgeting's tools and techniques are the same tools and techniques of the Cost Estimating process: analogous estimating, parametric modeling, bottom-up estimating, and computerized tools.

18. C. Future period operating costs are considered ongoing costs and are not part of project costs.

19. B. The cost baseline is displayed as an S-curve because of the way project spending occurs. Spending begins slowly, picks up speed until the spending peak is reached, and then tapers off as the project winds down.

20. A. All of the Project Plan Development inputs come from other planning processes, but not all the inputs are outputs of other processes (historical information, for example).

Chapter 8

Developing the Project Team

THE PMP EXAM CONTENT FROM THE
PROJECT EXECUTION PERFORMANCE
DOMAIN COVERED IN THIS CHAPTER
INCLUDES:

- ✓ 1. Committing resources
- ✓ 2. Implementing resources
- ✓ 3. Managing progress
- ✓ 4. Communicating progress

This chapter begins the project Executing process group. We'll cover three processes in the project Executing group: Project Plan Execution, Team Development, and Information Distribution. You'll get a reprieve in this chapter: there is only one math equation you need to memorize.

Project Plan Execution is the action process so to speak. This is where you'll put the plans into action and begin working on the project activities. Execution also involves keeping the project in line with the original project plan and bringing wayward activities back into alignment.

Several things happen during the Executing processes. The majority of the project budget will be spent during this process, and often the majority of the project time is expended here as well. The greatest conflicts you'll see during the project Executing process are schedule conflicts. In addition, the product description will be finalized here and contain more detail than it did in the Planning process.

Project Plan Execution is the only core process in the Executing process group. All the other processes we'll discuss are facilitating processes to Project Plan Execution. The facilitating processes assist you with executing the project plan.

Hang with me during this chapter, because there are several references to the next process—the Controlling process group—that are inputs to the Execution process group. These are the only two process groups that serve as inputs to each other. Since we can't discuss both of them at the same time, we'll tell you when there's something specific from the Controlling process that will be discussed in a later chapter.

This chapter starts with the Project Plan Execution process and then discusses Team Development and communication processes. There might be several exam questions from every process within the Executing process group. You'll find the majority of questions are about the Project Plan Execution process, the Team Development process, and the Contract Administration process, which we'll talk about in the next chapter. Don't skip studying the other processes, however, as roughly a quarter of the exam questions concern the entire Executing process group. Are you ready to dive into Executing? Let's go.

Executing the Project Plan

The purpose of the *Project Plan Execution* process is to carry out the project plan. This is where your project comes to life and the work of the project happens. Activities are clarified, and the work is authorized to begin. Resources are committed and carry out their assigned activities to create the product or service of the project. This process is where the rubber meets the road. If you've done a good job planning the project, things should go relatively smoothly for you during this process. The deliverables and requirements are agreed to, the resources have been identified and are ready to go, and the stakeholders know exactly where you're headed because you had them review, agree to, and approve the project plan.

Some project managers think this is the time for them to kick back and put their feet up. After all, the project plan is done, everyone knows what to do and what's expected of them, and the work of the project should almost carry itself out because your project plan is a work of genius—wrong! You must stay involved. Your job now is a matter of overseeing the actual work, staying on top of issues and problems, and keeping the work lined up with the project plan.

Exam Spotlight

The project plan serves as the project baseline. During the Executing processes, you should continually compare and monitor project performance against the baseline so that corrective actions can be taken and implemented at the right time to prevent disaster.

One of the most difficult aspects of this process is coordinating and integrating all the elements of the project. While you do have the project plan as your guide, there are still a lot of balls in the air. You'll find yourself coordinating and monitoring many project elements—occasionally all at the same time—during the course of the Project Plan Execution process. You may be negotiating for team members at the same time you're negotiating with vendors at the same time you're working with another manager to get a project component completed so your deliverable stays on schedule. Risks and risk triggers should be monitored closely. The Procurement planning process may need intervention or cause you delays. The organizational, technical, and interpersonal interfaces may require intense coordination and oversight. And of course, you should always be concerned about the pulse of your stakeholders. Are they actively involved in the project? Are they throwing up roadblocks now that the work has started?

Later in this chapter we'll also talk about team building, because this is an integral part of the Project Plan Execution process as well. You'll want to monitor the team's performance, the status of their work, and their interactions with you and other team members as you execute the project plan.

As you can see, your work as project manager is not done yet. There are many elements to the project that require your attention, so let's get to work.

Executing Inputs

Project Plan Execution has five inputs:

- Project plan
- Supporting detail

- Organizational policies
- Preventive action
- Corrective action

Supporting detail was discussed earlier in this book; it includes constraints and assumptions. There are a few new concepts to add to organizational policies, so we'll look at that input again, along with the others.

Project Plan

The *project plan* is the output of the Planning process group, specifically the Project Plan Development process. The important thing to note here is that all the management plans we discussed during the Planning process—the scope management plan, the schedule management plan, the resource management plan, and so on, plus the cost budgeting baseline and the schedule baseline—are used throughout the Executing process to manage the project and keep the performance of the project on track with the project objectives. If you don't have a project plan, you'll have no way of managing the process. You'll find that even with a project plan, project scope has a way of changing. Stakeholders and others tend to sneak in a few of the "Oh, I didn't understand that before" statements and hope that they slide right by you. With that signed, approved project plan in your files, you are allowed to gently remind them that they read and agreed to the project plan and you're sticking to it. They can request a formal change, but that's another topic, which we'll get to shortly.

Organizational Policies

It's important for the project manager to understand *organizational policies*, because they may impact Project Plan Execution. For example, the organization may have purchasing approval processes that must be followed. Perhaps orders for goods or services that exceed certain dollar amounts need different levels of approval. As the project manager, you need to be aware of policies like this so you're certain you can execute the project smoothly. It's very frustrating to find out after the fact that you should have followed a certain process or policy, and now because you didn't, you've got schedule delays or worse. You could consider using the "Sin now, ask forgiveness later" technique in extreme emergencies, but you didn't hear that from me. By the way, that's not an authorized PMI technique.

The project manager and the project team will be responsible for coordinating all the organizational interfaces for the project, including technical, human resource, purchasing, finance, and so on. It will serve you well to understand the policies and politics involved in each of these areas in your organization.

My organization is so steeped in policy (a government organization steeped in policy...go figure!), we have to request the funds for large projects at least two years in advance. There are mounds and mounds of request forms, justification forms, approval forms, routing forms—you get the idea. But my point is if you miss one of the forms or don't fill out the information correctly, you can set your project back by a minimum of a year, if not two. Then once the money is awarded, there are more forms and policies to follow. Again, if you don't follow the policies correctly, you can jeopardize future project funds. Many organizations have a practice of not giving you all the project money up front in one lump sum. In other words, you must meet major milestones or complete a project phase before they'll fund your next phase. Once the milestone is met or the phase is complete, you'll get the funding for the next phase and so on for the remainder of the project. Know what your organizational policies are well ahead of time. Talk to the people that can walk you through the process and ask them to check your work to avoid surprises.

Preventive Action

Preventive action involves anything that will reduce the potential impacts of risk events should they occur. Contingency plans and risk responses are examples of preventive action. These and other risk responses are described in the Risk Response Planning process discussed in Chapter 6, "Establishing Project Planning Controls." You should be aware of contingency plans and risk responses so that you're ready to implement them at the first sign of trouble.

Corrective Action

In my organization, a corrective action means an employee has big trouble coming. Fortunately, this isn't what's meant here. *Corrective actions* are taken to get the anticipated future project outcomes to align with the project plan. Maybe you've discovered one of your programmers is adding an unplanned feature to the software project because he's friends with the user. You'll have to redirect him to the activities assigned him originally to avoid schedule delays. Perhaps your vendor isn't able to deliver the laboratory equipment needed for the next project phase. You'll want to exercise your contract options (hopefully there's a clause in the contract that says they must provide rental equipment until they can deliver your order), put your contingency plan into place, and get the lab the equipment they need to keep the project on schedule.

Corrective actions are outputs of processes in the Controlling process group, but they serve as inputs to the Project Plan Execution process. We'll talk more about corrective actions in Chapter 10, "Controlling Change."

Exam Spotlight

For the exam, remember that the Executing and Controlling process outputs are inputs to each other.

Meetings and More

As with the Project Plan Development process, almost everything you've done to date is utilized by the Project Plan Execution process. The primary output here is work results, meaning actually accomplishing the activities leading to completion of the product or service you set out to produce. Without having completed the prior processes, you wouldn't know what the work of the project should look like. Several tools and techniques are used to facilitate the work results. We'll look at all of them, with the exception of project management information system, which we've covered previously.

General Management Skills

You learned about general management skills back in Chapter 1, "What Is a Project?" These include skills like general business knowledge, budgeting, organizational skills, problem solving skills, and so on. What's important to note here is that the general management skills of leadership, negotiation, and communications are especially useful during Project Plan Execution. We'll talk more about leadership in the next section, "Developing the Project Team," as there are some new terms and techniques you'll want to know for the exam.

 One other thing to consider regarding this tool and technique is that other departments will have assignments on the project that you're responsible for monitoring. For example, the Finance department and the Marketing department may have project activities, and as the project manager, you'll manage their progress. This implies that you'll need general knowledge management skills to understand what the assignments entail and strong leadership skills to influence the departments to stay on schedule.

Product Skills and Knowledge

Product skills and knowledge are needed by the project team members to understand the product or service of the project. If, for example, your project is constructing a mass spectrometer and no one on your team knows what a mass spectrometer looks like, you've got a problem. Key team members should have knowledge, skills, and experience with the products of the project.

Work Authorization System

Work authorization systems clarify and initiate the work of each work package or activity. This is a formal procedure that authorizes work to begin in the correct sequence and at the right time. Work authorization systems are usually written procedures defined by the organization. They might include e-mail, intranet-based, or paper-based systems. Verbal instructions may work well with small projects. Understand the complexity of the project and balance the cost of instituting a work authorization system against the benefit you'll receive from it. This may be overkill on small projects, and as stated earlier, verbal instructions might work just as well.

Work is usually authorized using a form that describes the task, the responsible party, anticipated start and end dates, special instructions, and whatever else is particular to the activity or project. Depending on the organizational structure, the work is assigned and authorized by either the project manager or the functional manager.

Status Review Meetings

Status review meetings are important functions of Project Plan Execution. The purpose of the status meeting is to provide updated information regarding the progress of the project. These are not show-and-tell meetings. If you have a prototype to demo, set up a different time to do that. Status meetings are meant to exchange information and provide project updates. They are a way to formally exchange project information. I've worked on projects where it's not unusual to have three or four status meetings conducted for different audiences. They can occur between the project team and project manager, the project manager and stakeholders, the project manager and users or customers, the project manager and the management team, and so on.

Notice that the project manager is always included in status review meetings. Take care that you don't overburden yourself with meetings that aren't necessary or could be combined with other meetings. Any more than three or four status meetings is unwieldy.

Regular, timely status meetings prevent surprises down the road, because you are keeping stakeholders and customers informed of what's happening. Team status meetings alert the project manager to potential risk events and provide the opportunity to discover and manage problems before they get to the uncontrollable stage.

The project manager is usually the expediter of the status meeting. As such, it's your job to use status meetings wisely. Don't waste your team's time or stakeholders' time either. Notify attendees in writing of the meeting time and place. Publish an agenda prior to the meeting and stick to the agenda during the meeting. Every so often, summarize what's been discussed during the meeting. Don't let side discussions lead you down rabbit trails, and keep irrelevant conversations to a minimum. It's also good to publish status meeting notes at the conclusion of the meeting, especially if any action items resulted from the meeting. This will give you a document trail and serves as a reminder to the meeting participants of what actions need to be resolved and who is responsible for the action item.

It's important that project team members are honest with the project manager and that the project manager is in turn honest about what they report. A few years ago, a department in my agency took on a project of gargantuan proportions and unfortunately didn't employ good project management techniques. One of the biggest problems with this project was that the project manager did not listen to their highly skilled project team members. The team members warned of problems and setbacks, but the project manager didn't want to hear of it. The project manager took their reports to be of the "Chicken Little" ilk and refused to believe the sky was falling. Unfortunately, the sky *was* falling! The project manager, because they didn't believe it, refused to report the true status of the project to the stakeholders and oversight committees. Millions of dollars were wasted on a project that was doomed for failure, while the project manager continued to report that the project was on time and activities were completed when in fact they were not.

There are hundreds of project stories like this, and I'll bet you've got one or two from your experience as well. Don't let your project become the next bad example. Above all, be honest in your reporting. No one likes bad news, but bad news delivered too late along with millions of dollars wasted is a guaranteed career showstopper.

Organizational Procedures

Organizational procedures are very similar to organizational policies, except organizational policies are an input and organizational procedures are a tool and technique of this process.

The project manager should take organizational procedures into consideration when doing the work of the project. Maybe your finance department requires special requisitions for certain purchases, or your human resources department requires formal hiring procedures for full-time employees and a different set of hiring procedures for contract personnel. Be aware of procedures like this ahead of time so that they don't interfere with the project Executing process.

Resulting Outputs

We've already touched on the outputs of the Project Plan Execution process. Obviously, the activities that produce the product or service of the project are your end result. *A Guide to the PMBOK* calls this work results. The second output of the Project Plan Execution process discussed in this section is change requests.

Work Results

During Project Plan Execution, you'll gather and record information regarding the outcomes of the work, including activity completion dates, milestone completions, the status of the deliverables, the quality of the deliverables, costs, schedule progress and updates, and so on. Deliverables aren't always tangible. For example, perhaps your team members require training on a piece of specialized equipment. Completion of the training is recorded as a work result as well. All of this information gets used during the Performance Reporting process, which we'll discuss during the Controlling process.

Project Executing and Controlling are two processes that work hand in hand. As you gather the information from work results, you'll measure the outputs and take corrective actions where necessary. This means you'll loop back through the Executing process to put the corrections into place. *A Guide to the PMBOK* breaks these processes up for ease of explanation, but in practice, you'll work through several of the Executing and Controlling processes together.

Change Requests

As a result of working through activities and producing your product or service, you will inevitably come upon things that need to be changed. This might encompass schedule changes, scope changes, or requirements or resource changes. The list really could go on. Your job as project manager, if you choose to accept it (wasn't that a movie theme?), is to collect the change requests and make determinations about their impact to the project. We'll discuss change requests in the coming chapters. Change requests are an output of the Project Plan Execution process and an output of the Performance Reporting process in the Controlling process group. Remember that Executing and Controlling outputs feed each other as inputs.

Project Plan Execution is the primary process, and the only core process, in the Executing process group. The work of the project is performed here, and the project plan is put into action and carried out. In this process, the project manager is like an orchestra conductor signaling the instruments to begin their activities, monitoring what should be winding down, and keeping that smile going to remind everyone that they should be enjoying themselves. I recommend that you know the tools and techniques and the outputs of the Project Plan Execution process for the exam.

Developing the Project Team

Projects exist to create a unique product or service within a limited time frame. Projects are performed by people, and most projects require more than one person to perform all of the activities. If you've got more than one person working on your project, you've got a team. And if you've got a team, you've got a wide assortment of personalities, skills, needs, and issues in the mix. Couple this with part-time team members, teams based in functional organizations whose loyalty lies with the functional manager, or teams based in matrix organizations that report to you for project-related activities and another manager for their functional duties, and you could have some real challenges on your hands. Good luck—okay, I won't leave you hanging like that.

Team Development, according to *A Guide to the PMBOK*, is about creating an open, encouraging environment for stakeholders to contribute as well as developing your team into an effective, functioning, coordinated group. Projects are performed by individuals, and the better they work together, the smoother and the more efficient the execution of the project will be.

Proper development of the team is critical to a successful project. Since teams are made up of individuals, individual development becomes a critical factor to project success. Individual team members need the proper development and training to perform the activities of the project or to enhance their existing knowledge and skills. The development needed will depend on the project. Perhaps you have a team member who's ready to make the jump into a lead role, but they don't have any experience at lead work. Give them some exposure by assigning them a limited amount of activities in a lead capacity, provide them some training if needed, and be available to coach and mentor where needed. The best option is to work with the management team to provide this person with the development they need prior to the start of the project (if you're lucky enough to know that early on who your resources might be and what their existing skills are).

Team Development inputs include project staff (from the Staff Acquisition process), project plan (from the Project Plan Development process), staffing management plan (from the Organizational Planning process), performance reports, and external feedback. All of the inputs have been discussed elsewhere, with the exception of performance reports and external feedback.

Performance reports tell you how the project is performing compared to the project plan. Chapter 9, "Measuring and Controlling Project Performance," discusses performance reports in more detail.

External feedback, as its name implies, is information relayed to the project team from those outside of the project team regarding performance expectations. This feedback might come from stakeholders, the management team, users, customers, etc.

The tools and techniques of Team Development include team-building activities, general management skills, reward and recognition systems, collocation, and training. We'll cover all these tools and techniques next, with the exception of general management skills, which were discussed earlier in this chapter. As I said earlier, there could be a lot of exam questions regarding team building, so dig out all your favorite memorization techniques and put them to use.

Team-Building Activities

Many times, project teams are made up of folks who don't know each other. They aren't necessarily aware of the project objectives and may not even want to be a part of the team. The project manager may not have worked with the people assigned to the project team before either. Sound like a recipe for disaster? It's not. Thousands of projects are started with team members and project managers who don't know each other and come to a successful completion. How is that done? It's a result of the project manager's team-building and communication skills.

The project manager's job is to bring the team together, get them all headed in the right direction, and provide motivation, reward, and recognition to keep the team in tip-top shape. This is done using a variety of team-building techniques and exercises. *Team building* is simply getting a diverse group of people to work together in the most efficient and effective manner possible. This may involve management events as well as individual actions designed to improve team performance. There are entire volumes on this subject, and it's beyond the scope of this book to go into all the team-building possibilities. The exam tends to focus more on the theories behind team building and the characteristics of effective teams, so that's what we'll spend our time looking at.

All newly formed teams go through four stages of development:

- Forming
- Storming
- Norming
- Performing

You've probably seen this elsewhere, but since these stages are on the exam, you'll want to memorize them. Let's take a brief look at each of them.

Forming This one's easy. Forming is the beginning stage of team formation, when all the members are brought together, introduced, and told the objectives of the project. This is where team members learn why they're working together. During this stage, team members tend to be formal and reserved and take on an "all-business" approach.

Storming Storming is where the action begins. Team members become confrontational with each other as they're vying for position and control during this stage. They're working through who is going to be the top dog and jockeying for status.

Norming Now things begin to calm down. Team members know each other fairly well by now. They're comfortable with their position in the team, and they begin to deal with project problems instead of people problems. In the norming stage, they confront the project concerns and problems instead of each other. Decisions are made jointly at this stage, and team members exhibit affection and familiarity with one another.

Performing Ahh, perfection. Well, almost, anyway. This is where great teams end up. This stage is where the team is productive and effective. The level of trust among team members is high, and great things are achieved. This is the mature development stage.

Exam Spotlight

Different teams progress through the stages of development at different rates. When new team members are brought onto the team, the development stages start all over again. It doesn't matter where the team is in the forming process—a new member will start the cycle all over again.

 Real World Scenario

Micro-Robotics Research and Development

Micro-Robotics is working on a prototype microscopic robot that's inserted into inoperable brain tumors. The robot is controlled using a remote control joystick device that allows a trained brain surgeon to excise the brain tumor. You are the project manager for this project and have recently assembled your team.

You've got a diverse group of highly skilled team members, including medical doctors, medical researchers, computer programmers, and biomechanical engineers.

You've held a few project meetings and have called the next one to order. The agenda has been read, and you're discussing the progress of one of the computer programs that controls the robot.

"I did hear what you said, Amiel," Noelle the brain surgeon says. "And it won't work like that."

Amiel is the lead computer programmer on the project. "But when we met last week, you said…"

Noelle interrupts, "How many brain surgeries have you performed? Fix it or I'm off this team."

You tell everyone to take five. It occurs to you that this really isn't unusual behavior. Highly skilled experts are sometimes difficult to manage, but all teams go through certain stages prior to hitting the peak performance stage. You realize this team is in the storming stage and will benefit from some team-building exercises. A few off-site team-building activities are just what the doctor ordered.

Team Focus

Have you ever watched any of those old pirate movies on late-night TV? Remember the scenes where the captain goes down into the bowels of the ship to check on the teams of rowers? He scrutinizes the crew and literally whips the rowers who aren't pulling their weight into shape. I don't recommend this as a team-building technique, but imagine for a minute that your project team members are like those rowing teams. If the members on the left are rowing one way and the members on the right are rowing another, you're creating a lot of energy and looking very busy, but in the end you aren't making any progress.

It's paramount that the team members know and understand the goals and objectives of the project. They should all understand the direction you're headed and work toward that end. After all, that's the reason they've been brought together in the first place. Keep in mind that people see and hear things from their own perspective. A room full of people attending a speech will each come away with something a little different, because what was said speaks to their particular situation in life at the time. In other words, their own perceptions filter what they hear. It's your job as project manager to make certain the team members understand the project goals and their own assignments correctly. The whip was effective for the captain in the old movies, but I suggest you use solid communication skills to get your point across. Ask your team members to tell you in their own words what they believe the project goals are. This is a great way to know if you've got everyone on board and a great opportunity for you to clarify any misunderstandings regarding the project goals.

Effective Team Characteristics

Effective teams are typically very energetic teams. Their enthusiasm is contagious, and it feeds on itself. They generate a lot of creativity and become good problem solvers. Teams like this are every project manager's dream. Investing yourself in team building as well as relationship building—especially when you don't think you have the time to do so—will bring many benefits. Here's a sample of the benefits:

- Better conflict resolution
- Commitment to the project
- Commitment to the project team members and project manager
- High job satisfaction
- Enhanced communication
- A sense of belonging and purpose
- A successful project

Dysfunctional teams will typically produce the opposite results of the benefits just listed. Dysfunctional teams don't just happen by themselves any more than great teams do. Sure, sometimes you're lucky enough to get the right combination of folks together right off the bat. But usually, team building takes work and dedication on the part of the project manager. Even in the situations where you do get that dynamite combination of people, they will benefit from team-building exercises and feedback.

Unfortunately, sour attitudes are just as contagious as enthusiasm. Watch for these symptoms among your team members and take action to correct the situation before the entire team is affected:

- Lack of motivation or "don't care" attitudes
- Project work that isn't satisfying
- Status meetings that turn into whining sessions

- Poor communication
- Lack of respect and lack of trust for the project manager

No amount of team building will make up for poor project planning or ineffective project management techniques. Neglecting these things and fooling yourself into thinking that your project team is good enough to make up for the poor planning or poor techniques could spell doom for your project. And besides that, it's not fair to your project team to put them in that position.

Collocation

Team members are often located in the same physical location—for example, the same office building or office complex. This tool and technique is called *collocation*. Collocation enables teams to function more effectively than if they're spread out among different localities. Many times on large projects, the project manager will make provisions in the project budget to bring the team together at the same location. (It's difficult, but not impossible, to manage project team members who are not physically located together.) One way to achieve collocation might be to set aside a common meeting room, sometimes called a war room, for team members who are located in different buildings or across town to meet and exchange information.

Multiple locations can also be a big time waster for you as the project manager and for your team members. If some team members are located in one part of town and another set of team members are located across town, you'll find yourself in the car (or the bus) driving back and forth to make face-to-face contact and get status updates. Conducting team meetings also becomes a hassle as one set of team members or the other must drive to the other location (or both to a central location) to have a meeting.

There is a lot of value in face-to-face contact with your team members and stakeholders. I'm a huge e-mail fan—it's one of my favorite forms of communication—but e-mail cannot tell you tone of voice, facial expressions, and body language. Whenever possible, practice the technique of collocation and get your team together.

In reality, it's often difficult to get your team together physically. A good solution in lieu of having people relocate is conference calling. Team members scattered across the country all have access to the telephone and it's relatively easy to find a time everyone can meet over the phone.

Training

Training is a matter of assessing your team's skills and abilities, assessing the project needs, and providing the training necessary for the team members to carry out their assigned activities.

Training can sometimes be a reward as well. In the software industry, programmers seek out positions that offer training on the latest and greatest technologies, and they consider it a benefit or bonus to attend training on the company dollar and time.

Motivating the Team with Rewards and Recognition

Team building starts with project planning and doesn't stop until the project is completed. It involves employing techniques to improve your team's performance and keeping team members motivated. Motivation helps people work more efficiently and produce better results. If clear expectations, clear procedures, and the right motivational tools are used, project teams will excel.

Motivation can be extrinsic or intrinsic. Extrinsic motivators are material rewards and might include bonuses, the use of a company car, stock options, gift certificates, training opportunities, extra time off, and so on.

Intrinsic motivators are specific to the individual. Some people are just naturally driven to achieve—it's part of their nature. (I suspect this is a motivator for you since you're reading this book.) Cultural and religious influences are forms of intrinsic motivators as well. Reward and recognition—a tool and technique of the Team Development process—are examples of extrinsic motivators. We'll look at them next.

Reward and Recognition Systems

Reward and recognition systems are an important part of team motivation. They are formal ways of recognizing and promoting desirable behavior and are most effective when carried out by the management team and the project manager.

Reward and recognition should occur in proportion to the achievement. In other words, appropriately link the reward to the performance. For example, a project manager who has responsibility for the project budget and the procurement process and keeps the costs in line with the budget should get rewarded for this achievement. However, if these functions are assigned to a functional manager in the organization, it wouldn't be appropriate to reward the project manager, because they were not the one responsible for keeping the costs in line.

Team members should be rewarded for going above and beyond the call of duty. Perhaps they put in a significant amount of overtime to meet a project goal or spent nights round-the-clock babysitting ill-performing equipment. These types of behaviors should get rewarded and formally recognized by the project manager and the management team. On the other hand, if the ill-performing equipment was a direct result of mistakes made or if it happened because of poor planning, rewards would not be appropriate, obviously.

Consider individual preferences and cultural differences when using rewards and recognitions. Some people don't like to be recognized in front of a group; others thrive on it. Some people appreciate an honest thank-you with minimal fanfare, and others just won't accept individual rewards as their culture doesn't allow it. Keep this in mind when devising your reward system.

🌐 Real World Scenario

Baker's Gift Baskets

You're a contract project manager for Baker's Gift Baskets. This company assembles gift baskets of all styles and shapes with every edible treat imaginable. The company has recently experienced explosive growth, and you've been brought on board to manage their new project. They want to offer "pick-your-own" baskets that allow customers to pick the individual items they want included in the basket. In addition, they're introducing a new line of containers to choose from, including things like miniature golf bags, flowerpots, serving bowls, and the like. This means changes to the catalog and the website to accommodate the new offerings.

The deadline for this project is the driving constraint. The web changes won't cause any problems with the deadline. However, the catalog must go to press quickly to meet holiday mailing deadlines, which in turn are driving the project deadline.

Your team members put their heads together and came up with an ingenious plan to meet the catalog deadline. It required lots of overtime and some weekend work on their part to pull it off, but they met the date.

You decide this is a perfect opportunity to recognize and reward the team for their outstanding efforts. You've arranged a slot on the agenda at the next all-company meeting to bring your team up front and praise them for their cooperation and efforts to get the catalog to the printers on time. You'll also present each of them with two days of paid time off and a gift certificate for a dinner with their family at an exclusive restaurant in the city.

Motivational Theories

There are many theories on motivation. You may encounter questions on these theories on the exam, so know their names and their primary points.

Motivational theories came about during the modern age. Prior to today's information and service type jobs and yesterday's factory work, the majority of people worked the land and barely kept enough food on the table to feed their family. No one was concerned about motivation at work. You worked because you wouldn't have anything to eat if you didn't. Fortunately, that isn't the case today.

Today we have a new set of problems in the workplace. Workers in the U.S. today aren't concerned with starvation—that need has been replaced with other needs like job satisfaction, a sense of belonging and commitment to the project, good working conditions, and so on. Motivational theories present ideas on why people act the way they do, and how we can influence them to act in certain ways to get the results we want. Again, there are libraries full of books on this topic. We'll cover four of them here.

Maslow's Hierarchy of Needs

You have probably seen this classic example of motivational theory. Abraham Maslow hypothesized that humans have five basic needs arranged in hierarchical order. The first needs are physical needs like the need for food, clothing, and shelter. The idea is these needs must be met before the person can move to the next level of needs in the hierarchy, which includes safety and security needs. Here, the concern is for the person's physical welfare and the security of their belongings. Once that need is met, they progress to the next level, and so on. *Maslow's hierarchy of needs* theory suggests that once a lower-level need has been met, it no longer serves as a motivator and the next higher level becomes the driving motivator in a person's life. Maslow conjectures that humans are always in one state of need or another. Here is a recap of each of the needs, starting with the highest level and working down:

Self-actualization   Performing at your peak potential

Self-esteem needs   Accomplishment, respect for self, capability

Social needs   A sense of belonging, love, acceptance, friendship

Safety and security needs   Your physical welfare and your belongings

Basic physical needs   Food, clothing, shelter

The highest level of motivation in this theory is the state of self-actualization. The United States Army had a slogan a few years ago that I think encapsulates self-actualization very well: "Be all that you can be." When all the physical, safety, social, and self-esteem needs have been met, a person reaches a state of independence where they're able to express themselves and perform at their peak. They'll do good work just for the sake of doing good work. Recognition and self-esteem have already been fulfilled at lower levels; now the need for being the best they can be is reached.

Hygiene Theory

Frederick Herzberg came up with the *Hygiene Theory*, also known as the *Motivation-Hygiene Theory*. He postulates that there are two factors that contribute to motivation: hygiene factors and motivators. Hygiene factors deal with work environment issues. The thing to remember about hygiene factors is that they prevent dissatisfaction. Examples of hygiene factors are pay, benefits, the conditions of the work environment, and relationships with peers and managers. Pay is considered a hygiene factor, because Herzberg believed that over the long term, pay is not a motivator. Being paid for the work prevents dissatisfaction but doesn't necessarily bring satisfaction in and of itself. He believed this to be true as long as the pay system is equitable. If two workers performing the same functions have large disparities in pay, then pay can become a motivator.

Motivators deal with the substance of the work itself and the satisfaction one derives from performing the functions of the job. Motivators lead to satisfaction. The ability to advance, the opportunity to learn new skills, and the challenges involved in the work are all motivators according to Herzberg.

Expectancy Theory

The *Expectancy Theory* says that the expectation of a positive outcome drives motivation. People will behave in certain ways if they think there will be good rewards for doing so. Also note that this theory says the strength of the expectancy drives the behavior. This means the expectation or likelihood of the reward is linked to the behavior. For example, if you tell your two-year-old to put the toys back in the toy box and you'll give her a cookie, chances are she'll put the toys away. This is a reasonable reward for a reasonable action. However, if you promise your project team members vacations in Hawaii if they get the project done early and they know there is no way you can deliver that reward, there is little motivation to work toward that reward.

This theory also says that people become what you expect of them. If you openly praise your project team members and treat them like valuable contributors, you'll likely have a high-performing team on your hands. Conversely, when you publicly criticize people or let them know that you have low expectations regarding their performance, they'll likely live up (or down as the case may be) to that expectation as well.

Achievement Theory

Achievement Theory says that people are motivated by the need for three things: achievement, power, and affiliation. The achievement motivation is obviously the need to achieve or succeed. The power motivation involves a desire for influencing the behavior of others. And the need for affiliation is relationship oriented. Workers want to have friendships with their co-workers and a sense of camaraderie with their fellow team members. The strength of your team members' desire for each of these will drive their performance on various activities.

We'll cover two more theories in the leadership section, which is next. These deal specifically with how leaders deal with their project team members.

Leadership vs. Management

Chapter 1 talked about leaders versus manager. There's a bit more information to add here regarding leadership theories and the types of power leaders possess. Let's recap leadership and management first before we talk about those theories.

Recall that leadership is about imparting vision and rallying people around that vision. Leaders motivate and inspire and are concerned with strategic vision. Leaders have a knack for getting others to do what needs done.

Two of the techniques they use to do this are power and politics. *Power* is the ability to get people to do what they wouldn't do ordinarily. It's also the ability to influence behavior. *Politics* imparts pressure to conform regardless of whether the person agrees with the decision. Leaders understand the difference between power and politics and when to employ each technique. We'll talk more about power shortly.

Good leaders have committed team members who believe in the vision of the leader. Leaders set direction and time frames and have the ability to attract good talent to work for them. Leaders inspire a vision and get things done through others by earning loyalty, respect, and cooperation from team members. They set the course and lead the way. Good leaders are directive in their approach but allow for plenty of feedback and input. Good leaders commonly have strong interpersonal skills and are well respected.

Managers are generally task-oriented, concerned with things like plans, controls, budgets, policies, and procedures. They're generalists with a broad base of planning and organizational skills, and their primary goal is satisfying stakeholder needs. They also possess motivational skills and the ability to recognize and reward behavior.

Project managers need to use the traits of both leaders and managers at different times during the project. On very large projects, a project manager will act more like a leader inspiring the subproject managers to get on board with the objectives. On small projects, project managers will act more like managers, because they're responsible for all the planning and coordinating functions.

There are two theories that we'll discuss regarding leadership and management. They are McGregor's Theory of X and Y and the Contingency Theory. Then we'll end this section with a discussion of the types of power leaders use and the outputs of Team Development.

Theory X and Theory Y

Douglas McGregor defined two models of worker behavior, *Theory X* and *Theory Y*, that attempt to explain how different managers deal with their team members.

Theory X managers believe most people do not like work and will try to steer clear of it; they have little to no ambition, need constant supervision, and won't actually perform the duties of their job unless threatened. As a result, Theory X managers are like dictators and impose very rigid controls over their people. They believe people are motivated only by punishment, money, or position. Unfortunately for them, Theory X managers unknowingly also subscribe to the Expectancy Theory. If they expect people to be lazy and unproductive and treat them as such, their team members probably will be lazy and unproductive.

Theory Y managers believe people are interested in performing their best given the right motivation and proper expectations. These managers provide support to their teams, are concerned about their team members, and are good listeners. Theory Y managers believe people are creative and committed to the project goals, that they like responsibility and seek it out, and that they are able to perform the functions of their positions with limited supervision.

Contingency Theory

The Contingency Theory builds on a combination of Theory Y and the Hygiene Theory. The Contingency Theory, in a nutshell, says that people are motivated to achieve levels of competency and will continue to be motivated by this need even after competency is reached.

The Power of Leaders

As stated earlier, power is the ability to influence others to do what you want them to do. This can be used in a positive manner or a negative one. But that old saying of your grandmother's about attracting more flies with honey than vinegar still holds true today.

Leaders, managers, and project managers use power to convince others to do things a specific way. The kind of power they use to accomplish this depends on their personality, their personal values, and the company culture.

There are several forms of power that a project manager might use. We've already talked about reward power, which is the ability to grant bonuses or incentive awards for a job well done. Let's look at a few more:

Punishment power Punishment, also known as coercive or penalty power, is just the opposite of reward power. The employee is threatened with consequences if expectations are not met.

Expert power Expert power occurs when the person being influenced believes the manager, or the person doing the influencing, is knowledgeable on the subject or has special abilities that make them an expert. The person goes along just because they think the influencer knows what they're doing and it's the best thing for the situation.

Legitimate power Legitimate, or formal, power comes about as a result of the influencer's position. Because that person is the project manager, or executive vice president, or CEO, they have the power to call the shots and make decisions.

Referent power Referent power is inferred to the influencer by their subordinates. Project team members who have a great deal of respect and high regard for their project managers willingly go along with decisions made by the project manager because of referent power.

Punishment power should be used as a last resort. There are times when you'll have to use this method, but hopefully much less often than the other three forms of power. Sometimes, you'll have team members who won't live up to expectations and their performance suffers as a result. This is a case where punishment power is enacted to get the employee to correct their behavior.

Exam Spotlight

Know the Theory of X and Y, the Contingency Theory, and types of power for the PMP exam. Understand the circumstances when each type of power might be used.

Defining Team Development Outputs

We're now ready to close out the Team Development process. The outputs of this process are performance improvements and input-to-performance appraisals. These are pretty straightforward. As a result of positive team-building experiences, you'll see individuals improving their skills, team behaviors and relationships improving, conflict resolutions going smoothly, and team members recommending ways to improve the work of the project.

Performance appraisals are typically annual or semi-annual affairs where managers let their employees know what they think of their performance for the past year and rate them accordingly. Project managers should contribute to the performance appraisals of all project team members. In functional organizations, the functional manager is responsible for the performance appraisal. If project managers do not have an equal say, or at least some say in the employee's performance, it will cause the team member to be loyal to the functional manager and show little loyalty to the project or project manager.

 Project managers wear a lot of hats. This is one of the things that make this job so interesting. You need organization and planning skills to plan the project. You need motivation and sometimes disciplinary skills to execute the project plans. You need to exercise leadership and power where appropriate. And all the while, you have a host of relationships to manage, including team members, stakeholders, managers, and customers. It's a great job and brings terrific satisfaction.

Distributing Project Information

The *Information Distribution* process is concerned with getting stakeholders information about the project in a timely manner. This can come about in several ways: status reports, project meetings, review meetings, and so on. In the Information Distribution process, the communications management plan that was defined during the Communications Planning process is put into action. Communication and Information Distribution work together to report the progress of the project team.

The Information Distribution process inputs are:

- Work results
- Communications management plan
- Project plan

These inputs have all been discussed previously and there isn't any new information to add for this process.

The tools and techniques of this process are:

- Communication skills
- Information retrieval systems
- Information distribution methods

We'll look at communication skills next.

Developing Great Communication Skills

Every aspect of your job as a project manager will involve communications. It's been estimated that project managers spend as much as 90 percent of their time communicating in one form or another. Therefore, communication skills are arguably the most important skills a project manager can have. They are even more important than technical skills. Good communication skills foster an open, trusting environment. The ability to communicate well is a project manager's best asset.

Chapter 1 talked about how important good communication skills are. This section discusses the act of communication, listening behaviors, and conflict resolution. You'll employ each of these techniques with your project team, stakeholders, customers, and management team.

Information Exchange

Communication is the process of exchanging information. There are three elements to all communication: the sender, the message, and the receiver.

Sender

The sender is the person responsible for putting the information together in a clear and concise manner. The information should be complete and presented in a way that the receiver will be able to correctly understand it. Make your messages relevant to the receiver. Junk mail is annoying, and information that doesn't pertain in any way whatsoever to the receiver is nothing more than that.

Message

The message is the information being sent and received. It might be written, verbal, nonverbal, formal, informal, internal, external, horizontal, or vertical. Horizontal communications are messages sent and received to peers. Vertical communications are messages sent and received down to subordinates and up to executive management.

Make your messages as simple as you can to get your point across. Don't complicate the message with unnecessary detail and technical jargon that others may not understand. A simple trick that helps clarify your messages, especially verbal messages, is to repeat the key information periodically. Public speakers are taught that the best way to organize a speech is to first tell the audience what you're going to tell them; second, tell them; and third, tell them what you just told them.

Receiver

The receiver is the person the message is intended for. They are responsible for understanding the information correctly and making sure they've received all of the information.

This book is an example of the sender-message-receiver model. I'm the sender of the information. The message concerns topics you need to know to pass the PMP exam (and if I've done my job correctly, is written in a clear and easily understood format). You, the reader, are the receiver.

Keep in mind that receivers filter the information they receive through their knowledge of the subject, culture influences, language, emotions, attitudes, and geographic locations. The sender should take these filters into consideration when sending messages so that the receiver will clearly understand the message that was sent.

Methods of Information Exchange

Senders, receivers, and messages are the elements of communication. The way the sender packages or encodes the information and transmits it and the way the receiver unpacks or decodes the message are the methods of communication exchange.

Senders encode messages. Encoding is a method of putting the information into a format the receiver will understand. Language, pictures, and symbols are ways to encode messages. Encoding formats the message for transmitting.

Transmitting is the way the information gets from the sender to the receiver. Spoken words, written documentation, memos, e-mail, voicemail, and so on are all transmitting methods.

Decoding is what the receiver does with the information when they get it. They convert it into an understandable format. Usually, this means they read the memo, listen to the speaker, read the book, and so on.

Forms of Communication

Communication occurs primarily in written or verbal form. Granted, you can point to something or indicate what you need with motions, but usually you use the spoken or written word to get your message across.

Verbal communication is easier and less complicated than written communication, and it's usually a fast method of communication. Written communication, on the other hand, is an excellent way to get across complex, detailed messages. Detailed instructions are better provided in written form, because it provides the reader the ability to go back over information they're not quite sure about.

Both verbal and written communications might take a formal or an informal approach. Speeches or lectures are an example of formal verbal communications. Most project status meetings take more of a formal approach, as do most written project status reports. Generally speaking, the project manager should take an informal approach when communicating with stakeholders and project team members outside of the status meetings. This makes you appear more open and friendly and easier to approach with questions and issues.

Lines of Communication

Project communication will always involve more than one person, even on the tiniest of projects. As such, communication network models have been devised to try to explain the relationships between people and the number or type of interactions needed between project participants. What you need to remember for the exam is that network models consist of nodes with lines connecting the nodes that indicate the number of lines of communication. See Figure 8.1 for an example of a network communication circle with six participants.

FIGURE 8.1 Circular communication network

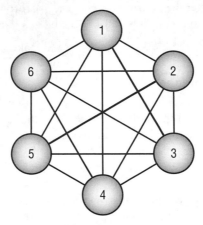

Nodes = participants
Lines = lines of communication between participants

The nodes are the participants, and the lines show the connection between them all. You'll need to know how to calculate the lines of communication when you take the exam. You could draw them out like this example and count up the lines, but there's an easier way. The formula for calculating the lines of communication is as follows:

(number of participants (number of participants less one)) divided by two

Here's the calculation in mathematical terms:

$(n \times (n - 1)) \div 2$

Figure 8.1 shows six participants, so let's plug that into the formula to determine the lines of communication:

$(6 \times (6 - 1)) \div 2 = 15$

Exam Spotlight

I recommend you memorize the lines of communication formula before taking the exam.

Effective Listening Skills

What did you say? Often we think we're listening when we really aren't. In all fairness, we can take in only so much information at one time. But it's important to perform active listening when someone else is speaking. As a project manager, you will spend the majority of your time communicating with team members, stakeholders, customers, vendors, and others. This means you should be as good a listener as you are a communicator.

There are several techniques you can use to improve your listening skills. There are books devoted to this topic, so we'll try to highlight some of the most common techniques here.

- Appear interested in what the speaker is saying. This will make the speaker feel at ease and will benefit you as well. By acting interested, you become interested and thereby retain more of the information being presented.

- Making eye contact with the speaker is another effective listening tool. This lets the speaker know you are paying attention to what they're saying and are interested.

- Put your speaker at ease by letting them know beforehand that you're interested in what they're going to talk about and that you're looking forward to hearing what they have to say. While they're speaking, nod your head, smile, or make comments when and if appropriate to let the speaker know you understand the message. If you don't understand something and are in the proper setting, ask clarifying questions.

- Another great trick that works well in lots of situations is to recap what the speaker said in your own words and tell it back to them. Start with something like this, "Let me make sure I understand you correctly, you're saying…," and ask the speaker to confirm that you did understand them correctly.

- Just like your mother always said, it's impolite to interrupt. Interrupting is a way of telling the speaker that you aren't really listening and you're more interested in telling them what you have to say than listening to them. Interrupting gets the other person off track, they might forget their point, and it may even make them angry.

Not to disagree with Mom, but there probably are some occasions where interrupting is appropriate. As an example, if you're in a project status meeting and someone wants to take the meeting off course, sometimes the only way to get the meeting back on track is to interrupt them. You can still do this politely. Start first by saying the person's name to get their attention. Then let them know that you'd be happy to talk with them about their topic outside of the meeting or add it to the agenda for the next status meeting if it's something everyone needs to hear. Sorry, Mom.

Resolving Conflicts

I said earlier in this chapter that if you have more than one person working on your project, you have a team. Here's another fact: If you have more than one person working on your project, you'll have conflict. I put conflict resolution in the communication section because conflict resolution involves communication, as you'll see in a moment.

Everyone has desires, needs, and goals. Conflict comes into the picture when the desires, needs, or goals of one party are incompatible with the desires, needs, or goals of another party (or parties). *Conflict*, simply, is the incompatibility of goals and one party resisting or blocking the attainment of those goals by the other party. Wait—this doesn't sound like a party!

There are five ways of resolving conflict that may show up on the exam: forcing, smoothing, compromise, confrontation, and withdrawal. Let's look at each of these in detail.

Forcing

Forcing is just like it sounds. One person forces a solution on the other parties. This is where the boss puts on the "Because I'm the boss and I said so" hat. While this is a permanent solution, it isn't necessarily the best solution. People will go along with it because, well, they're forced to go along with it. It doesn't mean they agree with the solution. This isn't the best technique to use when you're trying to build a team. This is an example of a win-lose conflict resolution technique. The forcing party wins, and the losers are those who are forced to go along with the decision.

Smoothing

Smoothing does not lead to a permanent solution. It's a temporary way to resolve conflict where someone attempts to make the conflict appear less important than it is. Everyone looks at each other and scratches their head and wonders why they thought the conflict was such a big deal anyway. As a result, a compromise is reached and everyone feels good about the solution until they get back to their desk and start thinking about the issue again. When they realize that the conflict was smoothed over and really is more important than what they were led to believe, they'll be back at it, and the conflict will resurface. This is an example of a lose-lose conflict resolution technique, because neither side wins.

Compromise

Compromise is achieved when each of the parties involved in the conflict gives up something to reach a solution. Everyone involved decides what they will give on and what they won't give on, and eventually through all the give and take, a solution is reached. Neither side wins or loses in this situation. As a result, neither side is really gung ho on the decision that was reached. They will drag their feet and reluctantly trudge along. If, however, firm commitments are made by both parties to the resolution, then the solution becomes a permanent one.

Confrontation

This technique is also called problem solving and is the best way to resolve conflict. A fact-finding mission results in this scenario. The thinking here is that one right solution to a problem exists and the facts will bear out the solution. Once the facts are uncovered, they're presented to the parties and the decision will be clear. Thus the solution becomes a permanent one and the conflict expires. This is the conflict resolution approach project mangers use most often and is an example of a win-win conflict resolution technique.

Withdrawal

Withdrawal never results in resolution. This occurs when one of the parties gets up and leaves and refuses to discuss the conflict. It is probably the worst of all the techniques, because nothing gets resolved. This is an example of a lose-lose conflict resolution technique.

Exam Spotlight

Know each of the conflict resolution techniques for the exam. Also remember that these techniques will not necessarily yield long-term results. The smoothing and withdrawal techniques have temporary results and aren't always good techniques to use to resolve problems. Forcing, compromise, and confrontation techniques tend to have longer-lasting results.

Keep in mind that group size makes a difference when you're trying to resolve conflict or make decisions. Groups of 5 to 11 people have been shown to make the most accurate decisions.

Use communication, listening, and conflict resolution skills wisely. As a project manager, you'll find that your day-to-day activities encompass these three areas the majority of the time. Project managers with excellent communication skills can work wonders. Communication won't take the place of proper planning and management techniques, but a project manager who communicates well with their team and the stakeholders can make up for a lack of technical skills any day, hands down. If your team and your stakeholders trust you, and you can communicate the vision and the project goals and report on project status accurately and honestly, the world is your oyster.

Information Retrieval Systems

Information retrieval systems are ways that project information is stored and shared among project team members. They include things like project management software, manual filing systems, intranet project sites, and electronic databases.

Information Distribution Methods

Information distribution methods are ways of getting the project information to the project team or stakeholders. As the name implies, these are ways to distribute the information and might include e-mail, hard copy, voicemail, videoconferencing, and so on.

Exam Spotlight

Don't confuse information retrieval systems with information distribution methods. Remember that retrieval systems are ways for the project team to get at project information, while distribution methods are ways of getting the information into the hands of the stakeholders or team members.

Outputs of Information Distribution

The first output of the Information Distribution process is *project records*. These include, as you might guess, memos, correspondence, and other documents concerning the project. The best place to keep information like this is in a project binder or in a set of project binders, depending on the size of the project. The project binders are ordinary three-ring binders where project information gets filed. They are maintained by the project manager or project office and contain all information regarding the project. You could also keep the information on a project website, the company intranet, or on CDs. If you're keeping the information electronically, make certain it's backed up periodically. Individual team members may keep their own project records as well in notebooks or electronically. These records serve as historical information once the project is closed.

Project reports, the second output of the Information Distribution process, include the project status reports and minutes from project meetings. If you're keeping an issues log, they would be included with the project reports as well.

The final output of this process is *project presentations*. These involve presenting project information to the stakeholders and other appropriate parties when necessary. The presentations might be formal or informal and depend on the audience and the information being communicated.

Project Case Study: New Kitchen Heaven Retail Store

Dirk Perrier logs on and finds the following e-mail addressed to all the stakeholders and project team members from you:

Project Progress Report

Project Name   Kitchen Heaven Retail Store

Project Number   081501-1910

Prepared by   Project Manager

Date   September 20, 2004

Section 1: Action Items

- Action Item 1: Call Cable Vendor—Responsible Party: Ricardo; Resolution Date: 9/12

- Action Item 2: T1 Connection Status—Responsible Party: Ricardo; Resolution Date: Pending

- Action Item 3: Build-Out Begins—Responsible Party: Jake; Resolution Date: Pending

Section 2: Scheduled and Actual Completion Dates

- Sign Lease—Scheduled: 8/20/04; Completed: 8/20/04

- Gomez Contract Signed—Scheduled: 9/11/04; Completed: 9/11/04

- Ethernet Cable Run—Scheduled: 9/18/04; Completed: 9/18/04

- Build-out Started—Scheduled: 9/20/04; Completed: Open

Section 3: Activity That Occurred in the Project This Week

The Ethernet cable run was completed without a problem.

Gomez construction started the build-out process. This task was fast tracked with the Ethernet cable run as planned.

Jill made initial calls regarding retail products order.

Section 4: Progress Expected This Reporting Period Not Completed

None. Project is on track to date.

Section 5: Progress Expected Next Reporting Period

Build-out will continue. Jake reports that Gomez expects to have electrical lines run and drywall started prior to the end of the next reporting period.

Ricardo should have a T1 update. There's a slim possibility that the T1 connection will have occurred by next reporting period.

Section 6: Issues

We had to start the build-out on the last day of the cable run (this is called fast tracking) to keep the project on schedule. Jake and Ricardo reported only minor problems with this arrangement in that the contractors got into each other's way a time or two. This did not impact the completion of the cable run, as most of day two this team was in the back room and Gomez's crew was in the storefront area.

A key member of the Gomez construction crew was out last week due to a family emergency. Gomez assures us that it will not impact the build-out schedule. They replaced the team member with someone from another project, so it appears so far that build-out is on schedule.

Ricardo is somewhat concerned about the T1 connection, because the phone company won't return his calls inquiring about status. We're still ahead of the curve on this one, because hardware isn't scheduled to begin testing until January 21. Hardware testing depends on the T1 connection. This is a heads-up at this point, and we'll carry this as an issue in the status report going forward until it's resolved.

One of the gourmet food item suppliers Jill uses regularly went out of business. She is in the process of tracking down a new supplier to pick up the slack for the existing stores and supply the gourmet food products for the new store.

"Good job on the status," Dirk says as you pick up the phone. "I was beginning to wonder when we'd see some action on the project, but it looks like things are underway."

"A lot has happened in just the past two weeks, as you can see. I'll publish these project status updates twice a month in conjunction with the regular project status meetings. Starting in January, I'll publish them once a week until project completion."

"Keep me posted on that T1 line. That isn't going to be a showstopper, is it?"

"We have a contingency plan in place," you reply. "We talked about that last week."

"Okay. I'll see you at the project meeting Friday."

"See you then," you say.

Project Case Study Checklist

Communication

- Sender makes it clear and concise.

- There's no unnecessary technical jargon.

- Formal written communication is provided.

- It's the receiver's responsibility to understand information.

- The status report is a vertical and horizontal communication method.

Project Plan Execution

- Status review meetings

- Work results

Team Development

Information Distribution

- Project information is delivered to stakeholders in a timely manner.

- The information distribution method is status reports via e-mail and project meetings.

- The status report is part of the project reports filed in the project binder or filed for future reference as historical information.

Summary

This chapter described three processes from the Executing process group: Project Plan Execution, Team Development, and Information Distribution.

In project Plan Execution, the project plans come to life. Activities are authorized to begin using a work authorization system, the product or service of the project is actually produced, and status review meetings are held to inform stakeholders of project progress and updates.

Team building involves creating an open, inviting atmosphere where stakeholders and project team members will become efficient and cooperative teams, increasing productivity during the course of the project. It's the project manager's job to bring the team together into a functioning, productive group.

There are four stages of Team Development: forming, storming, norming, and performing. All groups proceed through these stages, and the introduction of a new team member will always start the process over again.

Collocation is physically placing team members together in the same location. This might also include a common meeting room or gathering area where team members can meet and collaborate on the project.

Several motivational theories exist, including reward and recognition, Maslow's Hierarchy of Needs, the Hygiene Theory, the Expectancy Theory, and the Achievement Theory. These theories conjecture that motivation is driven by needs, anticipation of expected outcomes, or needs for achievement, power, or affiliation. The Hygiene Theory proposes that hygiene factors prevent dissatisfaction.

Leaders inspire vision and rally people around common goals. Theory X leaders think most people are motivated only through punishment, money, or position. Theory Y leaders think most people want to perform the best job they can. The Contingency Theory says that people naturally want to achieve levels of competency and will continue to be motivated by competency needs even after competency is reached.

Leaders exhibit five types of power: reward, punishment, expert, legitimate, and referent power.

Communication skills are the most important skills a project manager exercises. People who send messages are responsible for making sure the message is clear, concise, and complete. Receivers are responsible for understanding the message correctly and making sure they've received all of the information.

Listening skills put speakers at ease. Several techniques tell your speaker you're listening attentively, including making eye contact, nodding, asking clarifying questions, and limiting interruptions.

Information Distribution is a matter of getting project information out to the stakeholders. Information retrieval systems generally store project information and include project management software, filing cabinets, and electronic databases. Information distribution methods are ways to get the information to the stakeholders and include e-mail, paper, voicemail, or videoconferencing.

Exam Essentials

Be able to identify the distinguishing characteristics of Project Plan Execution. Project Plan Execution is the only core process in the Executing group, and the majority of the project budget is spent during this process.

Be able to name the four stages of group formation. The four stages of group formation are forming, storming, norming, and performing.

Be able to define Maslow's highest level of motivation. Self-actualization occurs when a person performs at their peak and all lower level needs have been met.

Be able to name the five levels of power. The five levels of power are reward, punishment, expert, legitimate, and referent.

Be able to differentiate between senders and receivers of information. Senders are responsible for clear, concise, complete messages, while receivers are responsible for understanding the message correctly.

Be able to identify the five styles of conflict resolution. The five styles of conflict resolution are forcing, smoothing, compromise, confrontation, and withdrawal.

Key Terms

Before you take the exam, be certain you are familiar with the following terms:

Achievement Theory	politics
collocation	power
communication	Project Plan Execution
conflict	project presentations
corrective actions	project records
Expectancy Theory	project reports
Hygiene Theory	reward and recognition systems
Information Distribution	status review meetings
information distribution methods	team building
information retrieval systems	Team Development
Maslow's hierarchy of needs	Theory X
Motivation-Hygiene Theory	Theory Y

Review Questions

1. You are a project manager for an international marketing firm. You are ready to assign resources to your new project using a work authorization system. All of the following statements are true except:

   A. Work authorization systems clarify and initiate the work for each work package.

   B. Work authorization systems are written procedures defined by the organization.

   C. Work authorization systems are tools and techniques of the Project Plan Execution process.

   D. Work authorization systems are an output of the Project Plan Execution process.

2. Your project is progressing as planned. The project team has come up with a demo that the sales team will use when making presentations to prospective clients. You will do which of the following at your next stakeholder project status meeting?

   A. Report on the progress of the demo and note that it's a completed task.

   B. Preview the demo for stakeholders and obtain their approval and sign-off.

   C. Review the technical documentation of the demo and obtain approval and sign-off.

   D. Report that the demo has been noted as a completed task in the information retrieval system.

3. All of the following are tools and techniques of the Project Plan Execution process except:

   A. Project management information system

   B. Work authorization system

   C. Organizational policies

   D. General management skills

4. You are a project manager for a growing dairy farm. They offer their organic dairy products regionally and are expanding their operations to the West Coast. They're in the process of purchasing and leasing dairy farms to get operations under way. You are in charge of the network operations part of this project. An important deadline is approaching that depends on the successful completion of the testing phase. You've detected some problems with your hardware in the testing phase and discover that the hardware is not compatible with other network equipment. You take corrective action and exchange the hardware for more compatible equipment. Which of the following statements is true?

   A. This is not a corrective action, because corrective action involves human resources, not project resources.

   B. Corrective action is taken here to make sure the future project outcomes are aligned with the project plan.

   C. Corrective action is not necessary in this case, because the future project outcomes aren't affected.

   D. Corrective action serves as the change request to authorize exchanging the equipment.

5. You are a project manager for a growing dairy farm. They offer their organic dairy products regionally and are expanding their operations to the West Coast. They're in the process of purchasing and leasing dairy farms to get operations under way. The subproject manager in charge of network operations has reported some hardware problems to you. You're also having some other problems coordinating and integrating other elements of the project. Which of the following statements is true?

   A. You are in the Project Plan Execution process.

   B. Your project team doesn't appear to have the right skills and knowledge needed to perform this project.

   C. You are in the Information Distribution process.

   D. Your project team could benefit from some team-building exercises.

6. Which of the following processes serve as inputs to each other?

   A. Executing and Controlling

   B. Planning and Executing

   C. Planning and Controlling

   D. Executing and Initiation

7. You are the project manager for a cable service provider. Your team members are amiable with each other and are careful to make project decisions jointly. Which of the following statements is true?

   A. They are in the smoothing stage of Team Development.

   B. They are in the norming stage of Team Development.

   C. They are in the forming stage of Team Development.

   D. They are in the forcing stage of Team Development.

8. You are the project manager for a cable service provider. Your project team is researching a new service offering. They have been working together for quite some time and are in the performing stage of Team Development. A new member has been introduced to the team. Which of the following statements is true?

   A. The Team Development process will start all over again with the storming stage.

   B. The team will continue in the performing stage.

   C. The Team Development process will start all over again with the forming stage.

   D. The team will start all over again at the storming stage but quickly progress to the performing stage.

9. You are the project manager for a cable service provider. Your project team is researching a new service offering. They have been working together for quite some time and are in the performing stage of Team Development. This stage of Team Development is similar to which of the following?

    A. Smoothing

    B. Achievement Theory

    C. Hygiene Theory

    D. Self-actualization

10. Receivers in the communication model filter their information through all of the following except:

    A. Culture

    B. Knowledge of subject

    C. Conflict

    D. Language

11. You've promised your team two days of paid time off plus a week's training in the latest technology of their choice if they complete their project ahead of schedule. This is an example of which of the following?

    A. Achievement Theory

    B. Expectancy Theory

    C. Maslow's Theory

    D. Contingency Theory

12. What are the outputs of the Team Development process?

    A. Performance improvements and input to performance appraisals

    B. Input to performance appraisals and reward and recognition systems

    C. Performance improvements, input to performance appraisals, and performance reports

    D. Work results, input to performance appraisals, and performance reports

13. Your team is split between two buildings on either side of town. As a result, the team isn't very cohesive, because the members don't know each other very well. The team is still in the storming stage because of the separation issues. Which of the following should you consider?

    A. Corrective action

    B. Collocation

    C. Training

    D. Conflict resolution

14. Your project team is a close group all busily working on project activities. They're close to approaching the performing stage of Team Development. All seven members must communicate frequently with each other. How many lines of communication are there?

A. 24

B. 21

C. 28

D. 20

15. Which conflict resolution technique do project managers use most often?

A. Smoothing

B. Confronting

C. Norming

D. Forcing

16. You are the project manager for a web development project. You hold regular project status meetings and publish status reports on a timely basis. You know that communication is one of your most important functions. As such, all of the following are true regarding your published status reports except:

A. Senders are responsible for sending clear, concise, complete messages.

B. Receivers are responsible for understanding the message.

C. Communication can be vertical or horizontal or both.

D. Effective communication techniques include making eye contact, nodding, and asking clarifying questions.

17. You are a fabulous project manager, and your team thinks highly of you. You are well respected by the stakeholders, management team, and project team. When you make decisions, others follow your lead as a result of which of the following?

A. Referent power

B. Expert power

C. Legitimate power

D. Punishment power

18. Theory Y managers believe which of the following?

A. People are motivated only by money, power, or position.

B. People will perform their best if they're given proper motivation and expectations.

C. People are motivated to achieve a high level of competency.

D. People are motivated by expectation of good outcomes.

19. You have accumulated project information throughout the project and need to distribute some important information you just received. All of the following are part of information distribution methods except:

   A. Electronic mail

   B. Videoconferencing

   C. Electronic databases

   D. Voicemail

20. You know that the next status meeting will require some discussion and a decision for a problem that has surfaced on the project. In order to make the most accurate decision, you know that the number of participants in the meeting should be limited to:

   A. 1 to 5

   B. 5 to 11

   C. 7 to 16

   D. 10 to 18

Answers to Review Questions

1.   D.   Work authorization systems are a tool and technique of the Project Plan Execution process. They formally initiate the work of each work package and clarify the assignments.

2.   A.   Status meetings are to report on the progress of the project. They are not for demos or show-and-tell. Answer C is not correct, because stakeholders are not concerned about the content of the technical documentation; they need to know that the technical documentation has been reviewed by a qualified technician and that the documentation task is accurate and complete.

3.   C.   Organizational policies are an input to this process. Organizational procedures are a tool and technique.

4.   B.   Corrective action brings anticipated future project outcomes back into alignment with the project plan. Since there is an important deadline looming that depends on a positive outcome of this test, the equipment is exchanged so that the project plan and project schedule are not impacted.

5.   A.   The most difficult aspect of the Project Plan Execution process is coordinating and integrating all the project elements. The clue to this question is the next-to-last sentence, which contains this wording.

6.   A.   The Executing process group and Controlling process group serve as inputs to each other.

7.   B.   Teams in the norming stage of Team Development exhibit affection and familiarity with one another and make joint decisions. Smoothing and forcing are conflict resolution techniques, not Team Development stages.

8.   C.   The introduction of a new team member will start the Team Development process all over again with the forming stage, which is the first stage of Team Development.

9.   D.   The performing stage is similar to Maslow's self-actualization. They are both at the peak of performance, concerned with doing good and being the best.

10.   C.   Receivers filter information through cultural considerations, knowledge of the subject matter, language abilities, geographic location, emotions, and attitudes.

11.   B.   The Expectancy Theory says that people are motivated by the expectation of good outcomes. The outcome must be reasonable and attainable.

12.   A.   Performance improvements and input to performance appraisals are the Team Development outputs.

13.   B.   Collocation would bring your team members together in the same location and allow them to function more efficiently as a team. At a minimum, team members meeting in a common room, such as a war room, for all team meetings would bring the team closer together.

14. B.   The formula to calculate lines of communication for this question is as follows: $(7 \times (7 - 1)) \div 2 = 21$.

15. B.   Confronting is a problem-solving technique that seeks to determine the facts and find solutions based on the facts. That results in a win-win resolution for all parties.

16. D.   Making eye contact, nodding, and asking clarifying questions are good communication skills but they don't apply to written communication.

17. A.   Referent power is power that is inferred on a leader by their subordinates as a result of the high level of respect for the leader.

18. B.   Theory Y managers believe that people will perform their best if they're provided with the proper motivation and the right expectations.

19. C.   Electronic databases are a type of information retrieval system, not a distribution method.

20. B.   Group sizes of 5 to 11 participants make the most accurate decisions.

Chapter

9

Measuring and Controlling Project Performance

THE PMP EXAM CONTENT FROM THE PROJECT EXECUTION PERFORMANCE DOMAIN COVERED IN THIS CHAPTER INCLUDES:

- ✓ 3. Managing progress
- ✓ 5. Implementing quality assurance procedures

THE PMP EXAM CONTENT FROM THE PROJECT CONTROL PERFORMANCE DOMAIN COVERED IN THIS CHAPTER INCLUDES:

- ✓ 1. Measuring performance
- ✓ 2. Refining control limits
- ✓ 3. Taking corrective action
- ✓ 4. Evaluating effectiveness of corrective action
- ✓ 5. Ensuring plan compliance

This chapter will wrap up the Executing process group and introduce the Controlling process group. The Executing processes covered in this chapter are Solicitation, Source Selection, Contract Administration, and Quality Assurance. You might find several questions on the exam that involve the Solicitation, Source Selection, and Contract Administration processes. These processes are usually performed in the order given here.

The Solicitation process obtains vendor proposals in the form of responses to requests for proposals (RFPs), requests for information (RFIs), and other documents. Source Selection marks the receipt of bids and proposals and selects a vendor from among the bidders. The Contract Administration process monitors the contract to ensure the vendor meets all the requirements of the contract.

The Controlling process group involves taking measurements and performing inspections to find out if there are variances in the plan. If variances are discovered, corrective action is taken to get the project back on track, and the affected project Planning processes are repeated to make adjustments to the plan as a result of the variances. We will examine two Controlling processes in this chapter: Scope Verification and Performance Reporting.

During Performance Reporting, we'll talk about performance measurements and look at the various techniques used to get to these measurements. We'll discuss the remaining Controlling processes in Chapter 10, "Controlling Change."

The Solicitation Process

Many times project managers must purchase goods or services to complete some or all of the work of the project. Sometimes the entire project is completed on contract. The *Solicitation* process is concerned with obtaining responses to bids and proposals from potential vendors.

There are two inputs to this process: procurement documents and qualified seller lists.

The procurement documents were prepared during the Solicitation Planning process. We talked about them in Chapter 6, "Establishing Project Planning Controls." Procurement documents include requests for proposals (RFPs), requests for information (RFIs), requests for quotation (RFQs), and so on. The vendors—or potential sellers—bear the majority of work in the Solicitation process by preparing responses to the RFPs. Depending on the RFP and the effort needed to respond, costs to the vendor can become quite substantial.

Qualified seller lists are lists of prospective sellers who have been preapproved or prequalified to provide contract services (or provide supplies and materials) for the organization. For example, your organization might require vendors to register and maintain information regarding their experience, offerings, and current prices on a qualified seller list. Vendors must usually go through the procurement department to get placed on the list. Project managers are then required to choose their vendors from the qualified seller list published by the procurement department. However, not all organizations have qualified seller lists. If a list isn't available, you'll have to work with the project team to come up with your own requirements for selecting vendors.

> The Solicitation process is only used if you're obtaining goods or services from outside your own organization. If you have all the resources you need to perform the work of the project within the organization, you won't use this process.

Remember that the purpose of the Solicitation process is to obtain responses to your RFP (or similar procurement document). The two tools and techniques of this process are actually designed to assist the vendors in getting their proposals to you. The tools and techniques are bidder conferences and advertising.

Bidder conferences are meetings with prospective vendors or sellers that occur prior to the completion of their response proposal. The meeting is prearranged by you or someone from your procurement department. The purpose is to allow all prospective vendors to meet with the buyers to ask questions and clarify issues they have regarding the project and the RFP. The meeting is held once, and all vendors attend at the same time. The bidder conference is held before the vendor prepares their responses so that they are sure their RFP response will address the project requirements.

Advertising is letting potential vendors know that an RFP is available. The company's Internet site, professional journals, or newspapers are examples of where advertising might appear.

Proposals are the only output of the Solicitation process. These are the vendor-prepared documents that describe how the vendor intends to meet the needs of your project. And if they've done their job correctly, the proposal should detail responses to each of your items as they were outlined in your RFP. These proposals become the input to the next process, Source Selection.

Exam Spotlight

A Guide to the PMBOK makes a distinction between the Solicitation process and the Source Selection process that you should know: Solicitation *obtains* bids and proposals; Source Selection is the *receipt* of bids and proposals and evaluating each in order to award a winner.

Selecting a Vendor

In the *Source Selection* process you evaluate the proposals you've received against your predefined evaluation criteria. Source Selection, as mentioned in the Exam Spotlight, is where you receive bids and proposals. Honestly, I cannot distinguish the difference between "obtaining" the bids and proposals in the Solicitation process and "receiving" them during this process, but *A Guide to the PMBOK* does.

Source Selection has three inputs:

- Proposals
- Evaluation criteria
- Organizational policies

Proposals, as mentioned, are obtained in the Solicitation process and used as an input to the Source Selection process. Organizational policies should always be considered when you're working with vendors. If your organization has specific policies such as choosing vendors from a qualified sellers list or specific evaluation procedures for appraising all the vendor proposals and you don't follow these policies, you could jeopardize the project.

Evaluation criteria are the criteria you'll use to compare proposals. You developed evaluation criteria as part of the Solicitation Planning process in Chapter 6. However, let's take a little closer look at this topic now, since you'll actually be using the criteria during this process.

 In practice, you will probably perform Solicitation Planning, Solicitation, and Source Selection all as one process.

Evaluation Criteria

Evaluation criteria are one method of rating and scoring proposals. Keep in mind this is an input to this process, not a tool and technique, even though you'll be using it like a tool and technique.

The types of goods and services you're trying to procure will dictate how detailed your evaluation criteria is. (Of course, if your organization has policies in place for evaluating proposals, then you'll use the format or criteria already established.) The selection of some goods and services may be price driven only. In other words, the bidder with the lowest price will win the bid. This is typical when the items you're buying are widely available.

When you're purchasing goods, you might request a sample from each vendor in order to compare quality (or some other criteria) against your need. For example, perhaps you need a special kind of paper stock for a project you're working on at a bank. This stock must have a watermark, it must have security threads embedded through the paper, and when printed, the ink must not be erasable. You can request samples of stock from the vendors with these qualities and then test them out to see if they'll work for your project.

It's always appropriate to ask the vendor for references, especially when you're hiring contract services. It's difficult to assess the quality of services, because it's not a tangible product. References can tell you if the vendor delivered on time, if they had the technical capability to perform the work, and if their management approach was appropriate when troubles surfaced. Create a list of questions to ask the references before you call.

Financial records may be requested to assure you—the buyer—that the vendor has the fiscal ability to perform the services they're proposing and that they can purchase whatever equipment is needed to perform the services. If you examine the records of the company and find they're two steps away from bankruptcy, they may not be a likely candidate for your project. (Remember those general management skills? Here's another example where they come into play.)

One of the most important criteria is the evaluation of the response itself to determine if the vendor has a clear understanding of what you're asking them to do or provide. If they missed the mark (remember they had an opportunity at the bidder conferences to ask clarifying questions), and didn't understand what you were asking them to provide, you'll probably want to rank them very low.

Now you can compare each proposal against the criteria and rate or score each proposal for its ability to meet or fulfill these criteria. This can serve as your first step in eliminating vendors that don't match your criteria. Let's say you received 18 responses to an RFP. After evaluating each one, you discover that six of them don't match all the evaluation criteria. Those six vendors are eliminated in this round. The next step is to apply the tools and techniques of this process to further evaluate the remaining 12 potential vendors.

Tools and Techniques of Source Selection

The following tools and techniques of Source Selection are used to further evaluate vendors:

- Contract negotiation
- Weighting systems
- Screening systems
- Independent estimates

Let's look at each one.

Contract Negotiation

In *contract negotiation*, both parties come to an agreement regarding the contract terms. Negotiation skills are put into practice here as the details of the contract are ironed out between the parties. At a minimum, contract language should include price, responsibilities, regulations or laws that apply, and the overall approach to the project.

You might see a term called *fait accompli* show up on the exam. This happens during contract negotiation when one party tries to convince the other party discussing a particular contract term that it is no longer an issue. It's a distraction technique, as the party practicing fait accompli is purposely trying to keep from negotiating an issue and claims the issue cannot be changed. For example, during negotiations the vendor tells you that the key resource they're assigning to your project must start immediately or you'll lose that resource and they'll get assigned work elsewhere. However, you don't know—because the vendor didn't tell you—that they can reserve this resource for your project and hold them until the start date. They used fait accompli to push you into starting the project, or hiring this resource, sooner than you would have otherwise.

Weighting Systems

Weighting systems assign numerical weights to evaluation criteria and then multiply them by the weights of each criteria factor to come up with total scores for each vendor. According to *A Guide to the PMBOK,* this tool and technique quantifies the qualitative data to keep personal biases to a minimum. Weighting systems are useful when you have multiple vendors to choose from, because they allow you to rank order the proposals to determine the sequence of negotiations.

There is an example of a weighted scoring system in Chapter 3, "Creating a Project Charter." These systems are commonly used to evaluate vendor proposals.

Screening Systems

Screening systems use predefined performance criteria to screen out vendors. Perhaps your project requires board-certified engineers. One of the screening criteria would be that vendors propose project team members who have this qualification. If they don't, they're eliminated from the selection process.

Weighting systems and screening systems are often used in combination to come up with a selection.

Independent Estimates

Your procurement department might conduct *independent estimates* (also known as *should cost estimates)* of the costs of the proposal and use these to compare to the vendor prices. If there are large differences between the independent estimate and the proposed vendor cost, one of two things is happening: The statement of work (SOW), or the terms of the contract, was not detailed enough to allow the vendor to come up with an accurate cost, or the vendor simply failed to respond to all the requirements laid out in the contract or SOW.

After all the RFPs are examined and scored, a vendor is selected and the contract is awarded and you move on to the output of the Source Selection process.

 Real World Scenario

Vendor Selection for Fitness Counts HR System

Amanda Jacobson is the project manager for Fitness Counts, a nationwide chain of gyms containing all the latest and greatest fitness equipment, aerobics classes, swimming pools, and such.

Fitness Counts is converting their human resources system. They have several requirements that were specifically addressed in the RFP, including the following:

- The new system must run on a platform that's compatible with the company's current operating system.

- Hardware must be compatible with company standards.

- Data conversion of existing HR data must be included in the price of the bid.

- Fitness Counts wants to have the ability to add their own custom modules using internal programmers.

- Training of Fitness Counts programmers must be included in the bid.

They are in the Source Selection process and have received bids based on the RFP published earlier this month. Fitness Counts is using a combination of selection criteria and weighted scoring model to choose a vendor.

One of the selection criteria said that the vendor must have prior experience with a project like this. Four vendors met that criteria and proceeded to the weighted scoring selection process.

Amanda is one of the members of the selection committee. She and four other members on the committee rated the four vendors who met the initial selection criteria. The results are shown in Tables 9.1 and 9.2 (following this sidebar).

Vendor C is the clear winner of this bid. Based on the weighted scoring model, their responses to the RFP came out ahead of the other bidders. Amanda calls them with the good news and also calls the other vendors to thank them for participating in the bid. Vendor C is awarded the contract, and Amanda moves on to the Contract Administration process.

TABLE 9.1   Example Weighted Scoring Model

Criteria	Weight*	Vendor A Weighting Factor	Vendor A Score	Vendor B Weighting Factor	Vendor B Score
Platform	5	*3*	15	*2*	10
Hardware	4	*3*	12	*3*	12
Data Conversion	5	*3*	15	*4*	20
Custom Modules/Training	4	*4*	16	*3*	12
Totals	—		**58**		**54**

*1–5; 5 highest

TABLE 9.2 Example Weighted Scoring Model

Criteria	Vendor C Weighting Factor	Vendor C Score	Vendor D Weighting Factor	Vendor D Score
Platform	4	20	3	15
Hardware	4	16	3	12
Data Conversion	4	20	2	10
Custom Modules/Training	3	12	4	16
Totals		68		53

*1–5; 5 highest

Contract Award

The contract is the only output of the Source Selection process. You may recall that a contract is a legally binding agreement between two or more parties typically used to acquire goods or services. Contracts have several names, including agreements, memorandums of understanding (MOUs), subcontracts, or purchase orders.

We talked about the types of contracts—fixed price, cost reimbursable, etc.—in Chapter 6 if you need a refresher.

Since contracts are legally binding and obligate your organization to fulfill the terms of the contract, they'll likely be subject to some intensive review, and often by several different people. Be certain you understand your organization's policies on contract review and approval before proceeding.

Contracts, like projects, have a life cycle of their own. You might encounter questions on the exam regarding the contracting life cycles, so let's look at this topic next.

Contracting Life Cycles

Contracts progress through four contract life cycles:

- Requirement
- Requisition
- Solicitation
- Award

These life cycles are closely related to the following processes from *A Guide to the PMBOK:*

- Solicitation Planning
- Solicitation
- Source Selection
- Contract Administration

A description of each of these life cycles follows.

Requirement

The requirement cycle is the equivalent of *A Guide to the PMBOK*'s Procurement Planning process, which was discussed in Chapter 6. The project and contract needs are established in this cycle, and the requirements of the project are defined. The SOW is used to define the work of the project, the objectives, and a high-level overview of the deliverables. A work breakdown structure (WBS) is developed, a make or buy analysis takes place, and cost estimates are determined.

The SOW is provided by the buyer when the project is performed under contract to describe the requirements of the project. The product description can serve as the SOW.

Requisition

The requisition cycle is similar to *A Guide to the PMBOK*'s Solicitation Planning process, discussed in Chapter 6.

In the requisition phase, the project objectives are refined and confirmed. Solicitation materials such as the request for proposals (RFP), request for information (RFI), and request for quotations (RFQ) are prepared during this phase. Generally, the project manager is the one responsible for preparing the RFP, RFI, and RFQ. A review of the potential qualified vendors takes place, including checking references and reviewing other projects the vendor has worked on that are similar to your proposed project.

Solicitation

Solicitation is where vendors are asked to compete for the contract and respond to the RFP. You will use the tools and techniques of *A Guide to the PMBOK*'s Solicitation process during this contract cycle. The resulting output is the vendor proposals.

Award

Vendors are chosen, and contracts are awarded and signed during the award cycle. *A Guide to the PMBOK* equivalent to the award cycle is the Source Selection process.

The project manager—or the selection committee depending on the organizational policy—receives the bids and proposals during the award phase and applies evaluation criteria to each in order to score or rank the responses. After ranking each of the proposals, an award is made to the winning vendor and the contract is written.

Once you have a contract, someone has to administer it. In large organizations, this responsibility will fall to the procurement department. The project manager should still have a solid understanding of administering contracts, because they'll work with the procurement department to determine the satisfactory fulfillment of the contract.

This brings us to our last contract topic for this chapter: Contract Administration.

Administering the Contract

The *Contract Administration* process entails monitoring the vendor's performance and ensuring that all the requirements of the contract are met. When there are multiple vendors providing goods and services to the project, Contract Administration entails coordinating the interfaces among all the vendors as well as administering each of the contracts. If vendor A has a due date that will impact whether or not vendor B can perform their service, the management and coordination of the two vendors becomes important. Vendor A's contract and due dates must be monitored closely, because failure to perform could impact other vendor's ability to perform, not to mention the project schedule. You can see how this situation could multiply quickly when you have six or seven or more vendors involved.

 It's imperative that the project manager and project team are aware of any contract agreements that may impact the project so the team does not inadvertently take action that violates the terms of the contract.

Depending on the size of the organization, administering the contract might fall to someone in the procurement department. This doesn't mean that you're off the hook as the project manager. It's still your responsibility to oversee the process and make sure the project objectives are being met, regardless of whether a vendor is performing the activities or your project team members are performing the activities. You'll be the one monitoring the performance of the vendor and informing them when and if performance is lacking. If administering the contract is your responsibility, you may have to terminate the contract when the vendor violates the terms or doesn't meet the agreed-upon deliverables. If the procurement department has this responsibility, you'll have to document the situation and provide this to the procurement department so that they can enforce or terminate the contract.

Administering the contract is closely linked with project management processes. You'll monitor the progress of the contract, execute plans, track costs, measure outputs, approve changes, take corrective action, and report on status, just as you do for the project itself. According to *A Guide to the PMBOK*, integration and coordination of the Project Plan Execution, Performance Reporting, Quality Control, and Change Control processes must be applied during Contract Administration.

Contracting Inputs

The inputs to Contract Administration are:

- Contract
- Work results
- Change requests
- Seller invoices

The contract is the output from the Source Selection process. We've already discussed contracts, so let's move on to work results.

Work Results

Monitoring work results involves an examination of the vendor's deliverables. This includes monitoring their work results against the project plan and making certain activities are performed correctly and in sequence. You'll need to determine which deliverables are complete and which ones have not been completed to date. You'll also need to consider the quality of the deliverables and the costs that have been incurred to date.

Exam Spotlight

Work results are also an output of the Project Plan Execution process. The results you gather here are actually collected as part of the Project Plan Execution work result output.

Change Requests

Sometimes as you get into the work of the project, you'll discover changes need to be made. This could entail changes to the contract as well. Change requests are used to process the project or contract changes and might include things like modifications to deliverables, changes to the product or service of the project, changes in contract terms, or termination for poor performance.

Changes that cannot be agreed upon are called *contested changes*. Contested changes usually involve a disagreement about the compensation to the vendor for implementing the change. You might believe the change is not significant enough to justify additional compensation, whereas the vendor believes they'll lose money by implementing the change free of charge. Contested changes are also known as *disputes*, *claims*, or *appeals*. These can be settled directly between the parties themselves, through the court system, or by a process called arbitration. *Arbitration* involves bringing all parties to the table with a third, disinterested party who is not a participant in the contract to try and reach an agreement. The purpose of arbitration is to reach an agreement without having to go to court.

Seller Invoices

Vendors request payment for the goods or services delivered in the form of *seller invoices*. Seller invoices should describe the work that was completed or the materials that were delivered, and should include any supporting documentation necessary to describe what was delivered. The contract should state what type of supporting documentation is needed with the invoice.

 Remember that seller invoices are an input to the Contract Administration process, not an output. Also, don't confuse seller invoices with the payment system, which is a tool and technique of this process.

Administering Contracts with Tools and Techniques

Administering the contract requires several tools and techniques:

- Contract change control system
- Performance reporting
- Payment system

Here's a description of each.

Contract Change Control System

Much like the management plans found in the Planning processes, the *contract change control system* describes the processes needed to make contract changes. Since the contract is a legal document, changes to it require the agreement of all parties. A formal process must be established to process and authorize (or deny) changes. (Authorization levels are defined in the organizational policies.)

The purpose of the contract change control system is to establish a formal process for submitting change requests. It documents how to submit changes, establishes the approval process, and outlines authority levels. It includes a tracking system to number the change requests and record their status. The procedures for dispute resolution are spelled out in the change control system as well.

The change control system, along with all the management plan outputs, becomes part of the Integrated Change Control process that we'll discuss in the next chapter.

Performance Reporting

Performance reporting is a large part of project management. This tool and technique entails providing your managers and stakeholders with information about the vendor's progress regarding the contract objectives. This information is also part of the Performance Reporting process that we'll discuss in depth later in this chapter.

Payment Systems

Vendors submit seller invoices as an input to this process, and the *payment system* is the tool and technique used to issue payment. The organization may have a dedicated department, such as accounts payable, that handles vendor payments, or it might fall to the project manager. In either case, follow the policies and procedures the organization established to track vendor payments.

Many times, contracts are written such that payment is made based on a predefined performance schedule. As an example, perhaps the first payment is made after 25 percent of the product or service is completed. Or maybe the payment schedule is based on milestone completion. In any case, as the project manager, you will verify that the vendor's work (or delivery) meets expectations before the payment is authorized. It's almost always your responsibility as the project manager to verify that the terms of the contract to date have or have not been satisfied. Depending on your organizational policies, someone from the accounting or procurement department may request written notification from you that the vendor has completed a milestone or made a delivery. Monitoring the work of the vendor is as important as monitoring the work of your team members.

Managing Contract Outputs

The outputs to the Contract Administration process include:

- Correspondence
- Contract changes
- Payment requests

These outputs relate to the tools and techniques just talked about and in practice, work hand in hand with them.

Correspondence

Correspondence is information that needs to be communicated in writing to either the seller or the buyer. An example might be changes to the contract, clarification of contract terms, or notification of performance issues. You would also use correspondence to notify a vendor that you're terminating the contract because performance is below expectations and is not satisfying the requirements of the contract.

Contract Changes

Contract changes are coordinated with the Project Plan Execution and Integrated Change Control process so that any changes impacting the project itself are communicated to the project team and appropriate actions are put into place to realign the objectives. This might also mean the project plan itself will require changes. That requires you to jump back to the Planning process group to bring the project plan up-to-date. Once the plan is up-to-date, the Project Plan Execution may require changes as well to get the work of the project in line with the new plan. Remember that project management is an iterative process and it's not unusual to revisit the Planning or Executing processes, particularly as changes are made or corrective actions are put into place.

Contract changes will not always impact the project plan, however. For example, late delivery of key equipment probably would impact the project plan, but changes in the vendor payment schedule probably would not. It's important that you are kept abreast of any changes to the contract so that you can evaluate whether the project plan needs adjusting.

Payment Requests

In the *payment requests* input, the payment is physically delivered to the vendor. Authorization to make the payment occurs through the payment system tool and technique, and then actual payment is made here.

WARNING Don't confuse payment systems (a tool and technique of Contract Administration) with payment requests (an output of Contract Administration). Payment systems include reviews and authorization to issue the check. In the payment request output, the check gets sent to the vendor.

Exam Spotlight

I recommend remembering the inputs, tools and techniques, and outputs of the contracting processes, including Solicitation, Source Selection, and Contract Administration. Be certain you understand the purposes of these processes and don't simply memorize their components.

Laying Out Quality Assurance Procedures

The Quality Planning process laid out the quality standards for the project and determined how those standards are satisfied. The *Quality Assurance* process involves performing quality audits to determine how the project is proceeding. Quality Assurance is concerned with making certain the project will meet and satisfy the quality standards of the project defined during the Quality Planning process.

Quality assurance has moved into the strategic realm and is concerned with integrating quality into the strategic-planning process so that quality becomes a company-wide theme. Your customers—whether internal or external—are the ones who should define quality. Quality Assurance is how you will know and guarantee the quality requirements of your project specifications will be met. Quality Assurance will also improve the quality of future projects, because the information gained from one project in the form of lessons learned can be applied to the quality process during the next project.

The Quality Assurance process integrates project scope, project costs, and project time. All three of these elements are brought together and measured during this process and throughout the life of the project. Quality Assurance, like many other processes, is not a one-time process. It should be performed throughout the life of the project.

Project team members, the project manager, and the stakeholders are responsible for the Quality Assurance of the project. The project manager will have the greatest impact on the quality of the project during this process.

Inputs to Quality Assurance

The inputs to Quality Assurance are what you use to measure the organizational project quality management processes against. The quality management processes were defined during Quality Planning. The inputs to the Quality Assurance process are:

- Quality management plan
- Results of quality control measurements
- Operational definitions

You've heard about the inputs to Quality Assurance before. They are very important elements of the Quality Assurance process and thus require revisiting.

Exam Spotlight

The most important thing to remember about Quality Assurance is that quality management processes are what you use to make certain the project satisfies the quality standards laid out in the project plan.

Quality Management Plan

The *quality management plan* talked about during Quality Planning defined the quality management processes that we'll use here. (Refer to Chapter 6 if you need a refresher on this topic.) You may recall that the quality management plan outlined quality improvements, quality control, and quality assurance. The quality management processes ensure that the project will satisfy the quality standards laid out in the plan.

Results of Quality Control Measurements

According to *A Guide to the PMBOK*, these results are quality control testing records and quality control measurements that are used to compare and analyze quality standards. Some of the tools you'll use to take quality measurements include inspecting, sampling, statistical sampling, and other monitoring techniques. We'll talk more about the tools and techniques of Quality Control in Chapter 10.

Operational Definitions

Operational definitions are an output of the Quality Planning process and become an input to the Quality Assurance process. You'll remember from Chapter 6 that operational definitions describe in detail what it is that's being measured and how to perform the measurements according to the Quality Control process.

Now let's take a look at the tools and techniques of this process, which will lead you to the final output—quality improvements.

Quality Tools and Quality Audits

There are only two tools and techniques of the Quality Assurance process: quality planning tools and techniques and quality audits.

We discussed Quality Planning tools and techniques during the Quality Planning process in Chapter 6. You'll recall that the tools and techniques are benefit/cost analysis, benchmarking, flowcharting, design of experiments, and cost of quality. These tools can be used during this process as well to measure project performance.

Quality audits serve a threefold purpose:

- Quality audits periodically review quality management activities and ensure that they're examining the right quality elements.

- Quality audits measure how the project is progressing and identify corrective actions when variances are detected in the measurements. You'll use the tools and techniques of this process to take performance measurements.

- Quality audits identify lessons learned for the benefit of the current project, future projects, or other projects in the organization currently in progress. *Lessons learned* allow project managers to learn from prior projects what things worked and what things didn't work so as not to repeat the same mistakes.

Exam Spotlight

Lessons learned are noted in *A Guide to the PMBOK* as the primary purpose for the Quality Assurance process.

Quality audits are performed on a regular schedule or at random depending on the organizational policies. Quality audits performed correctly will provide the following benefits:

- The product of the project is fit for use and meets safety standards.

- Applicable laws and standards are adhered to.

- Corrective action is implemented where necessary.

- The quality plan for the project is adhered to.

- Quality improvements are identified.

Quality audits are generally performed by experienced specialists. The specialist's job is to produce an independent evaluation of the quality process. Some organizations are large enough to have their own quality assurance departments or quality assurance teams; others may have to hire contract personnel to perform this function. Internal quality assurance teams report results to the project team and management team of the organization. External quality assurance teams report results to the customer.

Quality Improvements

Quality improvements are the only output of the Quality Assurance process. Quality improvements come about as a result of the quality audits. During the course of the audit, you may discover ways of improving the efficiency or effectiveness of the project, thereby increasing the value of the project and more than likely exceeding stakeholder expectations.

Quality improvements are implemented by submitting change requests or taking corrective action. Quality improvements interface with the Controlling processes because of the need to file change requests. We'll look at change requests and change request procedures in Chapter 10.

We've completed the Executing process group with the Quality Assurance section. Remember that the Executing and Controlling processes serve as inputs to each other and that Executing and Controlling are both iterative process groups. As your project progresses and it becomes evident controls need to be exercised to get the project back on track, you'll come back through the Executing process group to re-examine Project Plan Execution, Quality Assurance, and other processes and then proceed back through the Controlling processes again. Let's move on to the Controlling process group now and find out what it's all about.

Managing Project Progress

Managing and reporting on project progress is the primary focus of the Controlling processes. Many of the tools we talked about in the Project Plan Execution and the Information Distribution processes are used to manage and report project status. One of the Controlling processes that helps manage and control project progress is the *Scope Verification* process.

Exam Spotlight

The most important thing you should know about the Scope Verification process is that Scope Verification formalizes the acceptance of the project scope and is primarily concerned with the acceptance of work results. Don't confuse this process with the Quality Control process that we'll discuss in Chapter 10.

You can remember the difference between Scope Verification and Quality Assurance this way:

- Scope Verification = *accepting* work results

- Quality Control = *checking* for correct work results

Scope Verification involves evaluating the inputs of this process—work results, product documentation, WBS, scope statement, and project plan—to determine if the work is complete and if it satisfies the project objectives. Evaluation is performed using inspection, which is the only tool and technique of this process. You should perform Scope Verification—even if the project is canceled—to document the degree to which the project was completed. This serves as historical information, and if the project is ever started up again, you've got documentation that tells you what was completed and how far the project progressed.

The output of Scope Verification is formal acceptance. Stakeholders are the people who will accept the work results. Remember that stakeholders include customers, the project sponsor, the management team, etc. Document their acceptance with formal sign-off and file it in your project notebook.

Establishing Performance Measurements

The Controlling process group concentrates on monitoring and measuring project performance to identify variances from the project plan. Performance Reporting is the process where most of the monitoring and measuring occurs. Change requests are often generated as a result of the Controlling processes. Because of this, change control is a strong focus of the Controlling process group. (We'll discuss the change control processes in the next chapter.)

Performance Reporting is part of the Communications Management knowledge area. Thus it involves collecting and reporting information regarding project progress and project accomplishments to the stakeholders, project team members, management team, and other interested parties. Reporting might include information concerning project quality, costs, scope, project schedules, procurement, and risk.

The inputs to the Performance Reporting process—project plan, work results, and other project records—are used with the tools and techniques of this process to monitor and measure project performance. We have already discussed the project plan and work results. Other project records are any project documents that contain information that will help you monitor and measure project performance.

Performance measures are taken using the tools and techniques of this process. We'll look at them next.

Performance Reporting Tools and Techniques

There are five tools and techniques used in Performance Recording:

- Performance reviews
- Variance analysis
- Trend analysis
- Earned value analysis
- Information distribution tools and techniques

You'll need to fully understand the variance analysis, trend analysis, and earned value analysis techniques. We'll spend most of our time on the earned value analysis techniques in this section, which involve several formulas. I strongly recommend you memorize every formula I present. I'll pass on a memorization tip I used to commit these formulas to memory when we get to the earned value section.

Performance Reviews

Performance reviews are project status meetings held with the project team and stakeholders to collect status and report on project progress. Reports will take three forms: status reports, progress reports, and forecasting.

Status reports inform stakeholders about where the project is today in regard to project schedule and budget, for example. We covered the purpose and proper etiquette of status review meetings in Chapter 8.

Progress reports describe what the project team has accomplished to date. This report might include milestones completed to date, the percentage schedule completion, and what remains to be completed.

The third type of report concerns forecasting future project status and progress. This is where you inform the stakeholders of your prediction of milestone completion dates, the percentage of schedule completion on a certain date (maybe the end of the month or the end of the quarter, for example), and projected budget expenditures.

Variance Analysis

Variance analysis compares the expected project plan results with the actual results as the project progresses to determine if variances exist. Typically, the project schedule and project costs are the two areas most often measured. However, quality, performance specifications, risk, and project scope are measurable as well.

Exam Spotlight

Remember that variance analysis compares expected project results to actual results to determine variances.

Trend Analysis

According to *A Guide to the PMBOK*, *trend analysis* determines if project performance is improving or worsening over time by periodically analyzing project results. These results are measured with mathematical formulas that attempt to forecast project outcomes based on historical information and results. There are several formulas you can use to predict project trends, but it's outside the scope of this book to go into them. The exam expects you to understand the concept behind trend analysis, not the formulas used to calculate it. You'll want to remember that the results you've analyzed using trend analysis formulas are used to predict future project behavior or trends.

Earned Value Analysis

Earned value analysis is the most frequently used performance measurement method. Simply stated, it compares what you got to what you spent. Earned value looks at schedule, cost, and scope project measurements together. To perform the earned value calculations, you need to first determine three measurements: the planned value (PV), actual cost (AC), and earned value (EV).

Each of these measurements has been renamed in *A Guide to the PMBOK*. You may see their original names in other publications. Here is a quick reference in case you come across the original names of these measurements:

- PV = budgeted cost of work scheduled (BCWS)
- AC = actual cost of work performed (ACWP)
- EV = budgeted cost of work performed (BCWP)

Let's look at a definition of each of these before we dive into the actual calculations. I recommend you memorize each of these acronyms and make certain you understand the meaning of each before progressing.

Planned value   The *planned value (PV)* is the cost of work that's been budgeted for an activity or for the project during a certain time period. These estimates and budgets are established during the Planning process.

Actual cost   *Actual cost (AC)* is the cost of the work to date (or for a given time period), including direct and indirect costs. Later you'll see how to compare this to PV to come up with variance calculation results.

Earned value   *Earned value (EV)* is a measurement of the project's progress to date, or the value of the work completed to date.

Exam Spotlight

PV, AC, and EV are really easy to mix up. In their simplest forms, here's what each means:

- PV = The planned costs for activities scheduled during a given time period
- AC = Money that's actually been expended to date (or during a given time period)
- EV = The value of the work completed to date

EV is the sum of the cumulative budgeted costs for completed work for all activities that have been accomplished as of the measurement date. If your total budget is $1000 and 50 percent of the work has been completed as of the measurement date, your EV would equal $500. The PV, AC, and EV measurements can be plotted graphically to show the variances between them. If there are no variances in the measurements, all the lines on the graph remain the same, which means the project is progressing as planned. Figure 9.1 shows an example that plots these three measurements.

FIGURE 9.1 Earned value

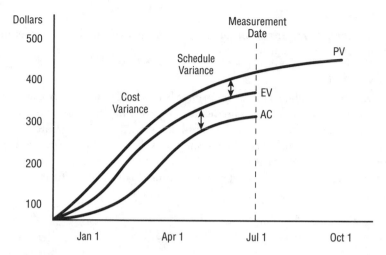

All of these measurements include a cost component. Costs are displayed in an S-curve, because spending is minimal in the beginning of the project, picks up steam toward the middle, and then tapers off at the end of the project. This means your earned value measurements will also take on the S-curve shape.

Now you can calculate whether the project is progressing as planned using a variety of formulas. Use Figure 9.1 as your example for the formulas that follow. Figure 9.1 totals are as follows: PV = 400; EV = 375; AC = 325.

Cost Variance

Cost variance is one of the most popular variances that project managers use, and it tells you if costs are higher than budgeted (with a resulting negative number) or lower than budgeted (with a resulting positive number).

The *cost variance (CV)* is calculated as follows:

CV = EV – AC

Let's calculate the CV using the numbers from Figure 9.1:

375 – 325 = 50

The CV is positive, which means you're spending less than what you planned as of July 1.

If you come up with a negative number as the answer to this formula, it means that costs are higher than what you'd planned as of July 1.

Schedule Variance

Schedule variance, also a popular variance, tells you if the schedule is ahead or behind what was planned for this period in time. The *schedule variance (SV)* is calculated as follows:

SV = EV – PV

Let's plug in the numbers:

$375 - 400 = -25$

The resulting schedule variance is negative, which means you are behind schedule, or behind where you planned to be as of July 1.

Performance Indexes

Cost and schedule performance indexes are primarily used to calculate performance efficiencies. They're often used in trend analysis to predict future performance. You'll need to know the calculations and what the results mean. If your result in either formula is greater than one, you've got better than expected performance. If the result is less than one, you've got poor performance. If it equals one, you're right on target.

The *cost performance index (CPI)*, the most commonly used cost efficiency indicator, is calculated this way:

$CPI = EV \div AC$

Let's plug in the numbers and see where you stand.

$375 \div 325 = 1.15$

This means cost performance is better than expected. You get an A+ on this assignment! The *schedule performance index (SPI)* is calculated this way:

$SPI = EV \div PV$

Again, let's see where you stand with this example:

$375 \div 400 = .94$

Uh oh, not so good. Schedule performance is not what you expected. Let's not grade this one.

Estimate at Completion

There are only a few calculations remaining that will help you finish up your analysis of project progress. EAC is the *estimate at completion*. This estimates (or forecasts) the total cost of the project at completion based on what you know today concerning project performance to date and risk quantification. It is typically the actual costs incurred to date plus a new estimate for the work that remains. It's the best estimate available to determine total costs at completion of the project.

This measurement is used during the Cost Control process, which we'll talk about in Chapter 10. However, I believe it's easier for you to review all these formulas in one place since they all use similar measurements. This should also help you when memorizing the formulas, which I recommend you do.

There are several ways to calculate EAC. *A Guide to the PMBOK* identifies three methods, which we'll cover here. The first one looks like this:

$EAC = AC + ETC$

The estimate to complete (ETC) formula is discussed in a later section. Essentially, it's the mathematical opposite of the EAC formula. ETC uses EAC, so we'll discuss EAC first.

The EAC formula calculates the actual cost of the project to date plus the cost estimate of the remaining work. Use this calculation when past estimating assumptions are no longer valid or you discover that they were flawed or incorrect.

The calculation for EAC using this formula looks like this when ETC = 50:

$$325 + 50 = 375$$

You will use this next EAC formula when you believe the current variances are not typical. In other words, you do not expect the variances that have occurred to date to continue to occur. The formula looks like this:

$$EAC = (AC + BAC) - EV$$

Budget at completion (BAC) is the remaining budget less the work that's been done to date. The exam will give you the BAC figure. Let's plug in the numbers and see what you get. Assume that BAC = 390.

$$(325 + 390) - 375 = 340$$

Only one more EAC formula to go. Use this version of EAC when you expect project performance to continue with the same type of variances occurring in the future as you've experienced to date:

$$EAC = AC + ((BAC - EV) \div CPI)$$

Putting the numbers into the formula, using BAC = 390, gives you the following:

$$325 + ((390 - 375) \div 1.15)) = 338 \text{ rounded to the nearest whole number.}$$

We'll look at two more formulas—variance at completion and estimate to complete—and then we'll recap them in an easy-to-memorize form.

Variance at Completion

Variance at completion (VAC) calculates the difference between the budget at completion and the estimate at completion. It looks like this:

$$VAC = BAC - EAC$$

Use the most optimistic EAC number:

$$390 - 375 = 15$$

Again, the positive number means you're doing better with costs than you anticipated.

Estimate to Complete

Estimate to complete (ETC) tells you how much more budget is required to finish the project if everything continues at the current levels of performance. This is your last formula, and you need to memorize it as well:

$$ETC = EAC - AC$$

One more time, let's put in the numbers using 375 as EAC:

$$375 - 325 = 50$$

This formula tells you that from July 1 through project completion on October 1, you'll need $50 more to complete the project if the project continues at the current level of performance.

Recap of Formulas

There are a lot of formulas to memorize. Keep in mind that you'll be given a calculator when you take the exam, so you don't have to do the math manually. Here are the formulas we've covered in this chapter:

$CV = EV - AC$

$SV = EV - PV$

$CPI = EV \div AC$

$SPI = EV \div PV$

$EAC = AC + ETC$ (use when past assumptions are incorrect)

$EAC = (AC + BAC) - EV$ (use when variances are not typical)

$EAC = AC + ((BAC - EV) \div CPI)$ (use when variances are expected to remain the same)

$ETC = EAC - AC$

$VAC = BAC - EAC$

Remember that there are nine formulas. You might want to devise an acronym for the first letters of each formula to help you memorize their order: C-S-C-S-E-E-E-E-V.

You'll be given some scratch paper when you go into the exam. I recommend that you write these calculations down on a piece of your scratch paper before you start answering questions and keep it handy. That way, the calculations are off your mind and you've got them in front of you to reference when you get to the portion of the exam where these questions appear.

One tool and technique remains, and then we'll get into the outputs of the Performance Reporting process.

Information Distribution Tools and Techniques

Once you've collected and calculated the variances for your project, you'll need to report on them. Information Distribution tools and techniques include:

- Communication skills
- Information retrieval systems
- Information distribution methods

We discussed each of these during the Information Distribution process in Chapter 8.

Performance Reporting Outputs

This process has two outputs: performance reports and change requests. We've already discussed change requests and will talk more extensively about them in Chapter 10.

Performance reports contain the information you've gathered from this process. You'll summarize the performance of the project and report on the analysis you've conducted, and then present it to the stakeholders, management team, and customers if appropriate, using reports that are distributed via the information distribution system. Remember that the communications management plan details the amount of information each stakeholder requires. Some performance reports need a deeper level of detail than others. Refer to the communications plan when you prepare your reports so that the right level of information is going to the appropriate stakeholders.

As a result of performance measures and corrective actions, changes are often needed. This requires that change control processes exist to deal with the changes as they happen. The next chapter will look at all of the change control processes.

Project Case Study: New Kitchen Heaven Retail Store

Your regularly scheduled status meeting is coming up. Stakeholders have asked for an updated status on the project schedule as well as a remaining cost projection. You decide to provide several performance figures for the project on the status report. You'll update these figures for every status report from now through the rest of the project. Let's see how the status meeting is progressing.

"Build-out is behind schedule. They were scheduled to be completed by the 24th of January, but they aren't going to finish up until the 31st."

"What's that do to my schedule?" Jill asks. "I'm starting interviews for the store positions on the 14th. I hope to have that wrapped up by the 19th even though the schedule gives me more time. As long as I have the majority of the staff hired by the 20th, we can have them stocking shelves starting the 22nd."

You tell Jill, "Let's finish up the status of the other items, and I'll come back to that."

"Gomez Construction has submitted a seller invoice for the work completed through December 31. Shelly in our contract management office manages the payment system and handles all payment requests. She'll get a check cut and out to Gomez by the end of this month. Thanks to Jake for overseeing the quality control of the build-out process.

"The contract management office used a fixed price contract on the hardware and IT supplies order. Ricardo's group will manage the quality control and testing once it's all arrived.

"Jill has ordered all the retail products, the cookware line, and has lined up the chef demos. The costs for the new gourmet supplier are higher than our original vendor. This impacts ongoing operations, but the hit to the project budget is minimal.

"I've calculated some performance measurements, including earned value measures, as follows (all figures are in millions of dollars):

$BAC = 2; PV = 1.86; EV = 1.75; AC = 1.70$

$CPI = 1.75 \div 1.70 = 1.03$

SPI = 1.75 ÷ 1.86 = .94

EAC = 1.70 + ((2 − 1.75) ÷ 1.03)) = 1.94

ETC = 1.94 − 1.70 = .24

"What is all this telling us?" Dirk asks.

"The cost performance index tells us we're getting a good return for the money spent on the project so far. In other words, we've experienced a $1.03 value for every dollar spent to date.

"The schedule performance index isn't as cheery, but it's not dreadful news either. This performance indicator says that work is progressing at 94 percent of what we anticipated by this point.

"The estimate at completion tells us that based on what we know today, the total project will cost $1.94 million. That's coming in under the original $2 million we had budgeted for completion, so we're on track with the project budget.

"The last figure is the estimated cost of the remaining work."

"It looks like we're a little behind schedule based on what you have figured here," Dirk says.

"Yes, that's correct," you reply. "That brings us back to Jill's question. I have two alternatives to propose. One, we overlap the schedule and allow Gomez's crew to complete their work while Jill's staff starts stocking shelves."

Jill says, "I don't like this option. We'll be tripping over each other, and I don't want merchandise damaged by workers who are still dragging equipment around inside the store. What's your other option?"

"We could ask Gomez to increase the crew size so that they complete on time according to the contract. We have a provision in the contract that stipulates they add crew members if they miss the scheduled completion date. I will instruct the contract management department to inform Gomez that we're requiring additional crew members."

"That will do the trick," Jill says. "We need the storefront to ourselves when stocking and preparing for opening. I'm glad you had that stipulation in the contract."

"Any other questions or concerns?" you ask. With that, the meeting is adjourned.

Project Case Study Checklist

Contract Administration

- Work results

- Seller invoices

- Payment systems

- Payment requests

Quality Assurance, quality audits

- Making certain the project will meet and satisfy the quality standards of the project

Scope Verification

- Acceptance of work results

Performance Reporting

- Performance reviews (status meetings)

- Earned value analysis

Summary

This chapter finished up the Executing process group and looked at the first process in the Controlling process group. We discussed Solicitation, Source Selection, Contract Administration, and Quality Assurance from the Executing process group and Scope Verification and Performance Reporting from the Controlling process group.

Solicitation, Source Selection, and Contract Administration are generally performed in that order. Solicitation is the process of requesting vendors to compete for the contract through RFPs, RFQs, and so on. The Solicitation process concerns obtaining vendor bids.

Source Selection involves choosing a vendor among the potential qualified vendors that bid on the project. Source Selection uses evaluation criteria, weighting systems, screening systems, and independent estimates to determine who will win the contract.

Contracts have cycles of their own, much like projects. Contracting life cycles include requirement, requisition, solicitation, and award. Contract Administration is concerned with monitoring the vendor's performance and making certain it adheres to the contract requirements. Changes to the contract are managed with change requests.

Changes that cannot be agreed upon are called *contested changes*. These take the form of disputes, claims, or appeals. They might be settled among the parties directly, through a court of law, or through arbitration.

Seller invoices are submitted as an input to the Contract Administration process. Payment systems process and track vendor invoices, while payment requests are the output of the Contract Administration process and result in the actual payment to the vendor.

During the Quality Assurance process, quality audits are performed to ensure the project will meet and satisfy the project's quality standards set out in the quality plan.

Scope Verification formalizes the acceptance of the work results. It determines if the work is complete and if it satisfies the project objectives. Performance Reporting is one of the core processes in the Controlling process group. This process collects and reports on project accomplishments. Stakeholders, team members, the management team, and the customer may all have interest in the performance progress reports. Performance reviews are status meetings where the performance measures are reported.

Performance reviews, variance analysis, trend analysis, earned value analysis, and information distribution tools and techniques are the tools and techniques of Performance Reporting. Variance analysis compares the expected results with the actual results. Trend analysis shows if the project is improving or worsening.

Earned value analysis is the most frequently used performance measurement method. It includes several calculations that show the status of the project based on three primary values: planned value, actual cost, and earned value.

Exam Essentials

Be able to describe the difference between the Solicitation process and the Source Selection process.   Solicitation obtains bids and proposals from vendors. Source Selection is the receipt of bids and proposals and the selection of a vendor.

Be able to name the tools and techniques of the Source Selection process.   The tools and techniques of the Source Selection process are contract negotiation, weighting systems, screening systems, and independent estimates.

Be able to describe the purpose of the Quality Assurance process.   It's a quality management process concerned with making certain the project meets and satisfies the quality standards of the project. It's concerned with making certain the project will meet and satisfy the quality standards of the project.

Be able to distinguish between seller invoices, payment systems, and payment requests.   Seller invoices are an input, payment systems are a tool and technique, and payment requests are an output of the Contract Administration process.

Be able to name the purpose of the Scope Verification process.   Scope Verification formalizes acceptance of project scope and acceptance of work results.

Be able to define the purpose of the Performance Reporting process.   The Performance Reporting process collects and reports information regarding project progress and project accomplishments. The technique used often to report on project performance is earned value analysis.

Key Terms

Before you take the exam, be certain you are familiar with the following terms:

actual cost (AC)

appeals

advertising

arbitration

bidder conferences

claims

contested changes

Contract Administration

contract change control system

contract negotiation

cost performance index (CPI)

cost variance (CV)

disputes

earned value (EV)

earned value analysis

estimate at completion (EAC)

estimate to complete (ETC)

evaluation criteria

Independent estimates

lessons learned

payment requests

payment system

Performance Reporting

performance reviews

planned value (PV)

qualified seller lists

Quality Assurance

quality audits

schedule performance index (SPI)

schedule variance (SV)

Scope Verification

screening systems

seller invoices

should cost estimates

Solicitation

Source Selection

trend analysis

variance analysis

variance at completion (VAC)

weighting systems

Review Questions

1. You are a project manager for Dakota Software Consulting Services. You're working with a major retailer that offers their products through mail-order catalogs. They're interested in knowing customer characteristics, the amounts of first-time orders, and similar information. As a potential bidder for this project, you worked on the RFP response and submitted the proposal. When the selection committee received the RFP responses from all the vendors bidding on this project, they used a weighted system to make a selection. In which process did this occur?

    A. Source Selection

    B. Solicitation

    C. Requisition

    D. Contract Administration

2. You have been asked to submit a proposal for a project that has been put out for bid. First, you attend the bidder conference to ask questions of the buyers and to hear the questions some of the other bidders will ask. Which of the following statements is true?

    A. Bidder conferences are a tool and technique of the Source Selection process.

    B. Bidder conferences are an output of the Source Selection process.

    C. Bidder conferences are an output of the Solicitation process.

    D. Bidder conferences are a tool and technique of the Solicitation process.

3. You have been asked to submit a proposal for a project that has been put out for bid. Prior to submitting the proposal, your company must register so that their firm is on the qualified seller list. Which of the following statements is true?

    A. The qualified seller list provides information about the sellers and is a tool and technique of the Solicitation process.

    B. The qualified seller list provides information about the project and the company that wrote the RFP and is an input to the Solicitation process.

    C. The qualified seller list provides information about the project and the company that wrote the RFP and is a tool and technique of the Source Selection process.

    D. The qualified seller list provides information about the sellers and is an input to the Solicitation process.

4. The tools and techniques of the Source Selection process include all of the following except:

    A. Contract negotiation

    B. Correspondence

    C. Independent estimates

    D. Screening system

5. Which of the following processes negotiates the sequence of award by rank ordering the proposals?

A. Source Selection

B. Solicitation

C. Contract Administration

D. Procurement

6. During the opening rounds of contract negotiation, the other party uses a fait accompli tactic. Which of the following statements is true about fait accompli tactics?

A. One party agrees to accept the offer of the other party but secretly knows they will bring the issue back up at a later time.

B. One party claims the issue under discussion was documented and accepted as part of Scope Verification.

C. One party claims the issue under discussion has already been decided and can't be changed.

D. One party claims to accept the offer of the other party, provided a contract change request is submitted describing the offer in detail.

7. Your procurement department has obtained independent estimates. The vendor's proposal is substantially different than the independent estimates. All of the following statements are true except:

A. The SOW was not detailed enough.

B. The vendor failed to respond according to the terms of the proposal.

C. The vendor failed to respond to all the items in the SOW.

D. The vendor failed to respond to all the items in the contract.

8. What are the tools and techniques of the Contract Administration process?

A. Contract change control system, payment system, and payment requests

B. Contract change control system, contract negotiations, and payment system

C. Contract change control system, contract negotiations, and contract changes

D. Contract change control system, performance reporting, and payment system

9. You are a project manager for an engineering company. Your company won the bid to add ramp-metering lights to several on-ramps along a stretch of highway at the south end of the city. You subcontracted a portion of the project to another company. The subcontractor's work involves digging the holes and setting the lamp poles in concrete. The subcontractor's performance is not meeting the contract requirements. All of the following are valid options except:

   A. You document the poor performance in written form and send the correspondence to the subcontractor.

   B. You terminate the contract for poor performance and submit a change request through Contract Administration.

   C. You submit a change request through Contract Administration to ask the subcontractor to comply with the terms of the contract.

   D. You agree to meet with the subcontractor to see if a satisfactory solution can be reached.

10. You are a project manager for an engineering company. Your company won the bid to add ramp-metering lights to several on-ramps along a stretch of highway at the south end of the city. You subcontracted a portion of the project to another company. The subcontractor's work involves digging the holes and setting the lamp poles in concrete. You've discovered the subcontractor's work is not correct because the poles are not buried to the correct depth. You review the work and note performance improvements that can be made on future projects as a result of this error. Which of the following is true?

   A. You are in the Quality Assurance process and have performed a quality audit to identify lessons learned.

   B. You are in the Scope Verification process and have performed a quality audit to ensure correctness of work.

   C. You are in the Contract Administration process and have completed a contract audit to ensure the subcontractor's performance meets the contract requirements.

   D. You are in the Performance Reporting process and have completed a performance review of the contractor's work.

11. The purpose of a quality audit includes all of the following except:

   A. Examines the work of the project and formally accepts the work results.

   B. Determines how the project is progressing and makes corrections.

   C. Identifies lessons learned.

   D. Reviews quality management activities to ensure the right quality elements are being examined.

12. You are a project manager for Dakota Software Consulting Services. You're working with a major retailer that offers their products through mail-order catalogs. They're interested in knowing customer characteristics, the amounts of first-time orders, and similar information. The stakeholders have accepted the project scope. Work has begun on the project, and you're confirming some of the initial work results with the stakeholders. You've asked for acceptance of the work results. Which process are you in?

A. Quality Assurance

B. Quality Control

C. Scope Verification

D. Performance Reporting

13. All of the following are tools and techniques of the Performance Reporting process except:

A. Variance analysis

B. Performance reporting

C. Information distribution tools and techniques

D. Performance reviews

14. This measurement is the value of the work that's been completed to date:

A. PV

B. AC

C. EV

D. EAC

15. You are a contract project manager for a wholesale flower distribution company. Your project is to develop a website for the company that allows retailers to place their flower orders online. You will also provide a separate link for individual purchases that are ordered, packaged, and mailed to the consumer directly from the grower's site. This project involves coordinating the parent company, growers, and distributors. You are preparing a performance review and have the following measurements at hand: PV = 300; AC = 200; and EV = 250. What do you know about this project?

A. The EAC is a positive number, which means the project will finish under budget.

B. You do not have enough information to calculate CPI.

C. The CV is a negative number in this case, which means you've spent less than what you planned as of the measurement date.

D. The CV is a positive number in this case, which means you're under budget as of the measurement date.

16. A negative result from an SV calculation means which of the following?

   A. PV is higher than EV.

   B. PV equals one.

   C. EV is higher than PV.

   D. EV is higher than AC.

17. You are a contract project manager for a wholesale flower distribution company. Your project is to develop a website for the company that allows retailers to place their flower orders online. You will also provide a separate link for individual purchases that are ordered, packaged, and mailed to the consumer directly from the grower's site. This project involves coordinating the parent company, growers, and distributors. You are preparing a performance review and have the following measurements at hand: PV = 300; AC = 200; and EV = 250. What is the CPI of this project?

   A. 0.80

   B. 1.25

   C. 1.5

   D. 0.83

18. You do not expect the types of variances that have occurred on the project to date to continue. If BAC = 300, ETC = 275, PV = 300, AC = 200, EV = 250, and CPI = 1.25, what is the EAC?

   A. 240

   B. 250

   C. 475

   D. 150

19. You know that BAC = 375, PV = 300, AC = 200, and EV = 250. Variances that have occurred on the project to date are not expected to continue. What is the ETC?

   A. 75

   B. 50

   C. 125

   D. 150

20. What are the outputs of the Performance Reporting process?

   A. Performance reports and change requests

   B. Performance reports and other project records

   C. Change requests and performance reporting

   D. Change requests and performance measurements

Answers to Review Questions

1. **A.** Source Selection involves the receipt of bids and proposals. Weighted systems are one of the tools and techniques of this process used to evaluate vendors based on selection criteria defined by the organization.

2. **D.** Bidder conferences are a tool and technique of the Solicitation process. In solicitation, proposals are submitted by vendors and obtained by the organization.

3. **D.** Qualified seller lists are an input to the Solicitation process. Their purpose is to provide information about the sellers.

4. **B.** Correspondence is an output of the Contract Administration process. One additional tool and technique of Source Selection not shown in this question is weighting systems.

5. **A.** Source Selection uses varying tools and techniques to rank order proposals in sequence, starting with the top scoring proposal.

6. **C.** Fait accompli is a tactic used during contract negotiations where one party convinces the other that the particular issue is no longer relevant or cannot be changed. Answer B is not correct because Scope Verification does not generally occur during contract negotiations since the work of the project has not yet been performed.

7. **B.** Estimates that differ from bids are the result of incomplete details in the SOW or the vendor failing to respond to the items in the SOW or the items in the contract.

8. **D.** The tools and techniques of the Contract Administration process are contract change control system, performance reporting, and payment system.

9. **C.** The contract change control system describes the processes you'll use to make changes to the contract. This might include contract term changes, date changes, and termination of a contract.

10. **A.** You have just performed a quality audit to identify lessons learned. Contract audits are not part of the Contract Administration process, so answer C is not correct. Answer D is not correct because performance reviews are status meetings, or similar meetings, that report on the performance of the project to stakeholders and other interested parties.

11. **A.** The acceptance of work results happens during the Scope Verification process, not during Quality Assurance.

12. **C.** The Scope Verification process is concerned with the acceptance of work results. It also formalizes the acceptance of the project scope.

13. **B.** Performance reporting is a tool and technique of the Contract Administration process. The other tools and techniques of Performance Reporting not listed in this question are trend analysis and earned value analysis.

14. C.   Earned value is referred to as the value of the work that's been completed to date.

15. D.   The CV is a positive number and is calculated by subtracting AC from EV as follows: 250 − 200 = 50. A positive CV means the project is coming in under budget, meaning you've spent less than what you planned as of the measurement date.

16. A.   The SV calculation is EV − PV. If PV is a higher number than EV, you'll get a negative number as a result.

17. B.   CPI is calculated as follows: EV ÷ AC. In this case, 250 ÷ 200 = 1.25.

18. B.   When variances are not expected to continue, or are atypical in nature, EAC is calculated as follows: (AC + BAC) − EV. Therefore, the calculation for this question looks like this: (200 + 300) − 250 = 250.

19. C.   To answer this question, you'll first have to calculate EAC because you need that result to plug into the ETC formula. The correct formula for EAC for this question is as follows: (AC + BAC) − EV. Therefore, EAC for this question is as follows: (200 + 375) − 250 = 325. ETC is calculated this way: EAC − AC. Therefore, ETC is as follows: 325 − 200 = 125.

20. A.   Performance Reporting outputs include performance reports and change requests.

Chapter 10

Controlling Change

THE PMP EXAM CONTENT FROM THE PROJECT CONTROL PERFORMANCE DOMAIN COVERED IN THIS CHAPTER INCLUDES:

✓ 1. Measuring performance

✓ 6. Reassessing control plans

✓ 7. Responding to risk event triggers

✓ 8. Monitoring project activity

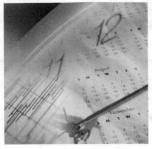

We started examining the Controlling processes with Performance Reporting and Scope Verification in Chapter 9, "Measuring and Controlling Project Performance." Performance reports, which are an output of the Performance Reporting process, serve as an input to every other Controlling process, except for Risk Monitoring and Control and Quality Control.

Performance reports are used during the Controlling processes, along with the tools and techniques of the Controlling processes, to measure project performance. These measurements and control tools allow the project manager to take corrective action during the Controlling processes to remedy wayward project results and realign future project results with the project plan.

We'll cover several processes in this chapter: Integrated Change Control, Scope Change Control, Schedule Control, Cost Control, Quality Control, and Risk Monitoring and Control.

Integrated Change Control lays the foundation for all of the change control processes. We'll spend time during this process to explain how change control works. The Scope Change Control, Schedule Control, and Cost Control processes are very similar to Integrated Change Control. There's no need to repeat the information from Integrated Change Control for the other processes. When we get to the Scope Change Control, Schedule Control, and Cost Control sections, we'll highlight any potential exam questions. Just remember when you're reading these sections that the information from the Integrated Change Control process applies to these areas as well.

Quality Control involves several new tools and techniques that may show up on the exam. Take some time here to understand them and to differentiate between Quality Planning tools and Quality Control tools. Some of the tools and techniques are used in both processes, but the others pertain only to the particular process where they're listed.

This chapter concludes the Controlling process group. From here, we move on to the Closing processes and wrap up the project. You've learned a lot about project management by this point and have just a few more things to add to your study list. Keep up the good work. You're getting closer to exam day.

Managing Integrated Change Control

The *Integrated Change Control* process is one of two core processes in the Controlling process group. (Performance Reporting is the other core process.) It serves as an overseer so to speak—the integrator of all the Control processes. This is where the project's change control process is established. Changes, updates, or corrective actions are common outputs across all the Controlling processes. (And don't forget that change requests are also an output of the Project Plan

Execution process, which is an Executing process.) These outputs often generate change requests that are managed through this process.

The inputs to the Integrated Change Control process are:

- Project plan
- Performance reports
- Change requests

We've discussed each of these inputs previously, but let's spend a little more time talking about changes and change requests.

Changes come about on projects for many reasons. It's the project manager's responsibility to manage these changes and see to it that organizational policies regarding changes are implemented. Changes don't necessarily mean negative consequences. Changes can produce positive results as well. It's important that you manage this process carefully, because too many changes—even one significant change—will impact cost, schedule, scope, and/or quality. Once a change request has been submitted, you've got some decisions to make. Ask yourself questions such as, "Should the change be implemented? If so, what's the cost to the project in terms of project constraints: cost, time, scope, and quality? Will the benefits gained by making the change increase or decrease the chances of project completion?"

Just because a change is requested doesn't mean you have to implement it. You'll always want to discover the reasons for the change and determine if they're justifiable, and you'll want to know the cost of the change. Remember that cost can take the form of increased time. Let's say the change you're considering increases the schedule completion date. That means you'll need human resources longer than expected. If you've leased equipment or project resources for the team members to use during the course of the project, a later completion date means your team needs the leased equipment for a longer period of time. All this translates to increased costs. Time equals money as the saying goes, so manage time changes wisely and dig deep to find the impacts that time changes might make on the budget.

How Change Occurs

As the project progresses, the stakeholders or customers may request a change directly. We'll talk about how they submit those change requests in the next major section, "Controlling Scope Changes."

Team members might recommend changes as the project progresses. Once the project is under way, they may discover more efficient ways of performing tasks or producing the product of the project and recommend changes to accommodate the new efficiencies.

Changes to the project may occur indirectly as a result of contingency plans, other changes, or team members performing favors for the stakeholders by making that one little change without telling anyone about it. Many times, the project manager is the last to know about changes like this one. There's a fine line here, because you don't want to discourage good working relationships between team members and stakeholders, yet at the same time, you want to ensure that all changes come through the change control process. If a dozen little changes slip through like this, your project scope suddenly exits stage left.

Change Control Concerns

Integrated Change Control, according to *A Guide to the PMBOK*, is concerned with three things:

- Influencing the factors that cause change and reaching agreement on their resulting change requests
- Determining that change is needed or has happened
- Managing change

Factors that may cause change include project constraints, stakeholder requests, team member recommendations, vendor issues, and many others. You'll want to understand the factors that are influencing or bringing about change and how the proposed change may impact the project if implemented. Performance measures and corrective actions may dictate that a project change is needed as well.

Modifications to the project are submitted in the form of change requests and managed through the change control process. Obviously, you'll want to implement those changes that are most beneficial to the project. We'll talk more about change requests later in this chapter.

Managing changes may involve making changes to the project plan, project schedule, or cost baseline, also known as the *performance measurement baselines*. It's your responsibility to maintain the reliability of the performance measurement baselines. If changes are not appropriately reflected in the baselines, they become meaningless. Changes that impact a previous project management process will require updates to those processes, which might mean additional passes through the appropriate Planning and Executing processes.

The management plans created during the Planning processes should reflect the changes as well. This requires a close eye on coordination among all the processes that are impacted. For example, a quality change may impact risk, schedule, cost, or other processes. Changes that impact product scope always require an update to the project scope.

Exam Spotlight

Managing changes involves maintaining accurate and reliable performance measurement baselines, coordinating all processes impacted as a result of the change, including revisiting Planning and Executing processes where needed and updating project scope to reflect any changes in product scope.

I caution you not to change baselines at the drop of a hat. Examine the changes, their justification, and their impacts thoroughly before making changes to the baselines.

Integrated Change Control Tools and Techniques

The Integrated Change Control process uses five tools and techniques to implement and manage change:

- Change control system
- Configuration management
- Performance measurement
- Additional planning
- Project management information system

Chapter 7, "Creating the Project Plan," covered the project management information system input, and Chapter 9, "Measuring and Controlling Project Performance," talked about performance measurements. Let's look at the remaining inputs next.

Change Control System

If you were to allow changes to occur to the project whenever requested, you would probably never complete the project. Stakeholders, the customer, and end users would continually change the project requirements if given the opportunity to do so. That's why careful planning and scope definition are important in the beginning of the project. It's your job as project manager to drive out all the compelling needs and requirements of the project during the Planning process so that important requirements aren't suddenly "remembered" halfway through the project. However, we're all human, and sometimes things are not known, weren't thought about, or simply weren't discovered until a certain point during the project. Stakeholders will probably start thinking in a direction they weren't considering during the Planning process, and new requirements will come to light. This is where the *change control system* comes into play.

The Purpose of the Change Control System

Change control systems are documented procedures that describe how to submit change requests, how to manage change requests, and the management impacts of the changes as they pertain to project performance. They can include preprinted change request forms that provide a place to record general project information such as the name and project number, the date, and the details regarding the change request.

The change control system also tracks the status of change requests, including their approval status. Not all change requests will receive approval to implement. Those changes that are not approved are also tracked and filed in the project notebook for future reference.

The change control system defines the level of authority needed to approve changes. Some change requests could receive approval based on the project manager's decision; others may need more formal approval or more levels of approval such as the project sponsor, executive management, and so on.

Procedures should be defined that detail how emergency changes are approved as well. For example, you and your team might be putting in some weekend hours and are close to the completion of a deliverable when you discover that thing one will not talk to thing two no matter what you do. The team brainstorms and comes up with a brilliant solution that requires a change request. Do you stop work right then and wait until the change control board or committee can meet sometime next week and make a decision, or do you—the project manager—make the decision to go forward with this solution and explain the change to the appropriate parties later? That answer depends on the change procedures you have in place to handle situations like this and the authority you have to make emergency changes as outlined in the change control system.

Many organizations have formal change control or change request systems in place. If that's the case, you can easily adopt those procedures and use the existing system to manage project change. But if no procedures exist, you'll have to define them.

Requirements for Change

There are two things you should require at the beginning of all projects regarding change. First, require that all change requests be submitted in writing. This is to clarify the change and make sure no confusion exists regarding what's requested. It also allows the project team to accurately estimate the time it will take to incorporate the change. Keep in mind that you will get verbal change requests as well.

According to *A Guide to the PMBOK*, change requests come in verbal or written forms, but it's good practice to require them in writing.

Second, all change requests must come through the formal change control system. Make sure no one is allowed to go directly to team members and request changes without the project manager knowing about it. Also make certain your stakeholders understand that this can cause schedule delays, cost overruns, and sacrifices to quality, and isn't good change management practice. Encourage them from the beginning of the project to use the formal procedures laid out in the change control system to request changes.

Configuration Control Board

In some organizations, a *configuration control board (CCB)* is established to review all change requests. They are given the authority to approve or deny change requests as defined by the organization. It's important that their authority is clearly defined and that separate procedures exist for emergency changes. The CCB may meet only once a week, once every other week, or even once a month, depending on the project. When emergencies arise, the pre-established procedures allow the project manager to implement the change on the spot. This will always require a follow-up with the CCB and the completion of a formal change request even though it's after the fact.

CCB members may include stakeholders, managers, project team members, and others who may not have any connection to the project at hand. Some organizations have permanent CCBs that are staffed by full-time employees dedicated to managing change for the entire organization, not just project change. You may want to consider establishing a CCB for your project if the organization does not have one.

Some organizations use other types of review boards that have the same responsibilities as the CCB. Some other names you might see are technical assessment board (TAB), technical review board (TRB), engineering review board (ERB), and change control board (CCB).

Configuration Management

Configuration management in most organizations is a subset of the change control process. Configuration management describes the characteristics of the product of the project and makes sure the description is accurate and complete. Configuration management controls changes to the characteristics of an item and tracks the changes made or requested and their status. Audits are performed as part of configuration management to determine if the requirements have been met. Sometimes the configuration management system *is* the change control system.

Exam Spotlight

The exam will expect you to know that configuration management involves identifying the physical characteristics of the product of the project (or of the individual components of the product) and documenting their functionality.

Additional Planning

As we've mentioned before, changes, updates, and corrective actions often require a trip down memory lane through the Planning and Executing processes. This is what the additional planning input refers to. As modifications come about, you might need to revise cost estimates (and the project budget as a result of revised cost estimates), the schedule may need to be modified, new activities might be identified that require resources, scheduling, and risk analysis, and so on. As the project evolves, count on additional planning activities.

Integrated Change Control Results

Project plan updates are the first output of the Integrated Change Control process. Changes to the project require updates to the project plan or the supporting detail of the project plan. These changes are noted as such in the project plan, and stakeholders are informed at the status meetings of the changes that have occurred, their impacts, and where the description of the changes can be found.

Project plan updates are the documented changes you made as a result of the additional planning you did in the tools and techniques section of this process. However, in practice, these steps probably occur all at the same time.

Two other outputs occur in the Integrate Change Control process: corrective action and lessons learned. You may recall that *corrective action* is any action taken to ensure that the product of the project, or future project performance, adheres to the requirements described in the scope document and to the project plan.

Exam Spotlight

Corrective action is an output of all of the change control processes (Integrated Change Control, Scope Change Control, Schedule Control, Cost Control, and Risk Monitoring and Control) except for Quality Control. Corrective action is an output of the Controlling processes and an input to the Executing processes.

Lessons learned document the causes of the variances that occur in the project. The corrective action taken and the justification for choosing that particular corrective action are noted as part of lessons learned as well. At the conclusion of the project, lessons learned become part of the historical information that is used as inputs to some of the Planning processes. When you take on a new project, it's a good idea to review the lessons learned of similar projects so that you can plan appropriately and avoid the variances that occurred in the first project.

 Real World Scenario

Mustang Enterprises' New Accounting System

You are a stakeholder of the New Accounting System project for Mustang Enterprises. The existing accounting system lives on a mainframe, and some of the programs used to process data on this system are over 15 years old. Your company decided to hire a contract software services firm to write a thin-client, browser-based version of the accounting system so that the mainframe programs could be retired.

The project is in the Controlling process, and the contract project manager keeps reporting everything is okay and on schedule. When you ask him detailed questions and request performance data, the project manager pats you on the back and says, "Don't worry, I've got everything under control."

You are a little worried, because some of the key project team members have come to you confidentially to inform you of the progress of the project.

After further investigation, you discover that the project manager has changed the database midway through the project and hasn't told anyone except the project team. The project scope states specifically that project development requires database product A. The change in database products changes the project scope and product scope without letting the stakeholders know.

This change has caused schedule delays, because the project team members have told you they need training in the new database development tools before they can proceed. Additionally, many of the programs already written were to interface with database A, not database B, and will have to be modified in order to work with database B. To add insult to injury, the database switch will impact the project budget in two ways. First, database B involves substantially more money than database A and requires the purchase of new development tools for the programming team. Second, several members of the programming staff will have to attend multiple training sessions on the new database product to fully integrate the programs and system. Training is currently running $2200 per session per person.

Since you're a key stakeholder, you decide to bring the information you've discovered out into the open at the next project status meeting. Additionally, you plan to meet with the project sponsor and the procurement department to determine what alternatives you have to request that the contracting firm replace the current project manager with a new project manager. This may cause further setback to the project, but the project plan and project schedule will require updates anyway as a result of the existing project manager's decisions. You also determine to document all that's happened as a lesson learned and to set up a change control process to prevent this from happening in the future.

Controlling Scope Changes

The Scope Management knowledge area includes Initiation, Scope Planning, Scope Definition, Scope Verification, and Scope Change Control. You'll recall that *project scope* describes the work required to produce the product or service of the project. This includes the requirements of the product, which describe the features and functionality of the product or service. *Product scope*, on the other hand, is the description of the product features. The product description is the document that defines the characteristics of the product or service of the project.

You can conclude from this that the *Scope Change Control* process involves changes to the project scope. Any modification to the agreed-upon WBS is considered a scope change. This means that the addition or deletion of activities or modifications to the existing activities on the WBS constitute a project scope change.

Changes in product scope will require changes to the project scope as well. Let's say one of your project deliverables is the design of a piece of specialized equipment that's integrated into your final product. Now let's say that due to engineering setbacks and some miscalculations, the specialized equipment requires design modifications. The redesign of this equipment impacts the end product, or product scope. Since changes to the product scope impact the project requirements, which are detailed in the scope document, changes to project scope are also required.

Scope Change Control Inputs

There are four inputs to the Scope Change Control process, all of which you've seen before:

- WBS
- Performance reports
- Change requests
- Scope management plan

Let's refresh your memory of each.

The WBS is a deliverables-oriented hierarchy that defines the total work of the project. Performance reports tell us which deliverables have been completed and if the project is proceeding as planned. When it's not proceeding as planned, change requests will result.

Change requests, according to *A Guide to the PMBOK*, come in written or verbal forms. (As stated earlier, I recommend that you require all change requests in written form. They are easier to track this way and provide an audit trail of the action taken.) It also states that change requests are direct or indirect, might come from inside or outside the organization, and may result from optional requests or from legal requirements.

The scope management plan details how scope changes get integrated into the project and how scope changes are managed as well.

Scope Change Control

There are three tools and techniques of the Scope Change Control process:

- Scope change control
- Performance measurements
- Additional planning

Scope change control is a system that tracks changes and—along with all the other change control systems explained in this chapter—is integrated with the integrated change control system. Depending on the size and complexity of the project, the integrated change control system may suffice for all changes to the project. If you are using a configuration management system to control product scope, the scope change control system must also integrate with it.

Scope change control is a lot like the integrated change control system. It tracks and records change requests, describes the procedures to follow to implement scope change, and details the authorization levels needed to approve the changes. When your project is performed under contract, scope changes will also require conformance to the provisions of the contract and the contract change system.

Scope Changes

The outputs of the Scope Change Control process are:

- Scope changes
- Corrective action

- Lessons learned
- Adjusted baseline

Let's take a look at scope changes and adjusted baseline.

Scope changes will likely require you to run back through the project Planning processes and make any needed adjustments. Scope changes include any changes to the project scope as defined by the agreed-upon WBS. This in turn may require changes or updates to project objectives, costs, quality measures or controls, or time in the form of schedule revisions. Scope changes always require schedule revisions.

Schedule revisions are always needed as a result of scope changes. But not all scope changes will necessarily cause increases to the project schedule. Some scope changes may reduce the number of hours needed to complete the project, which in turn may reduce the project budget.

When scope changes are requested, all areas of the project should be investigated to determine what the changes will impact. The project team should perform estimates of the impact and of the amount of time needed to make the change. Sometimes, however, the change request is so extensive that even the time to perform an estimate should be evaluated before proceeding. In other words, if the project team is busy working on estimates, they aren't working on the project. That means extensive change requests could impact the existing schedule because of the time and effort needed just to evaluate the change. Cases like these require you to make a determination or ask the CCB to decide if the change is important enough to allow the project team time to work on the estimates.

Changes in scope may require updates to the schedule, cost, or performance measurement baselines established during the Planning processes. When change is necessary, adjustments to the baselines are made, documented, and distributed to the stakeholders as needed. *Adjusted baseline* is the output where revisions to baselines are made.

Always remember to update your stakeholders regarding the changes you're implementing and their impacts. They'll want to know how the changes impact the performance baselines, including the project costs, project schedule, project scope, and quality.

Controlling Schedule Changes

According to *A Guide to the PMBOK*, scope changes will impact the project schedule and require schedule changes and revisions as a result. *Schedule Control* is the process that manages changes to the schedule.

Schedule Control inputs include:

- Project schedule
- Performance reports
- Change requests
- Schedule management plan

Remember that the schedule management plan details the process to implement schedule changes.

This process is very similar to the Integrated Change Control and Scope Change Control processes covered earlier. This process has a tool and technique called the *schedule change control system*. As you've probably already guessed, the schedule change control system works just like scope change control, except that it defines how changes to the schedule are made and managed. It tracks and records change requests, describes the procedures to follow to implement schedule changes, and details the authorization levels needed to approve the schedule changes.

Schedule changes may be potential hot buttons with certain stakeholders and can burn you if you don't handle them correctly. No one likes to hear that the project is going to take longer than originally planned. That doesn't mean you should withhold this information however. Always report the truth. If you've been keeping your stakeholders abreast of project status up until now, they should already know the potential for schedule changes exists. Nevertheless, be prepared to justify the reason for the schedule change, or start dusting off your resume'—one of the two.

The remaining tools and techniques of the Schedule Control process are:

- Performance measurements
- Additional planning
- Project management software
- Variance analysis

We'll look at variance analysis next.

Schedule Variances

Variance analysis is a tool and technique of the Schedule Control process that is a key factor in controlling project time, because this technique helps determine variances in schedule start and end dates. Comparing the estimated dates to the actual or forecasted dates will show you where variances have occurred—or may occur—and will allow you to implement corrective actions to keep the schedule on track.

Keeping the schedule on track means you're controlling time—one of the triple constraints.

Make sure to examine the float variance of the critical path activities. Remember that *float* is the amount of time you can delay starting an activity without increasing the amount of time it takes to complete the project. Because the activities with the least amount of float have the potential to cause the biggest schedule delay, examine float variance in ascending order of critical activities.

However, not all schedule variances will impact the schedule. For example, a delay to a non-critical path task will not delay the overall schedule and may not need corrective action. But delays to critical path tasks will always cause delays to the project completion date and do require corrective action. Careful watch of the variances in schedule start and end dates helps you control the total time element (or constraint) of the project.

Schedule Control Outputs

The outputs of the Schedule Control process are:

- Schedule updates
- Corrective action
- Lessons learned

Schedule updates involve adjusting activities and dates to coincide with approved changes and/or corrective actions. *A Guide to the PMBOK* calls changes to approved schedule start and end dates *revisions*. These generally occur as a result of a scope change or changes to activity estimates.

Rebaselining occurs when significant changes to the project schedule are made. This simply means a new schedule baseline is established that reflects the changed project activity dates. Once the new baseline is established, it is used as the basis for future performance measurements.

 Take care when rebaselining a project schedule because you may lose the original baseline information. Why do you care? Because the original baseline serves as historical information for future projects to reference. Make a backup copy of the original schedule so that you have a record of the original baseline as a reference. (Microsoft Project 2002 allows you to save up to ten baselines plus the original.)

Managing Cost Changes

The *Cost Control* process manages changes to project costs as outlined in the cost management plan. It's concerned with monitoring project costs to prevent unauthorized or incorrect costs from getting included in the cost baseline. The inputs to Cost Control are similar to the inputs you've seen for the other control processes and include:

- Cost baseline
- Performance reports
- Change requests
- Cost management plan

These inputs are examined using the tools and techniques of this process to determine if revised cost estimates or budget updates are required.

The tools and techniques of the Cost Control process are:

- Cost change control system
- Performance measurement
- Earned value management
- Additional planning
- Computerized tools

Cost variances are calculated using the performance measurement and earned value management tools and techniques. You'll recall from Chapter 9 that earned value management (EVM) continuously monitors the planned value, earned value, and actual costs expended to produce the work of the project. When variances that result in cost changes are discovered (including schedule variances and cost variances), those changes are managed using the cost change control system. Like the other processes we've examined so far, the cost change control system describes how changes are submitted, approved, and tracked, and is closely linked with the integrated change control system.

You may have to do some additional planning if your cost changes are significant. Remember that many times cost, scope, and schedule changes are closely linked. Cost changes may drive schedule changes due to budget cuts, poor-quality products, and so on. The Planning, Executing, and Controlling processes are iterative, and changes to one process may require changes to another process. Additional planning and computerized tools are the remaining tools and techniques of this process.

It's important to take the right corrective actions as a result of cost variances, because other problems can result from not dealing with cost issues. Impacts to the budget, quality, or schedule, or increased risk may result from incorrect responses to cost variances.

 Cost Control problems come about for many reasons, including incorrect estimating techniques, predetermined or fixed budgets with no flexibility, schedule overruns, inadequate WBS development, and so on. Good project management planning techniques during the Planning processes may prevent cost problems later in the project. At a minimum, proper planning will reduce the impact of these problems if they do occur.

Revising Costs

Cost Control has several outputs that involve revising your original cost estimates and calculating new estimates at completion. Cost Control outputs include:

- Revised cost estimates
- Budget updates

- Corrective action
- Estimate at completion
- Project closeout
- Lessons learned

We talked about estimate at completion (EAC) calculations in Chapter 9, so be certain to review them before taking the exam.

Exam Spotlight

EAC calculations determine the estimated total cost of the project at completion and are an output of the Cost Control process.

The corrective action, EAC, and lessons learned outputs were covered previously. We'll look at the revised cost estimates, budget updates, and project closeout outputs next.

Revised Cost Estimates

Revised cost estimates include updating original cost estimates and other areas of the project plan that these estimates may impact. As an example, perhaps the cost estimate for new hardware required for your project was recently revised. Suppose the cost estimate was needed because the equipment originally planned for in the project is no longer available and new equipment is ordered in its place. This may require revisions to other project activities, which will require you to revisit the project Planning and Executing processes.

Always inform appropriate stakeholders of revised cost estimates and any changes of significant impact to the project. Keep them updated on changes, status, and risk conditions during regularly scheduled project meetings.

Budget Updates

The Cost Control process tracks project performance to detect variances. Approved changes as a result of those variances are considered budget updates, which are a type of revised cost estimate. The cost baseline is changed as a result of the budget updates to reflect the new cost estimates. Significant updates to the budget as a result of corrective action or variances may require rebaselining of the project costs. Budget updates are usually revised as a result of scope changes.

Project Closeout

Make certain that you're familiar with the regulations and standards that are required for project closures and cancellations for your industry. Some industries require the costs of failed or cancelled projects be written off in a specific manner. Familiarize yourself with these standards. You may contact the American Institute of Certified Public Accountants for more information regarding accounting and finance standards for your particular industry.

Cost Control, like many of the other Controlling processes, is concerned with monitoring project performance for variances. As the project manager, keep a close eye on the factors that cause variance to keep their impacts to a minimum. An important thing to remember is that Cost Control makes certain all appropriate parties agree to any changes to the cost baseline. This process is ongoing and continues to manage cost changes throughout the project.

Utilizing Quality Control Techniques

Quality Planning, Quality Assurance, and Quality Control are part of the project Quality Management knowledge area. These processes work together to define and monitor the work of the project and to make certain the results meet the quality requirements laid out in the plan.

Quality Control is specifically concerned with monitoring work results to see if they comply with the standards set out in the quality management plan. Quality Control should be practiced and performed throughout the project to identify and remove the causes of unacceptable results. Remember that Quality Control is concerned with project results both from a management perspective, such as schedule and cost performance, and from a product perspective. In other words, the end product should conform to the requirements and product description defined during the Planning processes.

Quality Control inputs include:

- Work results
- Quality management plan
- Operational definitions
- Checklists

We've discussed each of these inputs previously, so let's move on to tools and techniques. There are several new tools and techniques in the Quality Control process:

- Inspection
- Control charts
- Pareto diagrams
- Statistical sampling
- Flowcharting
- Trend analysis

The primary purpose of each of these tools is to examine the product and/or the project processes for conformity to standards. Spend time understanding them and their individual uses, because there may be exam questions on each of them.

Inspection

Inspection involves physically looking at, measuring, or testing results to determine if they conform to the requirements or quality standards. It's a tool used to gather information and improve results. Inspections might occur after the final product is produced or at intervals during the development of the product to examine individual components.

Exam Spotlight

Don't confuse inspection with prevention, because they're two different things. Inspection keeps errors in the product from reaching the customer. *Prevention* keeps errors from occurring in the process. It always costs less to prevent problems in the first place than it does to fix problems built into the product after the fact. Rework, labor costs, material costs, and potential loss of customers are all factors to consider when weighing prevention costs versus the cost of rework. Philip Crosby developed the theory of zero defects, which deals with prevention costs. Loosely translated, zero defects means doing it right the first time.

Inspection may take actual measurements of components to determine if they meet requirements. Maybe a component part for your product must be exactly 5 mm in length. In order to pass inspection, the parts are measured and must meet the 5 mm length requirement. If they measure 5 mm, they pass; if they do not, they fail.

Measurements can vary even if the variances are not noticeable. Machines wear down, people make mistakes, the environment may cause variances, and so on. Measurements that fall within a specified range are called *tolerable results*. So, instead of 5 mm exactly, maybe a range between 4.98 mm and 5.02 mm is an acceptable or a tolerable measurement for our component. If the samples that are measured fall within the tolerable range, they pass; otherwise, they fail inspection.

One inspection technique uses measurements called *attributes*. The measurements determine whether the attributes meet one of two options, conforming or nonconforming. In other words, the measurements conform or meet the requirement, or they do not conform. This can also be considered a pass/fail or go/no-go decision.

Attribute conformity and inspections are not necessarily performed on every component part or every end product that's produced. That's time-consuming and inefficient when you're producing numerous components. Inspection in cases like this is usually performed on a sampling of parts or products where every X number of parts is tested for conformity or measurement specifics. This measurement technique is called statistical sampling. Statistical sampling is another tool and technique of the Quality Control process that we'll get to shortly.

Inspection will tell you where problems exist and give you the opportunity to correct them, thus leading to quality improvements. The other tools and techniques we'll talk about in this section also lead to quality improvements in the product or process, or both. Quality improvements are an output of the Quality Control process.

 Real World Scenario

The Never-Ending Bridge Project

One of the main thoroughfares into your city requires a bridge replacement. You were appointed the project manager for the city and have managed this project since its initiation 15 months ago.

The project entailed hiring a contractor to build and construct the new bridge and then managing the contract and the work of the contracting agency to bring the project to a successful completion.

Approximately 28,000 vehicles travel across this bridge on a daily basis, carrying commuters and college students back and forth to the downtown area. One of the requirements was the closure of no more than three of the six lanes of traffic at one time during construction. Another requirement stated that two coats of paint were to be applied to the steel before bringing it on-site, and a third coat of paint was to be applied at the site after construction. The paint is guaranteed to last 25 to 30 years.

You assisted the quality control department with a recent inspection. The inspection revealed that some of the paint was peeling. After further investigation, you discovered that the contractor did not allow the first coat of paint to cure properly, so when the second coat was applied, it didn't stick correctly and peeled and flaked in places.

You've instructed the contractor that according to the terms of the contract and the SOW specifications, they're required to apply three coats of paint to the bridge as part of the work of the project. Corrective action is needed to get this project back on track. As a result, the contract company decides to subcontract out the paint work to another company while they finish up their remaining tasks on the project.

Unfortunately, the subcontractor that was hired found they were in way over their heads and were not able to complete the paint job. Several months have passed, and the original project completion date was missed long ago. This obviously required revisions to the project schedule when it became clear that the subcontractor wasn't going to make the date. Now another revision to the project schedule is necessary due to the subcontractor's failure to complete the painting task.

The original contractor did some searching and found another subcontractor capable of completing the painting job. It's now the middle of winter. Because the temperatures are cold, the painting crew must hang insulated tarps between the bays on the bridge and use heaters to warm up small areas of steel to the proper temperature to apply the paint. This process has extended the completion date of this activity by over three times its original estimate and ultimately delayed the completion of the project by two years.

Corrective action was taken as a result of the inspection, and eventually the project was completed, but not without schedule delays, schedule changes, scope changes, and rework—not to mention the increased cost to the original contractor. Since the contract was a fixed-price contract, the contractor's profit was eaten away paying for the painting job. The cost to correct the quality issue did not impact the city, but it did impact the contractor. This is a case where an ounce of prevention would have been worth a pound of cure, as the old saying goes.

Control Charts

Control charts measure the results of processes over time and display the results in graph form. Control charts are a way to measure variances to determine if process variances are in control or out of control.

A control chart is based on sample variance measurements. From the samples chosen and measured, the mean and standard deviation are determined. Quality Control is usually maintained—or said to be in control—within plus or minus three standard deviations. In other words, Quality Control says that if the process is in control, you know that 99.73 percent of the parts going through the process will fall within an acceptable range of the mean. If you discover a part outside of this range, you should investigate and determine if corrective action is needed.

Figure 10.1 illustrates an example control chart.

FIGURE 10.1 Control chart

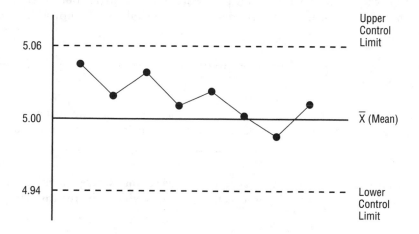

You've determined from your sample measurements that 5 mm is the mean in the example control chart. One standard deviation equals 0.02. Three standard deviations on either side of the mean becomes your upper and lower control points on this chart. Therefore, if all control points fall within plus or minus three standard deviations on either side of the mean, the process is in control. If points fall outside of the acceptable limits, the process is not in control and corrective action is needed.

Process Variances

Differences in results will occur in processes, because there is no such thing as a perfect process. When processes are considered in control, differences in results may occur due to common causes of variance or special cause variances.

Common causes of variances are a result of:

- Random variances
- Known or predictable variances
- Variances that are always present in the process

Random variations may be normal, depending on the processes you're using to produce the product or service of the project; but they occur as the name implies, at random. Known or predictable variances are variances that you know exist in the process. And the process itself will have inherent variability that is perhaps caused by human mistakes, machine variations or malfunctions, the environment, and so on, which are known as variances always present in the process.

Common cause variances that do not fall within the acceptable range are difficult to correct and usually require a reorganization of the process. This has the potential for significant impact, and decisions to change the process always require management approval.

Special cause variances come about as a result of circumstances or situations that are relatively unique to the process you're using and are easily controlled at the operational level. Perhaps a machine needs calibration or procedures for the process need refinement. Perhaps your process is very detailed, with specific procedures that are carried out to produce the output. Not following these detailed procedures could result in variances known as special cause variances.

Exam Spotlight

According to *A Guide to the PMBOK*, when a process is in control, it should not be adjusted. It's okay to change the process to bring about improvements, but it should not be adjusted.

Control charts are used most often in manufacturing settings where repetitive activities are easily monitored. For example, the process that produces widgets by the case lot must meet certain specifications and fall within certain variances to be considered in control. However, you aren't limited to using control charts only in the manufacturing industry. They can be used to monitor any output. You might consider using control charts to track and monitor project management processes. You could plot cost variances, schedule variances, frequency or number of scope changes, and so on to help monitor variances in the project management process.

Pareto Diagrams

You have probably heard of the 80/20 rule. Vilfredo Pareto is the person credited with discovering this rule. He observed that 80 percent of the wealth and land ownership in Italy was held by 20 percent of the population. Over the years, others have shown that the 80/20 rule applies across many disciplines and areas. As an example, generally speaking, 80 percent of the deposits of any given financial institution are held by 20 percent of its customer base. Let's hope that rule doesn't apply to project managers though, with 20 percent of the project managers out there doing 80 percent of the work!

According to Pareto, the 80/20 rule as it applies to quality says that a small number of causes (20%) create the majority of the problems (80%). Have you ever noticed that with your project or department staff? It always seems just a few people cause the biggest headaches. But we're getting off track.

Pareto diagrams are displayed as histograms that rank order the most important factors such as delays, costs, defects, or other factors by their frequency over time. His theory is you get the most benefit if you spend the majority of your time fixing the most important problems. The information shown in Table 10.1 is plotted on an example Pareto diagram shown in Figure 10.2.

TABLE 10.1 Frequency of Failures

Item	Defect Frequency	Percent of Defects	Cumulative Percent
A	800	.33	.33
B	700	.29	.62
C	400	.17	.79
D	300	.13	.92
E	200	.08	1.0

FIGURE 10.2 Pareto diagram

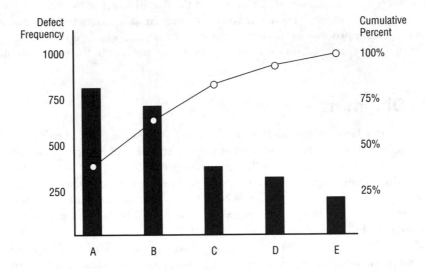

The problems are rank ordered according to their frequency and percentage of defects. The defect frequencies in this figure are shown as black bars, and the cumulative percentages of defects are plotted as circles. You can see in Figure 10.2 that problem A should receive priority attention, because the most benefit will come from fixing this problem.

Scatter Diagrams

You're probably checking the Quality Control tool and technique list now and have discovered that scatter diagrams are not on the list. You are correct. *A Guide to the PMBOK* does not list scatter diagrams as a tool and technique of Quality Control; however, you might encounter a question on the exam regarding them.

Scatter diagrams use two variables, one called an independent variable, which is an input, and one called a dependent variable, which is an output. Scatter diagrams display the relationship between these two elements as points on a graph. As an example, maybe your scatter diagram plots the ability of your employees to perform a certain task. Their experience performing this task in months is plotted as the independent variable on the X axis, and their score—the dependent variable—is plotted on the Y axis.

The important thing to remember about scatter diagrams is that they plot the dependent and independent variables. A sample scatter diagram is shown in Figure 10.3.

FIGURE 10.3 Scatter diagram

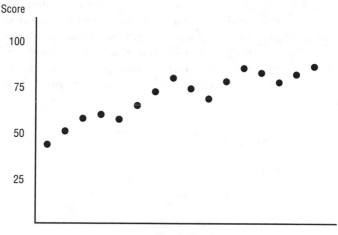

Statistical Sampling

Statistical sampling involves taking a sample number of parts from the whole population and examining them to determine if they fall within the variances outlined by the quality control plan. Perhaps you determine to statistically sample 25 parts out of a lot or run. The quality plan outlines that the lot will pass if four parts or fewer fall outside the allowable variance.

Statistical sampling may also involve determining the standard deviation for a process as discussed in the control chart tool and technique. The quality plan determines if plus or minus two standard deviations—95.44 percent of the population—is adequate, or if plus or minus three standard deviations—99.73 percent—is adequate.

Flowcharting

Flowcharting is also a tool and technique of the Quality Planning process. We discussed the different methods of flowcharting in Chapter 6, "Establishing Project Planning Controls," including cause-and-effect diagrams and system or process flowcharts. These show how various elements of a system relate. Flowcharts are used in the Quality Control process to examine how problems happen.

Trend Analysis

Trend analysis in the Quality Control process is a mathematical technique that uses historical results to predict future outcomes. Trend analysis often tracks variances in cost and schedule performance by monitoring the number of activities completed with significant variances within a certain time period. This information can then be used to forecast future performance. Trend analysis also tracks technical performance by determining the number of defects observed and the number of defects not corrected. Trend analysis is also a tool and technique of the Performance Reporting process.

Quality Control Outputs

Quality Control has several outputs:

- Quality improvement
- Acceptance decisions
- Rework
- Completed checklists
- Process adjustments

Quality improvements are also an output of the Quality Assurance procedure, as discussed in Chapter 9. Checklists were covered in the Quality Planning process discussed in Chapter 6. Let's take a quick look at the remaining Quality Control outputs.

Acceptance decisions are made when the work is inspected. The work is either accepted or rejected. When work is rejected, it might have to go back through the process for rework.

Rework will cause a project to take longer than originally planned or estimated to complete. You should try to keep rework to a minimum so as not to impact the project schedule. Rework has the potential to cause morale issues as well, especially if the team members thought they were doing a good job all along. Monitor quality periodically so that rework is kept to a minimum.

Process adjustments are made when corrective action or preventive measures are needed as a result of Quality Control variances. Remember, though, that processes in control can be changed to bring about improvements, but processes in control should not be adjusted. Processes out of control may require adjusting, but this should occur only as a result of a management decision and as part of the Integrated Change Control process.

Organizing Risk Response

Risk Monitoring and Control involves:

- Responding to risks as they occur
- Tracking and monitoring identified risks
- Identifying new risks

- Evaluating risk response plans that are put into action as a result of risk events
- Monitoring the project for risk triggers
- Ensuring that policies and procedures are followed
- Ensuring that risk response plans and contingency plans are put into action appropriately and are effective
- Bringing about corrective action

Risk Monitoring and Control is a busy process.

There are five inputs to this process:

- Risk management plan
- Risk response plan
- Project communication
- Additional risk identification and analysis
- Scope changes

You'll recall that the risk management plan details how risk is managed, and the risk response plan describes how you will implement plans and strategies in the event of an actual risk event. Keep in mind that some risk events identified in risk planning will happen and some will not. You will have to stay alert for risk event occurrences and be prepared to respond to them when they do occur.

Performance measurements taken during the Performance Reporting process and scope changes may identify new risks. Additional risk identification and analysis is an input to the Risk Monitoring and Control process, and the newly identified risks get documented here. Additional risk response planning may be needed to deal with the new risks or with expected risks whose impact was greater than expected. This may require repeating the Risk Response Planning process to create new contingency plans or alternative plans to deal with the risk, or it may require modification to existing plans.

Risk Monitoring and Control Tools and Techniques

The tools and techniques of Risk Monitoring and Control are used to monitor risks throughout the life of the project. Periodic reviews, audits, and new earned value analysis should be performed to check the pulse of risk activity and to make certain risk management is enacted effectively.

The tools and techniques of this process are:

- Project risk response audits
- Periodic project risk reviews
- Earned value analysis
- Technical performance measurements
- Additional risk response planning

Let's look at a few of these tools now.

Project Risk Response Audits

Risk audits are carried out during the entire life of the project by risk auditors. Risk auditors are not typically project team members and are expertly trained in audit techniques and risk assessment. These audits are specifically interested in looking at the implementation and the effective use of the transference, avoidance, and mitigation risk strategies.

Periodic Project Risk Reviews

Periodic, scheduled reviews of identified risks, risk responses, and risk priorities should occur during the project. The idea here is to monitor risks and their status and determine if their consequences still have the same impact on the project objectives as when they were originally planned. You may have to revisit the Qualitative and Quantitative Risk Analysis processes when new risk consequences are discovered or risk impacts are found to be greater than what was originally planned.

Technical Performance Measurements

This tool and technique compares the technical accomplishments of project milestones completed during the Executing processes to the technical milestones defined in the project Planning process. Variances may indicate that a project risk is looming, which you'll want to analyze and prepare a response to if appropriate. For example, a technical milestone for a new computer software project might require that the forms printed from a particular module include a bar code at the bottom of the page. If the bar code functionality does not work once the module is coded, a technical deviation exists, which means you should re-examine project risks. In this particular example, project scope is likely at risk.

Additional Risk Response Planning

When performing Risk Monitoring and Control, you are bound to discover new risks to the project. Risks require response plans, which mean additional risk response planning. You may also discover bigger impacts to existing risks as the project progresses, also requiring additional or revised risk response plans.

Risk Monitoring and Control Outputs

Risk Monitoring and Control should occur throughout the life of the project. Identified risks are monitored and plans are re-examined to determine if they will adequately resolve the risk as it approaches during this process. Several outputs may come about as a result of monitoring risks:

- Workaround plans
- Corrective action
- Project change requests
- Updates to the risk response plan
- Risk database
- Updates to the risk identification checklist

A *workaround* is an unplanned response to a negative risk event. It attempts to deal with the risk in a productive, efficient manner. If no risk response plan exists (this might be the case when you accept a risk event during the Planning process), or an unplanned risk occurs, workarounds are implemented to deal with the consequences of the risk.

Updates to the risk response plan should be made as the project progresses. Document the results of the response plans for the benefit of future projects and make sure to document risk events that do not occur as well. Re-examine your risk ratings and rankings periodically and determine if they are still appropriate given the information you know about the project now during the Controlling process group. If risk ratings change, update the risk response plans to accurately reflect the new rating or ranking.

Risk databases are a method of collecting and documenting information regarding risk events and they're also useful for lessons learned for future projects. Update the risk database as information is gathered.

Project Case Study: New Kitchen Heaven Retail Store

Ricardo submitted a change request regarding the hardware installation at the new store site. A new, much anticipated operating system was just released, and Ricardo has plans to upgrade the entire company to the new operating system. Since he must purchase new equipment for this store anyway, he contends that it makes sense to go ahead and purchase the hardware with the newest operating system already loaded. His staff won't have to upgrade this store as part of the upgrade project, because the store will already have the new operating system.

Ricardo's change request was submitted in writing through the change control system. A CCB was set up during the Planning stages of this project to handle change requests. At the CCB meeting, the following questions come up regarding Ricardo's request: Has the new operating system been tested with the existing system? Are there compatibility problems? If so, what are the severity and risk potential of getting the problems resolved and the equipment installed by opening day? Is the vendor ready to ship with the new operating system?

The CCB defers their decision for this request until Ricardo gives them answers to these questions.

During the next CCB meeting, the board reviews a change request from Jill Overstreet. The gourmet food supplier she used went out of business a month or so ago, and Jill contracted with a new vendor. She received a sample shipment from the new vendor and was very unhappy with the results. Upon inspecting the products, she found broken containers and damaged packaging. Meanwhile, Jill found another vendor, who has sent her a sample shipment. She is very pleased with the new vendor's products and service. However, this vendor's prices are even higher than the first replacement vendor she contracted with. Jill submitted a cost change request to the CCB because of the increased cost of the gourmet food product shipment. The change in cost does not have a significant impact on the budget, because the new EAC with this change is $1.90 million. The original project budget estimate was $2 million, so the project is still coming in under budget.

You hold a seat on the CCB and are aware of the change requests and their impacts to the project. Ricardo satisfactorily answered all the questions the CCB had, so his request and Jill's request are both approved during the meeting.

Project Case Study Checklist

Integrated change management

Change control systems

Formal change request procedures

Configuration control board

Cost change

Quality control

- Inspection

- Corrective action

Summary

We closed out the Controlling process group with this chapter by covering all the change control processes, with the exception of Performance Reporting. Change control is an important part of the project process. It's your responsibility as project manager to manage change and implement corrective action where needed to keep the project on track with the plan.

Integrated Change Control concerns influencing the things that cause change and managing the change once it has occurred. One or more of the triple constraints are generally affected when change occurs. Managing change may involve changes to the project plan, the project schedule, or the budget. Changes that impact processes you've already completed require updates to those processes. Corrective action is often a result of change and ensures that the future performance of the project lines up with the project plan.

Change control systems document the procedures to manage change and how change requests are implemented. Change requests may come in written or verbal forms, but ideally you should ask for all your change requests in writing. Change requests are processed through a formal change control system, and configuration control boards have the authority to approve or deny change requests.

Lessons learned are important for future projects and become part of the historical information used as inputs to the Planning processes on future projects. They also are used to document the causes of the variances that occur on the project.

Quality Control monitors work results to see if they fulfill the quality standards outlined in the quality management plan. Quality Control should occur throughout the life of the project. Quality Control uses many tools and techniques. Inspection measures results to determine if the results conform to the quality standards. Attributes are measurements that either conform or do not conform. Control charts measure the results of processes over time, and Pareto diagrams are histograms that rank order the most important quality factors by their frequency over time. You should not adjust processes that are in control; however, you can change these processes to realize improvements.

Risk Monitoring and Control responds to risks as they occur and implements workarounds for unplanned risk events. Some risks planned for during the Risk Response Planning process will occur, and some will not. Perhaps risks that were previously identified do occur, and their impacts are much greater than anticipated during the Risk Response Planning process. These will require updates to the risk management plan or workarounds.

Exam Essentials

Be able to name the Control processes that are integrated whenever a scope change occurs. The control processes that are integrated whenever a scope change occurs are Schedule Control, Cost Control, and Quality Control.

Be able to define the purpose of a change control system. Change control systems are documented procedures that describe how to submit change requests and how changes are tracked and approved, and they document the level of authority needed for approval.

Be able to describe a CCB. The configuration control board (CCB) has the authority to approve or deny change requests. Their authority is defined and outlined by the organization.

Be able to define configuration management. Configuration management is a subset of change control that describes the characteristics of the product of the project and ensures accuracy and completeness of the description.

Be able to name the tools and techniques of Quality Control. The tools and techniques of the Quality Control process are inspection, control charts, Pareto diagrams, statistical sampling, flowcharting, and trend analysis.

Key Terms

Before you take the exam, be certain you are familiar with the following terms:

adjusted baseline

attributes

change control system

common causes of variances

configuration control board (CCB)

configuration management

control charts

corrective action

Cost Control

float

inspection

Integrated Change Control

performance measurement baselines

prevention

product scope

project scope

Quality Control

rebaselining

revisions

rework

Risk Monitoring and Control

schedule change control system

Schedule Control

schedule updates

Scope Change Control

scope changes

special cause variances

statistical sampling

tolerable results

variance analysis

workaround

Review Questions

1. You are a project manager for Bluebird Technologies. Bluebird writes custom billing applications for several industries. A scope change has been requested. You know change is concerned with all of the following except:

   A. Managing change

   B. Verifying change

   C. Influencing causes of change

   D. Determining that a change occurred

2. You are a project manager for Bluebird Technologies. Bluebird writes custom billing applications for several industries. One of your users verbally requests changes to one of the screen displays. You explain to her that the change needs to go through the change control system. You explain that a change control system does all of the following except:

   A. Document procedures for change requests

   B. Track the status of change requests

   C. Describe the management impacts of change

   D. Determine if changes are approved or denied

3. Change control system, configuration management, performance measurement, additional planning, and project management information system are tools and techniques of which process?

   A. Integrated Change Control

   B. Scope Change Control

   C. Schedule Change Control

   D. Cost Change Control

4. You are a project manager for Star Light Strings. Star Light manufactures strings of lights for outdoor display. Their products range from simple light strings to elaborate lights with animal designs, bug designs, memorabilia, and so on. Your newest project requires a scope change. You have documented the characteristics of the product and its functionality using which of the following tools and techniques?

   A. Change control system

   B. Corrective action

   C. Configuration management

   D. Updates to the scope management plan

5. You are a project manager for Star Light Strings. Star Light manufactures strings of lights for outdoor display. Their products range from simple light strings to elaborate lights with animal designs, bug designs, memorabilia, and so on. Your newest project requires a change. One of the business unit managers submitted a change through the change control system, which utilizes a CCB. Which of the following is true regarding the CCB?

   A. The CCB describes how change requests are managed.

   B. The CCB requires all change requests in writing.

   C. The CCB approves or denies change requests.

   D. The CCB requires updates to the appropriate management plan.

6. You are working on a project that was proceeding well until a manufacturing glitch occurred that requires corrective action. It turns out the glitch was an unintentional enhancement to the product, and the marketing people are absolutely crazy about its potential. The corrective action is cancelled, and you continue to produce the product with the newly discovered enhancement. As the project manager, you know that a change has occurred to the product scope, because the glitch changed the characteristics of the product. Which of the following statements is true?

   A. Changes to product scope are reflected in the project scope.

   B. Changes to product scope are reflected in the integrated change control plan.

   C. Changes to product scope are a result of changes to the product description.

   D. Changes to product scope are a result of corrective action.

7. You are working on a project that was proceeding well until a manufacturing glitch occurred that requires corrective action. It turns out the glitch was an unintentional enhancement to the product, and the marketing people are absolutely crazy about its potential. The corrective action is cancelled, and you continue to produce the product with the newly discovered enhancement. As the project manager, you know that a change has occurred to the project scope. Which of the following statements is true?

   A. Project scope changes do not require CCB approval.

   B. Performance measurement baselines are affected by scope changes.

   C. Project scope change uses inspection to determine if change has occurred.

   D. Project scope change uses workarounds to correct unexpected problems with scope change.

8. Your project has recently experienced change. Some of the agreed-upon WBS elements have been changed as a result. What kind of change has occurred?

   A. Schedule change

   B. Risk response change

   C. Quality change

   D. Scope change

9. Your project has experienced some changes to the agreed-upon WBS elements. The changes were approved through the proper change control process. The WBS changes may in turn require which of the following?

    A. Scope changes

    B. Cost changes

    C. Schedule revisions

    D. Risk response changes

10. Which of the following statements is true regarding schedule variances?

    A. Schedule variances impact scope, which impacts the schedule.

    B. Schedule variances sometimes impact the schedule.

    C. Schedule variances always impact the schedule.

    D. Schedule variances never impact the schedule.

11. You are a project manager for Laurel's Theater Productions. Your new project is coming in over budget and requires a cost change through the cost change control system. The cost variance was projected using which of the following tools and techniques?

    A. Performance measurements

    B. Cost baseline measurements

    C. Computerized tools

    D. Performance reports

12. You are a project manager for Laurel's Theater Productions. Your new project is coming in over budget and requires a cost change through the cost change control system. You know all of the following statements are true regarding Cost Control except:

    A. Performance is monitored to detect variances.

    B. Changes are reflected in the cost baseline.

    C. Changes are monitored and reflected in the project scope.

    D. Changes are monitored so that inappropriate changes do not get into the cost baseline.

13. Which of the following might require rebaselining of the cost baseline?

    A. Corrective action

    B. Revised cost estimates

    C. Updates to the cost management plan

    D. Budget updates

14. You are working on a project to develop a new website for your company. You are monitoring the results of the project to determine if they comply with standards set out during the Planning processes. You are also taking steps to eliminate unsatisfactory results. This might mean rework in some cases. Which process are you in?

   A. Risk Monitoring and Control

   B. Quality Control

   C. Integrated Change Control

   D. Scope Change Control

15. This tool and technique of Quality Control keeps errors from reaching the customer:

   A. Inspection

   B. Prevention

   C. Corrective action

   D. Performance measurements

16. Common causes of variances are a result of all of the following except:

   A. Random variances

   B. Predictable variances

   C. Special variances

   D. Variances that are always present in the process

17. You are a project manager in the manufacturing industry. You are using sample variance measurements to monitor the results of the process over time. Which tool and technique of Quality Control are you using?

   A. Statistical sampling

   B. Scatter diagrams

   C. Control charts

   D. Pareto diagrams

18. All of the following statements are true regarding Pareto diagrams and Pareto theory except:

   A. Pareto diagrams are histograms.

   B. Pareto diagrams rank order factors.

   C. A small number of causes create the majority of problems.

   D. Pareto diagrams use two variables.

19. You are preparing a diagram that plots two variables—the dependent variable and the independent variable—to see the relationship between the two elements. What kind of diagram are you using?

A. Cause-and-effect diagram

B. Control chart

C. Flowchart

D. Scatter diagram

20. Your project progressed as planned up until yesterday. Suddenly, an unexpected risk event occurred. You quickly devised a response to deal with this negative risk event using which of the following outputs of Risk Monitoring and Control?

A. Risk management plan updates

B. Workarounds

C. Corrective action

D. Additional risk identification

Answers to Review Questions

1. B. Integrated Change Control, Scope Change Control, Schedule Control, and Cost Control are all concerned with three things: influencing the things that cause change, determining that change is needed or has happened, and managing the change.

2. D. Change control systems are documented procedures that describe how to submit change requests. They track the status of the change requests, document the management impacts of change, track the change approval status, and define the level of authority needed to approve changes. Change control systems do not approve or deny the changes—that's the responsibility of the configuration control board (CCB).

3. A. The tools and techniques of Integrated Change Control are change control system, configuration management, performance measurement, additional planning, and project management information system.

4. C. The key to this question was that the characteristics of the product were documented with this tool. Configuration management documents the physical characteristics and the functionality of the product of the project.

5. C. Configuration control boards (CCBs) review change requests and have the authority to approve or deny them. Their authority is defined by the organization.

6. A. Changes to product scope should be reflected in project scope.

7. B. Project scope change affects the performance measurement baselines, which may include schedule baselines and cost baselines.

8. D. Scope changes include changes to the agreed-upon WBS.

9. C. WBS element changes are scope changes. Schedule revisions are often required as a result of scope changes.

10. B. Schedule variances will sometimes—but not always—impact the schedule. Changes to non-critical path tasks will not likely impact the schedule, but changes to critical path tasks will always impact the schedule.

11. A. Performance measurements are a tool and technique of the Cost Control process and determine variances in cost using formulas discussed in the Performance Reporting process.

12. C. Cost Control tracks project performance to detect variances and reflect them in the cost baseline. It's also used to prevent inappropriate changes from getting into the cost baseline.

13. D. Budget updates may require cost rebaselining.

14. B. Quality Control is concerned with monitoring work results to see if they fulfill the quality standards set out in the quality management plan. Rework is an output of the Quality Control process.

15. A. Inspection is a tool and technique of the Quality Control process that keeps errors from reaching the customer. Prevention keeps errors from occurring in the process, but it is not a tool and technique of Quality Control.

16. C. Common causes of variances are a result of random variances, known or predictable variances, or variances that are always present in the process.

17. C. Control charts monitor repetitive activities like those in the manufacturing industry. They are based on sample variance measurements and monitor the results of the process over time.

18. D. Pareto diagrams are displayed as histograms. They rank order the most important factors by their frequency over time. Pareto is known for the 80/20 rule; he also said that a small number of causes creates the majority of problems.

19. D. Scatter diagrams use an independent and a dependent variable and display the relationship between these two elements as points on a graph.

20. B. Workarounds are unplanned responses. Workarounds deal with negative risk events as they occur. As the name implies, workarounds were not previously known to the project team. The risk event was unplanned, so no contingency plan existed to deal with the risk event, and thus it required a workaround.

Chapter 11

Closing Out the Project

THE PMP EXAM CONTENT FROM THE PROJECT CLOSING PERFORMANCE DOMAIN COVERED IN THIS CHAPTER INCLUDES:

- ✓ 1. Obtaining acceptance of deliverables
- ✓ 2. Documenting lessons learned
- ✓ 3. Facilitating closure
- ✓ 4. Preserving product records and tools
- ✓ 5. Releasing resources

You've made it to the homestretch. This chapter covers the last group of project processes. Most of the hard part is over, but you aren't quite done yet. Seven percent of the questions on the exam concern the Closing process group, so you'll want to study the main points of project closure.

The Closing process group has two processes, which are covered in this chapter: Contract Closeout and Administrative Closure. The Contract Closeout process is performed and completed before the Administrative Closure process begins. Contract Closeout and Administrative Closure are both concerned with verifying that the work of the project was completed correctly and to the stakeholders' satisfaction.

Project closeout is the most often neglected process of all the project processes. Once the project is over, it's easy to pack things up, throw some files in a drawer, and start moving right into planning the next project. However, don't be so quick to chuck your project just yet. There are a few things to take care of during this process that might make life easier for you on the next project.

One of the most important functions of this process is obtaining formal acceptance of the product of the project from stakeholders and customers. You'll want to get an official sign-off from the stakeholders acknowledging acceptance of the product and then file this with the project documents.

Formulating Project Closeout

All good projects must come to an end, as the saying goes. Hopefully, you've practiced all the things we've talked about that have led up to this point, and you've delivered a successful project to the stakeholders and customers. You've also put some of the vital tools of project management into play—planning, executing, controlling, and communicating—to help you reach that goal. But how do you know when a project has ended successfully? Delivering the product or service of the project doesn't mean it's been completed satisfactorily. Remember back in the opening chapters that I said a project is completed successfully when it meets or exceeds stakeholders' expectations and satisfies the goals of the project. During the Closing process, you'll document acceptance of the product of the project with a formal sign-off and file it with the project records for future reference. This is how the stakeholders will indicate that the goals have been met and that the project meets or exceeds their expectations, so that the project ends.

Characteristics of Closing

There are a few characteristics common to all projects during the Closing process. One is that the probability of completing the project is highest during this process and risk is lowest. You've already completed the majority of the work of the project—if not all of the work—so the probability of not finishing the project is very low.

Stakeholders have the least amount of influence during the Closing processes, while project managers have the greatest amount of influence. Costs are significantly lower during this process, because the majority of the project work and spending has already occurred. Remember those cost S-curves we talked about in Chapter 7, "Creating the Project Plan"? This is where they taper off as project spending comes to an end.

One last common characteristic of projects during Closing is that weak matrix organizations tend to experience the least amount of stress during the Closing process.

All projects do eventually come to an end. Let's examine a few of the reasons for project endings before getting into the Contract Closeout and Administrative Closure processes.

Project Endings

Projects come to an end for several reasons:

- They're completed successfully.
- They're canceled or killed prior to completion.
- They evolve into ongoing operations and no longer exist as projects.

There are four formal types of project endings you might need to know for the exam:

- Addition
- Starvation
- Integration
- Extinction

Let's look at each of these ending types in detail.

Addition

Projects that evolve into ongoing operations are considered projects that end due to *addition*; in other words, they become their own ongoing business unit. An example of this is the installation of an enterprise resource planning system. These systems are business management systems that integrate all areas of a business, including marketing, planning, manufacturing, sales, financials, and human resources. After the installation of the software, these systems can develop into their own business unit, because ongoing operations, maintenance, and monitoring of the software require full-time staff. These systems usually evolve into an arm of the business reporting system that no one can live without once it's installed.

A project is considered a project when it meets these criteria: It is unique, has a definite beginning and ending date, and is temporary in nature. When a project becomes an ongoing operation, it is no longer a project.

Starvation

When resources are cut off from the project or are no longer provided to the project, it's starved prior to completing all the requirements, and you're left with an unfinished project on your hands. *Starvation* can happen for any number of reasons:

- Other projects come about and take precedence over the current project, thereby cutting the funding or resources for your project.
- The customer curtails an order.
- The project budget is reduced.
- A key resource quits.

Resource starving can include cutting back or withholding human resources, equipment and supplies, or money. In any case, if you're not getting the people, equipment, or money you need to complete the project, it's going to starve and probably end abruptly.

This is one of those cases where documentation becomes your best friend. Organizations tend to have short memories. As you move on to bigger and better projects, your memory regarding the specifics of the project will fade. Six months from now when someone important wonders why that project was never completed and begins the finger-pointing routine, the project documents will clearly outline the reasons why the project ended early. That's one of the reasons why project documentation is such an important function. We'll talk more about documenting project details shortly.

Integration

Integration occurs when the resources of the project—people, equipment, property, and supplies—are distributed to other areas in the organization or are assigned to other projects. Perhaps your organization begins to focus on other areas or other projects, and the next thing you know, functional managers come calling to retrieve their resources for other, more important things. Again, your project will come to an end due to lack of resources, because they have been reassigned to other areas of the business or have been pulled from your project and assigned to another project.

The difference between starvation and integration is that starvation results in funding or resource cuts, while integration results in reassignment or redeployment of the resources.

Again, good documentation describing the circumstances that brought about the ending of a project due to integration should be archived with the project records for future reference.

Extinction

This is the best kind of project end, because *extinction* means the project has been completed and accepted by the stakeholders. As such, it no longer exists, because it had a definite ending date, the goals of the project were achieved, and the project was closed out.

 Real World Scenario

Pied Piper

Jerome Reeds is the project manager for Pied Piper's newest software project. His team is working on a program that will integrate the organization's human resource information, including payroll records, leave time accruals, contact information, and so on. His top two programmers, Lance and Kathy, are heading up the coding team and are in charge of the programming and testing activities.

Pied Piper recently hired a new CIO, who started working with the company just a few weeks ago. Jerome is concerned about his human resources project. It was the former CIO's pet project, but he's not sure where it falls on the new CIO's radar screen.

Jerome is in the computer room checking out the new hardware that just arrived for his project. Liz Horowitz, the director of network operations, approaches Jerome.

"That's a nice piece of hardware," Liz comments.

"It sure is. This baby is loaded. It's going to process and serve up data to the users so fast they'll be asking us to upgrade all the servers."

Liz replies, "You're right about that. I've asked Richard to burn it in and load the software."

"What software?" Jerome asks.

"You know, the new customer relationship management software. The CIO hired some vendor she's worked with before to come in and install their CRM system here. She said it was our top priority. I knew this new server was already on order, and it happens to be sized correctly for the new CRM system."

"I purchased this server for the human resources project. What am I supposed to use for that?"

Liz answers, "I've got a server over there on the bottom of the third rack that might work, or maybe you can order another one. But you should take this up with the CIO. All I know is she authorized me to use this server. She understood I was taking it from your project, so maybe she's thinking about going another direction with the human resources project."

"You probably should know I also asked to have Lance and Kathy assigned to the CRM project. Even though it's a vendor project, it still requires some of our coders. The CIO wanted the best, and they're the best we've got. It shouldn't take them long to make the changes I need, and then you can have them back for your project. In the meantime, they can give directions to your other programmers so they can keep working."

"I'm going to go see if the CIO is in," Jerome replies.

This is a case where Jerome's project ends by integration due to the reassignment of resources. The new CIO came on board and changed the direction and focus of the project priorities, making her new project a higher priority than the previous project. As a result, Jerome's hardware and his top two resources were reassigned to the new project. Had the CIO cut the resources and equipment on the original project altogether, it would have ended due to starvation.

Contract Closeout

Contracts have life cycles of their own—just like projects. We talked about the contract life cycles in Chapter 9, "Measuring and Controlling Project Performance." As such, contracts come to a close just like projects come to a close. As you might guess, *A Guide to the PMBOK* has a process that deals with contract closings called Contract Closeout.

The *Contract Closeout* process is concerned with completing and settling the terms of the contract. It also determines if the work described in the contract was completed accurately and satisfactorily. This process is called *product verification*.

Exam Spotlight

For the exam, remember that product verification performed during the Closing process determines if all of the work of the project was completed correctly according to the contract terms and satisfactorily according to stakeholder expectations. And remember that product documentation is verified and accepted during the Scope Verification process. One more note: When projects end prematurely, the Scope Verification process is where the level of detail concerning the amount of work completed gets documented.

Contract Closeout also updates records and archives the information for future reference. These records detail the final results of the work of the project. We'll look at the specifics of this when we examine the Contract Closeout outputs.

Contracts may have specific terms or conditions for completion and closeout. You should be aware of these terms or conditions so that project closure isn't held up because you missed an important detail. If you are not administering the contract yourself, be certain to ask your procurement department if there are any special conditions that you should know about so that your project team doesn't inadvertently delay contract or project closure.

Contract Closeout Inputs and Tools

Contract Closeout has one input and one tool and technique. The input to this process is contract documentation. This includes the contract itself and all the supporting documents that go along with the contract. These might include things such as the WBS, the project schedule, change control documents, technical documents, financial and payment records, quality control inspection results, and so on. This information—along with all the other information gathered during the project—is filed once the project is closed out, so that anyone considering a future project of similar scope can reference what was done.

Procurement Audits

The only tool and technique of Contract Closeout is *procurement audits*. Audits are reviews of processes to determine if they are meeting the right needs and are being performed correctly or according to standards. *A Guide to the PMBOK* says procurement audits are concerned with reviewing the procurement process, starting with Procurement Planning all the way through Contract Administration.

In practice, procurement audits should occur all the way through the Contract Closeout process. Closeout is where the project is formally accepted and the contract file is prepared for the Administrative Closure process and archiving. If you miss these steps, the procurement audit will discover that Contract Closeout was not completed and will allow you to correct it.

The primary purpose of the procurement audit is to identify lessons learned during the procurement process. Procurement audits examine the procurement process to determine areas of improvement and to identify flawed processes or procedures. This allows you to reuse the successful processes on other procurement items for this project, on future projects, or elsewhere in the organization. It also alerts you to problems in the process so that you don't repeat them.

Procurement audits may be used by either the buyer, or the vendor, or by both, as an opportunity for improvement. Documenting the lessons learned—including the successes and failures that occurred—allows you to improve other procurement processes currently under way on this project or other projects. It also gives you the opportunity to improve the process for future projects.

Contract Acceptance

One of the purposes of the Contract Closeout process is to provide formal notice to the seller—usually in written form—that the contract is complete. The output of Contract Closeout that deals with this is called *formal acceptance and closure*. It's your responsibility as project manager to document the formal acceptance of the contract. Many times the provisions for formalizing acceptance of the product and closing the contract are spelled out in the contract itself.

If you have a procurement department that handles contract administration, they will expect you to inform them when the contract is completed and will in turn follow the formal procedures to let the seller know the contract is complete. However, you'll still note the contract completion in your copy of the project records.

This process is your organization's way of formally accepting the product of the project from the vendor and closing out the contract. If the product or service does not meet expectations, the vendor will need to correct the problems before you issue a formal acceptance notice. Hopefully, quality audits have been performed during the course of the project, and the vendor was given the opportunity to make corrections earlier in the process than the Closing stage. It's not a good idea to wait until the very end of the project and then spring all the problems and issues on the vendor at once. It's much more efficient to discuss problems with your vendor as the project progresses, because it provides the opportunity for correction when the problems occur.

The other output of Contract Closeout is a *contract file*. This is simply a file of all the contract records and supporting documents. These records should be indexed for easy reference and included as inputs to the Administrative Closure process. Then, at the conclusion of Administrative Closure, project archives, which include the contract records, are filed for future reference.

Administrative Closure

The key activity of the *Administrative Closure* process is concerned with gathering project records and disseminating information to formalize acceptance of the product, service, or project, as well as to perform project closure. You'll want to review the project documents to make certain they are up to date. For example, perhaps some scope change requests were implemented that changed some of the characteristics of the final product. The project information you're collecting during this process should reflect the characteristics and specifications of the final product. Don't forget to update your resource assignments as well. Some team members will have come and gone over the course of the project; you need to double-check that all the resources and their roles and responsibilities are noted.

Once the project outcomes are documented, you'll request formal acceptance from the stakeholders or the customer. (We'll look at formal acceptance in the outputs section of Administrative Closeout.) They're also interested in knowing if the product or service of the project meets the goals the project set out to accomplish. If your documentation is up to date, you'll have the project results at hand to share with them.

Administrative Closeout is also concerned with analyzing the project management processes to determine their effectiveness and to document lessons learned concerning the project processes. And one of the other key functions of the Administrative Closeout process is the archiving of all project documents for historical reference.

Every project requires closure. According to *A Guide to the PMBOK*, the completion of each project phase requires Administrative Closure as well.

Administrative Closure verifies and documents the project outcomes, just like the Contract Closeout process. Keep in mind that not all projects are performed under contract, but all projects require Administrative Closure. Since verification and documentation of the project outcomes occur in both processes, projects that are performed under contract need to have project results verified only one time.

Administrative Closure Inputs

The Administrative Closure process gathers all the project records and verifies that they are up to date and accurate. The project records must correctly identify the final specifications of the product or service the project set out to produce. Administrative Closure is the place to ensure that this information accurately reflects the true results of the project.

The three inputs to the Administrative Closure process are:

- Performance measurement documents
- Product documentation
- Other project records

We talked quite extensively about performance measurements in Chapter 9, so we'll only recap them here.

Performance Measurement Documents

All of the performance measurements that were used to analyze project progress during the Controlling processes are included as part of the documentation for the Administrative Closure process. Any document that helped establish the basis for the performance measurements—the project plan, the cost budget, cost estimates, the project schedule, and so on—are also collected here. These documents are then reviewed to make certain the goals and objectives of the project were met.

You should make each of these documents available for review during the Administrative Closure process. Stakeholders, the executive management team, or the customer may request to see this information prior to formally accepting the project. You'll want to have these documents available in case they ask.

Product Documentation

The second input of Administrative Closure is product documentation. This documentation includes anything that details the product or service of the project. *A Guide to the PMBOK* includes elements like the requirements documents, specifications, plans, technical documents, electronic files, drawings, and so on. This input includes any information that details or lists product specifications or requirements. As with the performance documents, you should make these documents available for review.

Other Project Records

This last input is a catch-all input for the remaining documents not gathered in the first two inputs. It includes things like project reports, memos or correspondence generated during the project, and any other records that describe the work of the project.

Administrative Closure Tools and Techniques

You've seen all of the tools and techniques of Administrative Closure in other processes. They include:

- Performance reporting tools and techniques
- Project reports
- Project presentations

Here's a pop quiz. Without looking, can you name the nine performance measurements and their formulas?

$$CV = EV - AC$$

$$SV = EV - PV$$

$$CPI = EV \div AC$$

$$SPI = EV \div PV$$

$$EAC = AC + ETC \text{ (use when past assumptions are incorrect)}$$

$$EAC = (AC + BAC) - EV \text{ (use when variances are not typical)}$$

$$EAC = AC + ((BAC - EV) \div CPI) \text{ (use when variances are expected to remain the same)}$$

$$ETC = EAC - AC$$

$$VAC = BAC - EAC$$

So you've been studying. That's very good, because you should know these formulas for the exam. These same performance measurements that were examined throughout the Controlling process can be used during Administrative Closure to verify and document project outcomes. They are included with the project documents gathered and archived during this process. We'll look at project archives next.

Administrative Closure Outputs

Sometimes you'll work on projects where everything just clicks. Your project team functions at the performing stage, the customers and stakeholders are happy, and things just fall into place according to plan. I often find it difficult to close projects that have progressed particularly well, just because I don't want them to end. Believe it or not, the majority of your projects can fall into this category if you practice good project management techniques and exercise those great communication skills.

These are the last outputs of the last process of your project:

- Project archives
- Project closure
- Lessons learned

Project Archives

When all the work of the project is completed, the vendor is paid, the contract is closed, and the records are gathered, you'll create project archives. These include any project documents completed during the project. All of the inputs to this process we mentioned are included here, as well as the contract documents. Keep in mind that when projects are performed under contract, the archiving of financial records is especially important. These records may need to be accessed if there are payment disputes, so you need to know where it is and how it was filed. Projects with large financial expenditures also require particular attention to the archiving of financial records for the same reasons. Financial information is especially useful when estimating future projects, so again, make sure to archive the information so it's easily accessible.

All of these documents should be indexed for reference and filed in a safe place. Don't forget to include electronic databases and electronic documents as part of your project archives as well. These records can be stored on a network drive or copied onto a CD that's kept with the project binder.

Organizational policies will dictate how you should file your project records. If no policies exist, you'll have to create them. I recommend archiving all the information you have regarding your project.

Project Closure and Formal Acceptance

The project closure output concerns verifying that the product of the project meets all the requirements and obtains formal sign-off of the acceptance of the product. Formal acceptance also includes distributing notice of the acceptance of the product or service of the project by the stakeholders, customer, or project sponsor to stakeholders and customers. You should require formal sign-off indicating that the person or persons signing accepts the product of the project. Documenting formal acceptance is important, because it signals the official closure of the project and it is your proof that the project was completed satisfactorily.

Another function of sign-off is that it kicks off the beginning of the warranty period. Sometimes project managers or vendors will warranty their work for a certain time period after completing the project. Projects that produce software programs are often warranted from bugs for a 60- or 90-day time frame from the date of implementation or acceptance. Typically in the case of software projects, bugs are fixed for free during the warranty period. Watch out, because users will try to squeeze new requirements into the "bug" category mold. If you offer a warranty, it's critical that the warranty spells out exactly what is covered and what is not.

Lessons Learned

Lessons learned are the final output of the Administrative Closure process. The purpose of lessons learned is the same as you've seen before. They're used to document the successes and failures of the project. As an example, lessons learned document the reasons why specific corrective actions were taken, their outcomes, the causes of performance variances, unplanned risks that occurred, mistakes that were made and could have been avoided, and so on.

Unfortunately sometimes projects do fail. There are things that can be learned from failed projects as well as from successful projects, and this information should be documented for future reference. Most project managers, however, do not document lessons learned. The reason for this is that employees don't want to admit to making mistakes or learning from mistakes made during the project. And they do not want their name associated with failed projects or even with mishaps on successful projects.

 Lessons learned can be some of the most valuable information you'll take away from a project. We can all learn from our experiences, and what better way to have even more success on your next project than to review a similar past project's lessons learned document? But lessons learned will only be there if you document them now. I strongly recommend you not skip this step.

You and your management team will have to work to create an atmosphere of trust and assurance that lessons learned are not reasons for dismissing employees but are learning opportunities that benefit all those associated with the project. Lessons learned allow you to carry knowledge gained on this project to other projects you'll work on going forward. They'll also prevent repeat mistakes in the future if you take the time to review the project documents and lessons learned prior to undertaking your new project.

Post-implementation audits aren't an official output, but they are a good idea. These go hand in hand with lessons learned, as they examine the project from beginning to end and look at what went right and what went wrong. They evaluate the project goals and determine if the product or service of the project satisfies the objectives. Post-implementation audits also examine the activities and project processes to determine if improvements are possible on future projects.

Organizations that do not document lessons learned probably do conduct post-implementation audits. Documenting and gathering information during this procedure can serve the same function as lessons learned if you're honest and include all the good, the bad, and the ugly. Let's hope there's very little ugly.

⊕ **Real World Scenario**

Cimarron Research Group

The Cimarron Research Group researches and develops organic pesticides for use on food crops. They are a medium-sized company and have established a project management office (PMO) to manage all aspects of project work. The PMO consists of project managers and administrative staff who assist with information handling, filing, and disbursement.

Terri Roberts is the project manager for a project that has just closed. Terri diligently filed all the pertinent project documents as the project progressed and has requested the research files and engineering notes from the director of engineering to include them with the project archives as well. All information regarding the research on this project is included with the project archives. The engineering department chooses to keep their own set of research records as well, but it's important to keep a copy of these notes with the project archives so that all the information about the project is located in one place.

Terri's assistant has indexed all the project documents and recently sent notice of formal acceptance and approval of this project to the stakeholders, project sponsor, and management team. This notice officially closes the project. The next step is to archive the files onto CDs and store them.

Releasing Project Team Members

Releasing project team members is not an official process. However, it should be noted that at the conclusion of the project, you will release your project team members, and they will go back to their functional managers or get assigned to a new project if you're working in a matrix type organization.

You will want to keep the functional managers or other project managers informed as you get closer to project completion so that they have time to adequately plan for the return of their employees. Start letting them know a few months ahead of time what the schedule looks like and how soon they can plan on using their employees on new projects. This gives the other managers the ability to start planning activities and scheduling activity dates.

Celebrate!

I think it's a good idea to hold a celebration at the conclusion of a successfully completed project. The project team should celebrate their accomplishment, and you should officially recognize their efforts and thank them for their participation. Any number of ideas come to mind here—a party, a trip to a ballgame, pizza and sodas at lunch time, and so on. This shouldn't be the only time you've recognized your team, as discussed during the Team Development process, but now is the time to officially close the project and thank your team members.

A celebration helps team members formally recognize the project end and brings closure to the work they've done. It also encourages them to remember what they've learned and to start thinking about how their experiences will benefit them and the organization during the next project.

Project Case Study: New Kitchen Heaven Retail Store

Dirk strolls into your office maintaining his formal and dignified manners as always and then sits down in the chair beside your desk.

"I just want to congratulate you on a job well done," he says. "The grand opening was a success, and the store had a better-than-expected week the first week. I'm impressed you were able to pull this off and get the store opened prior to the Garden and Home Show. That was the key to the great opening week."

"Thank you, Dirk. Lots of people put in a lot of hard work and extra hours to get this job done. I'm glad you're happy with the results."

"I thought the banner with our logo, 'Great Gadgets for People Interested in Great Food,' was a wonderful touch."

"That was Jill's idea. She had some great ideas that made the festivities successful. As you know, though," you continue, "we did have some problems on this project. Fortunately, they weren't insurmountable, but I think we learned a thing or two during this project that we can carry forward to other projects."

"Like what?" Dirk asks.

"We should have contracted with Gomez Construction sooner so that we didn't have to pay overtime. We had a very generous budget, so the overtime expense didn't impact this project, but it might impact the next one.

"And we came fairly close to having a hardware disaster on our hands. Next time, we should order the equipment sooner, test it here at headquarters first, and then ship it out to the site after we know everything is working correctly."

"Good ideas. But that's old news. Now that this project is over, I'd like to get you started on the next project. We're going to introduce cooking classes in all of our retail stores. The focus is the home chef, and we might just call the classes the Home Chef Pro series. We'll offer basic classes all the way to professional series classes if the project's a hit. We'll bring in guest chefs from the local areas to give demos and teach some of the classes as well."

"I'm very interested in taking on this project and can't wait to get started. I'm thrilled that you want me to head this up. But I do have a few things here to wrap up before I start work on the new project," you reply.

Dirk says, "The project's over. The grand opening was a success. It's time to move on. Let Jill take over now; the retail stores are her responsibility."

"Jill has taken over the day-to-day operations. However, I've got to finish collecting the project information, close out the contract with Gomez, and make the final payment. Jake verified that all the work was completed correctly and to his satisfaction. Then I need to publish the formal acceptance notice to all of the stakeholders via e-mail. I will also create a document that outlines those things I told you earlier about that we should remember and reference during the next project; that document is called lessons learned. Then after all those things are completed, all of the project records need to be indexed and archived. I can have all that done by the end of the week and will be free starting Monday to work on requirements gathering and the charter document for the new project."

"This is just like the planning process discussion we got into with the tree, breakdown structure thing, and all the planning, I suspect. I do have to admit all the planning paid off. I'll give you until the end of the week to close out this project. Come see me Monday to get started on Home Chef Pro."

Project Case Study Checklist

Contract Closeout

- Product verification (work was correct and satisfactory)

- Formal acceptance and closure

Administrative Closure

- Product verification (work was correct and satisfactory)

- Collecting project documents

- Disseminating final acceptance notice

- Documenting lessons learned

- Archiving project records

Summary

Project closure is the most often neglected process of all the project management processes. The four most important tasks of closure are:

- Checking the work for completeness and accuracy
- Documenting formal acceptance
- Disseminating project closure information
- Archiving records and lessons learned

Closure involves checking that the work of the project was completed correctly and to the satisfaction of the stakeholders. Documenting formal acceptance of the product of the project is an important aspect of project closure as well. This assures that the stakeholder or customer is satisfied with the work and that it meets their needs.

Projects come to an end in one of four ways: addition, starvation, integration, or extinction. Addition is when projects evolve into their own business unit. Starvation happens because the project is starved of its resources. Integration occurs when resources are taken from the existing project and dispersed back into the organization or assigned to other projects. And extinction is the best end, because the project was completed, accepted, and closed.

The two processes in the Closing group are Contract Closeout and Administrative Closure. Contract Closeout is performed before Administrative Closure and is concerned with settling the contract and completing the contract according to its terms. Its two outputs are the contract file, and formal acceptance and closure.

Administrative Closure is performed at the end of each phase of the project as well as at the end of the project. Administrative Closure involves documenting formal acceptance and disseminating notice of acceptance to the stakeholders, customer, and others. All documentation gathered during the project and collected during this process is archived and saved for reference purposes on future projects.

Lessons learned document the successes and failures of the project. Many times lessons learned are not documented, because staff members do not want to assign their names to project errors or failures. You and your management team need to work together to assure employees that lessons learned are not exercises used for disciplinary purposes but benefit both the employee and the organization. Documenting what you've learned from past experiences lets you carry this forward to new projects so that the same errors are not repeated. It also allows you to incorporate new methods of performing activities that you learned on past projects.

Exam Essentials

Be able to name the purpose of the Closing process.   The purpose of the Closing process is to verify that the work was satisfactorily completed, to disseminate information, to document formal acceptance, to archive records, and to document lessons learned.

Be able to describe product verification.   Product verification confirms that all the work of the project was completed accurately and to the satisfaction of the stakeholder.

Be able to name the primary activity of the Closing process.   The primary activity of the Closing process is to distribute information that formalizes project completion.

Be able to describe when Administrative Closure is performed.   Administrative Closure is performed at the close of each project phase and at the close of the project.

Be able to define the purpose for lessons learned.   The purpose of lessons learned is to describe the project successes and failures and to use the information learned on future projects.

Key Terms

Before you take the exam, be certain you are familiar with the following terms:

addition

Administrative Closure

Contract Closeout

contract file

extinction

formal acceptance and closure

integration

procurement audits

product verification

starvation

Review Questions

1. You are the project manager for a top secret software project for an agency of the United States Government. Your mission—should you choose to accept it—is to complete the project using internal resources. The reason is because getting top secret clearances for contractors takes quite a bit of time and waiting for clearances would jeopardize the implementation date. Your programmers are 80 percent of the way through the programming and testing work when your agency appoints a new executive director. Slowly but surely your programmers are taken off this project and reassigned to the executive director's hot new project. Which of the following type of project ending is this?

    A. Starvation

    B. Extinction

    C. Addition

    D. Integration

2. You are the project manager for a top secret software project for an agency of the United States Government. Your mission—should you choose to accept it—is to complete the project using internal resources. The reason is because getting top secret clearances for contractors takes quite a bit of time and waiting for clearances would jeopardize the implementation date. Your programmers are 80 percent of the way through the programming and testing work when your agency appoints a new executive director. Your programmers are siphoned off this project to work on the executive director's hot new project. Which of the following addresses the purpose of Scope Verification in this case?

    A. Scope Verification determines the correctness and completion of all the work.

    B. Scope Verification documents the level and degree of completion.

    C. Scope Verification determines if the project results comply with quality standards.

    D. Scope Verification documents the correctness of the work according to stakeholders' expectations.

3. You are a project manager for Cinema Snicker Productions. Your company specializes in producing comedy films for the big screen. Your latest project has just been canceled due to budget cuts. Which of the following statements is true?

    A. This project ended due to starvation, because the funding was cut off.

    B. This project ended due to integration, because the resources were distributed elsewhere.

    C. This project ended due to starvation, because the resources were distributed elsewhere.

    D. This project ended due to integration, because the funding was cut off.

4. All of the following are types of project closures or endings except:

    A. Addition

    B. Integration

    C. Verification

    D. Extinction

5. You are a project manager for Cinema Snicker Productions. Your company specializes in producing comedy films for the big screen. Your latest project has just been completed and accepted. You've been given your next project, which starts right away. Which of the following statements is true?

   A. This project ended due to extinction, because it was completed and accepted.

   B. This project ended due to integration, because it was completed and accepted and the project manager moved on to a new project.

   C. This project ended due to addition, because it was completed and accepted and archived into the company's catalog of available films.

   D. This project ended due to integration, because it was completed and accepted.

6. Which of the following processes are performed in the Closing process group and in what order?

   A. Administrative Closure, then Contract Closeout

   B. Scope Verification, then Administrative Closure

   C. Contract Closeout, then Scope Verification

   D. Contract Closeout, then Administrative Closure

7. You are a project manager for Dutch Harbor Consulting. Your latest project involved the upgrade of an organization's operating system on 236 servers. You performed this project under contract. You are in the Contract Closeout process and know that you should document:

   A. Lessons learned

   B. Performance measurements

   C. Formal acceptance

   D. Product verification

8. Which of the following are the outputs of the Contract Closeout process?

   A. Project archives, formal acceptance and closure, and contract file

   B. Contract file, and formal acceptance and closure

   C. Project archives and contract file

   D. Contract file, formal acceptance and closure, and lessons learned

9. You are a project manager for Dutch Harbor Consulting. Your latest project involved the upgrade of an organization's operating system on 236 servers. You performed this project under contract. You are in the Closing process and know that product verification is for what purpose?

   A. To verify the goals of the project and ensure that the product of the project is complete

   B. To evaluate all the work of the project and compare the results to project scope

   C. To verify all the work was completed correctly and satisfactorily

   D. To evaluate project goals and ensure that the product of the project meets the requirements

10. You are a project manager for Dutch Harbor Consulting. Your latest project involved the upgrade of an organization's operating system on 236 servers. You performed this project under contract. You are in the Contract Closeout process and have reviewed the contracting process to identify lessons learned. What is the name of the tool and technique of Contract Closeout you used to perform this function?

    A. Procurement audits

    B. Performance reviews

    C. Performance audits

    D. Procurement reviews

11. All of the following are inputs to the Administrative Closure process except:

    A. Performance measurement documents

    B. Documentation of the product of the project

    C. Other documents

    D. Contract documents

12. You are a project manager for Penguin Software. Your company creates custom software programs for hospitals and large dental offices. You have just completed a project and are gathering the documentation of the product of the project. This might include all of the following except:

    A. Technical specifications

    B. Electronic files

    C. Programming plans

    D. Performance measurements

13. The outputs of the Administrative Closure process include all of the following except:

    A. Project archives

    B. Project closure

    C. Lessons learned

    D. Formal acceptance

14. You are a project manager for Penguin Software. Your company creates custom software programs for hospitals and large dental offices. You have just completed a project and are performing earned value analysis, trend analysis, and performance reviews. Which of the following statements is true?

    A. This is performance measurement documentation, which is an input to the Contract Closeout process.

    B. This is performance measurement documentation, which is an input to the Administrative Closure process.

    C. These are performance reporting tools and techniques of the Administrative Closure process.

    D. These are performance reporting tools and techniques of the Contract Closeout process.

15. You have collected the performance measurement documentation for your project to be included in the project archives. What is the purpose of the performance measurement documentation?

A. The performance measurement documentation is used as part of the formal acceptance process to verify contract expenditures.

B. The performance measurement documentation is reviewed to make certain the project goals and objectives were met.

C. The performance measurement documentation is included in the project archive documentation after confirming the accuracy of the measurements.

D. The performance measurement documentation is used as historical information for future projects that are similar in scope to this project.

16. Your project was just completed. Due to some unfortunate circumstances, the project was delayed, causing cost overruns at the end of the project. Which of the following statements is true?

A. You should document the circumstances as lessons learned.

B. You should pay particular attention to archiving the financial records for this project.

C. Your project ended due to starvation because of the cost overruns.

D. You should document the circumstances surrounding the project completion during the Scope Verification process.

17. Your project was just completed. Due to some unfortunate circumstances, the project was delayed, causing cost overruns at the end of the project. This information might be useful on future projects in all of the following activities except:

A. Cost estimating

B. Allocating resources

C. Product verification

D. Activity estimating

18. Your project was just completed, accepted, and closed. As is customary for your organization, you conduct a post-implementation audit. The purpose of this audit includes all of the following except:

A. Evaluating project goals and comparing them to the project's product

B. Reviewing successes and failures

C. Documenting the acceptance of the work results

D. Documenting possible improvements for future projects

19. Contract documentation is an input to the Contract Closeout process. Contract documentation might include all of the following except:

A. Supporting documents

B. Contract changes

C. Financial documents

D. Procurement audit documents

20. Procurement audits review what?

A. The procurement process from Procurement Planning through Contract Administration

B. The contract administration process from Solicitation Planning through Contract Administration

C. The procurement process from Procurement Planning through Contract Closeout

D. The contract administration process from Solicitation Planning through Contract Closeout

Answers to Review Questions

1. D. Integration occurs when resources, equipment, or property are reassigned or redeployed back to the organization or to another project.

2. B. Scope Verification should document the level and degree of completion of the project. If you come back at a later date and restart this project, Scope Verification will describe how far the project progressed and give you an idea of where to start.

3. A. Starvation occurs because the project no longer receives the resources needed to continue. Resources could include people, equipment, money, and the like.

4. C. Verification is not a type of project ending.

5. A. Extinction is the best type of project end, because it means the project was completed successfully and accepted by the sponsor or customer.

6. D. Contract Closeout and Administrative Closure are the processes in the Closing process group and are performed in that order.

7. C. The project manager is responsible for documenting the formal acceptance. This should be done during Contract Closeout when projects are performed under contract or during Administrative Closure if no work was performed under contract. In cases where part of the work was performed under contract and part with in-house staff, formal acceptance should occur in both of these processes. Lessons learned are an output of the Administrative Closure process, not the Contract Closeout process.

8. B. The contract file, and formal acceptance and closure are the only outputs of the Contract Closeout process.

9. C. Product verification examines all the work of the project and verifies the work was completed correctly and satisfactorily.

10. A. Procurement audits are the only tool and technique of the Contract Closeout process. They're used to review the procurement process and identify and document any lessons learned during the procurement process for future reference.

11. D. Contract documents are an input to the Contract Closeout process but are part of the project archives, which are an output of the Administrative Closure process.

12. D. Performance measurement documentation is an input to the Administrative Closure process and wouldn't be included in the documentation of the product of the project.

13. D. Formal acceptance is included in the project closure process and isn't a separate output.

14. C. Earned value analysis, trend analysis, and performance reviews are tools and techniques included in the performance reporting tools and technique of the Administrative Closure process.

15. B.   The performance measurement documentation is reviewed to make certain the project goals and objectives were met. This is an input to the Administrative Closure process.

16. A.   Lessons learned document the experiences, successes, and failures that occurred during this project for future reference. There isn't enough information in the question to determine if answer B or answer D is correct. Answer C is not correct because the project was completed.

17. C.   Product verification involves examining the work of the project for completeness and correctness. This process occurs on the existing project and isn't of much benefit to future projects, because you'll perform product verification on future project work at the close of the project. By definition, a project is unique and creates a unique product or service.

18. C.   Post-implementation audits are similar to lessons learned in that they review and document the project successes and failures, look for possible improvements for future projects, and evaluate the project goals and compare these to the end product.

19. D.   Procurement audits are a tool and technique of Contract Closeout and not an input. Contract documentation might include all of the other answers shown as well as the contract itself, technical documentation, quality inspection reports related to the contract, and so on.

20. A.   According to *A Guide to the PMBOK*, the procurement audit examines the procurement process from the Procurement Planning process through the Contract Administration process.

Chapter

12

Professional Responsibility

THE PMP EXAM CONTENT FROM THE PROFESSIONAL RESPONSIBILITY PERFORMANCE DOMAIN COVERED IN THIS CHAPTER INCLUDES:

✓ 1. Ensuring integrity

✓ 2. Contributing to knowledge base

✓ 3. Applying professional knowledge

✓ 4. Balancing stakeholder interests

✓ 5. Respecting differences

Congratulations! You've made terrific progress and are well-equipped to take the PMP exam. We've covered all of the *A Guide to the PMBOK* process groups, so the good news is you don't have any more inputs, tools and techniques, outputs, or formulas to memorize. However, there is one final area that the PMP exam will include: professional responsibility.

Once you've obtained the Project Management Professional (PMP) designation, you have an obligation to maintain integrity, apply your subject matter knowledge and project management knowledge, and maintain the code of conduct published by PMI. You'll also be required to balance the interests and needs of stakeholders with the organization's needs. The exam may include questions on any of these topics.

As a project manager, you'll find yourself in many unique situations, different organizations, and possibly even different countries. Even if you never get involved in international project management, you will still come in contact with others from different cultures and backgrounds than yours. If you work as a contract project manager, you'll be exposed to many different organizations that each have their own cultures and ways of doing things. You should always strive to act in a professional, nonoffensive manner in these situations.

We'll talk about each of these topics in this chapter.

Ensuring Integrity

As a project manager, one of your professional responsibilities is to ensure integrity of the project management process, the product, and your own personal conduct. We've spent the majority of this book discussing how to achieve project management integrity by following the project management processes. Accurately applying your knowledge of these processes to your next project will ensure the integrity of the process.

A product that has integrity is one that is complete and sound, or fit for use.

Again, the correct application of the project management processes you've learned will ensure the integrity of the product. You will accurately describe the product and the requirements of the product in the scope document. The project Planning, Executing, and Controlling processes, which include documenting scope, performing quality inspections. taking corrective actions, and so on, will also ensure that a quality product is produced by following the requirements, monitoring the process, and taking corrective action where needed. And as you learned in the last chapter, you will seek acceptance of the product from the stakeholders and customer during the Closing process.

Personal Integrity

Personal integrity means sticking to an ethical code. As a certified Project Management Professional, you are required to adhere to PMI's *Project Management Professional Code of Professional Conduct*. You can find a copy of this code at the PMI website: www.pmi.org.

You should read and understand this code, as you will be agreeing to adhere to its terms as part of the certification process. One of the aspects of personal integrity includes your truthfulness about your PMP application and certification, your qualifications, and the continued reporting you provide to PMI to maintain your certification.

Exam Spotlight

I recommend reading the *PMP Code of Professional Conduct* as part of your project management studies.

Personal Gain

Truthfulness and integrity involve not only information regarding your own background and experience, but regarding the project circumstances as well. For example, let's say you're a project manager working on contract. Part of your compensation consists of a bonus based on total project billing. Now let's suppose your project is finishing sooner than anticipated, and this means your personal profit will decrease by $1500. Should you stretch the work to meet the original contracted amount so that your personal bonus comes in at the full amount even though your project team is finished up? I think you know the answer is of course not.

Your personal gain should never be a consideration when billing a customer or completing a project. Personal gain should never be a factor in any project decision. If the project finishes sooner than planned, you should bill the customer for the work completed, not for the full contracted amount. Compromising the project for the sake of your personal gain shows a lack of integrity, which could ultimately cost you your PMP status and even your job.

Conflict of Interest

Another area the *PMP Code of Professional Conduct* discusses is your responsibility to report to the stakeholders, customers, or others any actions or circumstances that could be construed as a *conflict of interest*.

A conflict of interest is when your personal interests are put above the interests of the project or when you use your influence to cause others to make decisions in your favor without regard for the project outcome. In other words, your personal interests take precedence over your professional obligations, and you make decisions that allow you to personally benefit regardless of the outcome of the project. Let's take a look at a few examples.

Associations and Affiliations

Conflicts of interest may include your associations or affiliations. For example, perhaps your brother-in-law owns his own construction company and you are the project manager for a construction project that's just published an RFP. Your brother-in-law bids on the project and ends up winning the bid.

If you sat on the decision committee and didn't tell anyone about your association with the winning bidder, that is clearly a conflict of interest. If you influenced the bid decision so that it went to your brother-in-law, he benefited from your position. Therefore, you put your personal interests or the interests of your associations, in this case, above the project outcome. Even if you did not influence the decision in any way, when others on the project discover the winning bidder is your brother-in-law, they will assume a conflict of interest occurred. This could jeopardize the awarding of the bid and your own position as well.

The correct thing to do in this case would be, first, inform the project sponsor and the decision committee that your brother-in-law intends to bid on the project. Second, refrain from participating on the award decision committee so as not to unduly influence others in favor of your brother-in-law. And last, if you've done all these things and your brother-in-law still wins the bid, appoint someone else in your organization to administer the contract and make the payments for the work performed by him. Also, make certain you document the decisions you make regarding the activities performed by him and keep them with the project files. The more documentation you have, the less likely someone can make a conflict of interest accusation stick.

Vendor Gifts

Many professionals work in situations where they are not allowed to accept gifts in excess of certain dollar amounts. This might be driven by company policy, the department manager's policy, and so on. In my organization, it's considered a conflict of interest to accept anything from a vendor including gifts no matter how small, meals, even a cup of coffee. Vendors and suppliers often provide their customers and potential customers with lunches, gifts, ballgame tickets, and the like. It's your responsibility to know if a policy exists that forbids you from accepting these gifts. It's also your responsibility to inform the vendor if they've gone over the limit and you are unable to accept the gift.

The same situation can occur here as with the brother-in-law example earlier. If you accept an expensive gift from a vendor and later award that vendor a contract or a piece of the project work, it looks like and probably is a conflict of interest. This violates PMI guidelines and doesn't look good for you personally either.

Using the "I didn't know there was a policy" reasoning probably won't save you when there's a question of conflict of interest. Make it your business to find out if the organization has a conflict of interest policy and understand exactly what it says. Get a copy and keep it with your files. Review it periodically. Put a note on your calendar every six months to reread the policy to keep it fresh in your mind. This is a case where not knowing what you don't know can hurt you.

Don't accept gifts that might be construed as a conflict of interest. If your organization does not have a policy regarding vendor gifts, set limits for yourself depending on the situation, the history of gift acceptance by the organization in the past, and the complexity of the project. It's always better to decline a gift you're unsure about than to accept it and later lose your credibility, your reputation, or your PMP status because of bad judgment.

Stakeholder Influence

Another potential area for conflict of interest comes from stakeholders. Stakeholders are usually folks with a good deal of authority and an important position in the company. Make certain you are not putting your own personal interests above the interests of the project when you're dealing with powerful stakeholders. They may have the ability to promote you or reward you in other ways. That's not a bad thing, but if you let that get in the way of the project or let a stakeholder twist your arm with promises like this, you're getting mighty close to a conflict of interest. Always weigh your decisions with the objectives of the project and the organization in mind—not your own personal gain.

Keep in mind that you may not always be on the receiving end of the spectrum. You should not offer inappropriate gifts or services or use confidential information you have at your disposal to assist others, because this can also be considered a conflict of interest.

Acting Professionally

Acting in a professional manner is required of most everyone who works in the business world. While you are not responsible for the actions of others, you are responsible for your own actions and reactions. Part of acting professionally involves controlling yourself and your reactions in questionable situations. For example, a stakeholder or customer may lash out at you but have no basis for their outburst. You can't control what they said or did, but you can control how you respond. As a professional, your concern for the project and the organization should take precedence over your concern for your own feelings. Therefore, lashing out in return would be unprofessional. I don't have room here to go into all the different situations that relate to an example like this, but you get the idea. Maintain your professional demeanor and don't succumb to shouting matches or ego competitions with others.

Team Members

As project manager, you have a good deal of influence over your project team members. One of the items on the agenda at the project team kickoff meeting should be a discussion of where the team members can find a copy of organizational policies regarding conflict of interest, cultural diversity, standards and regulations, and policies on customer service and standards of performance. Better yet, have copies with you that you can hand out at the meeting or have website addresses available where they can find these documents.

When you see project team members acting out of turn or with less-than-desirable customer service attitudes, coach and influence those team members to conform to the standards of conduct expected by you and your organization. Your team members represent you and the project. As such, they should act professionally. It's your job as the project leader to ensure they do.

 You probably remember another saying your mother always told you that goes something like this: Actions speak louder than words. Always remember that you lead by example. Your team members are watching. If you are driven by high personal ethics and a strong desire to produce excellent customer service, those who work for you will likely follow your lead.

 Real World Scenario

The Golf Trip

Amanda Lewis is a project manager for a network upgrade project for her organization. This project will be outsourced to a vendor. Amanda will manage the vendor's work. She also wrote the RFP and is a member of the selection committee.

The project consists of converting the organization's network from 100MB Ethernet to Gigabit Ethernet. This requires replacing all of the routers and switches. Some of the cabling in the buildings will need to be replaced as well. The RFP requires that the vendor who wins the bid install all the new equipment and replace the network interface cards in each of the servers with Gigabit Ethernet cards. The grand total for this project is estimated at $1.2 million.

Don James is a vendor whom Amanda has worked with in the past. Don is very interested in winning this bid. He drops in on Amanda one day shortly after the RFP is posted.

"Amanda, it's good to see you," Don says. "I was in the neighborhood and thought I'd stop in to see how things are going."

"Just great, Don," Amanda replies. "I'll bet you're here to talk to me about that RFP. You know I can't say anything until the whole process closes."

"You bet we bid on the project. I know you can't talk about the RFP, so I won't bring it up. I wanted to chat with you about something else. My company is sending 15 lucky contestants and one of their friends to Scottsdale, Arizona, for a 'conference.' The conference includes the use of the Scottsdale Golf Club, green fees paid of course, and all hotel and meal expenses are on us for the length of the trip. I know Scottsdale is one of your favorite places to golf, so I thought of you. What do you say?"

Amanda sits forward in her chair and looks at Don for a minute. "That sounds fabulous, and I do love Scottsdale. But you and I both know this isn't a conference. I wouldn't feel right about accepting it."

"Come on, Amanda. Don't look a gift horse in the mouth. It is a conference. I'll be there and so will the top brass from the company. We have some presentations and demonstrations we'd like to show you while you're there, no obligation of course, and then you're free to spend the rest of the time however you'd like."

"I appreciate the offer. Thanks for thinking of me, but no thanks. I'm on the selection committee for the RFP, and it would be a conflict of interest if I attended this conference. Besides, the value of the conference is over the $100 limit our company sets for vendor gifts and meals," Amanda says.

"Okay. We'll miss you. Maybe next time."

Applying Professional Knowledge

Professional knowledge involves the knowledge of project management practices as well as specific industry or technical knowledge required to complete an assignment.

As a PMP, you should apply project management knowledge to all your projects. Take the opportunity to educate others regarding project management practices by keeping others up to date on project management practices, training your team members to use the correct techniques, and informing stakeholders of the correct processes and then sticking to those processes throughout the course of the project. This isn't always easy, especially when the organization doesn't have any formal processes in place. But once the stakeholders see the benefits of good project management practices, they'll never go back to the "old" way of performing their projects.

Project Management Knowledge

Project management is a growing field. Part of your responsibility as a PMP is to stay abreast of project management practices, theories, and techniques. There are many ways to do this, one of which includes joining a local PMI chapter. There are hundreds of local chapters in every state and in other countries as well. You can check the PMI website (www.pmi.org) to find a chapter near you.

Chapter meetings give you the opportunity to meet other project managers, find out what techniques they're using, and seek advice regarding your project. Usually guest speakers appear at each chapter meeting and share their experiences and tips. Their stories are always interesting, and they give you the opportunity to learn from someone else's experiences and avoid making wrong turns on your next project. You may have a few stories of your own worth sharing with your local chapter. Volunteer to be a speaker at an upcoming meeting and let others learn from your experiences.

One of the things you'll get when you join the PMI organization and pay your yearly dues is their monthly magazine. This publication details real-life projects and the techniques and issues project managers have to deal with on those projects. Reading the magazine is a great way to learn new project management techniques or reinforce the information you already know. You might discover how to apply some of the knowledge you've already learned in more efficient ways as well.

PMI offers educational courses through their local chapters and at the national level as well. These are yet another way for you to learn about project management and meet others in your field.

Honesty Is the Best Policy

We talked about honesty earlier in this chapter, but it's worth repeating: Don't mislead others regarding your experience in the project management field. The *PMP Code of Professional Conduct* requires that you honestly report your qualifications, your experience, and your past performance of services to potential employers, customers, PMI, and others.

Be honest about what you do know and what you don't know. For example, the Quality Control processes as described in *A Guide to the PMBOK* are used extensively in the manufacturing industry. However, the information technology field looks at quality issues in different ways. If you're a project manager in the information technology field, you've probably never used control charts and cause-and-effect diagramming techniques. Don't lead others to believe that you have used techniques you haven't used or that you have experience you don't have.

Emphasize the knowledge you do have and how you've used it in your specific industry and don't try to fudge it with processes and techniques you've never used. Potential clients and employers would much rather work with you and provide training where you might need it than think they've got someone fully experienced with the project or industry techniques needed for this project when they don't.

If you're working on contract or you're self-employed, you have a responsibility to ensure that the estimates you provide potential customers are accurate and truthful. Make certain you clearly spell out what services you're providing and let the customer know the results they can expect at the end of the project. Accurately represent yourself, your qualifications, and your estimates in your advertising and in person.

PMI Certification Policy

PMI has a program that allows you or your organization to become a Registered Education Provider (R.E.P.). This allows you—once you're certified—to conduct PMI-sanctioned project management training, seminars, and conferences. The best part is your attendees are awarded professional development units (PDUs) for attending the training or seminar. As a PMP, and especially as an R.E.P., you have a responsibility to the profession and to PMI to provide truthful information regarding the PMI certification process, the exam applications, PDU requirements, and so on. Keep up to date on PMI's certification process by periodically checking their website.

Industry Knowledge

Contributing and applying professional knowledge goes beyond project management experience. You likely have specific industry or technical experience as well. Part of applying your professional knowledge includes gaining knowledge of your particular industry and keeping others informed of advances in these areas.

Information technology has grown exponentially over the last few years. It used to be that if you specialized in network operations, for example, it was possible to learn and become proficient with all the knowledge out there related to this area. Today that is no longer the case. Each specialized area within information technology has grown to become a knowledge area in and of itself. Many other fields have either always had individual specialties or just recently experienced this phenomenon, including the medical field, bioengineering, manufacturing, pharmaceuticals, and so on. You need to stay up to date regarding your industry so that you can apply that knowledge effectively. Today's fast-paced advances can leave you behind fairly quickly if you don't stay on top of things.

I mentioned in the beginning of the book that as a project manager you are not required to be a technical expert, and that still holds true. But it doesn't hurt to stay abreast of industry trends and knowledge in your field and have a general understanding of the specifics of your business. Again, you can join industry associations and take educational classes to stay on top of breaking trends and technology in your industry.

Truthful Reporting

As a project manager, you are responsible for truthfully reporting all information in your possession to stakeholders, customers, the project sponsor, and the public. Always be up front regarding the project's progress.

Nothing good will come of telling stakeholders or customers that the project is on track and everything looks great, when in fact the project's behind schedule or several unplanned risks have occurred that have thrown the project team a curveball. I've personally witnessed the demise of the careers of project managers who chose this route.

Tell the truth regarding project status, even when things don't look good. Stakeholders will likely go to great lengths to help you solve problems or brainstorm solutions. Sometimes, though, the call needs to be made to kill the project. This decision is usually made by the project sponsor and/or the stakeholders based on your recommendation and predictions of future project activities. Don't skew the reporting to prevent stakeholders from making this decision when it is the best solution based on the circumstances.

Truthful reporting is required when working with the public as well. When working in situations where the public is at risk, truthfully report the facts of the situation and what steps you're taking to counteract or reduce the threats. I recommend you get approval from the organization regarding public announcements prior to reporting the facts. Many organizations have public relations departments that will handle this situation for you.

Complying with Laws and Regulations

This may seem obvious, but since it's part of the *PMP Code of Professional Conduct*, we'll mention it here. As a professional, you're required to follow all applicable laws and rules and regulations that apply to your industry, organization, or project. This includes PMI organizational rules and policies as well. You should also follow any ethical standards and principles that may govern your industry or the state or country you're working in. Remember that rules or regulations you're used to in the United States may or may not apply to other countries and vice versa.

As a PMP, one of the responsibilities that falls into this category is the responsibility to report violations of the PMP code of conduct. In order to maintain integrity of the profession, PMPs must adhere to the code of conduct that makes all of us accountable to each other.

When you know a violation has occurred and you've verified the facts, notify PMI. Part of this process—and a requirement of the code of conduct—is that you'll comply with ethics violations and will assist PMI in the investigation by supplying information, confirming facts and dates, and so on. Violations include anything listed in the *PMP Code of Professional Conduct* such as conflicts of interest, truthful advertising and reporting of PMP experience and credentials, and so on, as well as appearances of impropriety. This one calls for some judgment on your part, but it's mostly based on common sense. For example, a PMP in most situations should not have a family member working on the project team reporting to them (unless they own and run a family business).

Respecting Confidential Information

Many project managers work for consulting firms where their services are contracted out to organizations that need their expertise for particular projects. If you work in a situation like this, you will likely come across information that is sensitive or confidential. Again, this may seem obvious, but as part of the *PMP Code of Professional Conduct*, you agree not to disclose sensitive or confidential information or use it in any way for personal gain.

Often when you work under contract, you'll be required to sign a nondisclosure agreement. This agreement simply says that you will not share information regarding the project or the organization with anyone—including the organization's competitors—or use the information for your personal gain.

However, you don't have to work on contract to come into contact with sensitive or private information. You may work full-time for an organization or a government agency that deals with information regarding its customer base or citizens. For example, if you work for a bank, you may have access to personal account information. If you work for a government agency, you may have access to personal tax records or other sensitive material. It would be highly unethical and maybe even illegal to look up the account information of individuals not associated with the project at hand just to satisfy your own curiosity. In my organization, that is grounds for dismissal.

 Don't compromise your ethics or your organization's reputation by sharing information that is confidential to the organization or would jeopardize an individual's privacy.

Company Data

While it may seem obvious that you should not use personal information or an organization's trade secrets for personal gain, sometimes the organization has a legitimate need to share information with vendors, governmental agencies, or others. You need to determine which vendors or organizations are allowed to see sensitive company data. In some cases, you may even need to determine which individuals can have access to the data. When in doubt, ask.

Here are some examples. Maybe the company you're working with has periodic mailings they send to their customer base. If one of your project activities includes finding a new vendor to print the mailing labels, your organization may require the vendor to sign a nondisclosure agreement to guard the contents of the customer lists. Discovering just who does have access to this information might be tricky.

Another example involves data on citizens that is maintained by the government. You might think that because the data belongs to one agency of the government—say the Internal Revenue Service—any other agency of the government can have access to the data. This isn't the case. Some agencies are refused access to the data even though they may have good reason to use it. Others may have restricted access, depending on the data and the agency policy regarding it. Don't assume that others should have access to the data because it seems logical.

Most organizations require vendors or other organizations to sign nondisclosure agreements when giving out sensitive company data. It's your responsibility to ensure that the proper nondisclosure agreements are signed prior to releasing the data. This function is often handled by the procurement department.

Intellectual Property

You are likely to come into contact with intellectual property during the course of your project management career. Intellectual property includes items developed by an organization that have commercial value but are not tangible. Intellectual property includes copyrighted material such as books, software, and artistic works. It may also include ideas or processes that are patented. Or it might involve an industrial process, business process, or manufacturing process that was developed by the organization for a specific purpose.

Intellectual property is owned by the business or person that created it. You may have to pay royalties or ask for written permission to use the property. Intellectual property should be treated just like sensitive or confidential data. It should not be used for personal gain or shared with others who should not have access to it.

Balancing Stakeholders' Interests

Projects are undertaken at the request of customers, project sponsors, executive managers, and others. Stakeholders are those who have something to gain or lose by implementing the project. As such, stakeholders have different interests and needs, and one of your jobs is to balance the needs of the stakeholders.

Customer satisfaction is probably the primary goal you're striving for in any project. If your customer is satisfied, it means you've met or exceeded their expectations and delivered the product or service they were expecting. You've got a winning combination when the customer is satisfied with the product, and you've also provided excellent customer service along the way. Satisfied customers tell others about your success and will most likely use your services in the future.

One of the key ways to assure that customer satisfaction is achieved is to employ appropriate project management techniques to your project. This includes taking the time to discover all the requirements of the project and documenting them in the scope statement. You will find that stakeholders who have a clear understanding of the requirements and have signed off on them won't suffer from faulty memory and pull the ever famous "I thought that *was* included" technique. Take the time to define your requirements and get stakeholder sign-off. You can't forget or fudge what's written down.

Competing Needs

Stakeholders come from all areas of the organization and include your customer as well. Because stakeholders do not all work in the same areas, they have competing needs and interests. One stakeholder's concern on a typical IT project might take the form of system security issues, while another stakeholder is concerned about ease of use. As the project manager, you will have situations where stakeholder needs compete with each other, and you'll have to decide between them and set priorities. Sometimes you'll be able to accommodate their needs, and sometimes you'll have to choose among them. You need to examine the needs against the project objectives and then use your negotiation and communication skills to convince the stakeholders of priorities.

Individual stakeholders may or may not have good working relationships with other stakeholders. Because of this, office politics will come into play. I advise you to stay away from the politics game, but get to know your stakeholders. You'll need to understand their business processes and needs in order to make decisions about stakeholder requirements.

Dealing with Issues and Problems

Problems will occur on your project—it's part of the process. We've talked throughout this book about how to deal with problems and risks and how to use conflict resolution techniques in handling problems. Balancing stakeholder needs comes into play here also.

You'll have to determine alternatives that will meet the key requirements of the project without jeopardizing the competing needs of other stakeholders. Once you're into the Executing process of the project and beyond, redefining scope becomes less and less of an option. So your responsibility is to resolve issues and determine alternative solutions to problems as they occur without changing the original objectives of the project. Enlist the help of your project team members and stakeholders during these times. Use some of the techniques we talked about in Chapter 6, "Establishing Project Planning Controls," like brainstorming and the Delphi technique to find solutions.

Another problem you might find with stakeholders is trying to make them understand your decision or the technical nature of a problem. Again, this is where communication skills help you immensely. Take the case of a technical problem that's cropped up on your project. You should not expect your stakeholder to understand the technical aspects of rocket science if they work in the finance department, for example. It's up to you to keep the explanation at a level they can understand without loading them down with technical jargon and specifications. Keep your explanations simple, yet don't skip important details they'll need to make decisions.

Balancing Constraints

Your toughest issues will almost always center on the triple constraints: time, cost, or quality. Because of the very nature of the constraints, one of these is the primary driver and one is the least important. Keep a close eye on stakeholders who want to switch the priority of the constraints for their own purposes. Let's say the project sponsor already told you that time is the primary constraint. Another stakeholder tells you that a requirement of the project is being overlooked and quality is suffering. Be careful that the stakeholder isn't trying to divert the primary constraint from time to quality to suit their own objectives.

 Real World Scenario

The Geographical Information System

Ryan Loveland is a project manager for a multinational company. He's working on a complex software project that involves rewriting the organization's mainframe accounting system to become a browser-based system running on thin-client architecture. A major problem with the existing system occurs when new accounts are entered into the system or account information changes. The accounts are tied to geographic areas, which are assigned to individual sales associates. Sales commissions are paid based on where the account resides. To date, the process of determining which territory an account belongs to has been done manually by looking at a map.

The project sponsor, Victor, requested a geographical information system (GIS) as part of the requirements of this project. The hope is that errors will be eliminated and commissions will get processed correctly. The sponsor is hoping that Ryan's internal team can write the GIS system that will tie to the accounting system. Let's drop in on Ryan and Victor's conversation.

"I just don't understand," Victor says. "I can go onto that Internet site and plug in an address and get directions from my house to anywhere in the country. It seems easy enough to me. Why can't your team write code like that?"

"It isn't that we can't write a program to do that. But there are several issues surrounding this request that I'd like to explain to you. I'd like you to understand why I'm asking to purchase a software product from an external vendor that will take care of these functions for us."

"Let's hear it," Victor says.

"One of the first problems is that our sales force is multinational. It would take us months just to obtain address information to populate the program. The second issue is that our sales districts are not divided by any known boundaries. Most GIS systems work off of latitude and longitude or geographic boundaries like county borders or zip code boundaries."

Victor interrupts, "Well, here's what we do. You give me a set of maps and I'll hand draw in the sales districts, and you can take that and put it into the system."

"Unfortunately, it's just not that easy. Our sales district boundaries are not consistent with known boundaries, and our existing address database is not standardized. For example, some addresses use the word *Street* spelled out; some use the abbreviation *St*. All of the addresses need to be standardized, and then we have to figure out which addresses belong to which territory.

"This process could take a great deal of time. There are vendors that specialize in GIS systems that could have us operational in a matter of weeks. I've already checked on a couple of the top vendors, and there aren't any problems interfacing with our new system. The time we'd save in the long run far outweighs the cost associated with purchasing this system from a vendor. And one last point: If I were to build this system internally, I'd have to take our top programming team off of existing project priorities to put them on this. GIS systems are extremely complicated. We're talking several months—if not a year or more delay—to get our programmers up to speed on GIS techniques and then write the programs."

Victor says, "If we're talking about a major delay in the schedule as you say, we can at least look at what these vendors have to offer. It's important that this system is accurate as well, and I think I hear you saying, 'Why reinvent the wheel.' Let's have a look at the costs."

Respecting Differences in Diverse Cultures

You have probably taken diversity or cultural differences training classes sometime during your career. Most organizations today require diversity training for all employees and contractors. Project managers who work on contract may find themselves taking these classes multiple times, as companies want to ensure that every employee and contractor has taken their own company's version of the class.

I won't attempt to repeat diversity training here, but I will point out some of the things you should know about working in other countries and about working with people who have backgrounds and belief systems that are different than yours.

Global Competition

More and more companies compete in the global marketplace. As a result, project managers with multinational experience are increasing in demand. This requires a heightened awareness of cultural influences and customary practices of the country where you're temporarily residing.

One thing I've witnessed when working in foreign countries is U.S. citizens who try to force their own culture or customs on those whom they're visiting or working with. That isn't recommended, and it generally offends those you're trying to impress. Don't expect others to conform to your way of doing things, especially when you're in their country. You know the saying, "When in Rome, do as the Romans do"? While you may not want to take that literally, the intent is good. For example, a quick kiss on both cheeks is a customary greeting in many countries. If that is the case and it's how you're greeted, respond with the same.

Culture Shock

Working in a foreign country can bring about an experience called *culture shock*. When you've spent years acting certain ways and expecting normal, everyday events to follow a specific course of action, you might find yourself disoriented when things don't go as you expected. This is known as culture shock.

One of the ways you can avoid this is to read about the country you're going to work in before getting there. The Internet is a great resource for information like this. Your local library is another place to research customs and acceptable practices in foreign countries.

When in doubt about a custom or what you should do in a given situation, ask your hosts or a trusted contact from the company you'll be working with to help you out. People are people all over the world, and they love to talk about themselves and their culture. They're also generally helpful, and they will respect you more for asking what's expected rather than acting as though you know what to do when you clearly do not.

Respecting Your Neighbors

Americans tend to run their lives at high speed and get right down to business when working with vendors or customers. It isn't unusual for a business person to board a plane in the morning, show up at the client site and take care of business, and hop another flight to the next client site that night.

You'll find that many other countries are not this way. People in other countries will expect you to take time to get to know them first, building an atmosphere of trust and respect. Some cultures build relationships first and then proceed to business. And don't expect to do that relationship building in a few hours. It could take several days, depending on the culture. They may even want you to meet their family and spend time getting to know each other. Resist the urge to get right down to business if that's not customary in that culture, because you'll likely spoil the deal or damage relationships past the point of repair.

Spend time building relationships with others. Once an atmosphere of mutual trust and cooperation is established, all aspects of project planning and management—including negotiating and problem solving—are much easier to navigate.

Training

Sometimes you may find yourself working with teams of people from different countries or cultures. Some team members might be from one country and some from another. The best way to ensure that cultural or ethical differences do not hinder your project is to provide training for all team members.

Team-building activities are a method of building mutual trust and respect and of bonding team members with differing backgrounds. Choose activities that are nonoffensive and ones where everyone can participate.

Diversity training makes people aware of differences between cultures and ethnic groups, and it helps them to gain respect and trust for those on their team. Provide training regarding the project objectives and the company culture as well.

Project objectives are why you are all together in the first place. Project objectives cut across cultural bounds and keep everyone focused on the project and tasks at hand.

Perceiving Experiences

All of us see the world through our own experiences. Your experiences are not someone else's experiences, and therefore what you perceive about a situation might be very different from what others believe. Keep this in mind when it appears that a misunderstanding has occurred or that someone you're working with didn't respond as you expected. This is especially true when you're working with someone from another country. Always give others the benefit of the doubt and ask for clarification if you think there is a problem. Put your feelings in check temporarily and remember that what you think the other person means is not necessarily as it appears.

Project Case Study: New Kitchen Heaven Retail Store

Jill Overstreet thought you did such a great job of managing this project that she's offered to buy you lunch at one of those upscale, white tablecloth–type French restaurants. The iced teas have just been delivered, and you and Jill are chatting about business.

"I'm impressed with your project management skills. This store opening was the best on record. And you really kept Dirk in line—I admire that. He can be headstrong, but you had a way of convincing him what needed doing and then sticking to it."

"Thanks," you reply. "I've got a few years of project management experience, so many of those lessons learned on previous projects helped me out with this project. I enjoy project management and read books and articles on the subject whenever I get the chance. It's nice when you can learn from others' mistakes and avoid making them yourself."

Jill takes a long drink of tea. She glances at you over the top of her glass and pauses before setting it down. The look on her face implies she's sizing you up and deciding whether to tell you what's on her mind.

"You know," Jill starts, "we almost didn't hire anyone for your position. Dirk wanted to do away with the project management role altogether. He had a real distaste for project management after our last project."

"Why is that?"

Jill explains, "The last project manager got involved in a conflict of interest situation. She was working on a project that involved updating and remodeling all the existing stores. Things like new fixtures, signs, shelving, display cases, and such were up for bid. And it was a very sizable bid. Not only did she accept an all-expenses-paid weekend visit to a resort town from one of the vendors bidding on the contract, she also revealed company secrets to them, some of which leaked to our competitors."

Your mouth drops open. "I can't believe she would accept gifts like that from a vendor. And revealing company secrets is almost worse. Conflict of interest situations and not protecting intellectual property violate the code of professional conduct that certified PMPs agree to adhere to. I can understand why Dirk didn't want to hire another project manager. Behavior like that makes all project managers look bad."

"I'm glad you kept things above board and won Dirk back over. The project management role is important to Kitchen Heaven, and I know your skills in this discipline are what made this project such a success."

"Jill, not only would I never compromise my own integrity through a conflict of interest situation, I would report the situation and the vendor to the project sponsor. It's better to be honest and let the project sponsor or key stakeholders know what's happening than to hide the situation or, even worse, compromise your own integrity by getting involved in it in the first place. You have my word that I'll keep business interests above my own personal interests. I'll report anything that even looks like it would call my actions into question just to keep things honest and out in the open."

"That's good to hear," Jill replies. "Congratulations on your new assignment. Dirk and I were discussing the new Home Chef Pro project yesterday. We're venturing into new territory with this project, and I'm confident you'll do an excellent job heading it up. Dirk made a good choice."

Project Case Study Checklist

Ensuring personal and professional integrity

Adhering to the *PMP Code of Professional Conduct*

Not placing personal gain above business needs

Avoiding conflict of interest situations

Truthfully reporting questionable situations and maintaining honesty

Protecting intellectual property

Summary

Project Management Professionals are responsible for reporting truthful information about their PMP status and project management experience to prospective customers, clients, and employers and to PMI. As a project manager, you're responsible for the integrity of the project management process and the product. In all situations, you are responsible for your own personal integrity.

Personal integrity means adhering to an ethical standard. As a PMP, you'll be required to adhere to the *PMP Code of Professional Conduct* established by PMI. Part of this code involves avoiding putting your own personal gain above the project objectives.

As a professional, you should strive to maintain honesty in project reporting. You're required to abide by laws, rules, and regulations regarding your industry and project management practices. You should also report any instances that might appear to be a conflict of interest. It's always better to inform others of an apparent conflict than to have it discovered by others and have your methods called into question after the fact.

You will very likely come across confidential information or intellectual property during your project management experiences. Respect the use of this information and always verify who may have permission to access the information and when disclosures are required.

Stakeholders have competing needs and business issues and as such will sometimes cause conflict on your project. You will be required to balance the needs and interests of the stakeholders with the project objectives.

Many project managers today are working in a global environment. It's important to respect and understand the cultural differences that exist and not try to impose your cultural beliefs on others. Culture shock is an experience that occurs when you find yourself in a different cultural environment than you're familiar with. Training is a good way to provide project team members with relationship management techniques regarding cultural and ethnic differences.

Exam Essentials

Be able to define integrity.   Integrity means adhering to an ethical standard.

Be able to name the ethical standard PMPs are required to adhere to.   The ethical standard PMPs are required to adhere to is described in the *PMP Code of Professional Conduct*.

Be able to describe the areas in which PMPs must apply professional knowledge.   PMPs must apply professional knowledge in the areas of project management practices, industry practices, and technical areas.

Be able to name the key activity that ensures customer satisfaction.   The key activity that ensures customer satisfaction is documenting project requirements.

Be able to define how multinational project managers must manage relationships.   Multinational project managers manage relationships by building relationships based on mutual trust and acceptance and recognizing and respecting diverse cultures and ethnic beliefs.

Key Terms

Before you take the exam, be certain you are familiar with the following terms:

conflict of interest   *Project Management Professional Code of Professional Conduct*

culture shock

Review Questions

1. As a project manager, you're responsible for maintaining and ensuring integrity for all of the following except:

   A. Personal integrity of others

   B. Project management process

   C. Personal integrity

   D. Product integrity

2. You are a project manager working on contract. You've performed earned value analysis and discovered that the project will be completed on time and under the original estimated amount. This means the profit to your company will decrease, as will your personal bonus. Which of the following should you do?

   A. Add activities to the project to increase the cost enough to meet the original estimated amount.

   B. Tell the customer you're adding additional requirements to the project that were originally cut because of cost constraints.

   C. Upon completion, inform the customer the project has come in under budget.

   D. Bill the customer for the full amount of the contract, because this was the original agreed-upon price.

3. Integrity in the project management field is accomplished through all of the following except:

   A. Training to learn how to manage relationships with others from different cultures

   B. Adhering to an ethical code

   C. Applying established project management processes

   D. Following the *PMP Code of Professional Conduct*

4. You are a project manager for a manufacturing firm that produces Civil War–era replicas and memorabilia. You discover a design error during a test production run on your latest project. Which of the following is the most likely response to this problem?

   A. Reduce the technical requirements so that the error is no longer valid.

   B. Go forward with production and ignore the error.

   C. Go forward with production but inform the customer of the problem.

   D. Develop alternative solutions to address the error.

5. You are a project manager for a telecommunications firm. You're working on a project that entails upgrading technical hardware and equipment. The estimated cost of the hardware and equipment is $1,725,000. You are reviewing products from three different vendors. One of the vendors invites you to lunch. What is the most appropriate response?

A. Thank them but let them know this could be a conflict of interest since you haven't made a decision about which vendor you're going to choose.

B. Thank them and decline. You know this could be considered personal gain, which could call your integrity into question.

C. Thank them and accept. You don't believe there is a conflict of interest or a personal integrity issue.

D. Thank them and decline. You believe this could be a conflict of interest on the part of the vendor, and you don't want to encourage that behavior.

6. You are a project manager for a telecommunications firm. You're working on a project that entails upgrading technical hardware and equipment. The estimated cost of the hardware and equipment is $1,725,000. You are reviewing products from three different vendors. One of the vendors offers you and your family the use of the company yacht for the upcoming three-day weekend. What is the most appropriate response?

A. Thank them and accept. You don't believe there is a conflict of interest or an integrity issue at stake.

B. Thank them and decline. You know this could be considered personal gain, which could call your integrity into question.

C. Thank them and accept. Immediately report your actions to the project sponsor so that your motives are not called into question after the fact.

D. Thank them and decline. You know this could be considered an integrity issue on the part of the vendor.

7. You are a project manager working on contract with a company in a foreign country. At the project kickoff meeting, you are given an expensive-looking gift. The person who presented this to you said that it is customary in their country to give their business partners gifts. What is the most appropriate response?

A. Thank them and decline. Explain that this is considered personal gain, which is unacceptable in your country.

B. Thank them and accept. You don't believe there is a conflict of interest or an integrity issue at stake.

C. Thank them and decline. Explain that this is considered a conflict of interest, which is unacceptable in your country.

D. Thank them and accept since you know that it would be considered offensive to decline the gift in their culture. Immediately report the acceptance of the gift to the appropriate parties at your company so that your actions are not called into question later.

8. Life seems to be going very well for your close friend, a fellow PMP. She's taken a trip to France, bought a new car, and stocked her wine cellar with a half-dozen expensive bottles of wine, all within the last six months. After a few cocktails one evening, she tells you her secret. The vendor she's working with on the $4 billion project she's managing has given her all of these items as gifts. Which of the following should you do? Choose the best answer.

   A. You tell your friend these gifts probably aren't appropriate and leave it at that.

   B. You and your friend have a long conversation about the gifts and she decides to return them (with the exception of the trip) and not accept any more gifts in the future.

   C. You're happy for your friend and say nothing.

   D. Your friend doesn't see a problem with accepting these gifts at all. You know this is a conflict of interest situation and should be reported as a *PMP Code of Professional Conduct* violation.

9. As a project manager, you know that the most important activity to ensure customer and stakeholder satisfaction is which of the following?

   A. Documenting the requirements

   B. Documenting the performance measurements

   C. Reporting changes and updating the project plan and other project documents where appropriate

   D. Reporting project status timely and regularly

10. As a PMP, you will be required to comply with the *PMP Code of Professional Conduct*. This code refers to all of the following except:

   A. Reporting conflicts of interest

   B. Reporting experience and PMP status truthfully

   C. Complying with the stakeholder requirements

   D. Complying with the rules and standards of foreign countries

11. You are a contract project manager working with the State of Bliss. Your latest project involves rewriting the Department of Revenue's income tax system. One of the key stakeholders is a huge movie buff, and she has the power to promote you into a better position at the conclusion of this project. She's discovered that one of her favorite superstars lives in the State of Bliss and therefore must file income tax returns in that state. She asks you to look up the account of this movie star. What is the most appropriate response?

   A. Report her to the management team.

   B. Refuse to comply with the request, citing conflict of interest and violation of confidential company data.

   C. Look up the information she's requested. Since the data is considered part of the project, there is no conflict of interest.

   D. You believe that tax records are public information, so you comply with the request.

12. You are a contract project manager working with the State of Bliss. Your latest project involves rewriting the Department of Revenue's income tax system. As project manager, you have taken all the appropriate actions regarding confidentiality of data. One of the key stakeholders is a huge movie buff, and she has the power to promote you into a better position at the conclusion of this project. She's reviewing some report data that just happens to include confidential information regarding one of her favorite movie superstars. What is the most appropriate response?

A. Report her to the management team.

B. Request that she immediately return the information, citing conflict of interest and violation of confidential company data.

C. Do nothing, because she has the proper level of access rights to the data and this information showed up unintentionally.

D. Request that she immediately return the information until you can confirm that she has the proper level of access rights to the data.

13. As a PMP, you are required to comply with the *PMP Code of Professional Conduct*. Part of your responsibility concerns applying professional knowledge. All of the following are part of applying professional knowledge except:

A. Developing relationships based on mutual respect

B. Staying abreast of project management practices

C. Keeping up with industry trends and new technology

D. Honestly reporting your project management experience

14. You are a project manager with several years of experience in project management. You've just accepted your first project in a foreign country. You've been in the country a week or two and are experiencing some disoriented feelings. This is known as:

A. Collocation

B. Diversity shock

C. Global culturing

D. Culture shock

15. You are a project manager for a software manufacturing firm. The project you've just finished created a new software product that is expected to become a number-one seller. All pre-release of software is handled through the marketing department. A friend of yours is a certified software instructor. They have asked you for a copy of the software prior to the beta release so they can get familiar with it. What is the most appropriate response?

A. Since your friend is certified to teach your company's brand of software, provide them with a copy of the software.

B. Ask them to sign a nondisclosure agreement before releasing a copy of the software.

C. Decline the request, since you stand to gain from this transaction by receiving free training.

D. Decline the request, because the software is the intellectual property of the company.

16. Your upcoming project includes project team members from a foreign country. In order to make certain that cultural differences don't interfere with team performance, thereby affecting the success of the project, your first course of action is to do which of the following?

    A. Provide diversity training to all the team members.

    B. Collocate the project team.

    C. Perform team-building exercises.

    D. Inform the team members of the organization's rules and standards.

17. You are a project manager for Pizza Direct, which is a retail pizza delivery store. Your company is competing with another retail store for the option of opening two new stores in a foreign country. You have been invited to dinner with the prospective foreign business partners and their spouses upon your arrival. You know that all of the following statements are generally true except:

    A. You should spend time building relationships with your prospective foreign business partners before getting down to business.

    B. You should explain your company's rules, standards, and operating policies at your first meeting with the prospective foreign business partners.

    C. You should build an atmosphere of mutual trust and cooperation.

    D. You should respect the cultural differences you'll encounter when working with your prospective foreign business partners.

18. You are a project manager for Pizza Direct, which is a retail pizza delivery store. Your company is competing with another retail store for the option of opening two new stores in a foreign country. You've been told that it is culturally unacceptable to eat certain foods in this country. You know that one of these foods happens to be a secret ingredient in the pizza sauce. What is the most appropriate response?

    A. Inform the potential partners that your sauce recipe is secret, but you're certain there are no forbidden ingredients in it.

    B. Inform the potential partners that you suspect there might be a forbidden ingredient in the sauce and you'll request an investigation to determine if any of them exist in the sauce.

    C. Inform the potential partners that a forbidden ingredient exists in the sauce and determine to work with them to come up with another ingredient to replace that one.

    D. Don't tell the potential partners about the ingredient, because the sauce they'll be using in the stores is shipped to them already prepared in cans. They won't know the ingredient is in the sauce.

19. You are a project manager for Pizza Direct, which is a retail pizza delivery store. Your company is competing with another retail store for the option of opening two new stores in a foreign country. You know, but have not yet informed your company, that you are going to go to work for the competitor, which happens to be bidding for this same opportunity. What is the most appropriate response?

    A. You decline to participate in the initial meetings with the foreign business partners due to a conflict of interest.

    B. You've not yet received an official offer from the competing company for your new job opportunity, so you choose to participate in the initial meetings with the foreign business partners.

    C. You decide to participate in the initial meetings with the foreign business partners, because any information you gain now will help you when you make the move to the new company.

    D. You inform the foreign business partners that you're going to be working with a new company and that you know the deal they'll receive from the competing company is better than the one this company is proposing.

20. You are the project manager for a new construction project in your city. Your longtime personal friend is bidding on the project. They've asked you to give them an indication of the budget for this project so that they do not overbid and lose the deal. What is the most appropriate response?

    A. Give the information to your friend. You know their character and can trust that they won't tell anyone.

    B. Tell your friend that after all this time, they should know you better than to think you'd put your personal integrity on the line or compromise your job due to a conflict of interest. Decline to give them the information.

    C. Tell your friend you'll give them the information if they'll promise not to tell anyone and if they'll agree to help you out with some materials on your basement-refinishing project.

    D. Give the information to your friend and inform the project sponsor so that the information can be shared with the other bidders as well.

Answers to Review Questions

1. **A.** You are not responsible for the personal integrity of others, but as project manager you do have influence over others such as your project team members.

2. **C.** Integrity means you'll honestly report project outcomes and status. Your personal gain should not be placed above the satisfaction of the customer.

3. **A.** Diversity training is used to help you manage project teams that are made up of people from other countries or cultures. Integrity is accomplished by following an ethical code and applying project management practices.

4. **D.** The best answer to this problem is to develop alternative solutions to address design error. Reducing technical requirements might be an alternative solution, but it's not one you'd implement without looking at all the alternatives. Ignoring the error and going forward with production will result in an unsatisfactory product for the customer.

5. **A.** A luncheon date could be considered a conflict of interest prior to awarding a contract to a vendor. Consider what a competitor of this vendor would think if they spotted you having lunch together.

6. **B.** The best response to this situation is to thank the vendor and decline based on the fact that this could be considered personal gain on your part. Answer D may seem correct, but remember, you're not responsible for the integrity of others. And it's often common business practice for vendors to offer gifts to potential customers.

7. **D.** The best response in this case is to accept the gift, because it would cause great offense to the other party if you were to decline. Report the gift and the circumstances as soon as possible to the appropriate parties at your company.

8. **D.** This is a conflict of interest situation and should be reported as a violation of the *PMP Code of Professional Conduct*.

9. **A.** Documenting the requirements is one of the key things you can do to ensure customer satisfaction. The requirements describe what the customer is looking for, and the final product is compared against them to determine if all of the requirements were met.

10. **C.** Stakeholder requirements are needed to determine if the project is successful and are not a part of the professional code.

11. **B.** The situation presented here requires you to put the interest of the company and the confidentiality of the data above your own personal interests or those of your stakeholders. Answer D is not the most correct response, because it says you believe the information is public. This implies you haven't verified whether the data is private or public. Until you know, treat the data as confidential. In this case, the information is confidential and should be shared only with those who have a valid reason for using it.

12. C.   As project manager, it's your responsibility to make sure the people you will be sharing data with have the proper permissions to see the data; this question indicated that you did that. In this case, answer D is not correct, because it implies you did not verify ahead of time that the stakeholder had the proper level of approvals to use the data.

13. A.   Applying professional knowledge involves staying abreast of project management practices, industry trends, and new technology and honestly reporting your experiences.

14. D.   Culture shock is the disoriented feeling that people may experience when working in a foreign country.

15. D.   The most appropriate response is to deny the request. Software is considered intellectual property and should not be used for personal gain or given to others without prior consent from the organization. This question states that the release of the beta software is handled through the marketing department, so you should not give your friend a copy of the software outside of this process.

16. A.   The most correct response is to first provide training to your team members to teach them how to respect and work with others from different cultures. Collocation may not be possible when you're working with team members from two different countries. Team-building exercises are a good idea as well but are not your first course of action.

17. B.   Your first meeting with foreign partners should be spent getting to know them. Many cultures like to spend time building relationships first and then talking business. Since you've been invited to dinner upon your arrival and the dinner includes the spouses of your prospective partners, chances are they want to spend some time getting to know you personally first.

18. C.   The most appropriate response is to inform the potential partners that an ingredient exists in the sauce that is not acceptable and determine to come up with a solution to the problem. As a professional, you're required to be honest in your reporting. Not telling them, or stalling by promising an investigation, is not an honest response.

19. A.   The most appropriate response is to decline to participate due to a conflict of interest.

20. B.   This situation is clearly a conflict of interest and should be avoided. Decline to provide your friend this information.

Appendix A

Process Inputs and Outputs

Throughout this book, *PMP: Project Management Professional Study Guide*, we've discussed the inputs and outputs to the PMI processes. In this appendix you'll find the inputs, tools and techniques, outputs, and knowledge areas of the project management processes listed by process. I think you'll find that it's very convenient to have all of this information in one location. Enjoy!

Initiation Processes

The following table lists the inputs, tools and techniques, outputs, and knowledge areas for the Initiation process group.

TABLE A.1 Initiation Process Group

Process Name	Inputs	Tools and Techniques	Outputs	Knowledge Area
Initiation	Product description	Project selection methods	Project charter	Scope
	Strategic plan	Expert judgment	Project manager identified/assigned	
	Project selection criteria		Constraints	
	Historical information		Assumptions	

Planning Processes

The following table lists the inputs, tools and techniques, outputs, and knowledge areas for the Planning process group. We'll start with the core processes.

TABLE A.2 Core Processes for the Planning Process Group

Process Name	Inputs	Tools and Techniques	Outputs	Knowledge Area
Scope Planning	Product description	Product analysis	Scope statement	Scope
	Project charter	Benefit/cost analysis	Supporting detail	
	Constraints	Alternatives identification	Scope management plan	
	Assumptions	Expert judgment		
Scope Definition	Scope statement	Work breakdown structure (WBS) templates	Work breakdown structure (WBS)	Scope
	Constraints	Decomposition	Scope statement updates	
	Assumptions			
	Other planning outputs			
	Historical information			
Resource Planning	Work breakdown structure (WBS)	Expert judgment	Resource requirements	Cost
	Historical information	Alternatives identification		
	Scope statement	Project management software		
	Resource pool description			

TABLE A.2 Core Processes for the Planning Process Group *(continued)*

Process Name	Inputs	Tools and Techniques	Outputs	Knowledge Area
	Organizational policies			
	Activity duration estimates			
Activity Definition	Work breakdown structure (WBS)	Decomposition	Activity list	Time
	Scope statement	Templates	Supporting detail	
	Historical information		Work breakdown structure (WBS) updates	
	Constraints			
	Assumptions			
	Expert judgment			
Activity Sequencing	Activity list	Precedence diagramming method (PDM)	Project network diagrams	Time
	Product description	Arrow diagramming method (ADM)	Activity list updates	
	Mandatory dependencies	Conditional diagramming methods		
	Discretionary dependencies	Network templates		
	External dependencies			
	Milestones			

TABLE A.2   Core Processes for the Planning Process Group *(continued)*

Process Name	Inputs	Tools and Techniques	Outputs	Knowledge Area
Activity Duration Estimating	Activity list	Expert judgment	Activity duration estimates	Time
	Constraints	Analogous estimating	Basis of estimates	
	Assumptions	Quantitatively based durations	Activity list updates	
	Resource requirements	Reserve time (contingency)		
	Resource capabilities			
	Historical information			
	Identified risks			
Risk Management Planning	Project charter	Planning meetings	Risk management plan	Risk
	Organization's risk management policies			
	Defined roles and responsibilities			
	Stakeholder risk tolerances			
	Template for the organization's risk management plan			
	Work breakdown structure (WBS)			

TABLE A.2   Core Processes for the Planning Process Group *(continued)*

Process Name	Inputs	Tools and Techniques	Outputs	Knowledge Area
Cost Estimating	Work breakdown structure (WBS)	Analogous estimating	Cost estimates	Cost
	Resource requirements	Parametric modeling	Supporting detail	
	Resource rates	Bottom-up estimating	Cost management plan	
	Activity duration estimates	Computerized tools		
	Estimating publications	Other cost estimating methods		
	Historical information			
	Chart of accounts			
	Risks			
Cost Budgeting	Cost estimates	Cost budgeting tools and techniques	Cost baseline	Cost
	Work breakdown structure (WBS)			
	Project schedule			
	Risk management plan			
Schedule Development	Project network diagrams	Mathematical analysis	Project schedule	Time

TABLE A.2   Core Processes for the Planning Process Group *(continued)*

Process Name	Inputs	Tools and Techniques	Outputs	Knowledge Area
	Activity duration estimates	Duration compression	Supporting detail	
	Resource requirements	Simulation	Schedule management plan	
	Resource pool description	Resource-leveling heuristics	Resource requirement updates	
	Calendars	Project management software		
	Constraints	Coding structure		
	Assumptions			
	Leads and lags			
	Risk management plan			
	Activity attributes			
Project Plan Development	Other planning outputs	Project planning methodology	Project plan	Integration
	Historical information	Stakeholder skills and knowledge	Supporting detail	
	Organizational policies	Project management information system (PMIS)		
	Constraints	Earned value management (EVM)		
	Assumptions			

The following table lists the inputs, tools and techniques, outputs, and knowledge areas of the Planning Facilitating processes in the Planning process group.

TABLE A.3 Planning Facilitating Processes for the Planning Process Group

Process Name	Inputs	Tools and Techniques	Outputs	Knowledge Area
Quality Planning	Quality policy	Benefit/cost analysis	Quality management plan	Quality
	Scope statement	Benchmarking	Operational definitions	
	Product description	Flowcharting	Checklists	
	Standards and regulations	Design of experiments	Inputs to other processes	
	Other process outputs	Cost of quality		
Organizational Planning	Project interfaces	Templates	Role and responsibility assignments	Human Resource
	Staffing requirements	Human resource practices	Staffing management plan	
	Constraints	Organizational theory	Organization chart	
		Stakeholder analysis	Supporting detail	
Staff Acquisition	Staffing management plan	Negotiations	Project staff assigned	Human Resource
	Staffing pool description	Preassignment	Project team directory	
	Recruitment practices	Procurement		

TABLE A.3 Planning Facilitating Processes for the Planning Process Group *(continued)*

Process Name	Inputs	Tools and Techniques	Outputs	Knowledge Area
Procurement Planning	Scope statement	Make-or-buy analysis	Procurement management plan	Procurement
	Product description	Expert judgment	Statement(s) of work	
	Procurement resources	Contract type selection		
	Market conditions			
	Other planning outputs			
	Constraints			
	Assumptions			
Solicitation Planning	Procurement management plan	Standard forms	Procurement documents	Procurement
	Statement(s) of work	Expert judgment	Evaluation criteria	
	Other planning outputs		Statement of work updates	
Communications Planning	Communications requirements	Stakeholder analysis	Communications management plan	Communications
	Communications technology			
	Constraints			
	Assumptions			
Risk Identification	Risk management plan	Documentation reviews	Risks	Risk

TABLE A.3 Planning Facilitating Processes for the Planning Process Group *(continued)*

Process Name	Inputs	Tools and Techniques	Outputs	Knowledge Area
	Project planning outputs	Information-gathering techniques	Triggers	
	Risk categories	Checklists	Inputs to other processes	
	Historical information	Assumptions analysis		
		Diagramming techniques		
Qualitative Risk Analysis	Risk management plan	Risk probability and impact	Overall risk ranking for the project	Risk
	Identified risks	Probability/ impact risk rating matrix	List of prioritized risks	
	Project status	Project assumptions testing	List of risks for additional analysis and management	
	Project type	Data precision ranking	Trends in qualitative risk analysis results	
	Data precision			
	Scales of probability and impact			
	Assumptions			
Quantitative Risk Analysis	Risk management plan	Interviewing	Prioritized list of quantified risks	Risk

TABLE A.3   Planning Facilitating Processes for the Planning Process Group *(continued)*

Process Name	Inputs	Tools and Techniques	Outputs	Knowledge Area
	Identified risks	Sensitivity analysis	Probabilistic analysis of the project	
	List of prioritized risks	Decision tree analysis	Probability of achieving the cost and time objectives	
	List of risks for additional analysis and management	Simulations	Trends in quantitative risk analysis results	
	Historical information			
	Expert judgment			
	Other planning outputs			
Risk Response Planning	Risk management plan	Avoidance	Risk response plan	Risk
	List of prioritized risks	Transference	Residual risks	
	Risk ranking of the project	Mitigation	Secondary risks	
	Prioritized list of quantified risks	Acceptance	Contractual agreements	
	Probabilistic analysis of the project		Contingency reserve amounts needed	
	Probability of achieving the cost and time objectives		Inputs to other processes	

TABLE A.3   Planning Facilitating Processes for the Planning Process Group *(continued)*

Process Name	Inputs	Tools and Techniques	Outputs	Knowledge Area
	List of potential responses		Inputs to a revised project plan	
	Risk thresholds			
	Risk owners			
	Common risk causes			
	Trends in qualitative and quantitative risk analysis results			

Executing Processes

The following table lists the inputs, tools and techniques, outputs, and knowledge areas for the Executing process group. We'll start again with the core processes.

TABLE A.4   Core Processes for the Executing Process Group

Process Name	Inputs	Tools and Techniques	Outputs	Knowledge Area
Project Plan Execution	Project plan	General management skills	Work results	Integration
	Supporting detail	Product skills and knowledge	Change requests	
	Organizational policies	Work authorization system		
	Preventive action	Status review meetings		
	Corrective action	Project management information system		
		Organizational procedures		

The following table lists the inputs, tools and techniques, outputs, and knowledge areas for the Executing Facilitating processes for the Executing process group.

TABLE A.5   Executing Facilitating Processes for the Executing Process Group

Process Name	Inputs	Tools and Techniques	Outputs	Knowledge Area
Quality Assurance	Quality management plan	Quality planning tools and techniques	Quality improvement	Quality
	Results of quality control measurements	Quality audits		
	Operational definitions			
Team Development	Project staff	Team-building activities	Performance improvements	Human Resource
	Project plan	General management skills	Input to performance appraisals	
	Staffing management plan	Reward and recognition systems		
	Performance reports	Collocation		
	External feedback	Training		
Solicitation	Procurement documents	Bidder conferences	Proposals	Procurement
	Qualified seller lists	Advertising		
Source Selection	Proposals	Contract negotiation	Contract	Procurement
	Evaluation criteria	Weighting system		
	Organizational policies	Screening system		

TABLE A.5 Executing Facilitating Processes for the Executing Process Group *(continued)*

Process Name	Inputs	Tools and Techniques	Outputs	Knowledge Area
		Independent estimates		
Contract Administration	Contract	Contract change control system	Correspondence	Procurement
	Work results	Performance reporting	Contract changes	
	Change requests	Payment system	Payment requests	
	Seller invoices			
Information Distribution	Work results	Communications skills	Project records	Communication
	Communications management plan	Information retrieval systems	Project reports	
	Project plan	Information distribution methods	Project presentations	

Controlling Processes

The following table lists the inputs, tools and techniques, outputs, and knowledge areas for the Controlling process group, starting with the core processes.

TABLE A.6 Core Processes for the Controlling Process Group

Process Name	Inputs	Tools and Techniques	Outputs	Knowledge Area
Performance Reporting	Project plan	Performance reviews	Performance reports	Communication
	Work results	Variance analysis	Change requests	

TABLE A.6   Core Processes for the Controlling Process Group *(continued)*

Process Name	Inputs	Tools and Techniques	Outputs	Knowledge Area
	Other project records	Trend analysis		
		Earned value (EV) analysis		
		Information distribution tools and techniques		
Integrated Change Control	Project plan	Change control system	Project plan updates	Integration
	Performance reports	Configuration management	Corrective action	
	Change requests	Performance measurement	Lessons learned	
		Additional planning		
		Project management information system		

The following table lists the inputs, tools and techniques, outputs, and knowledge areas for the Controlling Facilitating processes for the Controlling process group.

TABLE A.7   Controlling Facilitating Processes for the Controlling Process Group

Process Name	Input	Tools and Techniques	Outputs	Knowledge Area
Scope Verification	Work results	Inspection	Formal acceptance	Scope
	Product documentation			
	Work breakdown structure (WBS)			

TABLE A.7 Controlling Facilitating Processes for the Controlling Process Group *(continued)*

Process Name	Input	Tools and Techniques	Outputs	Knowledge Area
	Scope statement			
	Project plan			
Scope Change Control	Work breakdown structure (WBS)	Scope change control	Scope changes	Scope
	Performance reports	Performance measurement	Corrective action	
	Change requests	Additional planning	Lessons learned	
	Scope management plan		Adjusted baseline	
Schedule Control	Project schedule	Schedule change control system	Schedule updates	Time
	Performance reports	Performance measurement	Corrective action	
	Change requests	Additional planning	Lessons learned	
	Schedule management plan	Project management software		
		Variance analysis		
Cost Control	Cost baseline	Cost change control system	Revised cost estimates	Cost
	Performance reports	Performance measurement	Budget updates	
	Change requests	Earned value management (EVM)	Corrective action	
	Cost management plan	Additional planning	Estimate at completion (EAC)	

TABLE A.7   Controlling Facilitating Processes for the Controlling Process Group   *(continued)*

Process Name	Input	Tools and Techniques	Outputs	Knowledge Area
		Computerized tools	Project closeout	
			Lessons learned	
Quality Control	Work results	Inspection	Quality improvement	Quality
	Quality management plan	Control charts	Acceptance decisions	
	Operational definitions	Pareto diagrams	Rework	
	Checklists	Statistical sampling	Completed checklists	
		Flowcharting	Process adjustments	
		Trend analysis		
Risk Monitoring and Control	Risk management plan	Project risk response audits	Workaround plans	Risk
	Risk response plan	Periodic project risk reviews	Corrective action	
	Project communication	Earned value (EV) analysis	Project change requests	
	Additional risk identification and analysis	Technical performance measurement	Updates to the risk response plan	
	Scope changes	Additional risk response planning	Risk database	
			Updates to risk identification checklists	

Closing Processes

This final table lists the inputs, tools and techniques, outputs, and knowledge areas for the core processes of the Closing process group.

TABLE A.8 Core Processes for the Closing Process Group

Process Name	Inputs	Tools and Techniques	Outputs	Knowledge Area
Contract Closeout	Contract documentation	Procurement audits	Contract file	Procurement
			Formal acceptance and closure	
Administrative Closure	Performance measurement documentation	Performance reporting tools and techniques	Project archives	Communications
	Product documentation	Project reports	Project closure	
	Other project records	Project presentations	Lessons learned	

Glossary

acceptance   Acceptance is a tool and technique of the Risk Response Planning process. This strategy implies that the organization is willing to accept the consequences of the risk should it occur.

Achievement Theory   This motivational theory says people are motivated by the need for three things: achievement, power, and affiliation.

Activity Definition   This process identifies the activities of the project that need to be performed to produce the product or service of the project.

activity duration estimates   Activity duration estimates are a quantifiable estimate of the number of work periods needed to complete the activities listed on the WBS or on the subproject WBS. They are an output of the Activity Duration Estimating process.

Activity Duration Estimating   This process assesses the number of work periods needed to complete the project activities. Work periods are usually expressed in hours or days. Large projects might express duration in weeks or months.

activity list   An extension of the WBS that contains all the activities of the project and a description of each activity. The activity list is an output of the Activity Definition process.

activity on arrow (AOA)   A diagramming method that places activities on arrows, which connect to dependent activities using nodes. This is also known as the *arrow diagramming method*.

activity on node (AON)   A diagramming method that places activities on nodes, which connect to dependent activities using arrows. This is also known as the *precedence diagramming method*.

Activity Sequencing   This process sequences activities in logical order and determines if dependencies exist among the activities.

actual cost (AC)   The actual cost of work to date or during a given time period, including direct and indirect costs.

addition   A type of project ending where the project evolves into ongoing operations.

adjusted baseline   An output of the Scope Change process where changes in scope cause updates to the schedule, cost, or performance measurement baselines.

Administrative Closure   This process is concerned with gathering and disseminating information to formalize project closure. The completion of each project phase requires administrative closure also.

administrative costs   Administrative costs are the day-to-day costs of keeping an organization running, but they are not directly related to the project.

alternatives identification   A technique used to discover different methods or ways of accomplishing the project. Alternatives identification is a tool and technique of the Scope Planning process.

analogous estimating   This technique uses the actual duration of a similar, completed activity to determine the duration of the current activity. This is also called top-down estimating and is a form of expert judgment.

appeals   See *contested changes*.

arbitration   A negotiation technique used to settle contract disputes. All parties come to the table with a third, disinterested party who is not a participant in the contract to try and reach an agreement. The purpose of arbitration is to reach an agreement without having to go to court.

appraisal costs   Appraisal costs are associated with the cost of quality and are expended to examine the product or process and make certain the project requirements are being met.

arrow diagramming method (ADM)   A diagramming method that places activities on arrows, which connect to dependent activities using nodes. This is also known as *activity on arrow*.

assumption   An event or action believed to be true. Project assumptions should always be documented.

attributes   Measurements of deliverables (or certain characteristics of the deliverable) that meet one of two options: conforming or nonconforming. Conforming meets the requirement; nonconforming does not. This is an inspection technique that is a tool and technique of the Quality Control process.

avoidance   Avoidance is a tool and technique of the Risk Response Planning process. This strategy requires changes to the project plan in order to avoid or eliminate risk events and their impacts to the project objectives.

backward pass   A calculation used in CPM to determine late start and late finish dates for activities.

balanced matrix   A type of organizational structure where power is balanced between project managers and functional managers.

bar charts   A method of displaying schedule activities. See also *Gantt charts*.

baseline   A measurement used to determine project progress. Baselines are usually the original, approved project plan, schedule, or costs determined during the Planning processes. As the project progresses, measurements are made to determine how close the project is performing to the baseline. Significant scope, schedule, or cost changes may require the project to be rebaselined.

benchmarking   Compares previous similar activities to the current project activities to provide a standard to measure performance against. It's often used to derive ideas for quality improvements for the project.

benefit measurement methods   Benefit measurement methods are a category of project selection methods, which are a tool and technique of the Initiation process. They employ various forms of analysis and comparative approaches to make project decisions and include comparative approaches such as benefit/cost analysis, scoring models, benefit contribution methods, and economic models.

bidder conferences   Meetings with prospective vendors or sellers are held prior to the completion of their response proposal to clarify project objectives and answer questions. Bidder conferences are a tool and technique of the Solicitation process.

bottom-up estimating   Every activity or work item is individually estimated and then rolled up, or added together, to come up with a total project estimate. Bottom-up estimating is a very accurate means of estimating, provided the estimates at the work package level are accurate.

brainstorming   This is an information-gathering technique that is a tool and technique of the Risk Identification process. It involves assembling together in one place subject matter experts, team members, risk management team members, and anyone else who might benefit the process and querying them on possible risk events.

budget at completion (BAC)   Budget at completion is the remaining budget less the work that's been done to date. This figure is used in earned value analysis calculations.

buffer   See *reserve time*.

calculation methods   A category of selection methods outlined in the project selection methods tool and technique of the Initiation process. Calculation methods provide a way to calculate the value of the project. This value is used in the project selection decision-making process.

cardinal scale   Values that are linear or non-linear and referenced in the Qualitative Risk Analysis process.

cause-and-effect diagram   This diagram shows the relationship between the effects of problems and their causes. Depicts every potential cause and subcause of a problem and the effect that each proposed solution will have on the problem. This diagram is also called a fishbone diagram or an Ishikawa diagram.

change control system   Documented procedures that describe how to submit change requests and how to manage change requests. It tracks the status of change requests and defines the level of authority needed to approve changes. It describes the management impacts of the changes as they pertain to project performance.

chart of accounts   The coding system used to record and track project costs by category in the company's general ledger.

checklist   Provides a way to determine if the required steps in a process have been followed. Checklists are also used to help identify risks by compiling historical information from previous projects.

claims   See *contested changes*.

code of accounts   Unique, numeric identifiers assigned to each element of the WBS. This is also known as a *chart of accounts.*

collocated   Team members physically working at the same location or holding project meetings in a common area such as a war room.

common causes of variances   Process variances seen in control charts (a tool and technique of the Quality Control process) that are a result of random variances, known or predictable variances, or variances that are always present in the process.

communication   The process of exchanging information. There are three elements to all communication: the sender, the message, and the receiver. Communication can be written or verbal, and be formal or informal. A project manager spends 90 percent of their time communicating.

communications management plan   Documents the types of information needs the stakeholders have, when the information should be distributed, and how the information will be delivered.

Communications Planning   This Planning process determines the communication needs of the stakeholders, when and how the information will be received, and who will receive the information.

configuration control board (CCB)   A team established by the organization that's given the authority to review all change requests and approve them or deny them. This is also known as a *change control board.*

configuration management   Describes the characteristics of the product of the project and ensures that the description is accurate and complete. Configuration management controls changes to the characteristics of an item and tracks the changes made or requested and their status. It is usually a subset of the change control process in most organizations, or it may serve as the change control system.

conflict   The incompatibility of goals and one party resisting or blocking the attainment of those goals by the other party.

conflict of interest   Conflict of interest occurs when personal interests are put above the interests of the project. It also occurs when personal influence is used to cause others to make decisions in favor of the influencer without regard for the project outcome.

conflict resolution   The act of using one of the following five techniques to resolve conflict: forcing, smoothing, compromise, confrontation, or withdrawal.

constituent components   Constituent components are individual components that make up the deliverable. They are part of the Scope Definition process and should be defined in tangible, verifiable terms.

constrained optimization methods   Constrained optimization methods are a category of project selection methods, which are a tool and technique of the Initiation process. They are complex mathematical models that use linear, dynamic, integer, non-linear, and/or multi-objective programming in the form of algorithms, or in other words, a specific set of steps to solve a particular problem.

constraint   Anything that either restricts the actions of the project team or dictates the actions of the project team.

contested changes   Contract changes that cannot be agreed upon. They usually involve a disagreement about the compensation to the vendor for implementing the change.

contingency planning   This is a risk response strategy that involves planning alternatives to deal with the risks should they occur. Contingency planning is referenced in the Acceptance tool and technique of the Risk Response Planning process.

contingency reserves   This is a common contingency response (which is a risk response strategy). Contingency reserves hold project funds, time, or resources in reserve to offset any unavoidable threats that might occur to project scope, schedule, cost overruns, or quality.

contingency time   See *reserve time*.

contract   A legally binding agreement between two or more parties used to acquire products or services. Contracts can be made between two or more parties, and money is typically exchanged for goods or services. They are enforceable by law and require an offer and an acceptance.

Contract Administration   This process involves monitoring vendor performance and ensuring that all the requirements of the contract are met.

contract change control system   This describes the processes needed to make contract changes and is a tool and technique of the Contract Administration process.

Contract Closeout   This process is concerned with completing and settling the terms of the contract and determines if the work described in the contract was completed accurately and satisfactorily. This process is performed before Administrative Closure.

contract file   A contract file is a file of all the contract records and supporting documents. This is an output of the Contract Closeout process.

contract negotiation   Contract negotiation occurs when all parties discuss the terms of the contract and reach an agreement.

control charts   A tool and technique of the Quality Control process that measures the results of processes over time and displays them in graph form. Control charts measure variances to determine if process variances are in control or out of control.

corrective actions   Taking action to align the anticipated future project outcomes with the project plan.

cost baseline   The expected cost for the project. Cost baselines are produced during the Cost Budgeting process and are represented as S-curves.

Cost Budgeting   This process assigns cost estimates to activities and is used to create the cost baseline, which measures the variance and performance of the project throughout the project's life.

Cost Control   This process manages the changes to project costs using the cost change control system.

Cost Estimating   This process develops an approximation of the cost of resources needed for each project activity.

cost of quality   The total cost to produce the product or service of the project according to the quality standards. These costs include all the work necessary to meet the product requirements and the costs of work performed due to nonconforming quality requirements. The three costs associated with the cost of quality are prevention costs, appraisal costs, and failure costs.

cost performance index (CPI)   An earned value analysis technique that is used to calculate cost performance efficiencies. $CPI = EV \div AC$.

cost plus fixed fee (CPFF)   This contract type charges back all project costs to the seller and includes a fixed fee upon completion of the contract.

cost plus incentive fee   This contract type charges the costs associated with producing the goods or services of the project to the buyer and includes an incentive for exceeding the performance criteria laid out in the contract.

cost plus percentage of cost   See *cost plus incentive fee.*

cost reimbursable contract   This contract type charges the costs associated with producing the goods or services of the project to the buyer.

cost variance (CV)   An earned value analysis technique that determines if costs are higher or lower than budgeted during a given period of time. $CV = EV - AC$.

crashing   *Crashing* is a compression technique that looks at cost and schedule trade-offs. One of the things you might do to crash the schedule is add resources, from either inside or outside the organization, to the critical path tasks.

Critical Chain Method   This is a resource-leveling heuristics technique from the Schedule Development process that allows for modifying the project schedule due to limited or restricted resources. This is a technique that's designed to help manage the uncertainties of a project.

critical path (CP)   The longest path through the project that's made up of activities with zero float.

Critical Path Method (CPM)   Determines a single early and late start date and early and late finish date for each activity on the project.

critical success factors   Those elements that must be completed in order for the project to be considered complete.

culture shock   A disorienting experience that occurs when working in foreign surroundings or cultures that you are not familiar with.

decision models   A category of selection methods outlined in the project selection methods tool and technique of the Initiation process. Decision models are used to examine different criteria to help make a decision regarding project selection. (See also *calculation methods*.)

decomposition   The process of breaking project deliverables down into smaller, manageable components so that project tasks and activities can be planned and estimated.

deliverable   An output that must be produced to bring the phase or project to completion. Deliverables are tangible and can be measured and easily proved.

Delphi technique   A Risk Identification technique used to gather information. Similar to brainstorming, except participants don't usually know each other nor do they have to be present at the same location.

dependencies   See *logical relationships*.

design of experiments   This is a tool and technique of the Quality Planning process. It is a statistical technique that identifies the elements, or variables, that will have the greatest effect on overall project outcomes. This is used most often concerning the product of the project but can also be applied to project management processes to examine trade-offs.

discounted cash flow   Compares the value of the future cash flows of the project to today's dollars using time value of money techniques.

discretionary dependency   A dependency defined by the project management team as an input to the Activity Sequencing process. Discretionary dependencies are usually process- or procedure-driven. This is also known as *preferred logic, soft logic*, and *preferential logic*. See also *logical relationships*.

disputes   See *contested changes*.

duration compression   A tool and technique of the Schedule Development process that is a type of mathematical analysis used to shorten the project schedule without impacting project scope. See also *crashing* and *fast tracking*, two methods of duration compression.

earned value (EV)   A measurement of the project's progress to date, or the value of the work completed to date.

earned value analysis   The most commonly used performance measurement method. It looks at schedule, cost, and scope project measurements and compares their progress as of the measurement date against what was expected. The three measurements needed to perform earned value analysis are *planned value (PV), actual cost (AC)*, and *earned value (EV)*.

estimate at completion (EAC)   An earned value analysis technique that determines the expected cost of the work when completed.

estimate to complete (ETC)   An earned value analysis techniques that determines the additional expected costs to complete the activity (or project).

evaluation criteria   A method of rating and scoring vendor proposals. Evaluation criteria are an output of the Solicitation process.

Expectancy Theory   A motivational theory that states that the expectation of a positive outcome drives motivation and that people will behave in certain ways if they think there will be good rewards for doing so. The strength of the expectancy drives the behavior.

expert judgment   Expert judgment is a tool and technique of several of the Planning processes. Expert judgment relies on individuals or groups of people who have training, specialized knowledge, or skills concerning the inputs you're assessing.

external dependency   Dependencies that are external to the project. External dependencies are an input to the Activity Sequencing process. See also *logical relationships*.

extinction   A type of project ending where the work of the project is completed and accepted by the stakeholders.

failure costs   Failure costs are associated with the cost of quality tool and technique of the Quality Planning process. They result when problems occur and the project doesn't proceed according to plan. Internal and external costs are the two types of failure costs.

fast tracking   A schedule compression technique where two activities that were previously scheduled to start sequentially start at the same time. Fast tracking reduces schedule duration.

feasibility study   Feasibility studies are undertaken to determine if the project is a viable project, the probability of project success, and the viability of the product of the project.

fitness for use   This is a cost of quality theory developed by Joseph M. Juran that states that conformance to specifications is met or exceeded. This theory specifically reflects the customers' or stakeholders' view of quality.

fixed price contract   This contract sets a specific, firm price for the goods or services rendered based on a well-defined deliverable agreed on by the buyer and seller. The biggest risk is borne by the seller with this type of contract.

fixed price plus incentive   This contract sets a specific, firm price for the goods or services rendered (like the fixed price contract) and includes an extra incentive for exceeding agreed-upon performance criteria.

float   The amount of time you can delay the early start of a task without delaying the finish date of the project. This is also known as *slack time*.

float time   See *float*.

flowchart   A diagram that shows the logical steps that must be performed in order to accomplish an objective. A flowchart can also show how the individual elements of a system interrelate.

force majeure Catastrophic risks that are outside the scope of risk management planning such as earthquakes, meteorites, volcanoes, floods, civil unrest, and terrorism. This is referenced in the risk categories input of the Risk Identification process.

formal acceptance and closure Formal acceptance and closure involves providing formal notice to the seller—usually in written form—that the contract is complete. It's the organization's way of formally accepting the product of the project from the vendor and closing out the contract. This is an output of the Contract Closeout process.

forward pass A calculation used in CPM to determine early start and early finish dates for activities.

functional organization A form of organizational structure. Functional organizations are traditional organizations with hierarchical reporting structures. The functional manager has more authority in this type of organization than the project manager has.

Gantt charts A method of displaying schedule activities. Gantt charts might also show activity sequences, activity start and end dates, resource assignments, activity dependencies, and the critical path.

goals Describes what to do, accomplish, or produce. Goals should be stated in tangible terms that are specific, measurable, accurate, realistic, and time-bound.

Graphical Evaluation and Review Technique (GERT) A mathematical analysis technique in the Schedule Development process used to determine activity duration estimates. This technique allows for conditional branching and looping, and probabilistic treatment.

hammock A summary-level activity or aggregate activities shown as a summary activity on a project network diagram.

handoffs The process of ending one project life cycle phase and beginning the next.

hard dependency See *mandatory dependency*.

hard logic See *mandatory dependency*.

Hygiene Theory This theory was developed by Fredrick Herzberg. It's also known as the Motivation-Hygiene Theory. Hygiene factors and motivators contribute to motivation. Hygiene factors prevent dissatisfaction and deal with work environment issues.

historical information An input to several Planning processes that refers to information or records regarding past projects and their performance that are available for reference on the existing project.

human resource costs The costs associated with the personnel working on the project.

impact scale Assigns a value to depict the severity of a potential risk impact using a cardinal value or actual numeric value.

independent estimates   Comparing the costs of a vendor proposal with outside sources or other vendor prices to determine if estimates are reasonable. This is a tool and technique of the Source Selection process.

influence diagrams   A diagramming technique referenced in the Risk Identification process that shows the causal influences among project variables, the timing or time order of events, and the relationships among other project variables and their outcomes.

Information Distribution   This process is concerned with providing stakeholders with information regarding the project in a timely manner via status reports, project meetings, review meetings, e-mail, and so on. The communications management plan is put into action during this process.

information distribution methods   A tool and technique of the Information Distribution process that concerns getting the project information to the project team or stakeholders.

Information retrieval systems   A tool and technique of the Information Distribution process, retrieval systems describe ways that project information is stored and shared among project team members.

Initiation   This is the first process in a project life cycle. It acknowledges that the project, or the next phase in an active project, should begin.

inspection   A tool and technique of the Quality Control process that involves physically looking at, measuring, or testing results to determine if they conform to the requirements or quality standards.

Integrated Change Control   This process is concerned with influencing the things that cause change, determining that change is needed or has happened, and managing change. All other change control processes are integrated with this process.

integration   A type of project ending where the financial or human resources assigned to the project are diverted or reassigned elsewhere in the organization.

internal rate of return (IRR)   The discount rate when the present value of the cash inflows equals the original investment. Projects with higher IRR values are generally considered better than projects with lower IRR values. IRR assumes that cash inflows are reinvested at the IRR value.

interpersonal interfaces   A category of project interfaces that deals with the reporting relationships that exist among project team members and among other project participants.

iterative   To repeat processes more than once. The five process groups are repeated throughout the project's life due to change requests, responses to change, corrective action, and so on.

Kaizen   This is a cost of quality theory from Japan that means continuous improvement. All project team members and managers should be constantly watching for quality improvement opportunities. The Kaizen approach states that you should improve the quality of the people first and then improve the quality of the products or service.

lags   An input to the Schedule Development process used when scheduling activities with dependencies. Lags require the dependent activity to have time added either to the start date or to the finish date of the activity.

leaders   Leaders impart vision, gain consensus for strategic goals, establish direction, and inspire and motivate others.

leads   An input to the Schedule Development process used when scheduling activities with dependencies. Leads require time to be subtracted from the start date or the finish date of the dependent activity.

lessons learned   Information gained throughout the course of the project that can be used to benefit future projects or other projects currently being performed by the organization. Lessons learned should be documented and may include positive as well as negative lessons.

logical relationships   A dependency between two project activities whereby one activity must do something (finish or start) before another activity can be performed (start or finish). Logical relationships can also exist between an activity and a milestone. These are also known as *precedence relationships*. The four types of logical relationships are finish-to-start, finish-to-finish, start-to-start, start-to-finish.

make or buy analysis   An input to the Procurement Planning process that determines whether it's more cost-effective for the organization to purchase goods and services or to produce the goods and services itself. Make or buy analysis can also include capacity issues, skills, availability, trade secrets, and so on.

managers   Managers focus on results and are concerned with getting the job done according to the requirements.

mandatory dependency   Mandatory dependencies are directly related to the nature of the work being performed. They are also known as *hard dependencies* or *hard logic*. See also *logical relationships*.

Maslow's hierarchy of needs   A motivational theory that hypothesizes that people have five basic needs and they fall in hierarchical order: basic physical needs, safety and security needs, social needs, self-esteem needs, and self-actualization.

mathematical analysis   This is a tool and technique of the Schedule Development process that involves calculating early and late start dates and early and late finish dates for project activities. These calculations are performed without taking resource limitations into consideration, so the resulting dates are theoretical.

matrix organization   A form of organizational structure. Employees in a matrix organization report to one functional manager and at least one project manager. Functional managers assign employees to projects and carry out administrative duties, while project managers assign tasks associated with the project to team members and execute the project.

metrics   See *operational definitions*.

milestone A major deliverable or key event in the project used to measure project progress.

milestone chart A method to display project schedule information that shows the start and/or finish date of milestones.

mitigation This is a tool and technique of the Risk Response Planning process. Mitigation reduces the probability of a risk event and its impacts to an acceptable level.

Monte Carlo Analysis A tool and technique of the Quantitative Risk Analysis and Schedule Development processes that uses simulation to calculate a distribution of probable duration results.

Motivation-Hygiene Theory See *Hygiene Theory*.

needs analysis This is a process sometimes performed for projects prior to the beginning of the Initiation process. It's usually an informal process that is not considered part of the project work itself. Needs analysis (also called *needs assessment*) is typical for internal service-type projects and for projects that entail new product development.

needs assessment See *needs analysis*.

net present value (NPV) Net present value evaluates the cash inflows using the discounted cash flow technique, which is applied to each period the inflows are expected. The total present value of the cash flows is deducted from the initial investment to determine NPV. NPV assumes that cash inflows are reinvested at the cost of capital. Similar to *discounted cash flow*.

nominal group technique An interviewing and information-gathering technique similar to the Delphi technique that can be used during the Risk Identification process.

operational definitions Operational definitions are an output of the Quality Planning process that describes what is being measured and how it will be measured by the Quality Control process.

ordinal scale Values that are rank-ordered such as high, medium, or low. They are referenced in the Qualitative Risk Analysis process.

organizational breakdown structure (OBS) Relates the WBS elements, or the work package level for very large projects, to the organizational unit responsible for completing the work.

organizational interfaces A category of project interfaces that deals with the types of reporting relationships that exist within an organization's structure.

parametric modeling A mathematical model that uses parameters, or project characteristics, to forecast project costs.

payback period The length of time it takes the company to recover the initial cost of producing the product or service of the project.

payment requests An output to the Contract Administration process where payment is physically delivered to the vendor.

payment system   A payment system is the tool and technique of Contract Administration that is used to issue payment based on the input of seller invoices.

performance measurement baselines   The project plan baseline, schedule baseline, and cost baseline are collectively known as the performance measurement baselines.

Performance Reporting   This process concerns collecting information regarding project progress and project accomplishments and reporting it to the stakeholders, project team members, management team, and other interested parties. It also makes predictions regarding future project performance.

performance reviews   Gathering and reporting project status and progress to stakeholders, management, and team members. Reports include status reports, progress reports, and forecasting. Performance reviews are a tool and technique of the Performance Reporting process.

planned value (PV)   The cost of work that's been budgeted for an activity during a certain time period. (Note: PV also stands for present value.)

politics   A technique used to influence people to perform. It involves getting groups of people with different interests to cooperate creatively even in the midst of conflict and disorder.

power   A technique used to influence people to perform. It's the ability to get people to do things they wouldn't do otherwise, to change minds and the course of events, and to influence outcomes.

preassignment   This is a tool and technique of the Staff Acquisition process. This occurs when a project is put out for bid and specific team members are promised as part of the proposal, or when internal project team members are promised and assigned as a condition of the project.

precedence diagramming method (PDM)   A diagramming method that places activities on nodes, which connect to dependent activities using arrows. This is also known as *activity on node*.

precedence relationships   See *logical relationships*.

preferential logic   See *discretionary dependency*.

preferred logic   See *discretionary dependency*.

present value (PV)   A financial calculation that determines value in today's dollars. (Note: PV also stands for planned value.)

prevention   Keeps errors from occurring in the process. Prevention is a quality concern.

prevention costs   Costs associated with satisfying customer requirements by producing a product without defects. These costs are referenced in the cost of quality tool and technique in the Quality Planning process.

probability   The likelihood that an event will occur.

probability scale   A probability scale assigns a value to depict the probability that a risk event will occur. This value is expressed as a number between 0.0 and 1.0.

procurement   Procurement is a tool and technique of the Staff Acquisition process and involves hiring individuals or teams of people for project activities, either as full-time employees or as contract help during the course of the project or project phase or for specific project activities. Procurement is usually required when the organization does not have employees available to work on the project with the required skills and competencies.

procurement audits   A tool and technique of the Contract Closeout process that examines the procurement processes to determine the effectiveness of the processes. Procurement audits are performed on all the Project Procurement Management knowledge area processes except the Contract Closeout process.

procurement documents   Used to solicit vendors to bid on the project's procurement needs. Procurement documents may include documents such as a request for proposal (RFP), request for information (RFI), invitation for bid (IFB), or a request for quotation (RFQ).

procurement management plan   A document that describes how the procurement process will be managed, the type of contract to use, what authority the project team has, if more than one contractor will be used, and how the procurement process will be integrated with other project processes.

Procurement Planning   This process identifies what goods or services will be purchased from outside of the organization. Procurement Planning also uses make or buy analysis to determine if goods or services should be purchased or performed by the organization.

product analysis   A description of the product of the project that might include performing value analysis, function analysis, quality function deployment, product breakdown analysis, systems engineering techniques, value engineering, or function deployment techniques to further define and better understand the product or service of the project.

product verification   This determines if the work described in the contract was completed accurately and satisfactorily. It's one of the purposes of the Contract Closeout process.

product scope   A description of the product features typically documented in the product description.

program   A grouping of projects that are managed together. The individual projects are usually part of one bigger project and are therefore related.

Program Evaluation and Review Technique (PERT)   PERT uses expected value—or weighted average—of critical path tasks to determine project duration by establishing three estimates: most likely, pessimistic, and optimistic. PERT is used when activity duration estimates are highly uncertain.

progressive elaboration   The process of taking incremental steps to examine and refine the characteristics of the product of the project. Processes may be progressively elaborated as well.

project   Projects are temporary in nature, have definite start and end dates, create a unique product or service, and are completed when the goals and objectives of the project have been met and signed off on by the stakeholders.

project calendars   Project calendars are an input to the Schedule Development process. They concern all the resources involved in the project and specify the working periods for all resources.

project charter   An official, written acknowledgment and recognition that a project exists. The project charter is issued by senior management and gives the project manager the authority to assign organizational resources to the work of the project.

Project Communications Management   One of the nine knowledge areas of project management. Project Communications Management ensures proper and timely communications and includes these processes: Communications Planning, Information Distribution, Performance Reporting, and Administrative Closure.

Project Cost Management   One of the nine knowledge areas of project management. Project Cost Management ensures proper cost planning, budgets, and controls and includes these processes: Resource Planning, Cost Estimating, Cost Budgeting, and Cost Control.

Project Human Resource Management   One of the nine knowledge areas of project management. Project Human Resource Management ensures effective use of human resources and includes these processes: Organizational Planning, Staff Acquisition, and Team Development.

Project Integration Management   One of the nine knowledge areas of project management. Project Integration Management involves coordinating all aspects of the project and includes these processes: Project Plan Development, Project Plan Execution, and Integrated Change Control.

project life cycle   The grouping of project phases in a sequential order from the beginning of the project to the close.

project management   The process that's used to initiate, plan, execute, monitor, control, and close out projects by applying skills, knowledge, and project management tools and techniques to fulfill the project requirements.

project management knowledge areas   These nine project management groupings—known as knowledge areas—bring together common or related processes.

project management office (PMO)   Established by organizations to create and maintain procedures and standards for project management methodologies to be used throughout the organization.

Project Management Professional Code of Professional Conduct   An ethical code established by PMI to ensure personal and professional conduct on the part of PMPs.

project manager   The person responsible for applying the skills, knowledge, and project management tools and techniques to the project activities in order to successfully complete the project objectives.

project plan   A document—or assortment of documents—that constitutes what the project is, what the project will deliver, and how all the processes will be managed. The project plan is used as the guideline throughout the project Executing and Controlling process groups to track and measure project performance and to make future project decisions. It's also used as a communication and information tool for stakeholders, team members, and the management team.

Project Plan Development   This process takes the outputs from all the other Planning processes and brings them together in a concise, logical format as one main document with reference to other pertinent documents, or as several documents organized in a logical fashion. Its output is the project plan.

Project Plan Execution   This process involves carrying out the project plan. Activities are clarified, the work is authorized to begin, resources are committed and assigned to activities, and the product or service of the project is created. The largest portion of the project budget will be spent during this process.

project planning methodology   A formal, structured technique that the project manager uses to help develop the project plan.

project presentations   An output of the Information Distribution process that concerns presenting project information to the stakeholders and other appropriate parties.

Project Procurement Management   One of the nine knowledge areas of project management. Project Procurement Management concerns procurement and contract oversight. The processes included in this knowledge area are Procurement Planning, Solicitation Planning, Solicitation, Source Selection, Contract Administration, and Contract Closeout.

Project Quality Management   One of the nine knowledge areas of project management. Project Quality Management ensures that the quality requirements of the project are satisfied. The processes included in this knowledge area are Quality Planning, Quality Assurance, and Quality Control.

project records   Project records are all information regarding the project, including project reports, memos, project schedules, project plans, and other documents.

project reports   An output of the Information Distribution process that includes project information such as the project status reports and minutes from project meetings.

Project Risk Management   One of the nine knowledge areas of project management. Project Risk Management is concerned with identifying and planning for potential risks that may impact the project. Its processes include Risk Management Planning, Risk Identification, Qualitative Risk Analysis, Quantitative Risk Analysis, Risk Response Planning, and Risk Monitoring and Control.

project schedule   The project schedule determines the start and finish dates for project activities and assigns resources to the activities.

project scope   The project scope describes the work required to produce the product or the service of the project. This includes the requirements of the product, which describe the features and functionality of the product or service.

Project Scope Management   One of the nine knowledge areas of project management. Project Scope Management is concerned with the work of the project and only the work that is required to complete the project. Its processes include Initiation, Scope Planning, Scope Definition, Scope Verification, and Scope Change Control.

project selection criteria   This is an input to the Initiation process that's used to help select and prioritize projects. It's used to determine the value of the product of the project to the organization.

project sponsor   Usually an executive in the organization. The project sponsor has the authority to assign resources and enforce decisions regarding the project.

Project Time Management   One of the nine knowledge areas of project management. Project Time Management is concerned with estimating the duration of the project plan activities, devising a project schedule, and monitoring and controlling deviations from the schedule. Its processes include Activity Definition, Activity Sequencing, Activity Duration Estimating, Schedule Development, and Schedule Control.

projectized organization   A type of organizational structure focused on projects. Project managers generally have ultimate authority over the project. Sometimes, supporting departments like human resources and accounting might report to the project manager. Project managers are responsible for making project decisions and acquiring and assigning resources.

qualified seller lists   Lists of prospective sellers who have been preapproved or prequalified to provide contract services (or provide supplies and materials) for the organization. Qualified seller lists are an input to the Solicitation process.

Qualitative Risk Analysis   This process determines what impact the identified risks will have on the project and the probability that they'll occur, and puts the risks in priority order according to their effect on the project objectives.

Quality Assurance   This process performs quality audits to determine how the project is proceeding and is concerned with making certain the project will meet and satisfy the quality standards of the project. This process should be repeated throughout the project's remaining life.

quality audits   A periodic review of quality management activities that ensures that the right quality elements are being examined. Quality audits measure how the project is progressing and identify corrective actions when variances are detected in the measurements. They also identify lessons learned. Quality audits are a tool and technique of the Quality Assurance process.

Quality Control   This process is concerned with monitoring work results to see if they fulfill the quality standards set out in the quality management plan. The Quality Control process determines if the end product conforms to the requirements and product description defined during the Planning processes.

quality management plan   Describes how the project management team will enact the quality policy and documents the resources needed to carry out the quality plan, the responsibilities of the project team in implementing quality, and all the processes and procedures the project team and organization will use to satisfy quality requirements.

Quality Planning   This process identifies the quality standards applicable for the project and how to fulfill those standards.

Quantitative Risk Analysis   This process assigns numeric probabilities to each identified risk and examines their potential impact to the project objectives.

rebaselining   See *baseline*.

regulation   A mandatory rule or law almost always imposed by governments or institutions. Organizations may also have their own self-imposed regulations. Regulations require strict adherence. This is an input to the Quality Planning process.

requirements   The specifications of the goal or deliverable.

reserve time   A practice of adding a portion of time (percentage of total time or number of work periods) to an activity to account for schedule risk.

residual risk   A risk that remains after implementing a risk response strategy.

resources   All the physical resources required to complete the project, including people, equipment, supplies, materials, software, hardware, and so on.

resource capabilities   A description of the capabilities of the human and material resources you're assigning to the activity.

resource-based method   See *resource leveling*.

resource calendars   Calendars are an input to the Schedule Development process. Resource calendars refer to specific resources—or categories of resources—and their individual (or group) availability.

resource histogram   Displays resource usage in chart form, with project time along the horizontal axis and hours needed along the vertical axis.

resource leveling   Resource leveling attempts to smooth out the resource assignments, so that tasks are completed without overloading the individual and without negatively affecting the project schedule. Some ways to perform resource leveling include delaying the start of a task to match the availability of a key team member, giving more tasks to underallocated team members, and splitting tasks.

Resource Planning   This process defines all the resources needed and the quantity of resources needed to perform project activities.

resource rates   Resource rates are the unit cost of the resources being considered for the project. They are an input to the Cost Estimating process.

resource requirements   Resource requirements are an output of the Resource Planning process that describe the types of resources needed and in what quantity for each WBS work package level.

resource pool description   The resource pool description is an input to the Resource Planning process that lists the types of resources needed for the project.

resource or project costs   Resource or project costs are expenses directly related to the project. These might include expenses such as travel costs, long distance phone bills, vendor fees, equipment purchases, and so on. Any costs that are directly related to the project or to the work of the project are considered resource or project costs.

Responsibility Assignment Matrix (RAM)   The RAM ties roles and responsibilities with the WBS elements to ensure that each element has a resource assigned. A RAM is usually displayed in chart form.

reverse resource allocation scheduling   A resource-leveling heuristics technique used when key resources are required at a specific point in the project and they are the only resource, or resources, available to perform these activities. Reverse resource allocation scheduling requires that the resources be scheduled in reverse order, that is, from the end date of the project rather than from the beginning, in order to assign this key resource at the correct time.

revisions   Adjusting approved schedule start and end dates for activities to coincide with approved changes and/or corrective actions. This is another term for *schedule updates*.

reward and recognition systems   A tool and technique of the Team Development process, rewards and recognition systems are formal ways for the management team and the project manager to recognize and promote desirable behavior.

rework   An output of the Quality Control process that requires work be done again to make it conform to quality requirements or standards. Rework may increase the project schedule.

Risk   An event that poses a threat or an opportunity to the project.

Risk Identification   This process identifies the potential project risks and documents their characteristics.

risk management plan   Details how risk management processes will be implemented, monitored, and controlled throughout the life of the project. The risk management plan does not define responses to individual risks.

Risk Management Planning   This process determines how risks will be managed for a project.

Risk Monitoring and Control   This process involves responding to risks as they occur. The risk management plan details how risk is managed, and the risk response plan details how risk response strategies are implemented in the event of an actual risk event. This process implements risk response according to the plan.

risk register   See *risk response plan.*

risk response plan   An output of the Risk Response Planning process, the risk response plan describes the actions required should the identified risks occur. It includes all the identified risks, descriptions of the risks, and the area of the project in which the impact will occur.

Risk Response Planning   This process defines what steps to take to reduce threats and take advantage of opportunities, and assigns departments or individual staff members the responsibility of carrying out the risk response plans developed in this process.

schedule change control system   Defines how changes to the schedule are made and managed. Tracks and records change requests, describes the procedures to follow to implement schedule changes, and details the authorization levels needed to approve the schedule changes.

Schedule Control   This process involves documenting and managing changes to the project schedule.

Schedule Development   This process calculates and prepares the schedule of project activities, which becomes the schedule baseline. It determines activity start and finish dates, finalizes activity sequences and durations, and assigns resources to activities.

schedule performance index (SPI)   A performance index that calculates schedule performance efficiencies. $SPI = EV \div PV$.

schedule updates   Schedule updates are an output of the Schedule Control process and involve adjusting activities and dates to coincide with approved changes and/or corrective actions.

schedule variance (SV)   An earned value analysis technique that determines if the project schedule is ahead or behind what was planned for a given period of time. $SV = EV - PV$.

Scope Change Control   This process involves documenting and managing changes to project scope. Any modification to the agreed-upon WBS is considered a scope change. Changes in product scope will require changes to the project scope. (See also *product scope* and *project scope.*)

scope changes   Any change to the agreed-upon WBS. Scope changes may require changes or updates to project objectives, costs, quality measures or controls, or schedule revisions. Scope changes always require schedule revisions.

Scope Definition   This process breaks project deliverables down into smaller, manageable components so that project tasks and activities can be planned, estimated, and controlled. This is also known as *decomposition*, which is the primary purpose of this process.

scope management plan   The scope management plan analyzes the reliability and stability of the project scope and documents the process that manages project scope and changes to project scope.

Scope Planning   This process uses progressive elaboration to define the work of the project and culminates in the scope statement, which describes the project deliverables, objectives, and justification.

scope statement   The scope statement documents the project goals, deliverables, and requirements, which are used as a baseline for future project decisions. It also includes the project objectives and the business justification for the project.

Scope Verification   This process formalizes the acceptance of the project scope and is primarily concerned with the acceptance of work results.

scoring model   A project selection method used to score and rank project proposals. The scoring model is part of the input to the Initiation process called project selection methods. Scoring models may also be used in the Source Selection process.

screening systems   A set of predetermined performance criteria used to screen vendors. Screening systems are a tool and technique of the Source Selection process.

secondary risks   A risk that comes about as a result of implementing a risk response.

seller invoices   A request for payment of goods or services that should describe the work that was completed or the materials that were delivered. Seller invoices are an input to the Contract Administration process.

should cost estimates   See *independent estimates*.

simulation   Simulation is a tool and technique of the Schedule Development and Quantitative Risk Analysis process that uses various assumptions (based on risk or durations, for example) to calculate a distribution of probable results. See also *Monte Carlo Analysis*.

slack time   The amount of time you can delay the early start of a task without delaying the finish date of the project. This is also known as *float time*.

soft logic   See *discretionary dependency*.

Solicitation   This process involves obtaining bids and proposals from vendors in response to RFPs and similar documents prepared during the Solicitation Planning process.

Solicitation Planning   This process involves preparing solicitation materials such as RFPs, RFIs, and RFQs, and reviewing lists of potential qualified vendors.

Source Selection   This process involves the receipt of bids or proposals and choosing a vendor to perform the work or supply the goods or services.

special cause variances   Variances in the process that come about as a result of circumstances or situations that are unique to the process being used. They are easily controlled at the operational level. Special cause variances are a factor in the Quality Control process.

Staff Acquisition   This process involves attaining human resources and assigning them to the project. Human resources may come from inside or outside the organization.

staffing pool description   An input to the Staff Acquisition process that considers the previous experience, personal interest, personal characteristics, availabilities, and competencies of potential team members.

staffing requirements   A subset of resource requirements, which is an output of the Resource Planning process. Staffing requirements become an input to the Organizational Planning process. The staffing requirements list identifies the kinds of skills required, the competency levels, and the individuals or groups who might provide these skills to the project and should include the time frames during the project when these skills will be needed.

stakeholder   A person or organization who has a vested interest in the project and stands to gain or lose something as a result of the project.

standards   Rules, guidelines, or characteristics that should be followed and are approved by a recognized body. Standards are an input to the Quality Planning process.

starvation   A type of project ending where financial or human resources are cut off from the project.

statement of work (SOW)   A statement of work contains the details of a procurement item in clear, concise terms and includes the project objectives, a description of the work of the project, concise specifications of the product or services required, and a project schedule. Either the buyer or the seller may prepare the SOW.

statistical sampling   Taking a sample number of parts from the whole population and examining them to determine if they fall within the variances outlined by the quality control plan. Statistical sampling is a tool and technique of the Quality Control process.

status review meetings   Status meetings are a tool and technique of the Project Plan Execution process. The purpose of status meetings is to provide updated information regarding the progress of the project. They are not show-and-tell meetings.

steering committee   A group of high-level managers or executives in the organization who manage project prioritization and various project decisions. The steering committee typically represents functional areas or departments within the organization.

supporting detail   Supporting detail is an output of some of the project management processes and includes constraints, assumptions, and any information not specifically documented during the process.

team building   Team building activities are a tool and technique of the Team Development process. They involve getting a diverse group of people to work together in the most efficient and effective manner possible.

Team Development   This process concerns creating an open, encouraging environment for stakeholders to contribute as well as developing the project team into an effective, functioning, coordinated group.

Theory X   A motivational management theory that proposes that most people do not like work and will try to steer clear of it. It postulates that people have little to no ambition, need constant supervision, and won't actually perform the duties of their job unless threatened.

Theory Y   A motivational management theory that proposes that people are interested in performing their best given the right motivation and proper expectations.

time and materials (T&M) contract   A type of contract that is a cross between the fixed price contract and the cost reimbursable contract. Preset unit rates are agreed to at contract signing, but costs are charged to the buyer as they're incurred.

tolerable results   Quality measurements that fall within a specified range. Tolerable results are a concern of the Quality Control process. These are also known as *tolerances*.

top-down estimating   See *analogous estimating*.

transference   Transference is a tool and technique of the Risk Response Planning process. This strategy transfers the consequences of a risk to a third party. Insurance is an example of transference.

trend analysis   A forecasting technique that determines if project performance is improving or worsening over time by periodically analyzing project results. Trend analysis is a tool and technique of the Performance Reporting and Quality Control processes.

triggers   Risk symptoms that imply a risk event is about to occur.

variance analysis   Compares the expected project plan results with the actual project results to determine if variances exist. Variance analysis is a tool and technique of the Performance Reporting and Quality Control processes.

variance at completion (VAC)   An earned value analysis technique that calculates the difference between the budget at completion (BAC) and the estimate at completion (EAC). VAC = BAC – EAC.

WBS dictionary   The WBS dictionary contains WBS work component descriptions, particularly those at the work package level. Details regarding the activities within the work package are documented here. The WBS dictionary includes information such as costs, budgets, schedule dates, resource assignments, and activity descriptions.

weighted scoring model   See *weighting system*.

weighting system   A way to rank and score vendor proposals or project proposals. Weighting systems assign numerical weights to evaluation criteria, and then multiply this by the weight of each criteria factor to come up with total scores for each vendor. These systems keep personal biases to a minimum. Weighting systems are a tool and technique of the Source Selection process and are also used in the input to Initiation called project selection methods.

work breakdown structure (WBS)   A deliverables-oriented hierarchy that defines the total work of the project. Each WBS level has more detailed information than the previous level.

work package   The lowest level in a WBS. Team assignments, time estimates, and cost estimates can be made when this level represents tasks or activities. On very large projects, this level is handed off to subproject managers, who develop their own WBS to fulfill the requirements of the work package deliverable.

workaround   An unplanned response to a risk event that was unknown and unidentified or an unplanned response to a risk that was previously accepted. Workaround plans are an output of the Risk Monitoring and Control process.

zero defects   A cost of quality theory developed by Philip B. Crosby that states costs will increase when quality planning isn't performed up front. Prevention is the key to this theory, which ultimately prevents rework.

Index

Note to the Reader: Throughout this index **boldfaced** page numbers indicate primary discussions of a topic. *Italicized* page numbers indicate illustrations.

C

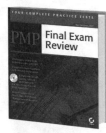

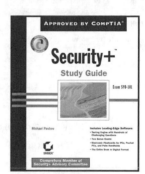

TELL US WHAT YOU THINK!

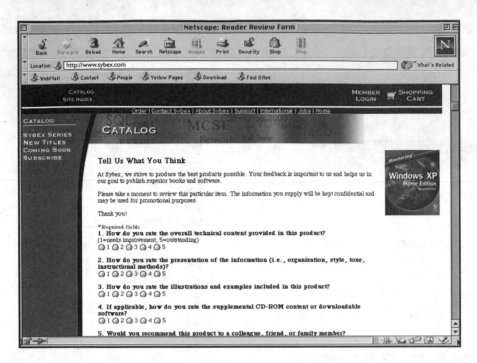

Your feedback is critical to our efforts to provide you with the best books and software on the market. Tell us what you think about the products you've purchased. It's simple:

1. Go to the Sybex website.
2. Find your book by typing the ISBN or title into the Search field.
3. Click on the book title when it appears.
4. Click **Submit a Review.**
5. Fill out the questionnaire and comments.
6. Click **Submit.**

With your feedback, we can continue to publish the highest quality computer books and software products that today's busy IT professionals deserve.

www.sybex.com

SYBEX Inc. • 1151 Marina Village Parkway, Alameda, CA 94501 • 510-523-8233

SYBEX®